Artificial Intelligence-Driven Decision Support Framework for Improving Energy Efficiency in Industry and Transportation

Zhipeng Ma

Artificial Intelligence-Driven Decision Support Framework for Improving Energy Efficiency in Industry and Transportation

Springer Vieweg

Zhipeng Ma
SDU Center for Energy Informatics,
the Maersk Mc-Kinney Moller Institute
University of Southern Denmark
Odense, Denmark

ISBN 978-3-658-51964-3 ISBN 978-3-658-51965-0 (eBook)
https://doi.org/10.1007/978-3-658-51965-0

This Springer Vieweg imprint is published by the registered company Springer Fachmedien Wiesbaden GmbH, part of Springer Nature.
The registered company address is: Abraham-Lincoln-Str. 46, 65189 Wiesbaden, Germany

Acknowledgements This PhD journey has been one of the most meaningful and transformative experiences of my life. Beyond learning how to approach and solve academic problems, this period has profoundly shaped my personal growth, strengthening my resilience, maturity, and outlook on life. The journey has never been walked alone, and I would like to express my heartfelt gratitude to everyone who has supported, guided, and inspired me along the way.

I am deeply grateful to my main supervisor, Professor Zheng Grace Ma, for her continuous guidance, encouragement, and trust throughout this research. Her insight, patience, and unwavering support have shaped both the direction of my PhD research and my development as a researcher. I am especially thankful for her guidance on how to navigate and contribute to an international research environment. My sincere appreciation also goes to my co-supervisor, Professor Bo Nørregaard Jørgensen, whose expertise, constructive feedback, and steady support have been invaluable during this journey. I am also thankful for the opportunity to join the SDU Center for Energy Informatics, which laid the foundation for beginning my academic career.

I am grateful for the opportunity to conduct my research within the DECODE and Driver Coach projects. Both projects are funded by the Energy Technology Development and Demonstration Programme (EUDP) in Denmark, whose financial support enabled my PhD employment and made this work possible. My sincere thanks go to all project partners for their valuable collaboration, data provision, domain insights, and contributions throughout the project.

My gratitude extends to my colleagues at the SDU Center for Energy Informatics, whose discussions, collaboration, and encouragement have created a stimulating and supportive research environment. I am also thankful for the institutional support and resources that enabled the progress of this PhD.

A special note of appreciation goes to the Institute for Technologies and Management of Digital Transformation at the University of Wuppertal, where I had the privilege to conduct my PhD exchange. I am thankful to Prof. Dr. Tobias Meisen and Dr. André Pomp for hosting my stay and providing a welcoming and productive research environment. My warmest thanks to Ali Rida Bahja and Dr. Andreas Burgdorf, with whom I collaborated closely on LLM research during the exchange. Their openness, insightful discussions, and collegiality made this period both enriching and memorable.

I am also grateful to the anonymous reviewers of my publications. Regardless of whether their decisions resulted in acceptance or rejection, their careful reading and constructive critiques have significantly improved the quality, rigor, and clarity of my research outputs.

To my grandma, parents, in-laws, and other family, thank you for your unconditional love, understanding, and encouragement. Your belief in me has been my greatest source of strength. Finally, and most importantly, thanks to the beloved of my life, Lu, who accompanied and cared for me throughout the journey. Without you, nothing is meaningful.

Odense, Denmark
November 14, 2025

Zhipeng Ma

Competing Interests The author has no competing interests to declare that are relevant to the content of this manuscript.

Abstract

Energy-intensive sectors such as industry and transportation are vital to economic development, yet remain major contributors to global energy consumption and greenhouse gas emissions. Enhancing their energy efficiency is essential to achieving climate resilience and meeting decarbonization goals. Despite abundant operational and sensor data, decision-making in these sectors often relies on heuristics and lacks systematic, transparent, and explainable analytical support. Existing Artificial Intelligence (AI)-based decision support methods frequently fall short in integrating robust data preprocessing, causal interpretation, and actionable recommendation generation, limiting their practical impact.

This thesis develops and validates an AI-driven decision support framework to improve energy efficiency in energy-intensive industrial and transportation systems. Guided by a three-cycle Design Science Research (DSR) methodology, the framework integrates complementary AI techniques into a modular, end-to-end architecture that transforms heterogeneous raw data into interpretable, actionable recommendations. It includes systematic data quality assessment and preprocessing pipelines, time-series segmentation, clustering key performance indicators for pattern recognition, causal inference methods to identify drivers of inefficiency, and a multimodal large language model (LLM)-based decision support module that translates analytical outcomes into domain-relevant strategies. Together, these components address challenges of data heterogeneity, causal ambiguity, and low interpretability, enabling adaptive and explainable decision support.

The framework's performance and adaptability are demonstrated through two real-world case studies: a metal foundry and a public transportation system. In the foundry case, the framework uncovers distinct furnace operation modes, quantifies the causal effects of process parameters, such as temperature control and charge scheduling, and generates actionable strategies to stabilize operations and reduce energy waste. In the transportation case, it identifies how driving behavior and environmental conditions influence fuel consumption, revealing the impacts of idling and acceleration patterns, and providing interpretable eco-driving recommendations. Across both domains, the proposed framework demonstrates the ability to handle complex real-world sensor data while maintaining analytical robustness and decision relevance. Its successful cross-domain application illustrates strong scalability and generalization potential.

The research makes three main contributions.

- Theoretically, it advances the integration of causal and explainable AI within decision support systems, bridging data-driven analytics and human-centric interpretability to foster sustainable decision-making.
- Methodologically, it provides a replicable DSR-based development process and extends traditional data science models such as CRISP-DM with novel modules for real-world data science projects.
- Practically, it delivers a validated AI-driven framework that supports operational and strategic decision-making in real industrial and transportation contexts, illustrating tangible pathways for energy and emission reduction.

Overall, this work demonstrates that coupling data understanding, pattern discovery, causal analysis, and LLM-based reasoning can transform complex industrial and transportation data into trustworthy decision intelligence. It lays the groundwork for future developments in adaptive, user-centered AI-driven decision support systems for sustainable operations. Future research should focus on real-time deployment, user interface development, and domain-specific LLM fine-tuning to enhance usability, interpretability, and measurable impact in live environments.

Resumé

Energikrævende sektorer som industri og transport er afgørende for den økonomiske udvikling, men udgør samtidig nogle af de største bidragydere til det globale energiforbrug og udledningen af drivhusgasser. Forbedring af energieffektiviteten i disse sektorer er derfor central for at opnå klimamæssig robusthed og realisere målene for dekarbonisering. På trods af store mængder drifts- og sensordata er beslutningstagningen i disse sektorer ofte baseret på heuristikker og mangler systematisk, gennemsigtig og forklarlig analytisk støtte. Eksisterende beslutningsstøttesystemer baseret på kunstig intelligens (AI) formår ofte ikke at integrere solid databehandling, kausal fortolkning og generering af handlingsorienterede anbefalinger, hvilket begrænser deres praktiske anvendelighed.

Denne ph.d.-afhandling udvikler og validerer en AI-drevet beslutningsstøtteramme, der har til at forbedre energieffektiviteten i energikrævende industrielle og transportmæssige systemer. Med udgangspunkt i en tre-cyklisk Design Science Research (DSR)-metodologi integrerer rammen komplementære AI-teknikker i en modulær og end-to-end arkitektur, der transformerer heterogene rå data til fortolkelige og handlingsorienterede anbefalinger. Rammen omfatter systematisk vurdering af datakvalitet, forbehandlingsprocesser, tidsseriebaseret segmentering, klyngedannelse af centrale præstationsindikatorer til mønstergenkendelse, kausal inferens til identifikation af årsagssammenhænge bag ineffektivitet samt et multimodalt beslutningsstøttemodul baseret på store sprogmodeller (LLM'er), der oversætter analytiske resultater til domænespecifikke strategier. Samlet set adresserer disse komponenter udfordringerne ved dataheterogenitet, kausal tvetydighed og lav fortolkelighed, hvilket muliggør adaptiv og forklarlig beslutningsstøtte.

Rammens ydeevne og tilpasningsevne demonstreres gennem to virkelige casestudier: et metalstøberi og et offentligt transportsystem. I støbericasen identificerer rammen forskellige driftsmønstre for ovnene, kvantificerer de kausale effekter af procesparametre såsom temperaturstyring og ladningsplanlægning samt genererer handlingsrettede strategier til at stabilisere driften og reducere energispild. I transportcasen afdækkes, hvordan køreadfærd og miljøforhold påvirker brændstofforbruget, herunder effekten af tomgang og acceleration, hvilket muliggør udviklingen af fortolkelige anbefalinger for energieffektiv kørsel. På tværs af begge domæner viser den foreslåede ramme evnen til at håndtere komplekse sensordata fra virkelige systemer samtidig med, at den opretholder analytisk robusthed og beslutningsrelevans. Dens succesfulde anvendelse på tværs af domæner illustrerer en stærk skalerbarhed og generaliserbarhed.

Afhandlingen bidrager med tre hovedbidrag:

- Teoretisk bidrager arbejdet til integrationen af kausal og forklarlig AI i beslutningsstøttesystemer ved at bygge bro mellem datadrevet analyse og menneskecentreret fortolkning for at fremme bæredygtig beslutningstagning.
- Metodologisk tilbyder afhandlingen en reproducerbar DSR-baseret udviklingsproces og udvider traditionelle data science-modeller som CRISP-DM med nye moduler til virkelighedsnære data science-projekter.
- Praktisk leverer afhandlingen en valideret AI-drevet ramme, der understøtter operationelle og strategiske beslutninger i reelle industrielle og transportmæssige kontekster, og som illustrerer konkrete veje til reduktion af energi- og emissionsforbrug.

Samlet viser arbejdet, at koblingen mellem dataforståelse, mønstergenkendelse, kausalanalyse og LLM-baseret ræsonnering kan transformere komplekse industrielle og transportrelaterede data til pålidelig beslutningsintelligens. Afhandlingen danner grundlaget for fremtidig udvikling af adaptive, brugercentrerede og AI-drevne beslutningsstøttesystemer til bæredygtig drift. Fremtidig forskning bør fokusere på implementering i realtid, udvikling af brugergrænseflader samt domænespecifik finjustering af store sprogmodeller for at øge anvendelighed, fortolkelighed og målbar effekt i praksis.

Publications

First-author Publications

Journal Articles	
[1]	**Z. Ma**, B. N. Jorgensen, and Z. G. Ma, "Data-Driven Causal Reasoning for Eco-Driving Behavior Analysis in Public Transportation Systems," *Complex & Intelligent Systems*, 2026, doi: https://doi.org/10.1007/s40747-026-02301-8.
[2]	**Z. Ma**, et. al, "Multi-Agent Multimodal Large Language Model Framework for Automated Interpretation of Fuel Efficiency Analytics in Public Transportation," Applied Sciences, vol. 15, no. 21, p. 11619, 2025, doi: https://doi.org/10.3390/app152111619.
[3]	**Z. Ma**, B. N. Jorgensen, and Z. G. Ma, "Discovering Operational Patterns Using Image-Based Convolutional Clustering and Composite Evaluation: A Case Study in Foundry Melting Processes," *Information*, vol. 16, no. 9, p. 816, 2025, doi: https://doi.org/10.3390/info16090816.
[4]	**Z. Ma**, B. N. Jorgensen, and Z. G. Ma, "A systematic data characteristic understanding framework towards physical-sensor big data challenges," *Journal of Big Data*, vol. 11, p. 84, 2024. doi: https://doi.org/10.1186/s40537-024-00942-5.
[5]	**Z. Ma**, B. N. Jørgensen, and Z. Ma, "A Scoping Review of Energy-Efficient Driving Behaviors and Applied State-of-the-Art AI Methods," *Energies*, vol. 17, no. 2, p. 500, 2024, doi: https://doi.org/10.3390/en17020500.

(continued)

(continued)

Conference Paper	
[6]	**Z. Ma**, B. N. Jørgensen, and Z. G. Ma, "Uncovering Causal Drivers of Energy Efficiency for Industrial Process in Foundry via Time-Series Causal Inference," in *Energy Informatics.Academy Conference 2025*, Kuala Lumpur, Malaysia, 2025, vol. 16394, in Lecture Notes in Computer Science, pp. 366–381, doi: https://doi.org/10.1007/978-3-032-19137-3_24.
[7]	**Z. Ma**, B. N. Jørgensen, and Z. G. Ma, "DataPro – A Standardized Data Understanding and Processing Procedure: A Case Study of an Eco-driving Project," in *Energy Informatics.Academy Conference 2024*, Bali, Indonesia, 2024, vol. 15271, in Lecture Notes in Computer Science, pp. 136–154, doi: https://doi.org/10.1007/978-3-031-74738-0_10.
[8]	**Z. Ma**, B. N. Jørgensen, and Z. Ma, "Fuel Efficiency Analysis of the Public Transportation System Based on the Gaussian Mixture Model Clustering," in *Progress in Artificial Intelligence, EPIA 2024*, Viana do Castelo, Portugal, 2024, vol. 14968, in Lecture Notes in Computer Science, pp. 209–219, doi: https://doi.org/10.1007/978-3-031-73500-4_18.
[9]	**Z. Ma**, B. N. Jørgensen, and Z. G. Ma, "Eco-driving Intelligent Systems and Algorithms: A Patent Review," in *The 8th International Conference on Power and Renewable Energy (ICPRE 2023)*, Shanghai, China, 2023: IEEE, doi: https://doi.org/10.1109/icpre59655.2023.10353603.
[10]	**Z. Ma**, B. N. Jørgensen, M. Levesque, M. Amazouz, and Z. G. Ma, "Decoding Digitalization Enabled Energy Efficiency and Flexibility in Industry: A Survey with Nine Case Studies," *in Energy Informatics.Academy Conference 2023*, São Paulo, Brazil, 2023, vol. 14467, in Lecture Notes in Computer Science, pp. 253–270, doi: https://doi.org/10.1007/978-3-031-48649-4_15.
[11]	**Z. Ma**, B. N. Jørgensen, and Z. G. Ma, "A Novel Hybrid Feature Importance and Feature Interaction Detection Framework for Predictive Optimization in Industry 4.0 Applications," in *IECON 2023–49th Annual Conference of the IEEE Industrial Electronics Society*, Singapore, 2023, pp. 1–6, doi: https://doi.org/10.1109/IECON51785.2023.10312491.

Co-author Publications

[12]	B. A. Tolnai, **Z. Ma**, B. N. Jørgensen, Z. G. Ma, "An Automated Domain-Agnostic and Explainable Data Quality Assurance Framework for Energy Analytics and Beyond," *Information*, vol. 16, no. 10, p. 836, 2025, doi: https://doi.org/10.3390/info16100836
[13]	D. A. Howard, M. Værbak, **Z. Ma**, B. N. Jørgensen, and Z. G. Ma, "Data-Driven Digital Twin Based Energy Flexibility Investigation for Commercial Greenhouse Production Process," in *Progress in Artificial Intelligence, EPIA 2024*, Viana do Castelo, Portugal, 2024, vol. 14968, in Lecture Notes in Computer Science, pp. 193-205, doi: https://doi.org/10.1007/978-3-031-73497-7_16.
[14]	D. A. Howard, M. Værbak, **Z. Ma**, B. N. Jørgensen, and Z. G. Ma, "Data-Driven Digital Twin for Foundry Production Process: Facilitating Best Practice Operations Investigation and Impact Analysis," in *Energy Informatics.Academy Conference 2024*, Bali, Indonesia, 2024, vol. 15271, in Lecture Notes in Computer Science, pp. 259-273, doi: https://doi.org/10.1007/978-3-031-74738-0_17.

Contents

Abbreviations

AI	Artificial Intelligence
BMC	Business Model Canvas
CAN bus	Controller Area Network bus
CCoT	Contrastive Chain of Thought
CH	Calinski-Harabasz
CI	Conditional Independence
CO_2	Carbon Dioxide
CoT	Chain of Thought
DAG	Directed Acyclic Graph
DB	Davies-Bouldin
DCAE	Deep Convolutional Autoencoder
DCE	Differentiable Causal Effect
DEC	Deep Embedded Clustering
DL	Deep Learning
DN	Data Narration
DSR	Design Science Research
DSS	Decision Support System
DTW	Dynamic Time Warping
EJ	Exajoules
EM	Expectation-Maximization
EMD	Earth Movers Distance
ETL	Extract, Transform, Load
FDR	False Discovery Rate
GHG	Greenhouse Gas

GMM	Gaussian Mixture Model
GPS	Global Positioning System
Gt	Gigaton
GUI	Graphical User Interface
i. i. d.	Independent and Identically Distributed
IDEC	Improved Deep Embedded Clustering
IEA	International Energy Agency
IIoT	Industrial Internet of Things
IoT	Internet of Things
IQR	Interquartile Range
ISO	International Organization for Standardization
KDE	Kernel Density Estimate
KL divergence	Kullback-Leibler divergence
KPI	Key Performance Indicator
LLM	Large Language Model
LMC	Local Markov Condition
MCI	Momentary Conditional Independence
ML	Machine Learning
MMD	Maximum Mean Discrepancy
MSE	Mean Squared Error
NN	Neural Network
PC	Peter-Clark
PCMCI	Peter-Clark Momentary Conditional Independence
RMS	Root Mean Square
SCM	Structural Causal Model
SEM	Structural Equation Model
SHD	Structural Hamming Distance
SIL	Silhouette
SotA	State-of-the-Art
SQL	Structured Query Language
TS-IDEC	Time-Series Image-based Deep Embedded Clustering
XAI	Explainable Artificial Intelligence
XDS	Explainable Decision Support

List of Figures

List of Tables

Listings

Introduction 1

1.1 Motivation

Energy-intensive sectors, such as industry and transportation, are fundamental to global economic development, yet they remain among the largest sources of greenhouse gas (GHG) emissions. According to the International Energy Agency (IEA), these two sectors consistently account for the highest share of final energy consumption and CO_2 emissions worldwide [1–3]. Enhancing energy efficiency within these domains is therefore critical to achieving net-zero emission targets, improving resource productivity, and fostering long-term climate resilience.

Recent years have witnessed a rapid digital transformation across both sectors, driven by the proliferation of sensors [4], Industrial Internet of Things (IIoT) platforms [5], and advanced automation systems [6]. Massive volumes of operational data are continuously generated from furnaces and process equipment in manufacturing plants [7, 8] to the Controller Area Network bus (CAN bus) and Global Positioning System (GPS) records [9, 10] in public transportation fleets. Despite this abundance of data, its potential value remains largely underexploited. Traditional decision-making frameworks are often limited by fragmented data management, low interpretability, and static operational rules [11, 12]. As a result, decision-makers struggle to identify energy-efficient operational strategies under uncertainty and to balance trade-offs among performance, reliability, and environmental objectives.

Decision-making in many energy-intensive end-user organizations remains largely heuristic and experience-driven [13, 14], with limited analytical integration and explainable intelligence. This gap underscores the need for data-driven systems that can effectively transform complex, high-dimensional datasets into

Z. Ma, *Artificial Intelligence-Driven Decision Support Framework for Improving Energy Efficiency in Industry and Transportation*,
https://doi.org/10.1007/978-3-658-51965-0_1

actionable insights. Artificial Intelligence (AI) offers transformative potential in this regard by enabling adaptive, transparent, and evidence-based decision-making [15]. Through its capacity to learn from data, recognize operational patterns, and perform predictive as well as prescriptive analyses, AI can significantly augment human expertise and improve the management of energy-intensive processes [16, 17].

The decision support system (DSS), traditionally designed to assist managerial, operational, and planning activities [18] provides a natural foundation for integrating AI into practical decision-making workflows. The emergence of intelligent, explainable, and data-centric DSS represents a paradigm shift in the digitalization of energy-intensive sectors under the Industry 5.0 vision. However, realizing this potential remains constrained by significant challenges, including data heterogeneity, methodological transparency, domain interpretability, and the alignment of AI outputs with real-world decision contexts.

This research is motivated by the need to establish a rigorous, interpretable AI-driven decision support framework that systematically bridges the gap between data analytics and operational decision-making in energy-intensive industrial and transportation systems. By integrating advanced data preprocessing, pattern recognition, and multi-criteria decision-support mechanisms, the proposed framework aims to enhance both analytical robustness and domain applicability. Ultimately, this thesis seeks to contribute to the development of transparent, explainable, and practically deployable AI-based decision systems that enable measurable improvements in energy efficiency and sustainability across critical sectors of the modern economy.

1.2 Target Challenges and Research Gaps

Based on the literature review and interviews with industrial stakeholders, several critical challenges and research gaps have been identified in applying AI-driven decision support for improving energy efficiency. Although the motivation highlights the transformative potential of AI and explainable systems in this context, realizing this potential remains constrained by key challenges observed in both research and practice. These challenges and research gaps form the focus of this thesis and are grouped into three main categories.

Challenge 1: Lack of integrated domain-agnostic and domain-aware data pipelines capable of managing heterogeneous, incomplete, and dynamic operational data.

Industrial and transportation systems generate large volumes of diverse sensors and process data characterized by varying structures, sampling rates, and quality. Missing, noisy, or misaligned data complicate model development and hinder reproducibility. Existing workflows often treat data preparation and modeling as independent tasks, resulting in fragmented, non-adaptive pipelines. Furthermore, the limited incorporation of domain knowledge in preprocessing reduces interpretability and constrains generalization across contexts.

Challenge 2: Lack of causal understanding of operational dynamics limits AI systems' ability to generate actionable, reliable, and trustworthy decision support.

Most existing data-driven approaches focus on identifying statistical associations rather than understanding the underlying mechanisms that drive energy inefficiencies. Without causal interpretability, it becomes difficult to determine which operational factors influence energy performance or to identify effective intervention strategies. As a result, AI-based systems often remain descriptive rather than prescriptive, offering limited support for evidence-based and explainable decisions in complex, evolving environments.

Challenge 3: Lack of transparent and user-centered explainability frameworks that align with domain reasoning and foster stakeholder trust.

Even high-performing AI systems are rarely adopted in practice if their outputs lack transparency or actionable interpretation. Many existing explainability methods are technical in nature and fail to communicate insights in a form meaningful to engineers, operators, or decision-makers. Moreover, few systems enable human feedback or iterative refinement of explanations, resulting in limited user engagement and confidence in AI-driven recommendations.

1.3 Research Aim, Questions, and Objectives

Building upon the challenges and research gaps identified in Sect. 1.2, this section defines the overall research aim, guiding research questions, and specific objectives that direct the study. Together, they establish the conceptual foundation and methodological orientation of the research, guiding the development of an AI-driven decision support framework to improve energy efficiency in industrial and transportation systems.

1.3.1 Research Aim

To address the identified research gaps, this thesis aims to **design, implement, and validate an explainable AI-driven decision-support framework that transforms abundant, heterogeneous sensor data into trustworthy, actionable insights, thereby advancing data-driven, human-centered decision-making to improve energy efficiency in energy-intensive industrial and transportation systems.**

This research aim reflects the methodological, theoretical, and practical ambitions of the thesis: to establish a scientifically grounded and operationally deployable framework that integrates a robust data quality pipeline, systematic pattern discovery, and causal reasoning, while ensuring interpretability, methodological rigor, and user-oriented decision support in real-world applications.

1.3.2 Research Questions

To fulfill the research aim, this study is guided by the following three research questions (RQs), which collectively define its conceptual scope and methodological focus.

RQ1: *How can artificial intelligence techniques be coherently integrated within a modular decision support framework to enable effective, data-driven enhancement of energy efficiency in industrial and transportation systems?*

This question addresses the architectural and conceptual foundation of this study. It examines how diverse AI components can be systematically organized into a unified, modular, and domain-aware framework. Addressing this question involves defining the design principles and integration strategies needed to connect heterogeneous data sources to interpretable, actionable decision outputs.

RQ2: *What data processing and analytical approaches are required to systematically capture, structure, and interpret heterogeneous operational data to uncover underlying patterns and causal relationships influencing energy performance?*

This question investigates the analytical dimension of the research. It focuses on developing data pipelines and AI-based analytical mechanisms that can handle noisy, incomplete, and dynamic datasets while maintaining methodological rigor and domain relevance. The goal is to enable the discovery of operational patterns and causal drivers that influence energy efficiency.

RQ3: *How can the proposed framework ensure reliability, explainability, and cross-domain adaptability of AI-driven analyses and recommendations, thereby enhancing stakeholder trust and practical applicability in various real-world decision contexts?*

This question concerns the human-centered and validation dimensions of the research. It explores how explainability, trust, and cross-domain transferability can be embedded within the framework to ensure that AI-generated analyses are transparent, traceable, and adaptable across different application domains. It also considers how decision support outputs can be effectively communicated to practitioners and validated through empirical case studies across different domains.

Together, these three research questions provide a coherent structure for the thesis. They guide the theoretical formulation, methodological development, and empirical validation of the proposed AI-driven decision support framework, ensuring that the research contributes both scientific rigor and practical value to the pursuit of energy efficiency in complex operational systems.

1.3.3 Research Objectives

To answer the three research questions, this study defines the following research objectives (ROs) and corresponding hypotheses (Hs). Each objective represents a major stage in the conceptualization, development, and validation of the proposed AI-driven decision support framework.

RO1: *Establish a rigorous methodological foundation that integrates Design Science Research (DSR) with a data-driven process model to guide the systematic design and development of the AI-driven decision support framework.*

H1: A structured methodological approach that combines DSR principles with a formalized data-processing model will provide a coherent foundation for designing, implementing, and evaluating AI-driven decision support systems, thereby ensuring both scientific rigor and practical relevance.

RO1 addresses RQ1, providing the theoretical and methodological basis for constructing a modular, transferable framework.

RO2: *Design a modular and unified AI-driven decision support framework architecture that integrates key analytical components, ensuring seamless interaction across the data-to-decision pipeline from data acquisition to interpretable recommendations.*

H2: A holistic and modular framework that integrates data preprocessing, pattern discovery, causal analysis, and explainable reporting within a unified structure will enhance the coherence, efficiency, and usability of decision-making processes compared with existing fragmented approaches.

RO2 also addresses RQ1, focusing on the framework's architectural design and integration logic.

RO3: *Develop and implement novel or adapted analytical modules that are both domain-agnostic and domain-aware for data understanding, pattern discovery, causal reasoning, and insights generation that enable systematic interpretation of operational dynamics and identification of energy efficiency drivers.*

H3: Advanced data- and AI-driven analytical methods that integrate domain-agnostic generalization with domain-aware adaptation will yield deeper insights and more reliable explanations of energy performance variations, enhancing the framework's robustness and interpretability across applications.

RO3 addresses RQ2, the analytical dimensions of the research.

RO4: *Embed explainability, reliability, and cross-domain adaptability into the framework to ensure transparent, trustworthy, and transferable AI-assisted decision support across diverse real-world contexts with varying data characteristics and operational constraints.*

H4: Incorporating explainability and cross-domain adaptability into the framework will enable transparent interpretation of AI-generated insights and support reliable adaptability across domains, ensuring consistent performance and trust in diverse operational environments.

RO4 aligns with RQ3, emphasizing stakeholder trust, explainability, and cross-domain generalization.

RO5: *Establish a rigorous evaluation and benchmarking strategy to assess the framework's performance, robustness, and practical utility through quantitative metrics and qualitative validation in real-world case studies.*

H5: Systematic evaluation across multiple criteria, including analytical accuracy, causal validity, interpretability, and decision-making effectiveness, will demonstrate that the proposed framework and its components outperform existing baselines, confirming their robustness, relevance, and contribution to energy-efficient operations.

RO5 supports RQ2 and RQ3, ensuring empirical validation and demonstrating the scientific and practical significance of both the overall decision support framework and the analytical sub-frameworks developed for its individual modules.

Together, the five research objectives and hypotheses translate the research aim into a coherent plan of inquiry, addressing the three research questions by establishing a rigorous methodological framework (RQ1), developing analytical modules for data interpretation and causal understanding (RQ2), and integrating explainability, adaptability, and evaluation mechanisms to ensure trust and cross-domain generalization (RQ3).

1.4 Research Methodology

The research objectives are addressed through the three-cycle DSR methodology [19], which serves as the overarching paradigm that guides and structures the entire research process.

In contrast to natural sciences, which aim to understand phenomena, DSR belongs to the sciences of the artificial and focuses on the design and evaluation of artifacts, such as algorithms, models, methods, constructs, or prototypes [20, 21]. Artifacts created in DSR are not end products but knowledge-generating tools that advance understanding through iterative design, implementation, and evaluation.

This study follows the well-established three-cycle DSR model [19], integrating relevance, rigor, and design cycles. The relevance cycle ensures practical grounding through collaboration with domain experts in industrial processing and public transportation to define system requirements and performance metrics. The rigor cycle provides theoretical grounding by drawing on established knowledge and analytical techniques from data science and AI, including data understanding, clustering, causal inference, and explainable modeling. At the core, the design cycle iteratively develops and evaluates the proposed AI-driven decision support framework and its modular components, enhancing functionality, accuracy, and interpretability until predefined success criteria are met.

Overall, the three-cycle DSR methodology ensures an iterative, rigorous, and contextually relevant research process that balances theoretical contribution with practical impact. Further details on the research design process and framework development procedure are provided in Chap. 4.

1.5 Research Significance and Expected Contributions

This thesis addresses a critical need at the intersection of AI, data science, and energy informatics: transforming abundant, heterogeneous sensor data into trustworthy, explainable, and actionable insights that support energy-efficiency decisions in real-world operations. By integrating DSR with advanced data analytics, the study contributes to both scientific knowledge and practical innovation in energy-intensive sectors.

- **Scientific and Theoretical Significance**
  The research advances understanding of how explainable and causal AI, including large language models (LLMs), can be systematically embedded within decision support systems. It establishes a conceptual bridge between data-driven analytics and design science theory, demonstrating how methodological rigor and contextual relevance can coexist. The proposed framework contributes to the theoretical advancement of energy informatics as an interdisciplinary field that unites information systems design, artificial intelligence, and sustainability objectives.
- **Technical and Methodological Significance**
  Methodologically, the thesis adopts the three-cycle DSR process as a replicable roadmap for developing AI-driven artifacts. It introduces the DataPro model, which provides a standardized procedure for data understanding and processing, extending the CRISP-DM model to ensure data quality and methodological consistency. Technically, the research proposes a novel integrated architecture that connects data profiling, clustering-based pattern discovery, causal reasoning, and LLM-based narration within a modular,

scalable framework, thereby advancing transparent, human-centered decision support.

- **Societal and Industrial Significance**
  Empirically, the framework is validated in two domains: industrial foundry operations and public transportation. The results demonstrate that AI can enhance operational sustainability, reduce energy waste, and strengthen decision confidence among engineers and managers. The research contributes to the broader goals of decarbonization and digital transition in manufacturing and transport systems.

This thesis is expected to deliver the following reinforcing contributions across theoretical, methodological, algorithmic, and practical dimensions.

- **Theoretical Contributions**

  o Advancing conceptual understanding of causal and explainable AI within the context of energy-efficiency decision support.
  o Proposing an integrated AI-driven decision support framework architecture that provides a structured end-to-end pathway from raw sensor data to actionable managerial insights, ensuring methodological coherence and alignment with energy efficiency objectives.

- **Methodological Contributions**

  o Establishing a reproducible three-cycle DSR process for the systematic development and validation of AI artifacts.
  o Developing the DataPro model, a standardized data understanding and processing procedure that extends the CRISP-DM model and introduces a novel data pipeline tailored to energy-intensive domains.

- **Algorithmic Contributions**

  o Designing and implementing a suite of data- and AI-driven analytical modules that form the core of the proposed decision support framework.
  o Developing the STREAM data collection pipeline and a sensor data characterization procedure for systematic understanding of operational data characteristics and quality.
  o Proposing the TS-IDEC time-series clustering algorithm for identifying operational patterns in high-dimensional energy data.

  - o Advancing causal analysis through the Bagging DAGMA-DCE and Integrated PCMCI + causal discovery algorithms for robust identification of causal relationships.
  - o Proposing a causal reasoning framework for root-cause analysis.
  - o Developing an LLM-based multimodal narration framework for generating explainable, human-centered insights.

- **Practical Contributions**

  - o Formulating design principles and operational guidelines for deploying responsible and human-centered AI in energy-intensive systems.
  - o Demonstrating the framework's scalability, robustness, and interpretability through cross-domain validation in industrial and transportation case studies.

1.6 Thesis Structure

The overall structure of the thesis, illustrated in Fig. 1.1, follows the three-cycle DSR framework [19].

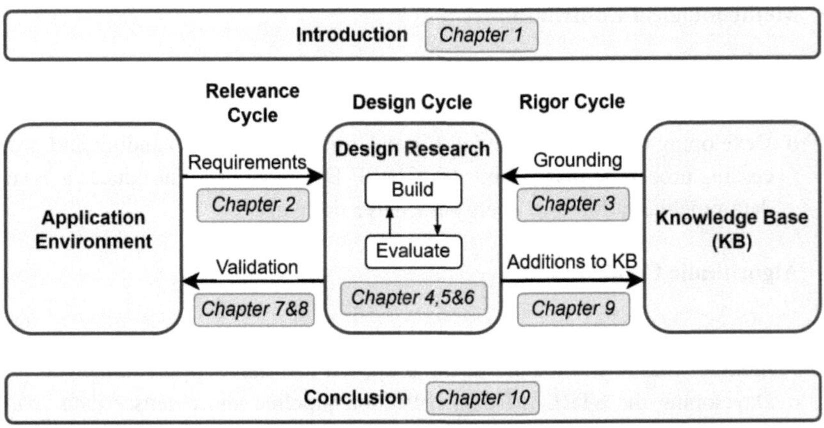

Fig. 1.1 The structure of the thesis following the three-cycle DSR framework [19]

The thesis is organized into the following ten chapters:

Chapter 1 introduces the research background, motivation, and challenges, and defines the research aim, objectives, and contributions, forming the foundation of the study.

Chapter 2 provides the contextual background situating the research within global and sectoral developments in sustainable energy and digitalization. It outlines the global context of energy efficiency and sustainability, analyzes energy-intensive sectors, and highlights efficiency challenges and opportunities in industry and transportation.

Chapter 3 reviews the state of the art in AI-driven decision support frameworks to identify methodological, conceptual, and technical gaps. It synthesizes key trends and challenges and outlines methodological directions relevant to framework development, including data quality assurance, clustering, causal inference, and multimodal decision narration.

Chapter 4 describes the research methodology based on the three-cycle DSR paradigm. It delineates the research process designed to support systematic scientific inquiry within data science and introduces the framework's development and verification methods, ensuring methodological rigor, validity, and reliability.

Chapter 5 presents the conceptual design and architecture of the proposed AI-driven decision support framework, comprising five interconnected modules and the DataPro model that guides the data pipeline. It provides an overview of the architecture and module interactions, introduces the DataPro process model for standardized data understanding and processing, and details the modular design, describing the high-level function and logic of each component.

Chapter 6 details the algorithmic implementation and empirical validation of the developed methods with comparative evaluations against state-of-the-art (SotA) baselines. It introduces the STREAM pipeline for real-world data acquisition, a systematic exploratory data analysis framework for data characterization and quality assessment, and clustering algorithms for identifying patterns in key performance indicators related to energy efficiency. It also outlines causal reasoning pipelines for uncovering and validating cause-effect relationships and an LLM-based multi-agent module that converts analytical results into interpretable narratives and actionable recommendations.

Chapters 7 and 8 present two case studies demonstrating the framework's cross-domain applicability. Chapter 7 focuses on the foundry industry, identifying operational patterns, causal drivers of energy consumption, and interpretable decision recommendations. Chapter 8 extends the analysis to public transportation, exploring behavioral and environmental factors influencing fuel efficiency and generating actionable eco-driving recommendations. Each chapter defines the case context, formulates the research problem, outlines methodological boundaries, presents the datasets, and demonstrates the framework's application and evaluation in terms of performance, robustness, and practical relevance.

Chapter 9 discusses the results in relation to the research objectives, synthesizes the theoretical and practical implications, and evaluates the framework's strengths, limitations, and contributions. It includes a cross-domain comparison of case studies, assesses generalization potential, addresses the research questions, and examines the study's validity.

Chapter 10 concludes the thesis by summarizing key findings, articulating generalized design principles for AI-driven decision support, highlighting scientific and practical contributions, and outlining future research directions.

Background

2

This chapter establishes the research background by situating it within the global context of sustainability and energy efficiency, addressing the requirements analysis phase of the relevance cycle in the three-cycle DSR model. It underscores the growing urgency to reduce GHG emissions, optimize resource use, and leverage digital transformation for data-driven decision-making in support of sustainable development. The chapter further justifies selecting industry and transportation as focal domains due to their high energy intensity and significant decarbonization potential. By integrating perspectives from energy systems and industrial operations, it highlights the practical and societal relevance of the research problem and lays the foundation for subsequent methodological development.

Section 2.1 explores the global context of energy efficiency and sustainability, while Sect. 2.2 analyzes energy-intensive sectors with emphasis on efficiency challenges and opportunities in industry and transportation. Section 2.3 concludes the chapter with a synthesis of key insights and introduces the conceptual linkage to the following chapter, which reviews the theoretical and methodological state of the art in AI-driven decision support for energy efficiency improvement.

2.1 Global Energy Efficiency and Sustainability Context

The intertwined challenges of climate change, energy demand, and sustainability continue to shape global development priorities. As energy consumption and GHG emissions remain on an upward trajectory, improving energy efficiency has become a fundamental pillar of strategies aimed at achieving net-zero emissions and ensuring long-term energy security [22].

Z. Ma, *Artificial Intelligence-Driven Decision Support Framework for Improving Energy Efficiency in Industry and Transportation*,
https://doi.org/10.1007/978-3-658-51965-0_2

Energy efficiency refers to the ability to generate more economic and social value from each unit of energy consumed [23]. It is widely recognized as one of the fastest and most cost-effective approaches to reducing emissions while sustaining economic growth [22]. Global transition pathways, such as those outlined by the IEA, highlight that accelerating efficiency improvements is essential for meeting the 2050 net-zero objective [24]. Recent analyses indicate that efficiency-related measures could deliver a large share of the projected reductions in oil and gas demand by 2030, comparable to the total energy use of several major economies [25]. These reductions are mainly driven by advances in vehicle electrification, improvements in fuel economy, better building insulation, and the modernization of industrial processes [25].

Between 2010 and 2022, improvements in global energy intensity, defined as the ratio of energy use to economic output, helped avoid approximately seven gigatons (Gt) of CO_2 emissions [25]. However, recent data suggest that global progress is slowing. Current projections indicate an annual improvement in energy intensity of about one percent, which is only half the average rate achieved in the previous decade. To address this slowdown, nearly 200 nations at the COP28 conference in Dubai in 2023 agreed to double the global rate of energy efficiency improvement by 2030, targeting an average annual gain of around four percent [25, 26].

Beyond emission reduction, energy efficiency provides multiple co-benefits. It enhances energy security by reducing dependence on imported fuels, lowers operational costs for industries and households, and contributes to improved public health through reduced air pollution [25]. The transition toward efficient and electrified technologies, including electric vehicles, smart buildings, and advanced manufacturing systems, also creates new employment opportunities and supports sustainable urban and industrial development [24, 25].

In summary, accelerating global progress in energy efficiency is indispensable for achieving sustainable energy systems. It represents a unifying strategy that aligns environmental objectives with economic competitiveness and social well-being, reinforcing its central role in the global clean energy transition.

2.2 Energy-Intensive Sectors and Energy Efficiency Challenges

Energy-intensive sectors are among the largest consumers of energy and emitters of greenhouse gases, making them critical to global decarbonization efforts. Their complex, high-energy processes present significant challenges for transitioning to low-carbon operations. The following subsections outline the characteristics of these sectors (Sect. 2.2.1) and introduce energy efficiency status in both industry (Sect. 2.2.2) and transportation (Sect. 2.2.3).

2.2.1 Overview

Energy end-users are the final consumers of energy in the economy, encompassing sectors, organizations, and individuals that utilize energy to perform specific activities rather than to transform or distribute it further [24]. This thesis focuses on the energy-intensive segments within these end-users, which represent a subset that consumes substantial amounts of energy per unit of economic output. Their operations rely heavily on energy as a core input for physical, chemical, or mechanical processes, making them both major energy consumers and significant sources of GHG emissions. According to analyses by the IEA, the industrial, transportation, and building sectors are the most energy-intensive end-use domains, warranting in-depth investigation to identify opportunities for improving energy efficiency [24, 25].

Figure 2.1 illustrates global final energy consumption and CO_2 emissions by sector.

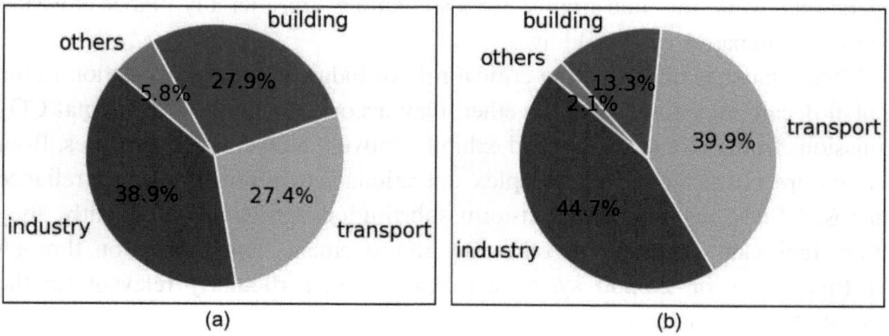

Fig. 2.1 Distribution of global final energy consumption and CO_2 emissions by sector in 2023 [24]. Sub-figure (a) illustrates the share of total final energy consumption attributed to major end-use sectors, including industry, transportation, building, and others. Sub-figure (b) presents the corresponding shares of CO_2 emissions from these sectors

Table 2.1 shows the CO_2 emissions intensity by sector in 2023.

Table 2.1 CO_2 emissions intensity by sector in 2023

Sector	Industry	Transport	Building
CO_2 emissions intensity (t CO_2 per TJ)	53.3	67.3	22.1

According to the IEA, total final energy consumption across all end-use sectors increased by 1.7% to about 445 exajoules (EJ) in 2023. Among these, the industry sector accounted for more than 170 EJ, followed by buildings with around 125 EJ, transportation with approximately 120 EJ, and agriculture and other non-energy uses contributing about 25 EJ. Direct energy use in these sectors generated roughly 55% of total energy-related CO_2 emissions, estimated at 37.7 Gt in 2023.

From a sectoral perspective, industry, transportation, and buildings together account for the majority of global energy use and emissions. As shown in Fig. 2.1, industry represents 38.9% of final energy consumption and 44.7% of CO_2 emissions, while transportation accounts for 27.4% of energy use and 39.9% of emissions. Buildings contribute 27.9% of energy consumption but only 13.3% of emissions, reflecting a lower emissions intensity. The corresponding CO_2 emission intensities presented in Table 2.1 indicate that transport activities release more carbon per unit of energy consumed than most industrial or building operations, while the industrial sector also exhibits considerably higher emission intensity compared with buildings.

These statistics underline the critical role of industry and transportation in the global decarbonization effort. Together, they account for over 70% of total CO_2 emissions from end-use sectors and exhibit relatively high energy intensities. Both sectors are characterized by complex operational environments, heavy reliance on fossil fuels, and limited short-term substitution options. Consequently, they offer significant potential for efficiency improvements and innovation through AI-driven decision-support systems, making them particularly relevant for the case studies conducted in this thesis.

2.2.2 Energy Efficiency in Industry

The industrial sector forms the backbone of global material production, supplying essential goods that underpin the economy and support the transition toward low-carbon technologies. However, it remains the most carbon-intensive end-use sector, contributing to nearly half of global final consumption emissions. In 2023, the sector's total final energy use reached approximately 170 EJ, representing about 39% of global consumption [24]. While energy demand rose by 2% compared to the previous year, the associated CO_2 emissions increased by less than 1%, reflecting gradual improvements in efficiency and the increasing adoption of cleaner technologies [24, 25].

The IEA categorizes industrial activities into energy-intensive (hard-to-abate) and less-intensive sectors [24]. Energy-intensive industries, such as iron and steel, cement, chemicals, and non-ferrous metals, are characterized by processes that require sustained high temperatures and pressures, often in facilities with long asset lifetimes. In contrast, less-intensive sectors, including food and beverages, textiles, and pulp and paper, operate under lower temperatures and pressures and typically have greater flexibility to implement energy-saving measures.

Industrial energy use is dominated by energy-intensive subsectors that rely heavily on high-temperature heat for chemical and material transformation [24, 25]. These industries consume nearly three-quarters of the sector's total energy but contribute only about one-fifth of total industrial value added [24], revealing the disproportionate relationship between energy input and economic output. Figure 2.2 presents the breakdown of industrial final energy consumption and associated CO_2 emissions by major subsector.

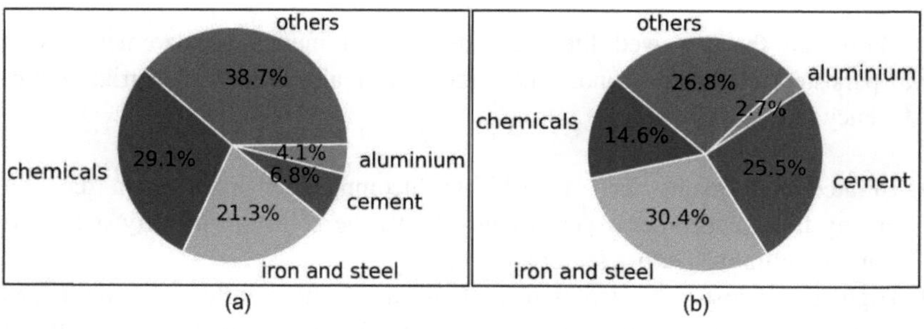

Fig. 2.2 Global distribution of industrial final energy consumption and CO_2 emissions by subsector in 2023 [24]. Sub-figure (a) illustrates the share of total final energy consumption attributed to major industrial subsectors, including chemicals, iron and steel, cement, aluminum, and others. Sub-figure (b) presents the corresponding shares of CO2 emissions from these subsectors

Figure 2.2 illustrates that the chemicals and iron and steel industries collectively account for nearly half of total industrial energy consumption, reflecting both the magnitude of their production volumes and the high thermodynamic requirements of their processes. In contrast, the cement industry, although responsible for a smaller share of energy use, generates disproportionately large CO_2 emissions. This is primarily due to process-related emissions from limestone calcination and the continued reliance on fossil fuels to supply high-temperature heat. The comparison highlights the heterogeneity of emission sources across industrial subsectors and underscores the need for effective decarbonization pathways tailored to the specific process characteristics and energy profiles of each industry.

Table 2.2 shows the CO_2 emissions intensity by industrial subsector in 2023. Cement production is the most carbon-intensive subsector, emitting over 200 tonnes of CO_2 per terajoule of energy. Iron and steel follow, with emissions mainly from coke combustion in blast furnaces, while aluminum's emissions are largely electricity related. The chemical sector, though energy-intensive, shows lower emission intensity. These variations highlight the complexity of industrial decarbonization and the need for data-driven, sector-specific strategies.

Table 2.2 CO_2 emissions intensity by industrial subsector in 2023

Sector	Chemicals	Iron and steel	Cement	Aluminium
CO_2 emissions intensity (t CO_2 per TJ)	26.7	76.0	201.3	35.4

Based on the reviewed literature, despite continuous improvements, several persistent challenges hinder the large-scale realization of industrial energy efficiency [24, 25, 27–31].

- Limited high-quality data availability: Incomplete or inconsistent data on energy flows and process performance limits the ability to identify optimization opportunities across sectors.
- High capital costs: The deployment of advanced, energy-efficient technologies often involves significant upfront investments that are prohibitive for small and medium-sized enterprises.
- Organizational resistance: Cultural and operational inertia can slow the adoption of energy-saving practices, particularly where short-term productivity concerns outweigh long-term sustainability gains.
- Quality assurance concerns: Some firms associate energy-efficiency interventions with risks to product quality or process stability, which discourages experimentation and innovation.

- Knowledge and awareness gaps: A lack of technical expertise and insufficient understanding of potential benefits hinder effective energy management in many industries.
- Policy and regulatory barriers: Weak policy incentives, limited carbon pricing mechanisms, and inconsistent enforcement frameworks constrain progress in several regions.

Addressing these barriers requires coordinated efforts combining technical innovation, digital transformation, capacity building, and supportive policy frameworks. Data-driven, AI-enabled decision-support systems offer new opportunities to optimize industrial processes, enhance transparency, and accelerate the transition to low-carbon manufacturing.

2.2.3 Energy Efficiency in Transportation

The transportation sector remains one of the largest and fastest-growing sources of global energy demand and CO_2 emissions. In 2023, total final energy consumption in transportation reached approximately 122 EJ, accounting for about 27% of global final energy use and generating around 8.2 Gt of CO_2 emissions [24]. This represents an increase of nearly 4% compared with the previous year, driven primarily by the rebound in aviation activity, which recovered to over 90% of pre-pandemic levels, and by sustained growth in road transport [24, 25]. The global passenger car fleet expanded by more than 20 million vehicles in 2023, mostly in China, India, and Southeast Asia, reflecting rising incomes and population growth [25].

Between 2010 and 2023, the sector's energy demand grew at an average annual rate of 1.45%, with the United States, the European Union, and China together accounting for nearly 44% of total transport energy consumption [24, 25]. Despite increasing electrification, energy use in transportation continues to rise, although efficiency gains and the growing market share of electric vehicles (EVs) have moderated the pace of emissions growth.

Figure 2.3 illustrates global final energy consumption and CO_2 emissions by transportation subsector. Road passenger light-duty vehicles account for the largest share of energy use at approximately 39%, followed by road freight trucks at around 23%. Aviation and navigation bunkers together contribute about 20%, while the remaining portion is attributed to other modes such as rail and pipeline transport. A similar pattern is observed for CO_2 emissions, with road freight trucks being major contributors due to diesel dependence and long-haul operations. Aviation exhibits a slightly higher emissions intensity relative to its energy use, reflecting the high carbon intensity of jet fuel and the limited availability of low-carbon alternatives.

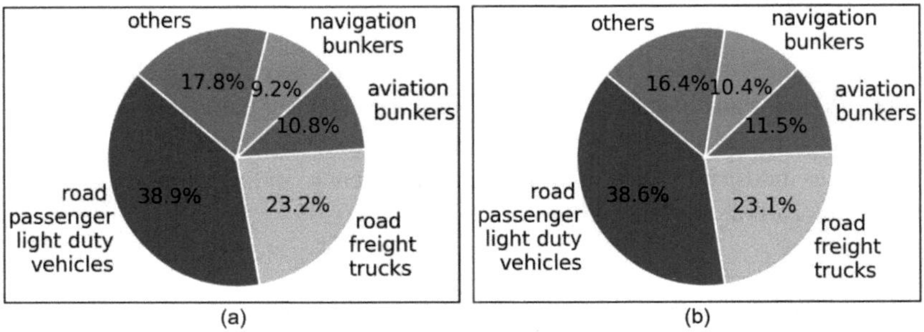

Fig. 2.3 Global distribution of transportation final energy consumption and CO_2 emissions by subsector in 2023 [24]. Sub-figure (a) illustrates the share of total final energy consumption attributed to major transportation subsectors, including road passenger light-duty vehicles, road freight trucks, aviation bunkers, navigation bunkers, and others. Sub-figure (b) presents the corresponding shares of CO_2 emissions from these subsectors

Table 2.3 shows the CO_2 emissions intensity by transportation subsector. Maritime and aviation bunkers exhibit the highest CO_2 emissions per unit of energy, at 76.0 and 71.3 t CO_2 per TJ, respectively, reflecting the use of high-carbon fuels and the limited availability of scalable alternatives. Road passenger and freight transport show slightly lower but still significant intensities, largely driven by internal combustion engines powered by gasoline and diesel. Although the growing penetration of electric and hybrid vehicles has improved average fleet efficiency, heavy-duty vehicles and aviation remain largely dependent on fossil fuels.

Table 2.3 CO_2 emissions intensity by transportation subsector in 2023

Sector	Road passenger light-duty vehicles	Road freight trucks	Aviation bunkers	Navigation bunkers
CO_2 emissions intensity (t CO_2 per TJ)	66.7	67.2	71.3	76.0

By the end of this decade, overall energy demand in transportation is projected to rise by nearly 10%, with road transport and aviation as the primary contributors. However, efficiency gains and electrification are expected to temper this growth. Despite these advances, substantial challenges remain in enhancing energy efficiency and reducing emissions across the transportation sector based on the reviewed literature [24, 25, 32–35]:

- Limited high-quality data availability: Incomplete or inconsistent data on energy flows and performance hampers accurate assessment and optimization across transport modes.
- Operational inefficiencies and data gaps: Poor fleet management, congestion, and limited system integration restrict opportunities for fuel savings.
- Technological and infrastructure limitations: Insufficient charging infrastructure, lack of standardization, and slow fleet renewal impede large-scale adoption of cleaner transport technologies.
- Economic and financial constraints: High vehicle costs, limited financing, and long payback periods discourage investment in efficient and electric transport systems.
- Behavioral and social resistance: Strong preference for private vehicles and low awareness of sustainable mobility options reduce adoption of energy-efficient transport behaviors.
- Institutional and policy barriers: Weak coordination and inconsistent regulatory frameworks limit strategic planning and hinder long-term investments in sustainable mobility.

Addressing these challenges requires integrated strategies that unite technical innovation, supportive policies, and digital transformation. AI-driven decision-support frameworks can play a pivotal role by enabling data-informed optimization of operations, route planning, fleet management, and maintenance. These systems enhance efficiency and sustainability, accelerating the transition to low-carbon, energy-efficient transportation.

2.3 Summary

This chapter has established the research's contextual foundation by examining the global drive toward energy efficiency and its critical role in the transition to sustainable energy systems. It highlights how improving efficiency has become a cornerstone of global and regional strategies to mitigate climate change, enhance energy security, and support long-term economic resilience. The analysis of energy-intensive sectors, particularly industry and transportation, demonstrates their dominant share of global energy use and emissions, as well as the structural, technical, and organizational barriers that continue to impede large-scale efficiency gains. Despite growing policy attention and technical progress, these sectors still require innovative, data-driven solutions to optimize performance and accelerate decarbonization.

By situating the study within these real-world challenges, the chapter has clarified the practical relevance and problem orientation of the research within the relevance cycle of the three-cycle DSR model. The insights presented here establish the application foundation for developing advanced analytical methods capable of addressing complex, data-rich decision environments.

Building upon this contextual background, Chap. 3 transitions to the rigor cycle, offering a comprehensive review of the theoretical and methodological foundations for AI-driven decision support. It examines the state of the art in AI-driven DSS and identifies key research gaps that motivate the design of the proposed AI-driven decision support framework.

Literature Review and State of the Art 3

Chapter 2 has established the contextual and practical relevance of this research by analyzing the global and sectoral challenges associated with energy efficiency and sustainability, which fulfills the requirement analysis step within the relevance cycle of the three-cycle DSR model. Building upon that, this chapter addresses the grounding stage of the rigor cycle by establishing the theoretical and methodological foundations for developing the proposed AI-driven decision-support framework. It critically reviews the foundational theories, methodological advancements, and state-of-the-art (SotA) research that underpin modern DSS enhanced by AI techniques.

Through this literature review, the chapter identifies scientific principles and existing knowledge gaps essential to designing a robust, interpretable, and human-centered framework that supports data-driven decision-making in complex industrial and energy systems. The review systematically examines both classical and emerging approaches, evaluating their conceptual foundations, technical methods, and practical limitations to inform the framework's methodological design and system architecture in subsequent chapters.

To provide a coherent overview of the multi-layered components constituting AI-driven decision support, the chapter is organized as follows. Section 3.1 reviews existing AI-driven decision-support frameworks, outlining their objectives, architectures, and underlying AI techniques, and synthesizes key challenges and emerging research trends. Section 3.2 discusses data understanding and quality assurance, emphasizing their role as prerequisites for reliable and valid analytics. Section 3.3 focuses on clustering and pattern-discovery methods for identifying latent operational behaviors. Section 3.4 examines causal inference and reasoning as the foundations for explainable, trustworthy decision support. Section 3.5 explores multimodal decision narration, highlighting the role

Z. Ma, *Artificial Intelligence-Driven Decision Support Framework for Improving Energy Efficiency in Industry and Transportation*,
https://doi.org/10.1007/978-3-658-51965-0_3

of LLMs in translating analytical results into interpretable narratives for stakeholders. Finally, Sect. 3.6 provides a summary of insights and methodological implications drawn from the reviewed literature.

3.1 AI-Driven Decision Support Frameworks

AI-driven decision-support frameworks are intelligent systems that leverage advanced data science and AI techniques to assist human decision-making in complex engineering environments. These systems combine data management, analytical modeling, and knowledge-based reasoning to support evidence-driven decisions across industrial, energy, and transportation domains. The concept and architecture of DSS form the theoretical foundation of this research and underpin the development of the proposed AI-driven framework.

3.1.1 Fundamentals of Decision Support Systems

A DSS is an interactive, computer-based environment designed to help decision-makers address unstructured or semi-structured problems by integrating data, analytical models, and expert knowledge [18, 36]. Rather than replacing human judgment, DSS enhances the decision process through analytical support, visualization, and scenario evaluation, thereby improving the quality and consistency of managerial and operational decisions [18].

DSS are particularly useful for complex and non-routine decisions that require balancing quantitative data and qualitative reasoning. They integrate management-science methodologies with computational tools to facilitate modeling, simulation, and optimization [18]. Flexibility and adaptability are essential features, ensuring that DSS remain responsive to evolving organizational structures, decision contexts, and technical developments [36].

Figure 3.1 illustrates the general DSS architecture [18, 36, 37]. The technical core, comprising data management, model management, and a knowledge engine, constitutes the analytical backbone of this PhD research:

- Data management oversees the collection, storage, and retrieval of relevant internal or external data.
- Model management develops and maintains analytical or optimization models aligned with decision objectives.

- Knowledge engine embeds domain rules and reasoning logic to enhance analytical depth.
- These components interact through a user interface that allows decision-makers to visualize outcomes, test scenarios, and interpret recommendations.

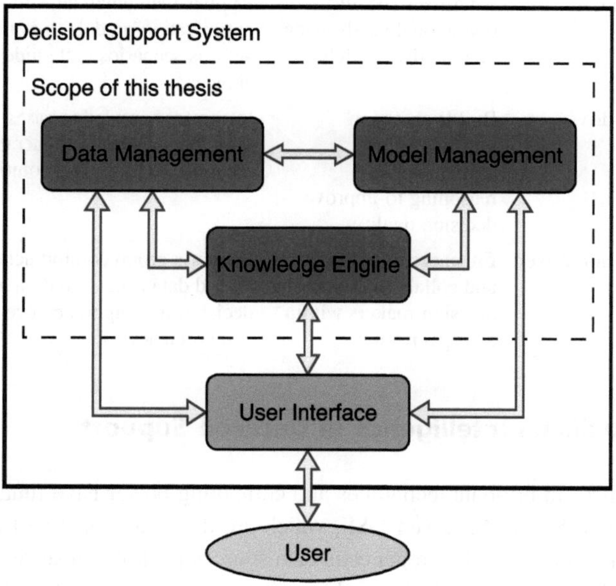

Fig. 3.1 General architecture of a decision support system [18, 36, 37]. The blue components represent the technical core for data processing and reasoning, which defines the main focus of this PhD thesis. The green component denotes the user interface for interaction and visualization, while the yellow component represents the end users and decision-makers

Table 3.1 summarizes major DSS categories [36–38], classified by their main intelligence source and analytical mechanism.

Table 3.1 Categories of decision support systems [36–38]

Category	Description	Operational mechanism
Data-driven	Utilizes extensive internal and external datasets to support decision-making.	Employs data mining and machine learning techniques to extract insights, identify patterns, and predict outcomes.
Model-driven	Addresses specific operational needs using quantitative models.	Applies mathematical, simulation, or optimization models to evaluate various scenarios and guide strategic choices.
Knowledge-driven	Builds on expert knowledge and domain-specific reasoning to improve decision quality.	Integrates knowledge bases, rules, and inference engines to generate tailored recommendations and solutions.
Communication-driven	Enhances coordination and collaboration among decision-makers within an organization.	Supports group communication, shared data access, and interactive decision-making to achieve consensus and efficiency.

3.1.2 Artificial Intelligence in Decision Support

Rapid advances in big-data techniques and computing power have fundamentally transformed DSS into AI-driven DSS, which are dynamic, adaptive frameworks capable of learning from heterogeneous data sources [39]. AI enhances the scope and speed of human reasoning by enabling faster, more consistent, and evidence-based decision-making [39, 40].

Among the many AI paradigms, three foundational techniques have been pivotal: Machine Learning (ML) [41], Deep Learning (DL) [42], and Natural Language Processing (NLP) [43]. ML provides predictive and prescriptive capabilities; DL extends learning to high-dimensional and unstructured data; and NLP enables semantic understanding and human-system interaction. Recent developments in LLMs and multimodal LLMs [44–46], further expand these capabilities by integrating reasoning across text, numerical, and visual modalities, thereby improving interpretability and user accessibility.

Table 3.2 summarizes the primary AI techniques used in DSS, highlighting their analytical focus and key contributions to enhancing decision-making in application domains.

Table 3.2 Overview of AI techniques in decision support [41–44]

AI technique	Learning paradigm	Core capability	Typical DSS applications
ML	• Supervised learning • Unsupervised learning	• Learning patterns and relationships • Predicting outcomes • Clustering outcomes	• Predictive maintenance • Demand forecasting • Process segmentation
DL	• Neural networks (NN)	• Hierarchical feature extraction • Nonlinear pattern recognition	• Fault detection • Visual inspection • Complex demand forecasting
NLP	• Rule-based methods • Representation learning • DL	• Semantic understanding • Human-system interaction	• Semantic modeling • Text mining • Information extraction
LLM	• Transformer-based generative AI	• Natural language understanding, reasoning, and generation	• Knowledge retrieval • Report summarization • Conversational DSS
Multimodal LLM	• Cross-modal reasoning with LLM	• Integrates and interprets multi-source data for reasoning	• Same application with LLM but with multimodal inputs

Machine learning enables DSS to learn directly from data rather than rely solely on predefined rules [47]. Supervised learning (e.g., decision trees, random forests, SVM) maps process parameters to outcomes such as equipment health or quality [48]. Unsupervised learning (e.g., k-means, hierarchical clustering, PCA) discovers latent structures [49–51], supporting anomaly detection and operational segmentation. However, traditional ML depends on structured features, limiting scalability for high-dimensional or multimodal data [52, 53].

DL overcomes this by automatically extracting hierarchical features from raw data [42]. CNNs are applied in image-based inspection and defect detection [54]; RNNs and transformers handle sequential data for time-series forecasting [55]. Reinforcement learning (RL) optimizes sequential decisions based on feedback, enabling adaptive scheduling, control, and energy management [56–60].

LLMs, exemplified by GPT-4 [61], Claude [62], and Gemini [63], extend DSS capabilities by enabling natural language interaction and reasoning. They convert unstructured textual data, such as manuals, reports, and maintenance logs, into structured, queryable knowledge [44]. Techniques such as chain-of-thought (CoT) prompting [64] and retrieval augmented generation (RAG) improve interpretability and factual grounding [65]. Multimodal LLMs [66–68] integrate textual, visual, and sensor inputs, allowing simultaneous reasoning across modalities, e.g., diagnosing a machine fault using images, sensor data, and maintenance records.

3.1.3 State of the Art and Applications

AI-driven DSS have achieved significant progress across engineering fields, leveraging large-scale data to identify hidden correlations, optimize operations, and improve efficiency. Representative studies are summarized in Table 3.3, covering manufacturing, transportation, energy, and other industrial sectors.

The methodological diversity in AI-based DSS reflects the need to select analytical techniques that align with the specific requirements and challenges of each application domain. ML, DL, and fuzzy logic constitute the core algorithmic foundations that enable DSS to process large-scale data and derive actionable insights.

Table 3.3 Overview of SotA AI-driven decision support studies across application domains

Application sector	Objectives	Methodologies	Ref.
Manufacturing	Predictive maintenance	Feature engineering; Random forest	[47]
	Predictive maintenance	Statistical analysis with domain knowledge; Decision tree	[69]
	Intelligent decision making	LLM	[70]
	Process quality improvement	Explainable AI (XAI) with SHAP	[71]
	Production planning	Fuzzy logic algorithm; Decision tree	[72]
Transportation	Forecasting electric vehicles' power requirement	Exponential smoothing	[73]
	Evaluating autonomous vehicle integration scenarios	Multi-criteria decision-making (MCDM); Random forest	[74]
	Warning and driver assistance	LLM	[75]
	Navigation strategy	Fuzzy logic-based dynamic decision-making	[76]
	Vessel trajectories prediction	GMM clustering; Linear discriminant analysis; Deep learning	[77]
Energy	Solar energy management	NN; Delphi method	[78]
	Energy-efficiency management in buildings	Data management; Multiple AI algorithms	[79]
	Energy consumption prediction in buildings	NN; Parametric modeling	[80]
Construction	Equipment selection and Maintenance	Feature engineering; Comparison of multiple supervised learning algorithms	[81]

(continued)

Table 3.3 (continued)

Application sector	Objectives	Methodologies	Ref.
	Autonomous real-time interpretation and decision-making support	Deep learning; AI-based digital twin	[82]
Agriculture	Precision agriculture	Hybrid AI algorithms	[83]
	Crop recommendation and soil nutrient analysis	MSVM-DAG-FFO classification algorithm	[84]
Production management	Product classification sales forecast	Decision tree; NN	[85]
Automotive industry	Assembly line balancing	Genetic algorithm	[86]
Infrastructure system	Infrastructure operation and maintenance	Feature engineering; Random forests; Bayesian networks	[87]
Mining	Promote sustainable mining practices	Fuzzy logic-based dynamic decision-making	[88]
Three industry scenarios	Professional semantic understanding; Judgment and decision making	LLM	[89]
IoT	Anomaly detection	Deep learning	[90]
Water	Water quality management	Statistical analysis; Comparison of multiple supervised learning algorithms	[91]
Environment	Landslide susceptibility modeling	Integrated machine learning models with the bagging ensemble	[92]
Smart cities	Support complex urban decision-making processes	LLM	[93]

ML methods, particularly supervised and unsupervised learning, have been widely applied across fields, where models learn from historical datasets to detect patterns, classify outcomes, and forecast future events [47–49]. In the manufacturing section, for instance, ML algorithms trained on industrial process and production data have improved the analysis of production quality and machine maintenance [47, 69]. DL, as an advanced subset of ML, can extract hierarchical features from unstructured data such as images, text, and speech [42].

This capability has driven major progress in complex domains requiring high accuracy, including product or machine images, natural language understanding, and autonomous systems [94, 95]. Fuzzy logic contributes to AI-based DSS by enabling reasoning under uncertainty and vagueness, conditions typical in energy, environmental, and industrial management [72, 76, 88]. Unlike binary logic, fuzzy systems model gradations of truth, allowing decisions to be made based on incomplete or imprecise information [72, 76, 88, 96]. This capacity makes fuzzy approaches particularly valuable in domains characterized by dynamic operating conditions and limited data availability, supporting more flexible and human-like reasoning within decision processes [96].

A critical advancement toward transparency and accountability in AI-based DSS is the emergence of XAI [97]. XAI techniques aim to make model outputs interpretable by elucidating how and why specific decisions are produced [97]. This is particularly significant in safety- or regulation-sensitive domains such as transportation and energy sectors, where understanding the rationale behind recommendations is essential [97–99]. Integrating XAI into DSS mitigates the "black-box" problem associated with complex ML and DL models, thereby enhancing user trust, credibility, and system adoption. Explainable DSS extends this concept by embedding interpretability directly into the decision-making framework, thereby transforming opaque predictive models into transparent and justifiable systems that support human oversight [71, 97].

Recently, LLMs have emerged as a new frontier for decision support[44]. Pretrained on massive text corpora, LLMs demonstrate exceptional capability in understanding and generating natural language, enabling new forms of human-AI interaction [44, 70, 75, 89, 93]. In engineering contexts, LLMs can process maintenance reports, technical manuals, or sensor data summaries to provide context-aware recommendations and explanations in real time [89, 93]. Their ability to integrate domain-specific data with general knowledge allows them to act as adaptive, language-based decision assistants. By enabling users to query complex systems in natural language, LLMs enhance accessibility and interpretability, while fine-tuning and retrieval-augmented techniques improve their factual precision and domain relevance [44].

Building upon the advanced AI techniques discussed above, AI-driven DSS are deployed across a spectrum of analytical and operational functions in engineering, each of which imposes distinct methodological requirements and trade-offs involving accuracy, interpretability, and computational cost. These tasks include predictive maintenance, forecasting, classification and diagnostic analysis, and decision-making. The following reviews these functional categories and the associated AI techniques.

Predictive Maintenance

Predictive maintenance aims to estimate equipment failure risks or remaining useful life (RUL) based on sensor and operational data [100]. Supervised learning algorithms, such as decision trees, random forests, and ensemble methods, are widely adopted for failure prediction due to their robustness in handling heterogeneous sensor features and their capacity to rank important predictors [47, 69]. For instance, random forests can highlight vibration variance or temperature as critical indicators of machine degradation, providing both prediction and interpretable insight [47]. More recently, deep learning architectures, such as Long Short-Term Memory (LSTM) [101] and transformer [102], have been applied to capture temporal degradation patterns in sequential sensor data, yielding improved RUL forecasting accuracy at the cost of interpretability. In scenarios with limited data or strong expert knowledge, fuzzy logic and rule-based systems are often integrated to encode expert-defined thresholds or warning conditions [103, 104]. Hybrid predictive maintenance frameworks increasingly combine data-driven models with knowledge-based rules and XAI tools to balance accuracy, safety, and transparency [69].

Forecasting

Forecasting underpins many engineering decisions, such as demand prediction in supply chains [85], load forecasting in power systems [80], and performance prediction in infrastructure management [87]. Deep learning methods excel at learning nonlinear temporal dependencies in multivariate time series, capturing seasonality and anomalies that conventional models may overlook [94, 95]. However, when data are limited or interpretability is a priority, ensemble approaches such as gradient boosting, e.g., XGBoost, and tree-based regression models remain competitive, offering shorter training times and interpretable feature importance metrics [85, 87, 105]. Hybrid methods that incorporate physical constraints or simulation-based features into ML models are increasingly popular, ensuring forecasts remain consistent with first-principles behavior [77, 87]. The method choice typically depends on data richness, complexity of the temporal patterns, and stakeholder requirements for transparency.

Classification and Diagnosis

Many DSS applications involve classification tasks, such as identifying fault types, assessing product quality, or diagnosing system states. Classical models such as Support Vector Machines (SVM) and decision trees remain prevalent in industrial fault diagnosis due to their interpretability and strong performance on medium-sized datasets [106–108]. As data dimensionality increases, e.g., through high-resolution sensor arrays or defect images, deep learning approaches such as CNNs and autoencoders have achieved SotA accuracy in detecting anomalies and classifying surface defects [90]. Despite their predictive power, the opacity of deep models often necessitates XAI integration to ensure accountability and user trust [97, 109]. Methods like SHAP [110] or LIME [111] are commonly used to explain feature contributions in ML, bridging the gap between black-box models and human understanding. In practice, hybrid diagnostic frameworks often layer complex models for detection with interpretable or rule-based systems for confirmation, maintaining both high detection accuracy and operational reliability [71, 91].

Decision-Making Methods

Decision-making models constitute a core component of AI-driven DSS, providing the analytical foundation for selecting optimal actions under uncertainty. Among these, MCDM is widely adopted for balancing conflicting objectives, such as cost, time, and quality, across complex domains like logistics, supply chain management, and energy planning [74, 112]. MCDM frameworks systematically evaluate and rank alternatives, supporting transparent and evidence-based decision processes [74, 112]. For instance, in energy-intensive industries, MCDM can support the selection of optimal furnace operating conditions by evaluating alternatives against criteria including energy consumption, production quality, and CO_2 emissions [8]. Recent advancements emphasize XAI and LLM to enhance interpretability and user interaction. XAI clarifies how model outputs are derived, addressing the opacity of black-box systems in high-stakes areas such as industry and transportation [97–99]. LLMs extend this capability by enabling natural language reasoning, context-aware dialogue, and integration of textual knowledge into DSS, facilitating more intuitive and explainable decision interfaces [44, 89, 93]. Additionally, human-in-the-loop architecture combines AI recommendations with expert judgment to ensure accountability and contextual relevance [113]. Together, these models strengthen the transparency, adaptability, and trustworthiness of modern AI-based DSS.

The integration and impact of AI-driven DSS vary substantially across sectors, shaped by differences in operational complexity, data environments, and institutional requirements for transparency and accountability. Below, several domain-specific applications are briefly outlined.

Energy Systems

In energy systems, AI-based DSS contribute significantly to optimizing energy consumption and production efficiency [78–80]. These systems analyze large volumes of data from smart grids, renewable generation, and user consumption to support real-time decisions that enhance grid stability and resource utilization. AI integration has improved load balancing, demand forecasting, and the coordination of distributed energy resources, contributing to both economic and environmental objectives [78–80]. However, ensuring system reliability and adaptability remains critical, particularly under fluctuating conditions such as variable renewable output or sudden demand peaks [114]. Equally important is the transparency of AI-driven recommendations; energy operators and regulators should trust that decisions are based on sound data analysis and interpretable logic [114].

Industrial Manufacturing

Within industrial environments, AI-driven DSS are increasingly used for process optimization, quality control, and supply chain management [47, 69–72]. By extracting insights from complex, multi-stage production data, these systems enable manufacturers to improve efficiency, minimize downtime, and reduce operational costs [47, 69–72]. The dynamic nature of industrial operations requires DSS to operate in real time [72], adapting to changing process conditions and environmental factors. Ensuring transparency and explainability is crucial for maintaining operator trust, as AI-generated recommendations directly impact production strategies and equipment performance [114]. Therefore, hybrid approaches that combine predictive analytics with interpretable reasoning are often preferred for practical deployment in manufacturing contexts [71].

Transportation Systems

In transportation, AI-based DSS addresses both strategic planning and operational control [73, 74, 77]. Forecasting tasks, such as predicting electric vehicle charging demand, are supported by time-series models [73, 77]. Strategic decisions, such as evaluating autonomous vehicle scenarios, benefit from hybrid models integrating MCDM frameworks with ML techniques to balance safety, efficiency, and environmental impact [74, 76]. At the operational level, fuzzy logic supports adaptive navigation and routing under uncertain conditions [76], while deep learning combined with clustering techniques enhances trajectory prediction [77]. The recent application of LLMs in driver-assistance systems [75] further demonstrates the potential for natural language-enabled, context-aware interaction in intelligent transportation systems.

3.1.4 Key Challenges and Limitations of AI-Driven DSS

Despite substantial progress, the development and deployment of AI-driven decision support frameworks across industrial, transportation, and energy systems continue to face persistent challenges. Recent research reveals several recurring obstacles related to data management, model interpretability, and human-organizational integration [41, 97, 114].

Data Compartmentalization and Heterogeneity

In many organizations, data essential for decision-making remains fragmented across isolated systems or stored in incompatible formats [41]. For instance, Industry 4.0 environments collect data from IoT sensors, enterprise resource systems, and external platforms that differ in structure, semantics, and temporal resolution [47, 90, 95]. Such heterogeneity complicates data fusion and prevents the formation of a unified DSS knowledge base [41, 95]. The lack of interoperability also constrains cross-domain decision-making, such as integrating transportation and energy data for optimizing electric vehicle charging operations [114].

Addressing these challenges requires robust data integration strategies. Common approaches include data wrangling pipelines, semantic ontologies for aligning data definitions, and middleware architectures that enable real-time multi-source data fusion [41]. While technically viable, these approaches are often constrained by legacy systems, institutional inertia, and insufficient data governance frameworks [41]. Overcoming compartmentalization is therefore as much an organizational as a technical challenge.

Data Quality and Corruption

The performance of AI-driven DSS depends on the quality of the input data. However, real-world industrial and infrastructural datasets are frequently noisy, incomplete, or corrupted due to sensor faults, manual entry errors, missing records, or malicious interference [115, 116]. Poor data quality directly undermines model accuracy. For example, an energy grid DSS trained on faulty sensor readings may misclassify network states, while a transportation DSS relying on outdated traffic data could recommend inefficient routing strategies.

To mitigate these issues, robust data governance mechanisms should ensure data integrity, accuracy, and timeliness [115, 116]. Techniques such as automated data cleaning, anomaly detection, and outlier correction are increasingly embedded in modern DSS architectures [41, 115, 116]. Nonetheless, many AI models still presuppose clean datasets, leaving them vulnerable to real-time data corruption or uncertainty [41, 117]. Designing systems that can maintain reliable performance under imperfect data conditions remains a major research gap.

Model Interpretability and Trust

Opaque or black-box AI models pose a significant barrier to adoption in high-stakes engineering applications [97]. Stakeholders such as engineers, operators, and regulators require transparency to justify and validate AI-driven recommendations [97, 114]. It is essential to make the internal mechanisms of AI-driven decision-making more understandable to end-users to enhance system transparency and foster user trust [114]. The integration of XAI techniques, such as SHAP and LIME, has been proposed to enhance interpretability by identifying the key factors influencing model predictions [99, 114]. However, most XAI methods remain post hoc, offering limited causal insight. The broader challenge lies in developing interpretable-by-design models that can convey meaningful reasoning to human users without sacrificing predictive performance. Without such transparency, even highly accurate DSS may see limited real-world uptake.

Human Factors and Organizational Challenges

Beyond technical capabilities, the success of an AI-DSS depends on its alignment with human workflows and organizational culture. A persistent challenge is trusting calibration, wherein users may either undertrust the system and dismiss valid recommendations or overtrust it and exhibit automation bias, both of which can result in suboptimal or unsafe decisions [114]. Building appropriate trust requires not only explainable models but also user training, iterative interface design, and mechanisms that communicate uncertainty [114]. Organizational resistance, lack of data literacy, and insufficient feedback loops further hinder effective adoption. Consequently, achieving human-AI collaboration in decision-making remains an open socio-technical challenge that extends beyond algorithmic performance.

3.1.5 Research Trends and Emerging Directions for AI-Driven DSS

Recent research directions reflect a concerted effort to overcome the challenges identified above. Emerging trends emphasize data integration, hybrid modeling, interpretability, trustworthiness, and human-AI collaboration as core enablers of next-generation decision support frameworks.

Improving Data Integration and Governance

To address data compartmentalization, researchers are developing more advanced frameworks for integrating heterogeneous data streams into coherent decision architectures [41]. Promising approaches include universal data standards, knowledge graph-based integration, and adaptive data fusion algorithms capable of handling structural and semantic heterogeneity [41]. Furthermore, there is a growing emphasis on enabling AI systems to operate reliably with imperfect data through anomaly-resilient modeling, data augmentation, and real-time quality monitoring [81, 87, 114]. Developing DSS that can reason under uncertainty or missing information remains a key frontier for safety-critical applications.

Hybrid and Multi-Method AI Frameworks

SotA DSS increasingly adopts hybrid modeling strategies that combine data-driven learning with domain knowledge [114]. Such approaches integrate statistical AI with symbolic or rule-based systems, leveraging their complementary strengths [69, 72, 91]. For example, a neural network (NN) may generate preliminary recommendations that are subsequently refined or validated by a rule-based module following engineering constraints [82]. Optimization algorithms can also fine-tune neural outputs or detect constraint violations [114]. This synthesis of physical modeling, heuristics, and learning is often referred to as knowledge-infused AI, enabling improved interpretability, generalization, and domain consistency [114].

Explainable and Trustworthy AI

Interpretability and trust have become defining characteristics of SotA AI-DSS research [97, 114]. Beyond generic explanation tools such as LIME and SHAP, domain-specific explainability methods are emerging, such as mapping predictions to known failure modes in structural engineering or code provisions in power systems [97, 99]. Techniques like surrogate modeling, rule extraction, and interactive visualization support transparent communication between models and users [97, 99]. Trustworthy AI extends these efforts by encompassing fairness, robustness, and security [114]. Recent standards in AI ethics emphasize bias assessment, adversarial robustness testing, and model accountability. In infrastructure and public systems, the need to ensure fairness, safety, and alignment with human values is becoming as critical as optimizing predictive performance [113]. These developments are fostering interdisciplinary collaborations among engineers, data scientists, and ethicists, marking a shift toward socially responsible AI in decision support.

Human-AI Interaction and Trust Calibration
As AI-DSS systems transition from research to operational environments, understanding human-AI interaction dynamics has become a key research priority [97, 114]. Studies increasingly investigate how different explanation formats, visualization designs, and confidence indicators influence user trust and decision quality [114]. The emerging concept of epistemic partnership envisions AI not merely as a decision tool but as a reasoning companion that presents alternatives, rationale, and confidence levels to augment human judgment [97, 113, 114]. Realizing this vision requires human-centered interface design, operator training, and adaptive trust calibration mechanisms that adjust AI behavior based on confidence or uncertainty levels [89, 93]. Embedding expert knowledge directly into AI architecture further enhances transparency, reduces data dependency, and promotes user acceptance [97, 114]. These developments point toward the evolution of AI-DSS from autonomous predictors to collaborative, context-aware decision partners.

In summary, the reviewed literature demonstrates a clear transition toward more integrated, explainable, and human-centered AI-driven DSS. However, persistent gaps remain in ensuring data quality and interoperability, maintaining reliable performance under uncertainty, and achieving transparent, trustworthy decision-making logic. These unresolved issues motivate the framework proposed in this PhD research, which focuses on data-driven and causality-informed decision support for energy-intensive systems. By addressing data heterogeneity, quality assurance, and interpretability through hybrid modeling and explainable analytics, the proposed work aims to bridge the gap between technical capability and practical deployment.

3.2 Data Characteristic and Quality Understanding

Note: Parts of this section are based on the author's first-author journal article: *"A systematic data characteristic understanding framework towards physical-sensor big data challenges"* [115].

Physical sensors generate vast streams of data that can be used for AI-driven DSS. These data are typically time-series readings, such as temperature, vibration and energy consumption, collected at high frequency and volume. The immense data volume, diverse data content, and complex data structure introduce unique computational and statistical challenges in big data. These include issues related to scalability and storage bottleneck, noise accumulation, spurious correlation, incidental endogeneity, and measurement errors [118, 119]. However, if the quality of sensor data is poor, the data become practically useless, and AI outputs can be misleading or even dangerous [120]. As a result, it is essential to develop techniques for comprehending the characteristics of big data, which extract valuable insights and assist in addressing the challenges posed by big data, ultimately enhancing the reliability and accuracy of data analytics.

In real-world applications, big data often fail to yield valuable insights due to the aforementioned challenges. Coping with big data problems requires substantial resources beyond simply adapting existing analytics algorithms. In data analytics, raw data is rarely immediately suitable for processing. Instead, it typically undergoes multiple stages, including cleansing, integrating, and transforming, before progressing to further refinement, evaluation, and preparation as it moves through its lifecycle [121].

Enhancing the capacity to comprehend, manage, and make informed decisions based on vast volumes of data is a crucial concern in big data analytics, which aims to advance the selection of techniques for extracting valuable insights from these substantial datasets to enable effective data processing. The vast amount of grown information hidden within datasets should be inferred and effectively managed to reveal the characteristics of big data, which should be the initial step before considering the application of any data-preprocessing and analytical techniques. Data characteristics are models on the "Vs" that describe the attribute and dimension information of data sources in detail [122, 123]. The number and selection of vs vary across studies based on distinct requirements. Volume, variety, and velocity are the three basic "Vs" showing big data characteristics [124, 125]. It can be extended to six "Vs" by adding veracity, value, and variability [126–128]. In addition to the 6 Vs framework, several other dimensions, such as validity [129], volatility [130], valence [129], and so on, have been developed in recent publications to encompass a more comprehensive representation of data characteristics. In recent research [129–133], several new criteria have been introduced to broaden the understanding of data characteristics, such as visualization, validity, vitality, etc. These novel criteria are currently still in the development stage and potentially overlap with the existing "Vs" concepts [134, 135]. Although the proposed "Vs" frameworks have provided precise and convincing definitions of all their dimensions, existing studies exhibit certain limitations when attempting to quantify these Vs to cover the comprehensive characteristics of large-scale data, primarily due to their sheer volume, multiple sources, and diverse formats [136].

The big data characteristics and challenges are defined as Vs, and the initial 3 Vs are named Volume (large scale of data), Variety (various data formats and sources), and Velocity (rapid data generation and interaction) [124, 125]. Afterward, the initial 3 Vs model, proposed to explain the technical and business implications of novel data management strategies, is extended to 6 Vs to capture intricate big-data characteristics by incorporating veracity (trustworthiness and reliability of data), value (data with huge value), and variability (consistency in data formats, units, and scales) [127, 137, 138]. In recent research [129–133], many new criteria have been proposed to broaden the data characteristic understanding, such as visualization, validity, vitality, etc. Table 3.4 outlines the different Vs in the analyzed literature. Such novel criteria are still in the development stage and potentially overlap with the existing Vs concepts [134]; therefore, the 6 Vs criteria are widely adopted in most literature to understand the big-data characteristics.

Although existing Vs-based frameworks have provided clear and systematic definitions of big data dimensions, several limitations remain in their practical quantification. Current studies often struggle to measure these dimensions in a way that fully captures the comprehensive characteristics of large-scale datasets, primarily due to the data's volume, heterogeneity, and multisource nature [136].

The characteristics of big data not only guide the selection of appropriate analytical methodologies but also expose the intrinsic challenges of data analytics. High dimensionality and large sample sizes introduce issues such as noise accumulation, computational complexity, and heterogeneity [139]. Each V-dimension conceptually corresponds to a specific challenge, but its qualitative nature limits detailed representation. The absence of quantitative indicators within Vs models constrains their ability to specify and compare data challenges across contexts. Developing measurable indicators is therefore essential for supporting informed decisions in data preprocessing, integration, and analytics.

While V-based frameworks are generally generic and applicable across sectors, physical-sensor data exhibit distinct characteristics shaped by machine configurations and system environments [5, 136]. The proliferation of measurement devices and multi-sensor networks within the IoT has led to the continuous generation of large-scale data through intelligent sensing and digital communication technologies [140, 141]. However, sensor malfunctions, synchronization errors, or communication delays often result in missing values, inconsistent records, and degraded data quality [142, 143].

Table 3.4 Vs summarization in literature study

Reference	Volume	Variety	Velocity	Veracity	Value	Variability	Visualization	Validity	Volatility	Valence	Vitality	Vincularity
[124]	✓	✓	✓									
[125]	✓	✓	✓									
[121]	✓	✓	✓	✓								
[123]	✓	✓	✓	✓	✓							
[135]	✓	✓	✓	✓	✓							
[126]	✓	✓	✓	✓	✓	✓						
[127]	✓	✓	✓	✓	✓	✓						
[128]	✓	✓	✓	✓	✓	✓						
[122]	✓	✓	✓	✓	✓							✓
[129]	✓	✓	✓	✓	✓			✓	✓	✓	✓	✓
[131]	✓	✓	✓	✓	✓	✓	✓					
[132]	✓	✓	✓	✓	✓	✓	✓					
[130]	✓	✓	✓	✓	✓			✓	✓			
[133]	✓	✓	✓	✓	✓	✓			✓			

Moreover, a substantial portion of physical-sensor data is recorded as time-series measurements, where temporal attributes, such as timestamps and sampling intervals, play a crucial role in defining data quality and analytical reliability. Irregular intervals, duplicate timestamps, or missing temporal records can distort analyses and model outcomes [144]. Despite this, current data characterization frameworks rarely incorporate time-related indicators, limiting their applicability to dynamic IoT and industrial contexts. Integrating temporal characteristics into data quality assessment is thus crucial for achieving a comprehensive, context-aware understanding of the challenges posed by physical sensor data.

3.3 Clustering for Pattern Analysis

Note: Parts of this section are based on the author's first-author journal article: *"Discovering Operational Patterns Using Image-Based Convolutional Clustering and Composite Evaluation: A Case Study in Foundry Melting Processes"* [145].

Clustering is a fundamental unsupervised learning technique for pattern analysis, grouping data into clusters such that similarity is high within each cluster and low between clusters. In the context of AI-driven decision support, clustering enables the discovery of latent patterns or segments in data without prior labels, providing insights that can inform decision-making. This section reviews the literature on clustering methods for pattern analysis, covering both static clustering for time-invariant data and time-series clustering for temporal data, as well as the clustering evaluation methods.

3.3.1 Static Data Clustering

Static clustering identifies inherent structures in datasets without considering temporal dynamics. Classical approaches can be divided into partitional, hierarchical, density-based, and model-based techniques, each with distinct assumptions and computational properties [146]. Table 3.5 summarizes key categories, advantages, and limitations.

Table 3.5 Overview of static clustering methods

Category	Representative algorithms	Principle	Advantages	Limitations
Partitional	k-means, k-medoids	Partition data into k clusters by minimizing within-cluster variance	Efficient and easy to interpret	Requires predefined k; Sensitive to initialization and outliers
Hierarchical	agglomerative, divisive, single/ complete linkage	Build the dendrogram by iterative merging or splitting	Multi-level granularity; No need to predefine k	$O(n^2)$ complexity; Poor scalability
Density-based	DBSCAN, OPTICS, HDBSCAN	Identify dense regions separated by sparse areas	Detects arbitrary shapes; Robust to noise	Sensitive to density parameters; Struggles with varying densities
Model-based	GMM, Bayesian mixtures	Assume data from a mixture of probability distributions	Probabilistic interpretation; Supports soft assignments	Computationally intensive; Model-selection required

Partitional methods, such as k-means and k-medoids, divide data into k non-overlapping clusters [146]. K-means iteratively minimizes within-cluster variance, offering simplicity and computational efficiency [147]. K-medoids, in contrast, uses actual data points as centroids, improving robustness to outliers and interpretability [147]. The main limitation of both methods is the need to predefine k, which is often non-trivial without prior knowledge [146].

Hierarchical clustering constructs a nested dendrogram through agglomerative merging or divisive splitting, providing multi-level cluster granularity [148]. It does not require a predefined number of clusters, but suffers from $O(n^2)$ computational complexity, which limits scalability for large datasets. Despite this, hierarchical methods remain valued for interpretability and have been applied, for instance, to group process models in manufacturing [149].

Density-based methods, particularly DBSCAN (Density-Based Spatial Clustering of Applications with Noise) [150], identify clusters as dense regions separated by sparse areas. DBSCAN detects clusters of arbitrary shape, handles noise effectively, and avoids specifying k [151]. Variants such as OPTICS and

HDBSCAN extend the capability to multi-scale and parameter-robust clustering, proving effective in spatial and anomaly detection contexts [151].

Model-based clustering assumes that data originate from a mixture of probability distributions estimated via maximum likelihood or Bayesian inference [146]. The GMM algorithm [152], for example, employs the Expectation-Maximization (EM) algorithm to assign soft cluster membership. Extensions, including Bayesian mixtures and non-parametric models, have expanded applicability to heterogeneous data [153].

3.3.2 Time-Series Clustering

Time-series clustering introduces additional complexity due to sequential dependencies, temporal variation, and high dimensionality [154]. Existing approaches can be categorized into similarity-based, feature-based, model-based, and representation-learning methods [154]. Table 3.6 summarizes key categories, advantages, and limitations.

Table 3.6 Overview of time-series clustering methods

Category	Representative algorithms	Principle	Advantages	Limitations
Similarity-based	DTW, soft-DTW, weighted-DTW	Measure similarity directly between sequences using distance functions	Preserves full temporal shape; handles time misalignment	High computational cost; Sensitive to noise
Feature-based	Statistical features, catch22	Represent sequences as fixed-length feature vectors	Efficient; Interpretable; Scalable	Loss of temporal detail; Manual feature design

(continued)

Table 3.6 (continued)

Category	Representative algorithms	Principle	Advantages	Limitations
Model-based	ARIMA, HMM	Cluster via parameters of fitted models	Captures process dynamics; Interpretable	Sensitive to model choice and estimation error
Representation-learning	DEC, IDEC, CAE	Learn latent embeddings optimized for clustering	Scalable; Handles complex, multivariate data	Requires large data; Limited interpretability

Similarity-based approaches measure pairwise similarity directly between time series. While Euclidean distance is simple, it is sensitive to phase shifts and misalignments. Dynamic Time Warping (DTW) [155] remains foundational for aligning sequences of varying length and speed, computing an optimal non-linear alignment that preserves shape-based similarity. Extensions such as soft-DTW [156] and weighted DTW [157] improve smoothness and robustness to noise, broadening applicability in process control and machine diagnostics. However, DTW's quadratic time complexity limits scalability without approximation or pruning strategies [154]. In practice, DTW is often integrated with k-means or hierarchical clustering to identify recurring operational patterns [8]. To improve efficiency, k-shape [158] adapts k-means with a shape-based distance metric derived from normalized cross-correlation, enabling clustering based on global trends while remaining invariant to amplitude shifts.

Feature-based methods transform time series into compact feature vectors that capture statistical, spectral, or shape characteristics [154]. This reduces dimensionality and computational cost while enabling the use of static clustering algorithms. In energy analytics, for example, daily electricity consumption profiles can be effectively clustered using extracted temporal features. Domain-agnostic feature sets such as catch22 [159] provide interpretable representations, although some temporal fidelity may be lost.

Model-based clustering represents each time series through the parameters of fitted models, such as ARIMA and the hidden Markov model (HMM) [154]. Clustering in model parameter space captures process similarity and temporal dynamics but depends heavily on model specification and estimation accuracy [154].

Representation-learning and deep clustering methods combine neural feature extraction with clustering objectives [145]. Autoencoders, recurrent networks, and transformers learn latent embeddings that encode temporal structure, while Improved Deep Embedded Clustering (IDEC) [160] jointly optimizes reconstruction and clustering losses for greater separability. Convolutional autoencoders (CAE) extend this idea by converting sequences into two-dimensional representations for localized temporal feature extraction [161]. Alternative paradigms [145], including GAN-based and topology-aware frameworks, explore generative or geometric perspectives, though training instability and computational cost currently limit industrial deployment.

3.3.3 Clustering Evaluation Methods

Evaluating clustering quality is essential yet challenging, particularly because ground-truth labels are typically unavailable in unsupervised learning. Cluster validation, therefore, relies on two main approaches: internal and external evaluation indices [145].

External validation indices are used when a reference partition or ground-truth labels are available [146]. The Adjusted Rand Index (ARI) measures similarity between two partitions while correcting for chance, with $ARI = 1$ representing perfect agreement and $ARI \approx 0$ indicating random correspondence [162]. Other indices, such as Jaccard, Fowlkes-Mallows, and F-measure, evaluate pairwise co-assignment accuracy [146]. Although valuable for benchmarking algorithms, external metrics are often impractical in real-world industrial settings where true labels are unavailable.

Internal validation indices assess the structural quality of clusters based on data alone, quantifying cohesion (intra-cluster similarity) and separation (inter-cluster dissimilarity) [145]. Table 3.7 summarizes commonly used internal metrics, including their advantages and limitations.

Table 3.7 Comparison of internal clustering evaluation metrics [145]

Metric	Range	Principle	Advantages	Limitations
Silhouette (SIL) index	$[-1,1]$	Balance between cohesion and separation	Intuitive; Interpretable; Shape-agnostic	Suffers in high dimensions; May penalize nonconvex clusters
Calinski-Harabasz (CH) index	$[0, +\infty)$	Ratio of between- to within-cluster variance	Computationally efficient; Works well for spherical clusters	Biased toward higher cluster counts; Assumes isotropic structure
Davies-Bouldin (DB) index	$[0, +\infty)$	Average similarity between each cluster and its nearest	Low values favor compact, well-separated clusters	Sensitive to outliers and centroid instability
Dunn index	$[0, +\infty)$	Ratio of minimum inter-cluster to maximum intra-cluster	Encourages compactness and separation	Highly sensitive to noise and outliers; Rarely stable

In industrial applications, where labels are rarely available, internal validation becomes particularly critical. However, these metrics often produce inconsistent results across datasets and cluster structures. For instance, the CH index tends to favor a higher number of clusters in high-dimensional spaces, while the SIL index penalizes over-segmentation by emphasizing compactness. DB index is sensitive to outliers and non-uniform cluster densities. Such inconsistencies become more pronounced in time-series clustering, where temporal misalignment, noise, and sparse sampling distort the assumptions underlying distance-based methods. Divergent outcomes are common: CH index may report high scores for amplitude-separated sequences even with weak temporal similarity, whereas SIL index penalizes alignment variations caused by time warping. Similarly, the CH index emphasizes global separation, while the DB index prioritizes local compactness, often leading to conflicting optima. In feature-encoded time-series data, SIL index performance can degrade further due to the curse of dimensionality.

Given that no single index consistently performs well across data types or domains, recent studies advocate composite evaluation frameworks. A large-scale comparison of over 30 indices concluded that combining multiple measures enhances reliability [163]. More recent ensemble-based approaches integrate results through rank aggregation, majority voting, or weighted averaging [164], improving robustness but still facing issues of scale mismatches, outlier sensitivity, and limited adaptation to noisy, high-dimensional time-series data. These limitations underscore the need for domain-specific, explainable cluster evaluation frameworks that account for the characteristics of real-world industrial data.

3.4 Causal Inference in Data-Driven Systems

Note: Parts of this section are based on the author's first-author publications: *"Data-Driven Causal Reasoning for Eco-Driving Behavior Analysis in Public Transportation Systems"* [165] and *"Uncovering Causal Drivers of Energy Efficiency for Industrial Process in Foundry via Time-Series Causal Inference"* [166].

Understanding causality is fundamental to transforming data-driven analysis from correlation toward explanation and reasoning. Causal inference provides a theoretical and methodological foundation for identifying cause-effect relationships that underline observed data patterns. In the context of AI-driven decision support, causal inference allows decision-makers to understand why an outcome occurs and how interventions may alter it. This section reviews the principal approaches to causal inference. It first discusses static causal discovery methods, followed by time-series causal discovery, and concludes with intervention-based approaches that enable causal reasoning.

3.4.1 Static Causal Discovery

Learning Directed Acyclic Graphs (DAGs) is a fundamental approach for uncovering causal structures within structural causal models (SCMs). A DAG provides a compact graphical representation of variable dependencies, where directed edges encode potential cause-effect relationships. However, learning DAGs from data is an NP-hard problem due to the combinatorial nature of the acyclicity constraint, which is difficult to enforce efficiently [167]. As a result, developing scalable and accurate DAG-learning algorithms remains a major challenge in causal inference. The DAG learning algorithms can be categorized into constraint-based and score-based methods [168]. Table 3.8 summarizes the key categories, advantages, and limitations of the static causal discovery algorithms.

Table 3.8 Overview of static causal discovery methods

Category	Representative algorithms	Principle	Advantages	Limitations
Constraint-based	PC algorithm and its extensions	Iteratively remove edges using conditional independence tests	Interpretable; Statistically grounded	Sensitive to noise; May produce globally inconsistent graphs
Score-based	NOTEARS	Continuous optimization; Gradient-based scoring	Efficient; Differentiable; Scalable	Limited for nonlinear systems
	DAGMA	Log-determinant acyclicity constraint using M-matrix	Stable gradients; Fast convergence; Accurate structure recovery	Lacks causal interpretability
	DAGMA-DCE	Differentiable causal effects via Jacobian matrix	Interpretable causal weights; Applicable to differentiable models	High computational Cost

Constraint-based approaches infer graph structures by performing conditional independence (CI) tests on the empirical joint distribution. The PC algorithm [169, 170] is one of the most established frameworks. It begins with a fully connected undirected graph, iteratively removes edges based on CI tests, and then orients the remaining edges using decision rules to produce a DAG. Variants employ kernel-based, NN-based, or GAN-based CI tests [171–173], improving flexibility for nonlinear relationships. Constraint-based methods are computationally efficient and interpretable because they rely on well-founded statistical tests.

However, since local independence decisions are made sequentially, they can sometimes yield globally inconsistent or spurious structures when conditional tests are unreliable or when data are noisy or high-dimensional.

In contrast, score-based approaches treat DAG learning as a global optimization problem. Candidate DAGs are evaluated using a scoring function, and the optimal structure maximizes this score under an acyclicity constraint. A breakthrough in this area is the NOTEARS algorithm [174], which reformulates the combinatorial optimization of DAG learning into a continuous optimization problem with a differentiable acyclicity constraint. This allows efficient gradient-based learning and enables the use of standard machine learning optimizers. Although NOTEARS achieves significant efficiency gains, it assumes linear structural equation models (SEMs) with least-squares loss, limiting its ability to model complex nonlinear dependencies.

Subsequent score-based developments extend this framework. Nonparametric variants generalize the acyclicity characterization to NN-based and orthogonal basis expansions [175], allowing flexible modeling of nonlinear relationships. Deep generative DAG models [176] have also been proposed to better approximate real-world data distributions. Building upon these, the DAGMA method introduces a new log-determinant acyclicity function using M-matrix theory, yielding more stable gradients and improved accuracy while significantly reducing runtime [177].

Despite these advances, many score-based methods suffer from limited interpretability. The weighted adjacency matrices learned by such models often lack direct causal meaning, as the weights do not correspond to consistent causal effects [178]. To address this, the DAGMA-DCE method introduces a differentiable causal effect (DCE) metric, where each edge weight corresponds to the root-mean-square entry of the Jacobian matrix between variables [179]. Although backward propagation through Jacobians increases computational cost, the method provides a theoretically interpretable measure of causal strength and can be efficiently estimated via Monte Carlo approximations in differentiable models.

In summary, DAG-based causal discovery has evolved from classical independence testing toward differentiable, gradient-based, and generative modeling frameworks. The key research trend focuses on integrating interpretability, computational efficiency, and nonlinear modeling capability to achieve reliable static causal inference.

3.4.2 Time-Series Causal Discovery

Causal discovery in time series aims to uncover how past values of one or more variables influence the future behavior of others. Unlike static data, temporal datasets exhibit autocorrelation, lagged dependencies, and confounding effects across multiple time scales, making causal reasoning more challenging [180, 181]. Table 3.9 summarizes the algorithms, advantages, and limitations of time-series causal discovery.

Table 3.9 Overview of time-series causal discovery methods

Algorithms	Principle	Advantages	Limitations
GC	Test whether one time series improves the prediction of another using autoregressive modeling	Simple; Interpretable; Foundational causal measure	Assume linearity; Sensitive to noise; Limited to bivariate systems
Extended GC (TF-CGC, CGCI, PDC)	Incorporate frequency-domain and multivariate extensions	Handle spectral and zero-lag effects; Suitable for multivariate systems	Computationally intensive; Limited scalability
NGC	Embed GC principles in deep learning	Capture nonlinear and high-dimensional dependencies	Require large data; Interpretability challenges
TE	Measure nonlinear information transfer via conditional mutual information	Non-parametric; Model-free; Detect nonlinear causality	High computational cost; Dimensionality issues
CCM	Identify causality through manifold reconstruction and cross-mapping	Effective for nonlinear, chaotic systems	Sensitive to noise and short time series
PCMCI/PCMCI +	Use CI tests with optimized conditioning sets	Robust to autocorrelation; Scalable; Capture instantaneous effects	Require sufficient data; Complex parameter tuning

The foundation of time-series causality lies in the Granger causality (GC) test, which determines whether one time series improves the forecast of another [182]. The GC has become one of the most influential methods for causal inference in dynamic systems. However, the classical formulation assumes linearity and bivariate relationships based on autoregressive models. It does not account for noise or nonlinear dependencies, which may lead to false causal detections in complex systems [183].

To overcome these limitations, several extensions of GC have been developed [183]. The two-phase extended GC procedure [184] detects zero-lag correlations and assigns causal directions using non-Gaussian estimation. The time-frequency conditional GC (TF-CGC) [185] integrates Geweke's spectral measure with time-varying autoregressive modeling, enhancing accuracy for multivariate systems. Similarly, the conditional GC index (CGCI) [186] and partial directed coherence (PDC) [187] expand GC into nonlinear and frequency-domain contexts, enabling causal connectivity analysis for multivariate and spectral data.

Beyond classical statistics, recent progress has integrated deep learning architectures into causal inference. Neural Granger Causality (NGC) [188] introduces nonlinear modeling using structured multilayer perceptron (MLP) or RNNs with sparsity-inducing regularization to identify relevant causal connections. The CAUSE framework [189] infers event-level dependencies using neural point processes and derives Granger-like statistics through attribution mechanisms. Other architectures [190] combine LSTM, AE, and CNNs to capture complex temporal dependencies while maintaining interpretability.

An alternative line of research uses information-theoretic approaches to model directional information flow. Transfer Entropy (TE) is a non-parametric measure of conditional mutual information that quantifies nonlinear causal dependencies without assuming specific functional forms [191]. It generalizes GC to nonlinear systems and performs better when the underlying processes deviate from Gaussianity. Under Gaussian assumptions, TE and GC are equivalent [192], linking autoregressive and information-theoretic causality. However, TE suffers from the curse of dimensionality when estimating high-dimensional probability densities. To address this, recent frameworks [193–195] decompose TE into finite-dimensional contributions or reformulate it using copula entropy, improving computational efficiency while maintaining interpretability.

The Convergent Cross Mapping (CCM) [196] method approaches causality through nonlinear state-space reconstruction. It assumes that if a variable X causally influences Y, the historical states of Y can reconstruct those of X through cross-mapping on attractor manifolds. CCM is particularly effective in detecting causality in nonlinear, chaotic, or ecological systems.

The PCMCI (Peter-Clark Momentary Conditional Independence) algorithm [197] and its extension PCMCI + [198] represent SotA approaches for high-dimensional and nonlinear time series. PCMCI combines conditional-independence tests with optimized conditioning-set selection to handle strong autocorrelation effectively [197]. PCMCI + extends this framework to include contemporaneous causal links [198], thereby improving both recall and precision in complex temporal systems. By leveraging momentary conditional independence (MCI) tests [180], PCMCI and PCMCI + achieve robust detection of causal networks while controlling false positives.

3.4.3 Data-Driven Intervention Analysis

Causal reasoning extends beyond identifying causal associations to understanding the effects of deliberate interventions within a system. In causal inference, an intervention refers to a deliberate manipulation of a variable within a system to observe and analyze its effects on the distributions of other variables. The do-calculus introduced by Judea Pearl [199, 200] provides a formal framework for deriving causal relationships based on such interventions. Specifically, the do-operator, denoted as $do(X = x)$, encapsulates an intervention where the variable X is forcibly set to a specific value x, irrespective of its prior dependencies. The inference rules within do-calculus respect this interpretation, treating the intervention as a modification of the relevant functional relationships within the causal model, thereby enabling the derivation of causal claims from both experimental and observational data.

Intervention analysis provides a systematic approach to addressing a range of causal questions. An approach based on graphical causal models [201] has been developed to identify the root causes of changes in the probability distribution of variables. The core concept is that, given a causal graph, the joint distribution of the variables can be factorized into a product of independent causal conditionals. Consequently, any change in the joint distribution or the marginal distribution of a target variable can be traced back to changes in specific causal conditions. This approach allows for precise attribution of observed distributional changes to their underlying causal mechanisms.

A permutation-based causal falsification test has been introduced in [202], representing another form of intervention in causal graphs. This approach involves developing a metric based on the sampling of node permutations of the causal graph to assess the validity of an estimated DAG on observed data. Two surrogate baselines are derived to compare the number of dependence violations observed in the given DAG, providing a measure of the causal graph's consistency.

3.5 Multimodal Decision Narration

Note: Parts of this section are based on the author's first-author journal article: *"Multi-Agent Multimodal Large Language Model Framework for Automated Interpretation of Fuel Efficiency Analytics in Public Transportation"* [203].

Multimodal decision narration is the automatic generation of explanatory narratives from data across multiple modalities, such as text, charts, images, or speech, to support decision-making. In data-intensive domains, experts have traditionally produced reports that combine textual explanations with visualizations to communicate analytical findings clearly [204]. This practice, known as data storytelling, integrates tables, charts, and narrative text to improve comprehension and engagement with complex information [204]. However, conventional reporting remains largely manual and produces fragmented outputs, such as separate figures, tables, and summaries that require human synthesis [205, 206]. Such fragmentation limits scalability, reproducibility, and consistency, as analysts should invest significant effort to integrate heterogeneous elements into coherent narratives [207].

The goal of AI-driven multimodal narration is to automate this synthesis by transforming heterogeneous data into unified, context-aware narratives that are accurate, interpretable, and tailored to diverse stakeholders. Automating data narration has been a longstanding objective in natural language generation research, often referred to as data-to-text generation. Early systems generated domain-specific textual reports from structured data using rule-based or template-driven methods. While effective in controlled environments like finance and sports analytics, these systems lacked flexibility and linguistic diversity.

Recent advances leverage neural language models that can produce more fluent and varied descriptions from structured or visual data. In parallel, the emergence of narrative visualization emphasized the alignment of textual commentary with visual representation. Benchmark datasets such as VisText [208] and Chart-Summ [209] have supported research in generating natural-language captions and summaries for visual data, including charts and graphs [206, 210]. These tasks, including chart captioning, chart summarization, and visual-textual grounding, serve as building blocks toward fully automated multimodal storytelling.

The current state of the art has been transformed by multimodal LLMs, which can process text, images, and structured data within a unified framework [211, 212]. These models can interpret visual inputs, such as charts and tables, and generate corresponding explanations, enabling AI systems to communicate analytical insights in a coherent, human-readable narrative that bridges visual and textual modalities for decision support.

3.5.1 Multimodal Large Language Models

Multimodal LLMs represent a significant evolution in AI, enabling the integration of diverse data modalities, such as text, images, and numerical data, within a unified processing framework. These models aim to perform complex reasoning tasks that require a deep understanding of heterogeneous inputs, thereby extending the application scope of LLMs across scientific, industrial, and creative domains. A core task in the development of multimodal LLMs lies in establishing effective mechanisms to support collaborative inference and cross-modal reasoning [213]. One of the most active areas of research involves integrating visual comprehension into LLMs, allowing them to process and interpret charts, diagrams, and other scientific visual content. This capability has garnered growing interest from the research community, as it paves the way for broader and more versatile applications of LLMs in domains such as education, scientific communication, and industrial analytics [214].

Recent SotA models such as GPT-4.1 [61], Claude Opus 4 [215], and Gemini 2.5 Pro [216] have demonstrated strong performance across tasks such as multimodal reasoning, visual question answering, and image-text alignment. These models benefit from advanced training techniques, such as reinforcement learning with human feedback (RLHF), which enhance their ability to understand and relate to multimodal content. However, the use of such high-performance commercial models often entails substantial cost, posing practical challenges for deployment. To address this, more cost-effective alternatives, such as GPT-4.1-mini [61], o4-mini [217], Claude 3.5 Haiku [62], and Gemini 2.5 Flash [63], have been developed. Therefore, selecting the appropriate model for a given application requires careful evaluation of the trade-offs between cost, computational efficiency, and inference accuracy during framework development.

Prompt engineering has emerged as a critical technique for enhancing the performance and adaptability of pre-trained LLMs. By crafting precise and contextually rich instructions, prompt engineering enables fine control over model outputs without requiring additional model training, thereby improving their effectiveness across a wide range of tasks and domains [218]. The significance of prompt engineering is underscored by its capacity to steer model responses, enhancing the adaptability and applicability of LLMs across diverse sectors.

Standard prompting strategies primarily include zero-shot and few-shot prompting. In zero-shot prompting [219], models are guided to perform tasks without any prior examples, relying solely on the prompt's phrasing. Few-shot prompting [220], by contrast, includes a small number of input-output examples within the prompt to help the model infer the desired task behavior. Even a few high-quality examples can substantially improve performance on complex or ambiguous tasks.

However, these standard strategies often fall short in scenarios that demand multi-step or structured reasoning. To address this limitation, Chain-of-Thought (CoT) prompting [64] has been introduced to enable LLMs to produce intermediate reasoning steps before arriving at a final answer. This method significantly enhances the logical coherence and interpretability of model outputs. Building on CoT, Chain-of-Table prompting [221] has been built for step-by-step tabular reasoning, where the model dynamically generates and executes the structured query language (SQL) or data frame operations. To further enhance reasoning robustness, the Contrastive Chain-of-Thought (CCoT) prompting [222] has been introduced, which provides both valid and flawed reasoning demonstrations. This contrastive learning framework enables models to distinguish between correct and incorrect logic, navigating a map with clearly marked right and wrong paths, ultimately fostering more reliable and explainable outputs.

Given the diversity of task types and data modalities involved in the framework, selecting an appropriate prompt strategy is essential to ensure both performance and interpretability.

3.5.2 Multimodal LLMs for Data Narration

Automated story generation is an open-ended task focused on producing coherent sequences of events based on predefined criteria or input data [223]. Recent advances in multimodal LLMs have significantly improved performance in this domain. These models can generate fluent, contextually appropriate narratives by iteratively incorporating information from both the narrative plan and the evolving state of the story into the prompt. Empirical studies [205, 210] have confirmed the effectiveness of LLMs in producing short, coherent, and natural-sounding stories, highlighting their potential for applications in dynamic content generation.

Related to narrative generation, recent research [208, 224, 225] has explored the ability of multimodal LLMs to interpret complex data-rich visuals, such as scientific charts, tables, and documents. Notably, studies examining visualizations in academic literature demonstrate the potential of these models to generate insightful narratives from structured and semi-structured data, enabling more scalable, nuanced approaches to scientific data analysis.

Complementing these developments, agent-based systems [205, 210] have emerged as a promising paradigm for automating narrative workflows. For instance, DS-Agent [226] integrates LLMs with case-based reasoning to automate data science tasks, significantly reducing manual intervention. Building on this concept, the study in [227] has introduced a multi-agent framework leveraging LLMs to generate animated data videos, further expanding the boundaries of automated data storytelling.

While recent work has advanced data narration using LLMs, most approaches rely on fine-tuning models for specific domains, limiting their generalizability. Few studies explore LLMs' zero-shot capabilities for leveraging global knowledge to generate narratives across diverse industrial contexts. Furthermore, existing research predominantly emphasizes descriptive output rather than actionable recommendations explicitly tailored to stakeholder needs. In cases such as improving fuel efficiency for public transportation, these limitations are significant: decision support requires both interpretable narratives and practical suggestions. This highlights the need for frameworks that combine zero-shot narration, automated evaluation, and stakeholder-aware recommendation generation toward integrated, real-world decision support.

3.6 Summary

This chapter has positioned the thesis within the rigor cycle of the three-cycle DSR model by establishing theoretical and methodological grounding for AI-driven decision support. It synthesizes the foundational theories, methodological developments, and SotA research that collectively form the conceptual and technical basis for developing a robust, interpretable, and human-centered decision-support framework. The review is structured around five interrelated components, including AI-driven decision-support frameworks, data characteristics and quality assurance, clustering and pattern discovery, causal inference and reasoning, and multimodal decision narration. Each section critically evaluates existing methods and discusses cross-cutting issues relevant to trustworthy, deployable decision support.

Several recurring challenges are identified, including fragmented and noisy data, limited quantification of data characteristics, instability in unsupervised evaluation, real-world constraints in causal discovery, and the continuing need for transparent and coherent AI-generated narratives. Addressing these issues is essential for advancing data-driven decision support.

From this synthesis, three overarching insights emerge that guide the subsequent methodological development:

- Data quality analytics linkage: connecting data-quality assurance with analytical robustness through quantified and temporally aware quality indicators.
- Integration of pattern discovery and causal reasoning: achieving a comparative understanding of unsupervised clustering and causal-inference methods to support algorithm selection and design for complex, data-rich environments.
- Bridging analysis and decision narration: creating an operational pathway from analytical results to automated, evidence-grounded, and human-interpretable multimodal decision support.

These insights define the key methodological requirements for the proposed AI-driven decision-support framework. Building on this rigor-grounded foundation, Chaps. 4–6 translate them into the framework's methodological design and system architecture.

Methodology

4

This chapter presents the overall research methodology and research process adopted for the progression of this thesis. The three-cycle design science research (DSR) framework [19] is employed as the overarching paradigm, guiding both the research activities and the structure of this thesis. Section 4.1 provides a detailed explanation of the three-cycle DSR framework. Section 4.2 outlines the research process developed to support the scientific investigation of this thesis in the field of data science, and it aligns with the progression of the three-cycle DSR framework. Next, Sect. 4.3 introduces the framework development and verification methods that ensure the scientific rigor, validity, and reliability of the proposed framework. Finally, Sect. 4.4 summarizes this chapter and highlights its relevance to the subsequent chapters.

4.1 Three-Cycle DSR Framework

The DSR methodology [20] is a constructive research approach that emphasizes problem-solving by creating innovative solutions to real-world challenges while simultaneously advancing theoretical knowledge. The primary objective of DSR is to develop theoretical methods that practitioners can leverage to design effective solutions for a special problem domain [21]. DSR achieves this by developing innovative and purposeful artifacts, such as models, algorithms, or frameworks [20]. These artifacts are informed by the operational context and grounded in existing theoretical foundations, thereby ensuring contributions to both theory and practice [228].

In this thesis, the DSR methodology is operationalized through the three-cycle DSR framework, as depicted in Fig. 4.1. This framework, comprising

Z. Ma, *Artificial Intelligence-Driven Decision Support Framework for Improving Energy Efficiency in Industry and Transportation*,
https://doi.org/10.1007/978-3-658-51965-0_4

the *relevance cycle*, the *rigor cycle*, and the *design cycle*, provides a structured approach for integrating scientific rigor with practical relevance [19]. It is particularly suited for research domains where practical problem-solving and theoretical advancement should coexist [228].

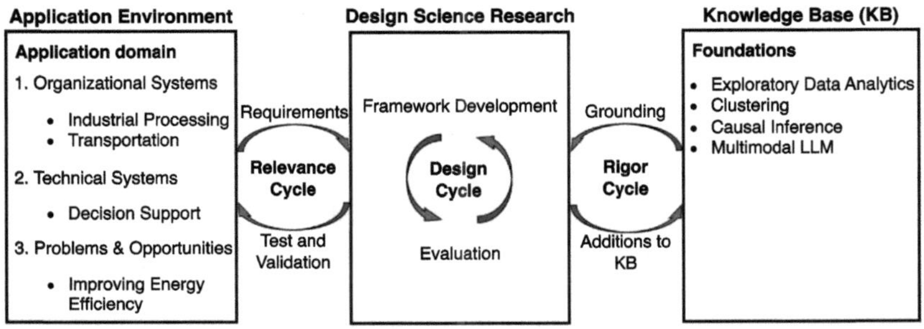

Fig. 4.1 The three-cycle DSR framework contextualized to the research topic of this thesis

The artifact development process follows an iterative approach, involving construction and refinement through successive *design cycles*. In each *design cycle*, an artifact is developed and evaluated to enhance the understanding of both the problem space and potential solutions [19]. Specifically, one *design cycle* in this thesis results in the development of algorithms or frameworks, such as a clustering algorithm and an LLM-based multi-agent system designed to address domain-specific challenges.

Before executing the *design cycles*, the *relevance and rigor cycles* are initiated. The *relevance cycle* begins with identifying a significant real-world research problem, eliciting requirements, and defining acceptance criteria for prospective solutions [19]. In this thesis, this involves collaborating with end users in the industrial processing and transportation domains to derive requirements for successful decision support systems and establish success metrics focused on improving energy efficiency. The second phase of the *relevance cycle* includes testing and validating the developed artifacts in their intended application environments. The results of this validation determine whether additional iterations are required or if the research objectives have been satisfactorily achieved, allowing the *relevance cycle* to be closed [19].

The *rigor cycle* complements these activities by ensuring theoretical soundness throughout the research process [19]. It involves systematically reviewing and integrating existing theories and methods to inform design decisions. This thesis includes drawing on exploratory data analytics, clustering, causal reasoning, and multimodal LLMs. Upon completion of the final artifact, the *rigor cycle* concludes with the derivation of new theoretical insights or design principles, which contribute to the broader knowledge base of the discipline [19].

4.2 Research Process

This section outlines the step-by-step research process employed in this thesis and illustrates how the three-cycle DSR framework is operationalized from problem identification through to evaluation. This research follows a structured and iterative process designed to ensure methodological rigor, theoretical robustness, and contextual relevance within the field of data science research. It comprises five stages: (1) problem identification and research framing; (2) research objective formulation and theoretical grounding; (3) methodological design, implementation, and analysis; (4) application context analysis and case study integration; and (5) scientific evaluation and validation of research contributions. Figure 4.2 maps the five stages onto the three DSR cycles and Fig. 4.3 details the components and interconnections within the overall research process.

As illustrated in Fig. 4.2, the *rigor cycle* anchors the research in existing knowledge by informing Stage 1 (problem identification and research framing), Stage 2 (research objective formulation and theoretical grounding), and Stage 5 (scientific evaluation and validation of research contributions) through engagement with prior literature, theories, and methodological standards. The *relevance cycle* ensures contextual alignment and practical applicability by connecting Stage 1 and Stage 5 to real-world needs and situating Stage 4 (application context analysis and case study integration) within the empirical environment. The *design cycle*, focused on the iterative development and refinement of artifacts, is operationalized through Stage 3 (methodological design, implementation, and analysis). Together, these mappings demonstrate how the research process integrates theoretical rigor, practical relevance, and systematic design to identify research questions and objectives, address the identified problem, and deliver validated contributions.

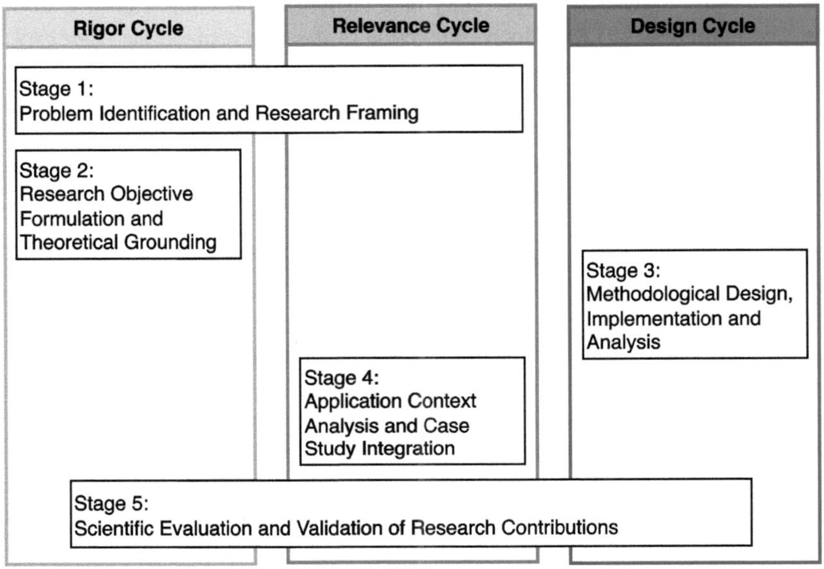

Fig. 4.2 Mapping research processes to the three-cycle DSR framework

Figure 4.3 illustrates how each stage of the research process is operationalized through a series of step-by-step activities and highlights the interconnections among these stages. In the following subsections 4.2.1–4.2.5, each of the five stages is described in detail, outlining their objectives, key activities, and outcomes, as well as their alignment with the three-cycle DSR framework. Subsection 4.2.6 further elaborates on the iterative and reflexive nature of the research process, emphasizing how continuous reflection and adaptation contribute to methodological rigor and contextual relevance.

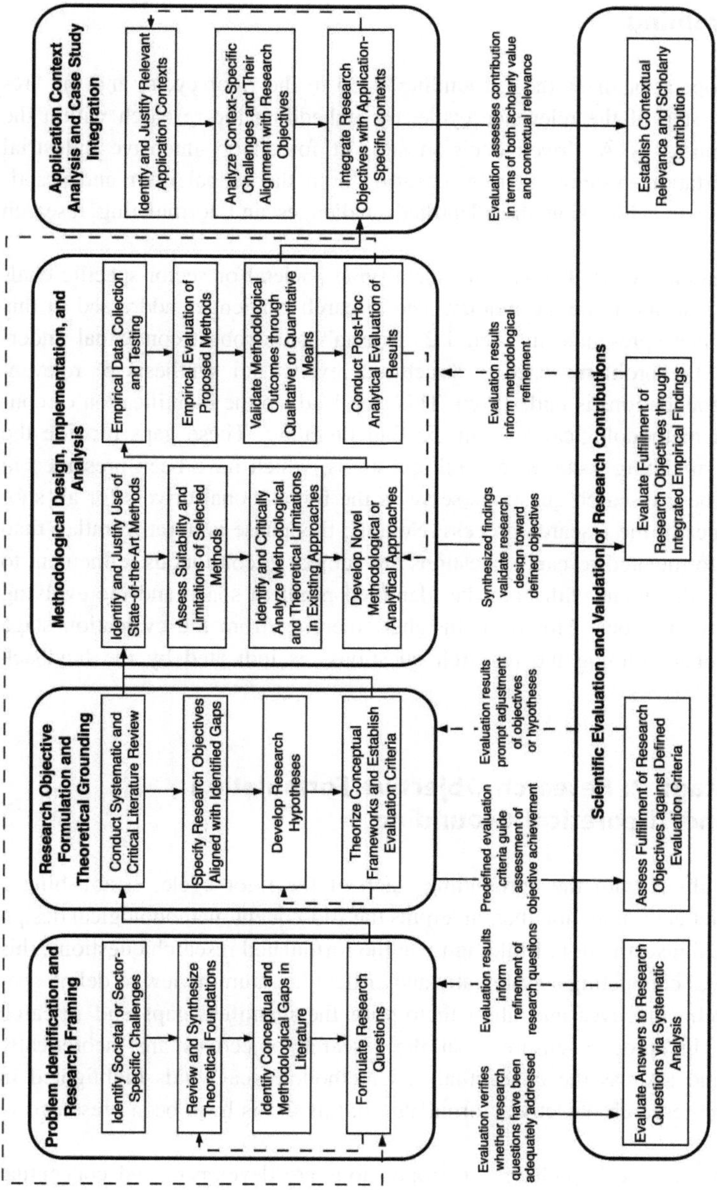

Fig. 4.3 Illustration of the structured research process adopted in this PhD study. The solid arrows represent the primary direction of the research workflow, while the dashed arrows denote the feedback loops that facilitate iterative refinement

4.2.1 Stage 1: Problem Identification and Research Framing

This stage operationalizes the "grounding" step in the rigor cycle, and the "requirements" step of the relevance cycle, by embedding the research within the concrete context of AI-driven decision support for energy-intensive industrial and transportation systems, thereby ensuring both theoretical rigor and practical relevance in addressing the identified challenges and formulating research questions.

The research process begins with identifying societal or sector-specific challenges that warrant academic inquiry. The research challenges addressed in this thesis have been presented in Sect. 1.2. To establish a robust contextual understanding of the problem space, a structured review and synthesis of relevant theoretical foundations is undertaken. This step leads to the identification of conceptual and methodological gaps in existing literature. These gaps provide the basis for formulating focused research questions, which have been presented in Sect. 1.3. These research questions serve as the foundational drivers for all subsequent stages of the research process. Notably, this phase is iterative rather than static. The formulated research questions are subject to continuous refinement to ensure their alignment with both the identified problem space and the evolving theoretical foundations. Moreover, insights emerging from the evaluation stage may necessitate refining the research questions, as indicated by the feedback loop.

4.2.2 Stage 2: Research Objective Formulation and Theoretical Grounding

This stage aligns with the "grounding" step of the rigor cycle, establishing a robust theoretical foundation that underpins the subsequent methodological design and empirical investigation. Building upon the formulated research questions, this stage involves conducting a systematic and critical literature review to define specific research objectives and align them with the identified gaps and research questions. This process ensures that the research objectives are theoretically grounded and address the conceptual and methodological voids highlighted in Stage 1. The research objectives formulated in this thesis have been presented in Sect. 1.3.

Subsequently, the hypotheses or propositions are developed, and conceptual frameworks are constructed to guide research design. The hypotheses developed in this thesis have been presented in Sect. 1.3. Additionally, evaluation criteria are formulated at this stage to serve as the basis for assessing the research outcomes in later stages. Evaluation criteria should ensure that methodological success is defined not only in academic terms but also in operational impact measures. Both the conceptual frameworks and hypotheses are subject to iterative refinement to ensure adequate explanatory and analytical capacity, with feedback from subsequent evaluation stages informing further adjustments where necessary.

The theoretical grounding combines design science research principles with selected bodies of knowledge from data science and AI. From this synthesis, the conceptual framework of this study is developed, mapping AI capabilities to sector-specific decision-support requirements.

4.2.3 Stage 3: Methodological Design, Implementation, and Analysis

This stage aligns with the design cycle of the three-cycle DSR framework. It represents the translation of the theoretical and conceptual foundations established in earlier stages into a coherent and rigorous methodological design.

The process begins with the identification and justification of SotA methods, followed by assessing their suitability in addressing the research objectives. Where limitations in existing approaches are identified, this stage facilitates the development of novel methodological or analytical tools, which constitute artifacts in the DSR process. These methods are subsequently operationalized through empirical data collection and testing, critically assessed within an evaluation framework, and rigorously validated using qualitative and quantitative criteria to ensure robustness and credibility. Afterward, post-hoc data analysis is conducted to derive deeper, more explanatory insights, supporting explainability and the iterative refinement of decision support. This step, in turn, may inspire iterative refinements of the developed artifacts. Furthermore, a feedback loop from the evaluation phase ensures that methodological adaptations can be informed by empirical findings, supporting the iterative and reflexive nature of the research process.

4.2.4 Stage 4: Application Context Analysis and Case Study Integration

This stage aligns with the relevance cycle of the three-cycle DSR framework. It ensures that the developed methods are not isolated technical artifacts but contextually integrated solutions. To ensure contextual relevance, the research is situated in a selected application domain. This involves identifying and justifying the chosen context, analyzing its unique challenges, and aligning these with the previously formulated research objectives. The integration of the developed methods and conceptual frameworks into real-world settings not only validates their practical utility but also reinforces their theoretical robustness through empirical application.

Furthermore, this integration facilitates the generation of new insights that can inform and enhance understanding of the application context, establishing an iterative feedback loop. Finally, the contributions are evaluated on both scholarly significance and contextual relevance, ensuring that the research addresses the imperatives of academic rigor and practical impact.

4.2.5 Stage 5: Scientific Evaluation and Validation of Research Contributions

The final stage focuses on the comprehensive evaluation and validation of the research contributions across all preceding stages (Stages 1–4), engaging with all three cycles of the DSR framework. First, it evaluates whether the research questions proposed in Stage 1 have been systematically addressed through rigorous analysis of empirical and theoretical outcomes. Second, the research objectives are assessed against the predefined evaluation criteria established in Stage 2. Third, the synthesized findings derived from the methodological design and application experiments in Stage 3 are evaluated to determine the extent to which they fulfill the research objectives. Finally, the overall contributions are validated and assessed by examining their contextual relevance and scholarly significance, ensuring alignment between the applied outcomes and theoretical constructions.

Crucially, this stage incorporates feedback loops to earlier stages of the research process, enabling iterative refinement of research framing, objectives, and methods in response to evaluative insights. This dynamic approach reinforces both methodological rigor and practical relevance, thereby ensuring that the research outcomes contribute meaningfully to both theory and practice.

4.2.6 Iterative and Reflexive Nature of the Research Process

The research process adopted in this PhD study is not linear, but iterative, reflexive, and responsive to emerging insights. While the overall trajectory progresses from problem framing to validation, each stage is designed to allow the revisiting of earlier stages in light of new understanding or empirical evidence. This dynamic approach ensures methodological coherence, theoretical robustness, and contextual relevance throughout the research journey.

Insights gained during empirical validation can prompt a re-examination of the original research problem. For instance, if the findings reveal unanticipated variables or dynamics, the research questions may need to be refined or reframed to better capture the phenomenon under investigation. Similarly, empirical results may reveal that certain objectives are too broad, overly narrow, or misaligned with observed real-world phenomena. Such outcomes may also highlight the need for adapting the theoretical framework to accommodate emergent findings, thereby supporting the theoretical maturation of the study.

When evaluation uncovers inconsistencies, unexpected behaviors, or performance limitations, these insights can inform methodological adjustments. Refinements may include parameter tuning, data augmentation, or even the development of alternative analytical or modeling approaches. Furthermore, deeper interpretive insights derived from post-hoc analysis may reveal new perspectives or variables relevant to the original context. This, in turn, can prompt further exploration or triangulation, contributing to a more nuanced understanding of the application domain and enhancing the relevance of the research within the case context.

Case-specific complexities and constraints may also challenge initial theoretical assumptions. Through iterative adaptation, the conceptual framework can be refined to better reflect empirical realities encountered in field or case study environments. This cyclical and reflexive design exemplifies the nature of high-quality doctoral research, where knowledge creation is not a linear endeavor but a continuous process of interrogation, adaptation, and integration. The deliberate interplay between theory, method, and application ensures that the research maintains coherence, rigor, and practical significance throughout its development.

4.3 Framework Development and Assessment Methods

The section outlines the methods and processes for developing and evaluating the AI-driven decision support framework, which constitutes the principal contribution of this thesis. Building upon the research process detailed in Sect. 4.2, this section is organized into two parts. Sect. 4.3.1 describes the high-level framework development procedure and Sect. 4.3.2 formalize the qualitative criteria employed in the framework evaluation.

4.3.1 Framework Development Procedure

The framework development procedure adopted in this PhD study adheres to the five-stage research process depicted in Fig. 4.3 and is guided by the three-cycle DSR paradigm presented in Fig. 4.1. Although the conceptual structure and detailed components of the proposed AI-driven decision support framework are introduced in Chaps. 5 and 6 for clarity, before presenting empirical results of case studies, the framework itself has been developed iteratively through in-depth engagement with case studies documented in Chaps. 7 and 8.

The initial step in the framework development involves identifying the key research challenges and existing knowledge gaps within the literature. Specifically, the fundamental gap identified for this study is the lack of an SotA explainable AI-driven decision support framework capable of transforming heterogeneous sensor data into trustworthy, actionable insights to enhance data-driven, human-centered decision-making for energy efficiency in energy-intensive systems. This critical gap is first recognized through an extensive preliminary literature analysis presented in Chaps. 2 and 3. Subsequently, research questions are formulated directly in response to these identified gaps, leading to a more systematic and critical literature review, detailed in Chap. 3. The outcomes of this comprehensive review directly inform the establishment of precise research objectives, hypothesis formulation, and the definition of rigorous evaluation criteria pertinent to both the framework design and the development of specific artifacts. Accordingly, before implementation, the SotA methods relevant to each module were systematically reviewed. Where existing methods are deemed adequate, they will be incorporated into the framework without modification. When methodological gaps are identified, novel algorithms or sub-frameworks will be developed to meet the defined functional and analytical requirements.

Each artifact incorporated into the overall framework is designed and developed in accordance with Stage 3 of the research process, as described in Fig. 4.3. Novel methodological and analytical approaches are systematically tested and validated using synthetic data, real-world datasets, or a combination thereof. To facilitate robust empirical validation and ensure generalizability, two distinct case studies are selected: one situated in industrial processing and the other within the transportation sector. These application domains are strategically chosen for their significant energy consumption profiles and substantial improvement potential, as initially introduced in Sect. 1.1. The selected case studies serve not only as testbeds for framework validation but also as practical environments that yield empirical insights and generate valuable artifacts, thereby concretely illustrating how advanced AI techniques effectively enhance decision-making capabilities for improved energy efficiency.

Throughout the iterative processes of framework development and validation, common design challenges, critical design decisions, and recurring data analytics methods are identified across different application domains. These empirically derived insights are methodically and systematically abstracted and synthesized into generalizable design principles, structured framework stages, standardized data analytics pipelines, and practical implementation guidelines. Collectively, these elements constitute the foundational architecture of the proposed decision support framework. This methodological approach reflects an inductive yet theory-informed development strategy, in which the framework is conceptually grounded in established theories and systematically refined through recurring empirical patterns rigorously validated across the diverse contexts of the selected case studies.

4.3.2 Framework Assessment Criteria

A systematic evaluation of the proposed AI-driven decision support framework is essential to establish its scientific validity, practical relevance, and adaptability across domains. Given the interdisciplinary nature of integrating artificial intelligence into decision support frameworks for improving energy efficiency, this study employs a set of qualitative assessment criteria recognized as scientifically robust within the field of data science and AI research [229–232]. These criteria are crucial for assessing how the framework performs in real-world organizational settings and how effectively it supports decision-making processes across various application domains. The selection and development of these criteria are informed by a comprehensive review of the relevant literature, ensuring their alignment with established evaluation practices [114, 229–233].

- ***Capabilities:*** the degree to which the framework provides a relevant breadth of decision-support functions and allows customization to stakeholder needs [233].
- ***Robustness:*** the degree to which the framework demonstrates consistent and reliable performance across a range of conditions, including the presence of previously unseen data and unexpected scenarios [229].
- ***Explainability:*** the degree to which the system delivers context-sensitive explanations that enable users to understand, verify, and justify recommendations [114, 230].
- ***Domain Integrity:*** The degree to which the framework embodies domain knowledge, constraints, and terminology required for credible energy-efficiency decisions [230].
- ***Iterative Validation Potential:*** the degree to which the design facilitates continuous testing, feedback incorporation, and improvement throughout the deployment lifecycle [114].
- ***Cross-Sector Applicability:*** the degree to which the framework can be transferred with minimal adaptation between distinct application contexts [114, 231].
- ***Adaptability and Scalability:*** the degree to which the framework accommodates varying data types, user groups, and operational volumes without performance loss [231].

The first five criteria, including capabilities, robustness, explainability, domain integrity, and iterative validation potential, are applied to assess the framework in each case study. By contrast, the remaining two criteria, including cross-sector applicability, and adaptability and scalability, are used to evaluate the framework after all case studies have been completed, thereby determining its generalizability beyond a single domain. Inevitably, trade-offs emerge among these dimensions: for example, maximizing domain integrity can constrain cross-sector applicability, while extensive customization to meet local stakeholder needs may reduce overall scalability. Recognizing and managing such trade-offs is therefore integral to the evaluation strategy, enabling a balanced appraisal of both domain-specific performance and broader applicability.

To enhance methodological rigor and enable reproducible validation, each qualitative criterion is complemented by at least one quantitative metric and a target benchmark. These metrics operationalize the qualitative definitions into measurable indicators, allowing both objective performance assessment and transparent comparison across case studies. However, these quantitative metrics do not fully capture contextual nuances. Therefore, the quantitative results are interpreted alongside qualitative assessments and discussions, providing a more comprehensive evaluation. Table 4.1 presents the integrated qualitative and quantitative evaluation framework used in this study.

Table 4.1 Integrated qualitative and quantitative evaluation criteria.

Criterion	Quantitative metrics	Target/ Benchmark
Capabilities	1) Decision-task coverage rate: *supported_tasks* ÷ *required_tasks* × *100%* 2) Customization rate: *customized_tasks* ÷ *supported_tasks* × *100%*	≥ 90% ≥ 80%
Robustness	1) Unexpected condition solving rate: *solved_unexpected_conditions* ÷ *unexpected_conditions* × *100%*	≥ 90%
Explainability	1) Rate of recommendations with traceable rationale: *traceable_recommendations* ÷ *all_recommendations* × *100%*	≥ 90%
Domain Integrity	1) Rate of compliance with domain rules: *compliant_domain_rules* ÷ *domain_rules* × *100%*	≥ 90%
Iterative Validation Potential	1) Iterative validation rate: *Tasks_can_be_validated* ÷ *supported_tasks* × *100%*	≥ 90%
Cross-Sector Applicability	1) Number of sectors tested without major redesign	≥ 2
Adaptability & Scalability	1) Number of data modalities supported 2) Maximum data volume processed	≥ 3 ≥ 10× 2) baseline

4.4 Summary

This chapter has established the methodological foundation of the thesis. Anchored in the three-cycle DSR framework, it articulates a five-stage research process specifically tailored to the data science research objectives of this study.

The process integrates the relevance, rigor, and design cycles to ensure a systematic balance between theoretical grounding, methodological robustness, and contextual applicability.

Based on this methodological foundation, the chapter has detailed the structured research procedures used to design, develop, and evaluate an AI-driven decision support framework. The framework development process is guided by iterative refinement through the DSR cycles, supported by comprehensive literature analysis and empirical validation across two application domains: industrial processing and transportation. The evaluation design incorporates both qualitative and quantitative criteria to ensure scientific validity, practical relevance, and cross-sectoral adaptability.

Through this systematic approach, the chapter demonstrates how the research methodology ensures coherence between conceptual foundations, methodological execution, and empirical validation. It thereby establishes a rigorous bridge between the theoretical and literature-based insights presented in Chaps. 1–3 and the framework specification, implementation, and case study validation discussed in Chaps. 5–8.

Conceptual Design and Architecture of the AI-Driven Decision Support Framework

5

This chapter presents the conceptual design and architecture of the proposed AI-driven decision support framework to improve energy efficiency. It emphasizes the framework's core concepts, terminology, and structural interactions, while also highlighting how it extends beyond conventional decision support approaches. By systematically integrating data analytics, causal reasoning, and narrative-driven decision support, the framework establishes a conceptual and theoretical foundation for AI-driven decision support. The chapter focuses on high-level design principles and guides the detailed implementation presented in Chap. 6.

The chapter is structured as follows. Section 5.1 establishes the conceptual foundations and design requirements of the framework. Section 5.2 provides a high-level overview of the architecture and its module interactions. Section 5.3 introduces the DataPro process model to standardize data understanding and processing, thereby ensuring methodological rigor and reproducibility. Section 5.4 details the modular design, describing the purpose and logic of each component. Finally, Sect. 5.5 concludes with a summary of the framework design.

Z. Ma, *Artificial Intelligence-Driven Decision Support Framework for Improving Energy Efficiency in Industry and Transportation*,
https://doi.org/10.1007/978-3-658-51965-0_5

5.1 Conceptual Foundations and Design Requirements of the AI-Driven Decision Support Framework

5.1.1 Defining Decision Support Framework and AI-Driven Decision Support

This section presents a clear, rigorous definition of an AI-driven decision-support framework, establishing the conceptual foundations for this research. Defining both "decision support framework" and "AI-driven decision support" is critical for clarifying the scope, boundaries, and key constructs of the proposed framework. These definitions provide a clear understanding of the core concepts, ensuring terminological precision and theoretical coherence as the framework's design and analysis unfold in subsequent sections.

Definition 5.1 (Decision Support Framework):
A decision support framework is a structured and conceptual model that provides a high-level blueprint for organizing and interrelating the processes, components, and relationships involved in decision support. It defines the theoretical architecture of key elements, such as data inputs, analytical mechanisms, and reasoning modules, and describes their logical relationships and layers of abstraction, while delineating the conceptual boundaries between the framework and its external environment. Unlike a fully implemented system, the framework remains at an abstract level, serving as a theoretical guide for structuring decision support activities. Its purpose is to support business or organizational decision-making by outlining how suitable and available techniques and methods may conceptually enhance the effectiveness of managerial and professional activities.

Definition 5.2 (AI-driven Decision Support):
AI-driven decision support is a conceptual approach in which AI methods, such as machine learning, predictive analytics, and reasoning algorithms, are integrated into a decision support framework to enhance its analytical and inferential capabilities. At a theoretical level, this integration enables the framework to process large and complex datasets, identify patterns and trends, and produce actionable insights that guide and augment human decision-making. By harnessing the conceptual power of AI, such frameworks redefine the decision-making paradigm, offering enhanced data-driven reasoning capabilities and supporting more effective, informed decisions across diverse industrial and organizational contexts.

5.1.2 Design Requirements for an AI-Driven Decision Support Framework

The following outline outlines the high-level requirements for designing AI-driven decision support frameworks. Clearly identifying these requirements provides a conceptual roadmap for framework development, guiding the design process and ensuring alignment with intended objectives and theoretical specifications.

Requirement 1: Clear Objectives and Contextual Alignment
A clear articulation of decision support objectives and their contextual parameters is essential at the outset of framework design. Effective AI-driven decision support frameworks begin by identifying specific problems and defining precise, measurable objectives. This requires a thorough understanding of the intended end users, the nature and scope of the supported decisions, and the conditions under which these decisions are made. Such clarity ensures the conceptual alignment of the framework with organizational needs and user expectations. By contextualizing decisions, including organizational constraints and criteria, the framework establishes a theoretical foundation that guides subsequent development stages. This process informs relevant data selection and the choice of appropriate analytical models. Academically, this prerequisite reflects the principles of established analytic methodologies, such as DataPro [234], underscoring that without well-defined objectives and context, even advanced AI frameworks may yield conceptually misaligned or practically inapplicable insights.

Requirement 2: Rigorous Data Quality and Conceptual Data Management
The foundation of any AI-driven decision support framework lies in access to high-quality data and the adoption of rigorous data management practices. Data quality extends beyond sheer volume; it should be accurate, relevant, consistent, and well-structured to support meaningful analysis. Poor or fragmented data risks producing flawed insights, with studies showing that inadequate data quality incurs significant organizational costs and undermines trust in AI-driven outcomes. To address this, the framework should conceptually embed robust data governance, effective integration, and comprehensive preprocessing strategies, including data cleansing, normalization, and validation, to ensure data integrity. At the conceptual level, such measures support the generation of reliable and actionable insights. Thus, systematic data quality management, encompassing collection, verification, updating, and theoretical safeguards for data handling, emerges as a critical prerequisite for the success and credibility of AI-driven decision support.

Requirement 3: Theoretically Appropriate AI Models and Analytical Methods

The selection of AI models and algorithms should be conceptually aligned with the decision problem and data characteristics to ensure robust analytical capabilities. An effective AI-driven decision support framework requires careful selection of algorithms well aligned with the task's characteristics. Model development, at a conceptual level, involves determining appropriate features and parameters to optimize analytical performance. Well-chosen models enable the framework to identify patterns, extract insights, and generate accurate predictions or recommendations. Conversely, poorly matched algorithms risk failing to capture essential data relationships or handle data complexity, thereby diminishing the framework's effectiveness. This requirement underscores the importance of methodological coherence between AI techniques and the decision context, supported by ongoing conceptual evaluation of model suitability and performance.

Requirement 4: Human-Centric Orientation in Decision Support

An AI-driven decision support framework should adopt a human-centric design philosophy, aiming to augment and complement human decision-making rather than replace or obscure it. In this paradigm, AI functions as an "algorithm-in-the-loop," supporting humans who remain the ultimate decision-makers. To ensure meaningful human involvement, the framework should avoid reducing users to passive acceptance of algorithmic outputs. Instead, it should conceptually support mechanisms that allow users to interpret AI-generated insights, apply their expertise, and exercise judgment aligned with their goals and values. At the design level, this entails considering usability and the seamless integration of the framework into human workflows, enabling informed oversight and user control. By keeping humans at the center of the decision process, the framework fosters trust, acceptance, and effective collaboration between AI and its users.

Requirement 5: Explainability of Decision Support

An AI-driven decision support framework should prioritize explainability, ensuring that human stakeholders can understand the reasoning behind AI-generated recommendations. Explainability is essential for building user trust and confidence, as it enables decision-makers to understand how and why specific outputs were produced. This is particularly critical in high-stakes domains, where opaque reasoning may lead to skepticism or rejection of AI support. Conceptually embedding explainability within the framework allows users to evaluate and justify decisions and to recognize potential errors or biases. In a framework design context, explainability is not a peripheral feature but a fundamental design principle, ensuring that the framework's outputs are interpretable and actionable within organizational decision-making processes.

5.1.3 Originality and Novelty of the Proposed Framework

To clarify the originality of the proposed framework, Table 5.1 contrasts conventional decision support frameworks with the AI-driven design developed in this thesis, based on the literature analysis in Chap. 3. Traditional frameworks tend to be descriptive or predictive, rely on ad-hoc processes, and offer limited opportunities for stakeholder engagement or interpretability. The proposed framework addresses these limitations by integrating data understanding, clustering, causal inference, and multimodal narration within a unified architecture informed by the DataPro model, thereby supporting methodological rigor and human-centric priorities, including explainability and iterative feedback.

Conventional DSS typically rely on pre-processed data and static predictive or rule-based models [18, 40]. The proposed design introduces an adaptive, data-driven pipeline that applies unsupervised clustering to uncover latent operational patterns and causal inference to identify underlying drivers of performance. An LLM-based narration layer further translates analytical outcomes into coherent, multimodal decision narratives that combine text, charts, and visuals, overcoming the fragmented reporting typical of legacy systems. These innovations address key gaps in existing frameworks, namely the absence of deep pattern discovery, causal transparency, and integrated interpretability. Table 5.1 summarizes these distinctions and demonstrates the framework's originality and its contribution to decision support in energy-efficiency contexts.

Building on the established design requirements, this thesis makes three original contributions at the framework level. First, it introduces a modular integration of pattern clustering, causal inference, and multimodal narration to support energy-efficiency decisions that unify descriptive, explanatory, and prescriptive insights. Second, it develops a process-oriented methodology by adapting the DataPro model to ensure standardization, reproducibility, and alignment with best practices in data science. Third, it embeds a human-centric orientation by incorporating explainability, transparency, and iterative stakeholder feedback directly into the framework's architecture.

Table 5.1 Comparison of conventional decision support frameworks and the proposed AI-driven framework

Dimension	Conventional decision support frameworks	Proposed AI-driven framework (this thesis)
Analytical methods	Predominantly supervised prediction or optimization models using fixed features	Integrates unsupervised clustering and causal inference to identify latent patterns and explain outcomes
Data integration	Primarily relies on preprocessed, structured data from isolated sources	Develops an automated understanding of data characteristics and quality, ensuring a reliable and context-aware foundation for analysis
Development process	Sequential lifecycle with limited stakeholder feedback	An iterative DataPro model for the data analytic process
Decision narration	Static dashboards and reports compiled manually, with separate visuals and text	Automated multimodal storytelling via LLMs, generating coherent narratives that combine charts, images, and explanations
Explainability & feedback	Opaque black-box models or simple post-hoc explanations with little interactive engagement	Explainable analytics and feedback mechanisms, enhancing transparency and trust

A key additional novelty lies in the framework's workflow design. The DataPro data processing model (Sect. 5.3) is developed to ensure that business objectives are continuously translated into technical requirements and that analytical outputs are validated in context. Explainability and user feedback are embedded by design, providing built-in interpretability and fostering trust through active human involvement.

In summary, the framework's originality is defined by three core contributions:

- Hybrid Analytic Integration: Combining unsupervised clustering with data-driven causal inference to reveal hidden operational segments and their drivers, extending beyond conventional predictive models.
- Adapted Process Model: Employing a DataPro-based workflow to maintain alignment between business goals and data-analytical execution.
- Human-Centric Narration and Interaction: Incorporating LLM-driven multimodal storytelling, explainability-by-design, and interactive feedback to enhance transparency and stakeholder engagement.

5.2 High-Level Architecture of the AI-Driven Decision Support Framework

This section provides a high-level overview of the proposed AI-driven decision support framework. The framework is designed in accordance with the five requirements introduced in Sect. 5.1.2. As shown in Fig. 5.1, it consists of five interconnected modules arranged in a bottom-up structure, progressing logically from data collection to deployment. Each module encompasses multiple stages of the data analytics process, collectively supporting the transformation of raw data into actionable insights for decision-making. Section 5.2.1 introduces the fundamental concepts and definitions of the proposed framework, and Sect. 5.2.2 outlines the overall workflow and both inter-module and intra-module interactions.

5.2.1 Core Concepts Underpinning the Framework Architecture

The structural foundation of the proposed framework rests on a set of core concepts that determine its architecture, data flow, and functional capabilities. To improve clarity, these concepts are grouped into four categories: (1) Data Foundations, (2) Data Preparation and Quality, (3) Causal Analysis, and (4) Decision Support and Interpretability. Together, they provide the terminology, mechanisms, and principles underpinning the modular design and ensure conceptual coherence throughout the framework.

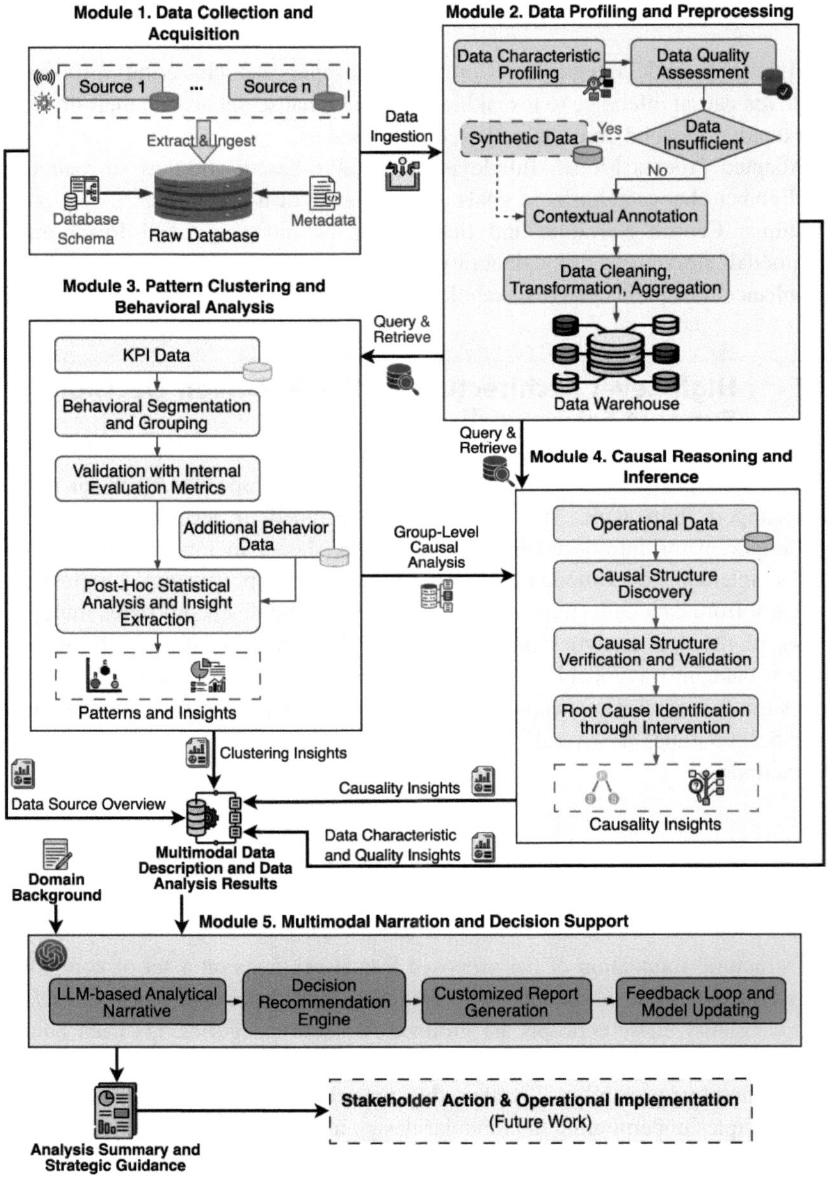

Fig. 5.1 Overview of the proposed AI-driven decision support framework. This framework involves five modules: (1) Data Collection and Acquisition, (2) Data Profiling and Preprocessing, (3) Pattern Clustering and Behavioral Analysis, (4) Causal Reasoning and Inference, and (5) Multimodal Narration and Decision Support

1) Data Foundations

This group covers the concepts necessary to capture, organize, and manage raw data from heterogeneous real-world environments, e.g., industry and transportation.

Definition 5.3 (Data Collection): the systematic process of identifying and recording relevant information from diverse sources to support downstream analysis. It specifies variables of interest, formats, and procedures to ensure accuracy and completeness.

Definition 5.4 (Data Acquisition): the technical process of retrieving and integrating data from internal and external sources into a centralized repository using communication protocols, scheduling mechanisms, and software tools.

Definition 5.5 (Metadata): structured descriptive information documenting data origin, format, schema, and quality indicators, which enables discoverability, interpretation, and governance.

Definition 5.6 (Database Schema): the logical structure that defines entities, attributes, relationships, and constraints within a database, ensuring consistency, validation, and efficient querying.

Definition 5.7 (Operational Data): time-stamped, sequential records generated by routine industrial or transportation processes (e.g., sensor readings, energy consumption logs). Such data primarily support monitoring, diagnostics, and performance analysis.

Definition 5.8: (Multimodal Data): datasets that combine multiple types of information (e.g., numerical values, text, images) aligned through shared temporal, spatial, or entity references. Within this framework, multimodal data enriches analytical perspectives and decision support.

2) Data Preparation and Quality

These concepts ensure that raw, heterogeneous data is transformed into high-quality, analysis-ready input for modeling.

Definition 5.9 (Data Profiling): the process of examining datasets to summarize structural patterns, distributions, and anomalies, providing insights into readiness and potential issues.

Definition 5.10 (Data Characteristic Profiling): a specialized form of profiling focusing on temporal and statistical features (e.g., autocorrelation, periodicity, skewness), guiding modeling assumptions and algorithm selection.

Definition 5.11 (Data Preprocessing): preparatory operations such as cleaning, normalization, imputation, and feature engineering to enhance quality, consistency, and suitability for analysis.

Definition 5.12 (Data Quality Assessment): systematic evaluation of datasets against defined quality dimensions, including accuracy, completeness, timeliness, validity, and consistency.

Definition 5.13 (Data Warehouse): a centralized, structured repository that integrates prepared datasets from multiple sources, ensuring stable schemas, historical persistence, and query performance.

Definition 5.14 (KPI Data): subsets of data used to compute Key Performance Indicators (KPIs), such as specific energy consumption or energy intensity, which quantify progress toward performance objectives.

3) Causal Analysis

This group introduces the concepts that enable the framework to move beyond correlations and towards explanatory and prescriptive insights.

Definition 5.15 (Causal Discovery): the algorithmic process of identifying potential causal structures among variables from observational data under explicit assumptions, typically represented as DAGs.

Definition 5.16 (Causal Reasoning): logical deduction of cause-effect pathways, including predictions of interventions ("what if"), explanations of observed outcomes ("why"), and evaluations of hypothetical scenarios ("what could have happened").

Definition 5.17 (Causal Inference): the estimation and validation of the strength and direction of causal effects, often using potential outcomes, graphical models, or structural equation models.

Definition 5.18 (Root Cause): a fundamental factor within a causal system whose alteration prevents the occurrence or recurrence of an undesired outcome, enabling targeted interventions.

4) Decision Support and Interpretability

The final group focuses on concepts that ensure analytical results are communicated clearly and made actionable for stakeholders.

Definition 5.19 (Data Narration): the automatic generation of structured and context-sensitive explanations that transform quantitative and multimodal outputs into human-readable narratives. By enhancing interpretability and transparency, data narration enables stakeholders to make informed decisions in complex operational environments.

Table 5.2 summarizes the core concepts and definitions of the proposed framework.

Table 5.2 Summary of core concepts and definitions of the proposed framework

No.	Concept	Concise definition	Role in framework
5.3	Data Collection	Recording relevant information from diverse sources	Ensures essential input is captured
5.4	Data Acquisition	Technical integration of data into a centralized system	Provides traceable and secure data ingestion
5.5	Metadata	Structured descriptive information about datasets	Enables governance, discoverability, and interpretation
5.6	Database Schema	Logical structure of stored data	Ensures consistency and efficient querying
5.7	Operational Data	Time-stamped sequential process data	Supports monitoring and diagnostics
5.8	Multimodal Data	Combined numerical, textual, and visual information	Enriches analytical scope
5.9	Data Profiling	Examination of datasets for properties and anomalies	Diagnoses readiness and guides preprocessing

(continued)

Table 5.2 (continued)

No.	Concept	Concise definition	Role in framework
5.10	Data Characteristic Profiling	Profiling focused on temporal and statistical features	Supports algorithm choice and interpretability
5.11	Data Preprocessing	Cleaning and transforming raw data	Produces analysis-ready datasets
5.12	Data Quality Assessment	Evaluation against quality dimensions	Ensures reliability and trustworthiness
5.13	Data Warehouse	Centralized structured repository	Provides a stable platform for data storage
5.14	KPI Data	Subset of data used for key performance indicators	Quantifies energy performance
5.15	Causal Discovery	Algorithmic identification of causal structures	Moves beyond correlation to explanation
5.16	Causal Reasoning	Deduction of cause-effect pathways	Supports "what if" and counterfactual reasoning
5.17	Causal Inference	Estimation of strength and direction of causal effects	Provides quantitative causal evidence
5.18	Root Cause	Fundamental causal factor preventing undesired outcomes	Enables targeted interventions
5.19	Data Narration	Automatic generation of explanatory narratives	Enhances interpretability and stakeholder engagement

5.2.2 Workflow and Inter-Module Interactions Within the Framework

As illustrated in Fig. 5.1, the proposed decision support framework consists of five modules, each encapsulating a key stage of the analytic process. While each module has a distinct function and set of internal processes, they operate in a coordinated manner. The outputs from one module serve as essential inputs to the other. This modular design enhances conceptual clarity by separating core components while maintaining seamless integration, enabling data and insights to flow progressively toward the final decision support outcome. The following presents a high-level overview of each module, outlining its purpose, internal structure, contribution to the overall framework, and its interactions with other modules.

Module 1: Data Collection and Acquisition serves as the data foundation for the AI-driven decision support framework, tasked with collecting and organizing all relevant data and metadata from heterogeneous sources. Its primary objective is to establish a high-fidelity and comprehensive raw data repository. The inclusion of this module is motivated by the need to consolidate fragmented, multi-format data, such as sensor measurements, equipment logs, and contextual variables, into a unified and analyzable form. This module initiates the data pipeline by executing a series of interrelated processes: source and sensor identification, interface and protocol integration, automated ingestion and logging, and metadata documentation. Together, these processes enable the systematic acquisition of raw data in native formats and facilitate initial schema alignment across sources. The main output of Module 1 is a raw dataset enriched with metadata, which serves as the analytical substrate for all downstream modules. Specifically, it provides input to Module 2 for data profiling and preprocessing, while also supplying the data's provenance and scope to Module 5 for narrative generation.

Module 2: Data Profiling and Preprocessing is dedicated to understanding, improving, and preparing raw data for downstream analytical tasks. Following data acquisition, raw datasets are rarely analysis-ready due to errors, missing values, inconsistencies, or uncharacterized structures. This module addresses such challenges through a twofold function: data profiling, which interrogates and summarizes the data's statistical properties and quality, and data preprocessing, which cleanses, transforms, and structures the data for reliable analysis. Key processes begin with data profiling and quality assessment, which involve generating descriptive statistics and identifying quality issues such as outliers, sparsity, or missing values. When data deficiencies are significant, synthetic data generation may be employed to support subsequent stages. Once the data is deemed adequate, it is enriched with contextual annotations, such as temporal, spatial, or operational labels, which embed domain knowledge into the dataset and enhance interpretability. Subsequent preprocessing steps include imputation, normalization, consistency checks, and other essential data refinement procedures. The output of this module consists of cleaned, structured datasets stored in a data warehouse, which form the foundation for Modules 3 and 4. In addition, data quality indicators and profiling insights are forwarded to Module 5 to support transparent data quality narratives and decision recommendations.

Module 3: Pattern Clustering and Behavioral Analysis aims to uncover latent structure in the cleansed dataset by grouping similar data points and analyzing associated behavioral patterns. The motivation for this module stems from the need to detect typical operational behaviors or anomalies that are not readily apparent from raw observations. Its core objective is to identify, validate, and interpret natural groupings (clusters) within KPI data that reflect energy-related behavior within the scope of this PhD study. The process begins with extracting KPI variables related to energy efficiency. These KPIs are segmented by operational cycle, e.g., manufacturing batches or transportation trips, to capture behavior at the unit level. The module then applies unsupervised learning techniques to group similar operational segments based on KPI patterns. Once clustering is completed, the performance of the resulting groups is assessed using internal clustering evaluation metrics. Additional behavioral variables may be integrated to enrich cluster profiles and enable more nuanced post-hoc analysis. Statistical tests and analyses are then conducted to assess significant differences between clusters across multiple indicators or dimensions, thereby enhancing the interpretability and diagnostic value of the identified patterns. The primary input is the structured dataset from Module 2. Outputs include cluster labels and behavioral summaries, which inform causal analysis in Module 4 and support narrative generation in Module 5 by illustrating distinct energy-related operational profiles.

Module 4: Causal Reasoning and Inference addresses the critical question of "why" observed patterns or outcomes occur. This module enhances the explanatory and prescriptive capabilities of the decision support framework. It concerns identifying the cause-and-effect relationships underlying system behavior. In decision support, correlation may suggest associations, but only causal understanding enables effective intervention, allowing decision-makers to act on the true drivers of performance. The module applies causal inference techniques to construct and validate a causal model of the system, typically represented as a DAG. Key processes include discovering an initial causal structure, refining it using domain knowledge and statistical verification, and simulating interventions to perform root cause analysis. For instance, the module tests how manipulating a particular factor might influence a downstream outcome. Inputs include operational data from Module 2 and pattern insights from Module 3, such as cluster assignments for stratified analysis. The outputs are validated causal relationships that identify key drivers and pathways. These insights feed directly into Module 5, ensuring that decision recommendations are grounded in robust causal mechanisms rather than statistical associations alone.

Module 5: Multimodal Narration and Decision Support serves as the integrative culmination of the framework, translating analytical results into actionable knowledge for decision-makers. Its primary function is to synthesize outputs from Modules 2–4 into a structured narrative, supported by visualizations and contextual information, to facilitate energy efficiency improvements. This module operationalizes the framework insights, ensuring they are communicated clearly, effectively, and in a decision-ready format. This module processes multimodal inputs, including structured data, visual outputs, and derived causal insights, using advanced multimodal LLMs. The key processes follow four sequential steps. First, multimodal analytical outputs are transformed into coherent and context-aware explanations. Second, user-oriented reports are generated in alignment with stakeholder needs. Third, evidence-based recommendations are formulated to provide actionable guidance grounded in analytical results. Fourth, the feedback loop captures outcomes and user responses, enabling iterative refinement and ensuring continuous alignment with real-world practice. The outputs consist of decision support artifacts that combine narrative text with visual elements, such as graphs, tables, and causal diagrams. The inputs originate from all preceding modules: contextual data from Module 1, data quality summaries from Module 2, behavioral patterns from Module 3, and causal findings from Module 4. Importantly, Module 5 integrates a feedback mechanism that feeds user actions and observed outcomes back into the system, enabling continuous refinement and alignment with real-world dynamics.

In future applications of the framework, end-users will implement recommendations, such as optimizing operational procedures or conducting targeted employee training, to improve energy efficiency. The observed outcomes and user feedback will be systematically collected and reintegrated into the framework, thereby supporting longitudinal validation, iterative learning, and refinement of the decision support process.

5.3 Process-Oriented Development Using the DataPro Model

Note: Parts of this section are based on the author's first-author conference paper: *"DataPro—A Standardized Data Understanding and Processing Procedure: A Case Study of an Eco-driving Project"* [234].

As the proposed decision support framework is fundamentally data-driven, its development should be guided by a systematic data analytics process that ensures consistency, rigor, and reproducibility. To address this need, this research proposes DataPro—a standardized data understanding and processing procedure, to support the construction of the AI-driven decision support framework. Informed by CRISP-DM [235, 236], the DataPro model is an enriched data understanding and processing framework for data science projects. Section 5.3.1 outlines the pipeline and core components of the DataPro model, and Sect. 5.3.2 demonstrates its application by mapping the model to the development of the proposed AI-driven decision support framework.

5.3.1 The DataPro Model: A Standardized Data Understanding and Processing Procedure

The DataPro model is a generic framework for data-driven decision support, an update and extension of the CRISP-DM model. Firstly, to provide a more comprehensive and logical arrangement of project execution activities, two additional phases, "technical understanding" and "implementation", are included. Secondly, the roles of data scientists and stakeholders are clearly defined and clarified in this model, facilitating effective communication to avoid misinformation. Thirdly, the eight phases are classified into five groups to better explain the objectives and activities of each phase.

The proposed DataPro model is demonstrated in Fig. 5.2. The gray cycle outlines the general explanation of the technical steps, which include "Define", "Refine", "Analyze", and "Delivery". In the "Refine" and "Analyze" stages, the "Validate" and "Verify" processes are applied for the necessary iterations. The eight blocks inside the circle correspond to the technical phases, with color-coding indicating the participants: orange for stakeholders and blue for data scientists. The black arrows linking the blocks indicate the information flow between the two phases.

This model extends the CRISP-DM framework by incorporating the "technical understanding" and "implementation" phases. The technical understanding phase converts business objectives into data science terminology. This translation facilitates data scientists' understanding of business requirements, ensuring their analytical efforts are precisely aligned with organizational goals. The implementation phase involves the practical deployment of the developed or selected models in real-world scenarios, including model application, parameter optimization, system integration, and related activities. This phase is crucial as it transitions

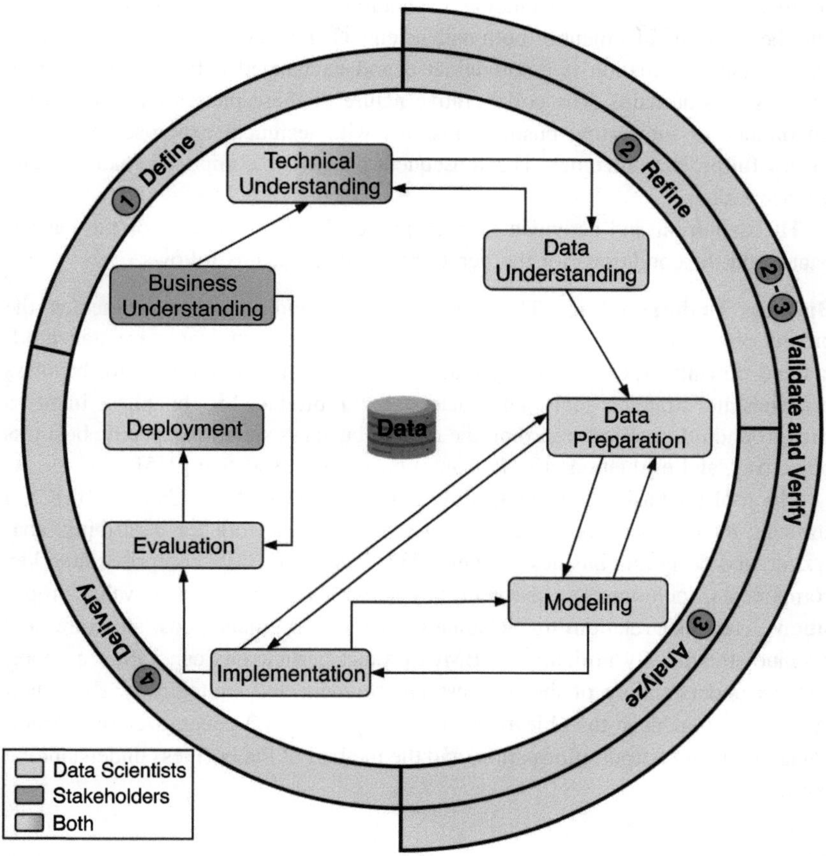

Fig. 5.2 The DataPro process model. The gray cycle outlines the general explanation of the technical steps. The eight blocks inside the circle correspond to the technical phases, with color-coded participants as indicated in the legend. The black arrows linking the blocks indicate the information flow between the two phases

the project from theoretical analysis to practical application, demonstrating the real-world value of the data science efforts.

Furthermore, the roles of distinct participants are highlighted in Fig. 5.2. The business understanding phase is carried out exclusively by the application partners, who are responsible for defining the project's business objectives. In contrast, the technical understanding, evaluation, and deployment phases necessitate the active involvement of both data scientists and stakeholders. In these three phases, the information is communicated and exchanged between data science and business domains. The collaborative nature of these phases underscores the importance of integrating business insights with technical expertise to achieve successful project outcomes. The subsequent phases are comprised solely of data science tasks.

The definition and activities of each phase, the detailed roles of the participants, and the conditions for the iterations are discussed as follows.

Business Understanding: The business understanding phase delineates the project objectives from the business perspective. The participants are stakeholders and domain experts, ensuring that the project objectives align with business priorities and strategic goals. The documentation produced in this phase involves background information regarding the current business situation, specific business objectives, and evaluation criteria from a business perspective [235].

The tool for business understanding is the Business Model Canvas (BMC), a strategic management tool that provides a visual framework for describing, analyzing, and designing business models [237, 238]. The BMC comprises nine key components, including key partners, key activities, key resources, value propositions, customer relationships, channels, customer segments, cost structure, and revenue streams. By utilizing the BMC, project participants can gain a comprehensive understanding of the business environment and strategically align their operations to achieve the objectives effectively. Table 5.3 generalizes the participants, input and output information, and the method of the business understanding phase.

Table 5.3 Inputs, participants, and outputs for the business understanding phase

Category	Details
Participants	Stakeholders and domain experts
Input Information	Background information on organizational goals, stakeholder requirements, operational context, constraints, and existing processes
Output Information	BMC results, including customer segments, value proposition, channels, customer relationships, revenue streams, key resources, key activities, key partners, and cost structure
Methods	BMC, stakeholder workshops, and structured interviews

Technical Understanding: The technical understanding phase is where business objectives and evaluation criteria are translated into a data science framework. This phase involves collaboration between stakeholders and data scientists. Data scientists focus on converting the business goals into technical terms, while stakeholders ensure that the translated objectives and evaluation criteria remain consistent with the original business intents.

In this phase, the technical understanding of a data science project is developed by defining the input and output variables, the constraint formulas, and the quantitative evaluation criteria. Input variables are the data used in the analysis, while output variables are the results the project aims to predict or explain. Constraint formulas establish the boundaries and limitations within which the data science models should operate. Finally, quantitative evaluation criteria are established to assess the effectiveness and accuracy of the data science solutions, ensuring they meet predefined business objectives. This translation process ensures that technical efforts are aligned with business goals, facilitating the integration of data science solutions into the broader business strategy.

The business understanding and technical understanding phases are both crucial components of the "Define" stage. In this stage, these two phases work together to establish clear and precise objectives and evaluation criteria. This collaboration ensures that business goals are aligned with technical capabilities, facilitating a comprehensive approach that addresses both business and data science challenges in the project. Table 5.4 lists the core aspects of the technical understanding phase.

Table 5.4 Inputs, participants, and outputs for the technical understanding phase

Category	Details
Participants	Data scientists and stakeholders
Input Information	BMC results from business understanding, data availability, and quality reports
Output Information	Defined input/output variables, constraint formulas, and evaluation criteria
Methods	Requirement engineering and technical scoping workshops

Data Understanding: The data understanding phase involves understanding data characteristics and evaluating data quality. This phase aims to identify and mitigate any potential issues during the subsequent data preparation phase. By thoroughly understanding the data's attributes, distribution, and potential anomalies, data scientists can preemptively address problems that might otherwise impede progress. To ensure a comprehensive understanding of data characteristics, the 6 Vs model can be adopted, which includes six dimensions: volume, variety, velocity, veracity, value, and variability [115]. This model provides a structured approach to examining data, facilitating more effective data management and utilization. When conducting data quality evaluations, it is essential to assess several key dimensions to ensure data integrity and utility, including completeness, timeliness, accuracy, consistency, validity, and uniqueness [115].

From the data understanding phase to the implementation phase, the participants involved are limited to data scientists, as these tasks require specialized technical expertise and do not rely on business understanding.

A feedback loop exists between data understanding and technical understanding, wherein data quality strongly influences the feasibility and success of technical objectives. This interdependence means that many technical goals cannot be achieved without first addressing data quality issues. Consequently, it is essential to adjust both the objectives and evaluation criteria in response to data quality challenges, such as incompleteness or invalidity.

Table 5.5 demonstrates the core aspects of the data understanding phase.

Table 5.5 Inputs, participants, and outputs for the data understanding phase

Category	Details
Participants	Data scientists
Input Information	Outputs from technical understanding, available datasets, and metadata
Output Information	Data characteristic and quality assessment results
Methods	Data characteristic profiling (6 Vs framework) and exploratory data analysis [115]

Data Preparation: The data preparation phase preprocesses the datasets based on the insights from the data understanding phase. Key activities in this phase include data cleaning, transformation, and integration. By performing these activities, the data preparation phase ensures that datasets are clean, accurate, and well-structured, thereby enhancing the effectiveness and efficiency of the subsequent modeling phases.

Data cleaning involves identifying and correcting errors and inconsistencies in the data, such as handling missing values, correcting inaccuracies, processing outliers, and removing duplicates. Furthermore, feature selection is another critical task in data cleaning, identifying and retaining the most relevant variables for analysis. This process enhances both the quality of the dataset and the performance of the data processing model in the subsequent phase. Data transformation methods convert data into a suitable format for analysis. Tasks include normalization, aggregation, and encoding categorical variables, ensuring the data is standardized and comparable. Data integration methods combine data generated from various sources to create a unified dataset. Tasks include merging datasets, reconciling data discrepancies, and ensuring consistency across the integrated data.

The data understanding and data preparation phases encompass the "Refine" stage, which focuses on improving the data quality for modeling. These phases ensure that the data is thoroughly understood and preprocessed, addressing inconsistencies and errors, and integrating data from various sources.

Table 5.6 presents the core aspects of the data preparation phase.

Table 5.6 Inputs, participants, and outputs for the data preparation phase

Category	Details
Participants	Data scientists
Input Information	Raw/synthetic datasets, data quality results, and feedback from modeling and implementation
Output Information	Preprocessed and structured datasets ready for modeling
Methods	Data cleaning, transformation, integration, and feature engineering

Modeling: In the modeling phase, multiple models are initially run with default parameters, and the best-performing model is selected. Following this, the parameters of the chosen model are fine-tuned to optimize its overall performance. This phase encompasses a range of models, including statistical methods such as causal inference and hypothesis testing, as well as machine learning and deep learning algorithms for tasks like prediction, classification, and clustering.

If necessary, the process may revert to the data preparation phase for additional data manipulations required by the chosen model. Therefore, there is a constant feedback loop between data preparation and modeling. As new issues and challenges arise during modeling experiments, data preprocessing strategies should be adjusted to better align the data with the model's requirements, thereby improving performance and accuracy.

Thus, the data preparation phase works together with the modeling phase within the "Analyze" stage. This collaboration is essential for continuously refining and improving the data, ensuring it is of the highest quality and suitable for modeling. By maintaining this iterative approach, organizations can better identify and address issues, ultimately leading to more reliable, robust models that provide valuable insights and support informed recommendations.

Table 5.7 demonstrates the core aspects of the modeling phase.

Table 5.7 Inputs, participants, and outputs for the modeling phase

Category	Details
Participants	Data scientists
Input Information	Preprocessed datasets, defined objectives, and evaluation criteria
Output Information	Selected models, tuned parameters, and performance metrics
Methods	Statistical analysis, machine learning/deep learning, and model evaluation metrics

Implementation: The implementation phase applies the models developed in the modeling phase to a real-world environment. Key activities include integrating the model into real-world systems, continuously monitoring its performance on diverse real-world datasets, and making necessary adjustments to ensure robustness and reliability. This phase also involves scaling the model to handle large volumes of real-world data and ensuring it operates efficiently under various usage conditions.

Additionally, the implementation phase relies on preprocessed datasets received from the data preparation phase for testing and validation. Moreover, continuous feedback loops between the modeling and implementation phases are essential for maintaining and improving model performance and for addressing issues that arise in the application environment. Overall, successful implementation ensures the model delivers actionable, reliable insights that can be effectively used for recommendations.

Table 5.8 lists the core aspects of the implementation phase.

Table 5.8 Inputs, participants, and outputs for the implementation phase

Category	Details
Participants	Data scientists and system engineers
Input Information	Selected models and parameters, and real-world datasets
Output Information	Integrated and deployed models, validation results, and monitoring reports
Methods	Model integration, system deployment, and real-world validation

Evaluation: During the modeling and implementation phases, the constructed models have been assessed against established technical evaluation criteria, ensuring they are technically sound and effective. Subsequently, during this evaluation phase, it is crucial to assess outcomes against the evaluation criteria defined in the business understanding phase. This dual-layered evaluation approach guarantees that technical accuracy is complemented by alignment with business objectives.

In the evaluation phase, the technical results need to be translated into operational recommendations. This translation is essential to bridge the gap between technical analytics and practical business insights, making the findings accessible and actionable for stakeholders, who are primarily concerned with the operational and strategic implications.

By converting technical results into understandable recommendations, business participants can effectively use the insights to drive decision-making. This collaborative approach not only enhances the overall effectiveness of the modeling process but also ensures that the technical and business perspectives are harmoniously integrated, fostering a comprehensive understanding and application of the results.

Table 5.9 demonstrates the core aspects of the evaluation phase.

Table 5.9 Inputs, participants, and outputs for the evaluation phase

Category	Details
Participants	Data scientists and stakeholders
Input Information	Business objectives, evaluation criteria, and deployed model results
Output Information	Evaluation reports and validated decision support recommendations
Methods	Quantitative and qualitative evaluation, user validation, and performance benchmarking

Deployment: The deployment phase is the final step of the data science project, delivering value to various stakeholders and concluding the project. The deployment phase includes two activities: planning and monitoring the deployment of results and producing a final report.

Planning and monitoring ensure a smooth, efficient deployment process aligned with stakeholders' expectations. This involves continuous oversight to address any issues that arise during implementation. Furthermore, the final report documents the project outcomes, methodologies, and insights, encompassing the models, technical results, and business recommendations. This report also includes a project review to assess the overall performance and identify lessons learned.

The implementation, evaluation, and deployment phases consist of the "Delivery" stage, which ensures that models are applicable in real-world scenarios and deliver business value. This stage is crucial for validating the practical applicability and alignment of models with operational goals and strategic objectives.

Table 5.10 presents the core aspects of the deployment phase.

Table 5.10 Inputs, participants, and outputs for the deployment phase

Category	Details
Participants	Data scientists, stakeholders, and decision-makers
Input Information	Evaluation results and validated recommendations
Output Information	Deployment reports, operational decision-support system, and stakeholder guidance
Methods	Deployment planning, monitoring, and reporting

5.3.2 Alignment of the Decision Support Framework with the DataPro Model

Figure 5.3 illustrates how the phases of the DataPro model correspond to the modules of the proposed AI-driven decision support framework. This mapping ensures that the framework is developed and operated within a standardized, systematic, and iterative process model, thereby avoiding ad-hoc design and reinforcing methodological rigor. Each module is anchored in one or more DataPro phases, ensuring alignment between data science best practices and decision support objectives.

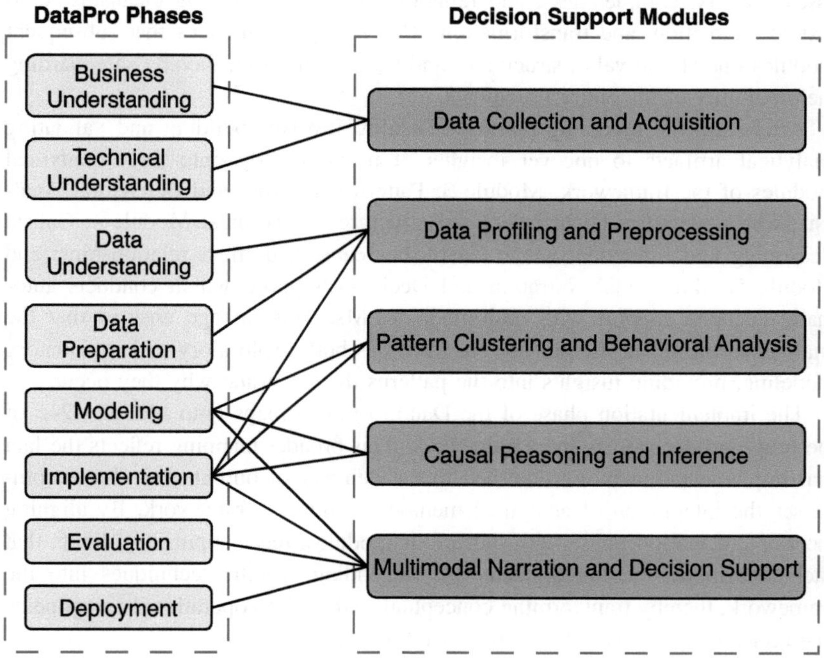

Fig. 5.3 The mapping between the phases of the DataPro model and the modules of the proposed AI-driven decision support framework. The yellow blocks on the left represent the phases of the DataPro model, while the green blocks on the right represent the modules of the decision support framework. The connecting lines illustrate the correspondence between DataPro phases and framework modules

The initial two phases of business and technical understanding in DataPro establish the problem context and define the project's technical requirements. These phases align with Module 1: Data Collection and Acquisition, ensuring that data gathering is guided directly by organizational objectives and technical feasibility. This linkage ensures that data sources are not selected arbitrarily but are purposefully chosen to address decision support needs in a manner consistent with resource and system constraints.

Next, DataPro emphasizes that meaningful analysis depends on deep knowledge of data characteristics and careful preparation, reflected in the phases of data understanding and data preparation. These phases correspond to Module 2: Data Profiling and Preprocessing, which interrogates the collected data to assess quality, completeness, and reliability, before performing cleansing, contextual annotation, and transformation. This linkage guarantees that subsequent modules operate on valid, structured, and trustworthy data, thereby safeguarding the credibility of the entire framework.

Afterward, the modeling phase of DataPro involves building and validating analytical artifacts to uncover insights. It maps directly onto three analytical modules of the framework: Module 3: Pattern Clustering and Behavioral Analysis, which identifies latent behavioral structures in the data; Module 4: Causal Reasoning and Inference, which establishes cause-and-effect relationships; and Module 5: Multimodal Narration and Decision Support, which conducts automatic decision support with multimodal LLMs. This linkage ensures that the analytical core of the framework encompasses both exploratory and explanatory modeling, providing insights into the patterns that exist and why they occur.

The implementation phase of the DataPro model maps onto Modules 2–5 of the proposed decision support framework. This broader mapping reflects the fact that implementation is not confined to the delivery of outputs but also encompasses the integration of analytical methods within the framework. By aligning the Implementation phase with these four modules, the mapping highlights that each contributes methodologically by embedding specific techniques into the framework, thereby transforming conceptual designs into operational components that collectively enable AI-driven decision support.

Finally, except for the implementation phase, the evaluation and deployment phases of the DataPro model are embodied in Module 5: Multimodal Narration and Decision Support. These phases stress the importance of translating analytical results into practical applications, assessing their utility, and maintaining adaptability through iterative refinement. Module 5 operationalizes these objectives by synthesizing outputs from earlier modules into coherent multimodal narratives, generating user-oriented reports, and formulating actionable, evidence-based recommendations. Crucially, it also incorporates a feedback mechanism that captures stakeholder responses and observed outcomes, reintegrating this information into the framework to support continuous learning.

Overall, each decision support module is conceptually and procedurally anchored in a corresponding DataPro phase, ensuring methodological rigor, process coherence, and seamless integration across the end-to-end pipeline.

5.4 Modular Design of the AI-Driven Decision Support Framework

This section provides a detailed account of the design of each module within the decision support framework. Unlike Sect. 5.2, which outlines the high-level concepts of the framework, including the information flow and interactions across modules, the present section focuses on the internal conceptualizations of each module. In doing so, it establishes a robust conceptual and theoretical foundation that informs both the framework's implementation and its subsequent application in case studies.

5.4.1 Module 1: Data Collection and Acquisition

The first module of the framework addresses the systematic collection and acquisition of data from real-world environments. To ensure rigor and traceability, this module employs the STREAM pipeline, a structured procedure that bridges the business and technical understanding phases of the DataPro model with the extract step of the ETL (extract, transform, load) process. The STREAM pipeline provides a principled approach for aligning sensor deployments with organizational objectives and ensuring that collected data is accurate, well-documented, and suitable for downstream analysis.

Definition 5.20 (Physical-Sensor Data): Physical-sensor data refers to quantitative measurements automatically generated by hardware devices that detect and record physical phenomena such as temperature, pressure, flow rate, vibration, or electrical current. These measurements are captured at the boundary between the physical and digital domains, typically as a time-stamped series of digital signals, and form the empirical basis for analyzing energy-related operational behaviors.

As illustrated in Fig. 5.4, the STREAM pipeline comprises six sequential stages: Specification of Objectives, Technical Requirements, Resource Mapping, Extraction from Sensors, Archival Metadata, and Migration to Database. Together, these stages establish a clear link between organizational goals and the resulting data infrastructure. At a conceptual level, they ensure that data acquisition is:

- Goal-oriented—objectives and performance indicators are defined upfront.
- Technically grounded—business requirements are translated into measurable parameters and sensor specifications.

- Systematic—sensors and resources are mapped to objectives in a coherent way.
- Traceable—metadata and contextual information are preserved for governance and reproducibility.
- Actionable—collected data is integrated into accessible repositories for subsequent processing.

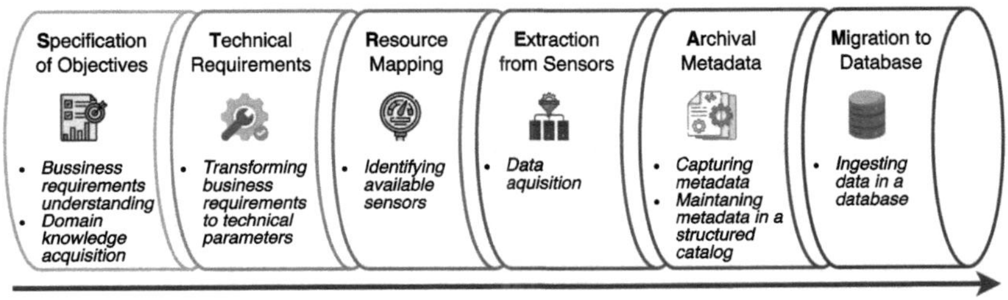

Fig. 5.4 The STREAM pipeline for data collection and acquisition. Each cylinder illustrates a distinct step of the pipeline. The upper segment contains the step name, while the lower segment summarizes its key activities

In summary, the STREAM pipeline provides the conceptual foundation for data collection in the framework. By integrating business objectives with technical execution, it ensures that physical-sensor data is systematically acquired, contextually documented, and securely stored, forming a robust basis for subsequent data profiling, preprocessing, and analysis. The implementation details of the STREAM pipeline are provided in Sect. 6.2.

5.4.2 Module 2: Data Profiling and Preprocessing

The second module of the framework ensures that raw sensor data acquired in Module 1 is systematically examined, evaluated, and prepared for analysis. Conceptually, this module bridges the data understanding and data preparation phases of the DataPro model with the transform-and-load steps of the ETL process. Its purpose is to transform heterogeneous and potentially noisy sensor data into reliable, structured, and analysis-ready datasets.

As illustrated in Fig. 5.5, the module follows a four-stage pipeline comprising data characteristic profiling, data quality assessment, contextual annotation, and data preprocessing. Together, these stages create a structured process that guarantees both the technical quality and semantic richness of the resulting datasets.

- Data Characteristic Profiling establishes a baseline understanding of the statistical and temporal properties of raw data, identifying potential issues that may hinder analysis.
- Data Quality Assessment evaluates the dataset against formal quality dimensions such as completeness, accuracy, timeliness, and consistency, ensuring that data is fit for purpose.
- Contextual Annotation enriches each record with metadata and operational context, embedding meaning and traceability to support interpretation and governance.
- Data Preprocessing integrates the outcomes of previous steps to produce a structured, consistent, and analysis-ready dataset suitable for downstream modules.

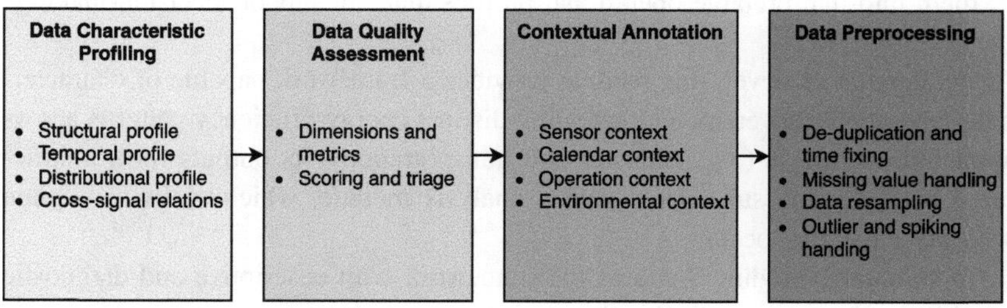

Fig. 5.5 The pipeline of data profiling and preprocessing. It comprises four sequential stages: data characteristic profiling, data quality assessment, contextual annotation, and data preprocessing

In summary, this module provides high-quality data for reliable and interpretable analytics. By combining statistical profiling, quality evaluation, contextual enrichment, and preprocessing, it ensures that raw sensor data is transformed into high-quality datasets that underpin the subsequent analytical stages of the decision support framework. The corresponding framework implementation is detailed in Sect. 6.3.

5.4.3 Module 3: Pattern Clustering and Behavioral Analysis

The third module of the framework focuses on pattern clustering and behavioral analysis, enabling the identification of recurring operational behaviors and their implications for energy efficiency. Conceptually, this module extends the framework from data preparation (Module 2) to analytical insight, helping uncover latent structures and behavioral patterns that are not immediately visible in raw data.

As illustrated in Fig. 5.6, the workflow integrates three key activities: data segmentation, clustering, and behavioral interpretation.

- Data segmentation ensures that continuous operational data (e.g., production cycles, transportation trips) is divided into meaningful analytical units, aligning with domain-specific operational boundaries.
- Clustering groups these segments based on similarity in energy-related performance indicators, revealing patterns of efficient and inefficient behaviors.
- Behavioral interpretation contextualizes the identified clusters, translating them into interpretable operational profiles that can support decision-making.

At the conceptual level, this module provides a framework capable of characterizing operational diversity and revealing distinct energy-efficiency patterns across application contexts (e.g., industry and transportation). Its outputs form a structured basis for the subsequent causal analysis module, which seeks to explain why these patterns occur.

In summary, Module 3 equips the framework with descriptive and diagnostic capabilities by systematically discovering and interpreting operational patterns regarding energy efficiency that inform both causal reasoning and decision support. Operational segmentation and post-hoc data analysis are domain-specific and therefore specialized within the case study chapters (Chaps. 7 and 8). The clustering algorithms underlying this module are described and validated in Sect. 6.4.

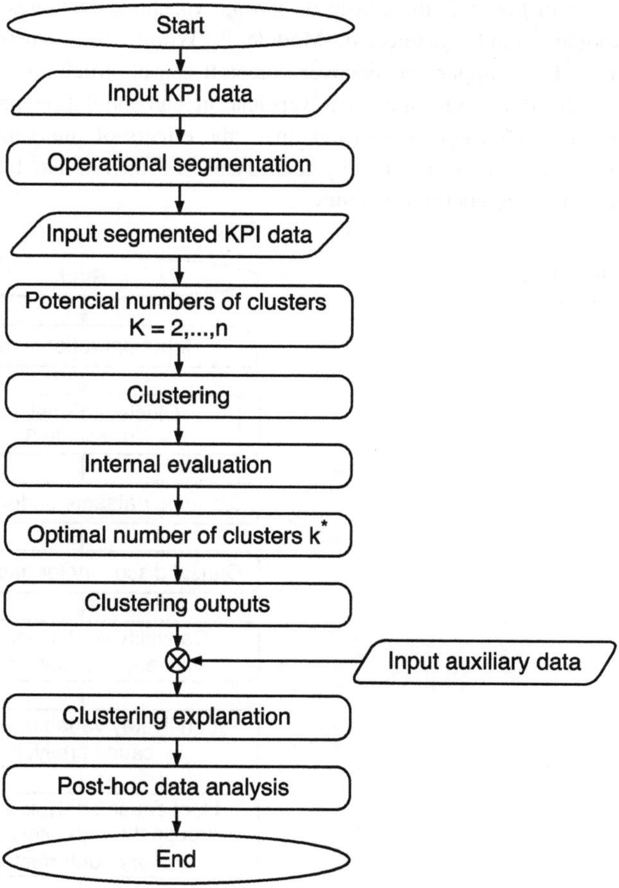

Fig. 5.6 Flowchart of pattern clustering and post-hoc analysis

5.4.4 Module 4: Causal Reasoning and Inference

The fourth module equips the framework to move beyond correlation and uncover cause-effect relationships that explain why specific operational patterns occur. This module provides explanatory and prescriptive capabilities that are essential for effective decision support in energy-intensive systems.

As illustrated in Fig. 5.7, the causal reasoning workflow integrates data prepared in Module 2 and clustered in Module 3. Within each cluster, causal discovery methods are applied to uncover potential causal structures, which are subsequently refined through statistical verification and validation procedures. Causal inference is then employed to estimate the effects of interventions and to conduct root-cause analysis, thereby identifying the operational factors that most strongly influence energy efficiency.

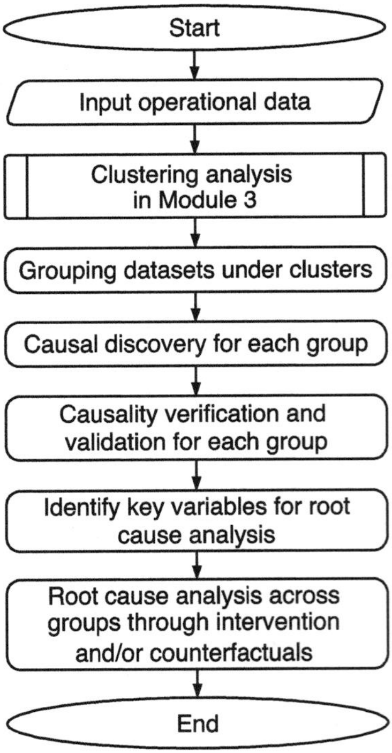

Fig. 5.7 The flowchart of causal reasoning and inference

The present framework adopts Pearl's theory of causal inference [199, 200, 239], which provides a rigorous language for representing causal assumptions, defining interventions, and reasoning about counterfactuals. Compared with alternative paradigms such as the Neyman-Rubin potential outcomes model [240], Pearl's framework offers a more comprehensive and transparent foundation. Its use of causal diagrams makes assumptions explicit, the do-operator formalizes interventions, and the do-calculus establishes general rules for identifiability.

SCMs provide the underlying formalism, offering both graphical and algebraic tools for encoding causal knowledge.

At the conceptual level, this module enables the framework to:

- Provide explanations for observed efficiency or inefficiency.
- Identify leverage points for intervention that can improve energy performance.
- Support robust decision-making by distinguishing genuine causal drivers from spurious correlations.

In summary, Module 4 introduces an explanatory dimension to the framework. By embedding causal reasoning and inference, it ensures that decision recommendations are grounded in cause-effect understanding rather than statistical associations alone. The insights generated here form the causal foundation for Module 5, where they are communicated and operationalized for decision support. The implementation details, including the causal discovery algorithms, the procedures for causal graph validation, and the methods for root-cause analysis, are presented and evaluated in Sect. 6.5.

5.4.5 Module 5: Multimodal Narration and Decision Support

The fifth module of the framework introduces a decision support layer that translates analytical results into interpretable, stakeholder-oriented outputs. Its primary role is to bridge the technical complexity of Modules 1–4 with the practical needs of decision-makers in application domains such as energy-intensive industries and transportation systems.

As illustrated in Fig. 5.8, this module integrates multimodal outputs from earlier stages, such as numerical results, tables, and visualizations, into structured narratives and actionable recommendations. By embedding data narration capabilities within the framework, the module ensures that decision support is not only data-driven but also transparent, interpretable, and contextually meaningful.

At the conceptual level, the narration process performs three key functions:

- Integration—collating outputs from data quality analysis, clustering, causal reasoning, and other data analytics into a coherent decision-support package.
- Translation—converting quantitative findings into domain-relevant explanations that can be readily understood by non-technical stakeholders.

- Recommendation—presenting actionable options, supported by evidence, to guide operational and strategic decision-making.

In addition, this module incorporates a feedback loop that enables stakeholders to interact with the generated narratives, provide corrections, and request further elaboration. In this way, the decision support process remains adaptive and human-centric, reinforcing the framework's emphasis on stakeholder engagement.

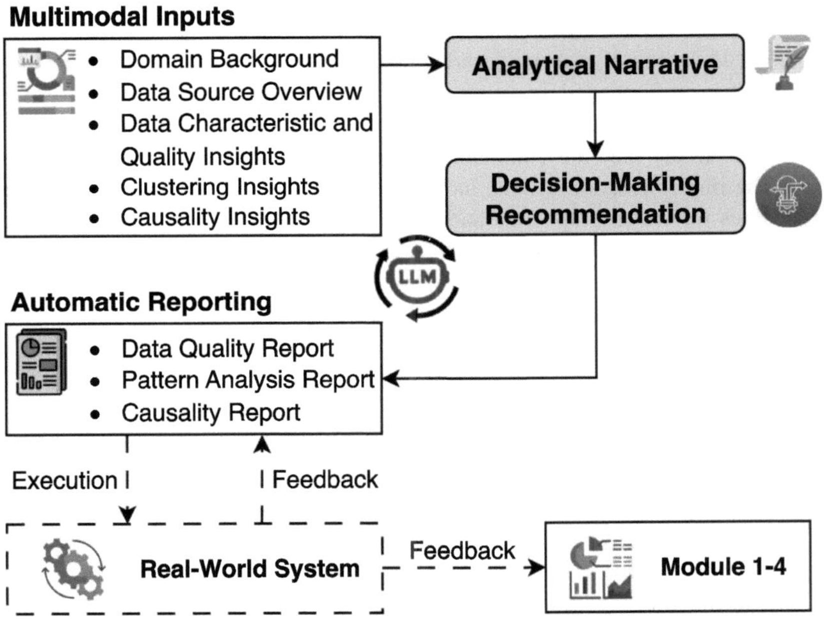

Fig. 5.8 Workflow of multimodal narration and decision support. The blocks and arrows with solid lines represent the processes developed and examined in this thesis, while the dashed elements indicate processes identified as directions for future work

In summary, Module 5 provides the interpretability and communication dimension of the framework. By embedding multimodal narration, it ensures that analytical insights are not only scientifically rigorous but also accessible and actionable for stakeholders, thereby completing the transformation from raw data to informed decision support in the real-world environment. The implementation of this module, including the framework utilizing multimodal LLMs for data narration and insight generation, is described and validated in Sect. 6.6.

5.5 Summary

This chapter has presented the conceptual design and modular architecture of the proposed AI-driven decision-support framework to improve energy efficiency. Structured into five sequential modules—from data acquisition and preparation to analysis and decision support—the framework provides a systematic pathway for transforming raw sensor data into actionable insights. The modular structure ensures conceptual clarity and operational flexibility, making the framework adaptable across diverse industrial and transportation contexts.

The framework's originality lies in its integration of the SotA AI techniques with human-centric decision support. Specifically, it combines (i) data characteristic and quality understanding, (ii) pattern discovery through clustering, (iii) causal reasoning for identifying root drivers of efficiency, and (iv) multimodal narration powered by LLMs to ensure interpretability and stakeholder engagement. This fusion of methodological sophistication with narrative-driven transparency advances decision-making practices beyond traditional data-driven approaches.

The originality of the framework can be summarized in three dimensions. First, it integrates SotA analytical components, including clustering for behavioral pattern discovery, causal reasoning for identifying efficiency drivers, and multimodal narration for stakeholder engagement, into a unified decision support architecture. Second, it introduces a methodologically rigorous development process, operationalized by adapting the DataPro model to ensure systematic data handling and iterative validation. Third, it emphasizes a human-centric design, where explainability and continuous feedback are not add-ons but core principles. Together, these contributions distinguish the framework from prior decision support approaches and establish a novel pathway for AI-driven decision-making in energy-intensive industrial and transportation domains.

The next chapter focuses on implementation and verification. It demonstrates how the conceptual framework is realized through the development or adaptation of algorithms and sub-frameworks, and evaluates their correctness, robustness, and efficiency through systematic experiments, ablation analysis, and sensitivity analysis.

6 Implementation and Empirical Verification of the Proposed Framework

This chapter implements the AI-driven decision support framework for improving energy efficiency proposed in Chap. 5. Its primary objective is to demonstrate and verify the methodological rigor and empirical superiority by developing and implementing analytical artifacts that correspond to each functional module in Fig. 5.1. Each artifact developed in this chapter undergoes rigorous evaluation against existing SotA methods, underscoring both its novelty and performance advantages.

- Section 6.1 provides an overview of this chapter, outlining the relationships between the modules in the proposed framework and the corresponding implemented algorithms or sub-frameworks. It also outlines the verification methods used to evaluate the effectiveness and reliability of each implementation.
- Section 6.2 introduces the STREAM pipeline for data collection and acquisition from real-world sensor deployments.
- Section 6.3 introduces a structured exploratory data analysis framework designed to systematically understand data characteristics and data quality, informing essential preprocessing steps.
- Section 6.4 details advanced clustering algorithms developed to uncover patterns within KPIs directly linked to energy efficiency, enhancing pattern recognition abilities.

Supplementary Information The online version contains supplementary material available at https://doi.org/10.1007/978-3-658-51965-0_6.

Z. Ma, *Artificial Intelligence-Driven Decision Support Framework for Improving Energy Efficiency in Industry and Transportation*,
https://doi.org/10.1007/978-3-658-51965-0_6

- Section 6.5 presents causality reasoning pipelines designed for robust identification and empirical validation of cause-effect relationships, and root causes for energy efficiency variables.
- Section 6.6 develops an LLM-based multi-agent framework that translates analytical results into coherent narratives and actionable recommendations, significantly improving the interpretability and practical usability of complex analytical outcomes for informed decision-making.
- Section 6.7 concludes this chapter by summarizing key contributions and linking them to subsequent case study applications.

6.1 Overview of Implementation and Verification Strategy

This section describes how the AI-driven decision support framework (Fig. 5.1, Chap. 5) maps to the implementation methods presented in this chapter. It delineates the correspondence between framework modules and the algorithms or sub-frameworks developed for each module, and it also outlines the verification methods used to evaluate these implementations. Table 6.1 summarizes these relationships and the associated verification procedures. For each module, Table 6.1 links the relevant implementation section, the developed specific algorithms or sub-frameworks, and the employed verification methods. This mapping ensures that the transition from conceptual framework to practical realization is both traceable and empirically justified. The implementations presented in this chapter are based either on SotA methods adopted from the literature or on novel algorithms developed where existing approaches proved insufficient.

Table 6.1 Mapping between the framework modules and their corresponding implementations, algorithms, and verification methods

Modules	Implementation	Algorithms or sub-framework	Verification
1. Data collection and acquisition	6.2 STREAM pipeline for structured data acquisition	The STREAM pipeline	• Comparative evaluation

(continued)

Table 6.1 (continued)

Modules	Implementation	Algorithms or sub-framework	Verification
2. Data profiling and preprocessing	6.3 Framework for data characteristic understanding	Data characteristic understanding framework	• Comparative evaluation
3. Pattern clustering and behavior analysis	6.4 Clustering approaches for pattern discovery	GMM clustering algorithm for static data and the internal evaluation method	• Discussion of method selection
		TS-IDEC algorithm for time-series clustering and the internal evaluation method	• Comparative evaluation • Parameter analysis • Ablation study
4. Causal reasoning and inference	6.5 Causal reasoning and inference pipeline	Bagging DAGMA-DCE algorithm for static causal discovery	• Comparative evaluation • Parameter analysis
		Integrated PCMCI+ algorithm for time-series causal discovery	• Comparative evaluation • Ablation study
		Method for evaluating causal graphs without ground truth	• Discussion of method selection
		Method for root cause analysis	• Discussion of method selection
5. Multimodal narration and decision support	6.6 Multimodal LLM-based framework for data narration and insight generation	LLM-based data narration and insight generation framework	• Comparative evaluation • Ablation study

Each implementation module in this chapter is structured into two parts: first, the design and realization of the algorithmic approach, and second, its evaluation through benchmarking against SotA methods. This consistent structure ensures that the originality of the developed methods is systematically assessed and that their advantages are demonstrated transparently. The evaluation process combines comparative experiments, parameter analysis, and ablation studies, enabling both fair comparisons and deep insights into methodological contributions. By maintaining this structure across all modules, the chapter provides a coherent basis for assessing the framework as an integrated solution.

The experimental process begins with the preparation of datasets. As this PhD research emphasizes real-world data analytics, real-world datasets are prioritized whenever appropriate evaluation protocols are available to assess algorithmic performance under practical conditions. When real-world evaluation is not feasible, synthetic datasets are generated to enable controlled, interpretable analysis of the proposed methods.

Evaluation of the implementations is conducted using three complementary strategies: comparative evaluation, parameter analysis, and ablation study. Comparative evaluation benchmarks the proposed algorithms or sub-frameworks against existing baselines and SotA methods, thereby demonstrating their empirical advantages and relevance. Parameter analysis explores how variations in key hyperparameters influence model behavior and performance. By systematically adjusting these parameters and analyzing the outcomes, this method helps identify whether the key hyperparameters are robust across different settings. The ablation study assesses the individual contributions of model components by systematically disabling or removing specific elements, thereby determining which components are essential to the model's overall functionality and which may be redundant.

Collectively, these verification strategies provide a robust, transparent framework for evaluating the effectiveness, efficiency, and reliability of the proposed algorithms or sub-frameworks under diverse conditions.

For Module 1, the STREAM pipeline is implemented to enable systematic data collection from real-world environments. By integrating business objectives with technical execution, it ensures that physical-sensor data are reliably acquired, contextually documented, and securely stored, thereby forming a robust foundation for subsequent data profiling and preprocessing. A comparative evaluation underscores the pipeline's superior effectiveness in real-world data acquisition and management compared with existing methods. Further implementation and evaluation details are provided in Sect. 6.2.

For Module 2, a structured data characteristic understanding framework is implemented to systematize exploratory data analysis and inform data preprocessing. Its implementation is justified by the critical role of high-quality, well-understood input data in ensuring the integrity and effectiveness of downstream analytical tasks. A comparative evaluation is conducted to assess the advantages of the proposed framework over existing profiling methods, demonstrating superior capability to reveal actionable insights and support preprocessing decisions. Further implementation and evaluation details are presented in Sect. 6.3.

In Module 3, two clustering algorithms are implemented to address both static and time-series KPI data. For static data, the GMM clustering algorithm is adopted, supported by a standard internal evaluation method to determine clustering quality and select the optimal number of clusters. As this method is well-established and widely used in practice, no further empirical validation is required beyond the contextual justification for its selection. For time-series data, a novel algorithm, TS-IDEC, is developed to overcome the limitations of existing clustering methods in handling temporal dependencies and real-world complexity. A tailored internal evaluation method is also introduced to assess clustering performance in this context. The real-world datasets are used in experiments. Given the novelty of this approach, multiple verification strategies are applied, including comparative evaluation, parameter sensitivity analysis, and ablation studies. A detailed discussion of these implementations and evaluations is provided in Sect. 6.4.

In Module 4, multiple algorithms are developed to support both static and time-series causal reasoning and inference. In the causal discovery task, as ground truth is not available in real-world causal data, synthetic datasets are generated to evaluate algorithmic performance in a controlled setting. For static data, a Bagging DAGMA-DCE algorithm is implemented to improve robustness and stability through ensemble learning, and its performance is verified via comparative evaluation and parameter analysis. For time-series data, the Integrated PCMCI+ algorithm is developed to identify temporal causal relationships, with verification conducted through comparative evaluation and ablation study. Additionally, two statistical methods are employed: one for validating and verifying causal graphs without ground truth, and another for identifying root causes of key variables. As both methods are well-established and rigorously validated in the literature, this study discusses only the rationale for their selection. Further implementation details are provided in Sect. 6.5.

For Module 5, a multimodal LLM-based multi-agent framework is implemented to translate complex analytical outputs into interpretable narratives and actionable recommendations. Comparative evaluation is conducted to benchmark different LLMs and prompting strategies using a set of designed evaluation metrics. Ablation studies are further used to assess the influence of specific components in the multi-agent framework. The details of implementation and evaluation are introduced in Sect. 6.6.

6.2 Module 1—STREAM Pipeline: Structured Data Collection and Acquisition

The STREAM pipeline provides a principled approach to aligning sensor deployments with organizational objectives, ensuring that collected data is accurate, well-documented, and suitable for downstream analysis. Section 5.4.1 introduces the high-level conceptions and functions of the STREAM pipeline (Fig. 5.4). This section provides the technical details of each step.

6.2.1 Pipeline Description and Stages

The STREAM pipeline comprises six sequential stages: Specification of Objectives, Technical Requirements, Resource Mapping, Extraction from Sensors, Archival Metadata, and Migration to Database.

Specification of Objectives (S):
This step translates business and research objectives into concrete analytical questions and performance indicators. The purpose is to ensure that the data acquisition process is directly aligned with the overarching decision-making requirements. By clarifying scope and defining measurable targets, the subsequent pipeline stages are grounded in well-structured objectives.

It involves a deep understanding of business requirements, in which stakeholders and domain experts define the problems to be solved or the decisions to be supported by sensor data. The aim is to articulate clear business objectives and questions that the data should answer, ensuring a comprehensive understanding of the organization's data needs. Equally important is the acquisition of domain knowledge during this phase. By gathering expertise in a specific domain or context (e.g., industrial manufacturing, transportation, environmental science), the most relevant data can be identified, avoiding the collection of irrelevant information. Strong domain knowledge guides the pipeline to focus on the most pertinent data streams, thereby improving efficiency and effectiveness. Together, understanding business goals and domain context establishes well-defined objectives for data collection, aligning the subsequent technical work with real-world needs.

Technical Requirements (T):

The second step reformulates the specified objectives in the first step into technical parameters. This includes defining the required variables, measurement units, sampling frequencies, and so on.

In this step, the specified goals are decomposed into measurable parameters and system design choices. The key activities involve identifying the types of sensors or data sources capable of fulfilling the objectives and defining the performance criteria that govern the data collection process. For example, if the objective is to analyze operational factors influencing energy efficiency, the technical requirements would delineate the relevant operational variables and corresponding sensors, together with the expected sampling frequency and data volume.

This step further requires specifying the constraints and standards that the system should satisfy, including parameters such as data precision, resolution, and reliability, as well as regulatory or organizational requirements related to compliance, privacy, and security. By the end of the Technical Requirements step, a comprehensive blueprint of the necessary techniques and system capabilities has been established. This technical specification serves as a bridge between high-level conceptual objectives and the practical design and implementation of the physical-sensor data-collection pipeline.

Resource Mapping (R):

At this step, available sensors are systematically identified and mapped to the technical requirements. Each relevant device is documented in terms of identifiers, calibration procedures, measurement ranges, installation contexts, and reliability characteristics. This mapping establishes a direct link between the high-level requirements and the physical data sources.

An inventory of existing sensors, devices, and supporting infrastructure is systematically compiled and assessed in this step to determine their capacity to generate the data required by the specified objectives. Where deficiencies are identified, additional sensors should be selected or complementary data sources incorporated to ensure comprehensive coverage of the defined requirements. Thereby, Resource Mapping entails translating abstract specifications into tangible system components—for example, associating each required measurement, such as temperature, pressure, or electricity consumption, with a specific sensor or IoT device capable of providing that observation. Upon completion, Resource Mapping produces a definitive alignment between technical requirements and physical resources, yielding a coherent design specification that ensures the subsequent extraction stage operates on verified, appropriately provisioned data sources.

Extraction from Sensors (E):
The fourth step is the direct acquisition of data streams from the physical sensors selected in the resource-mapping step. Depending on the operational context, this may be implemented via continuous streaming, scheduled polling, or batch extraction. All records are annotated with precise timestamps and device identifiers to preserve temporal integrity. Standardized naming and file conventions are applied to ensure consistency across sources.

At this step, the pipeline establishes connections to sensors, configures them to collect data at the desired frequency, and retrieves the sensor readings in a usable format. In practice, this extraction process involves using appropriate interfaces or communication protocols, such as IoT gateways, APIs, or direct sensor feeds, to capture the data of interest from each source. The data might be streaming continuously or collected in batches, but in all cases, the pipeline should reliably communicate with the operational sensor systems to pull data without loss. The system should ensure that raw sensor data is recorded accurately and timestamped, and that connectivity issues or outages are managed to avoid disruptions to data flow. In essence, sensor extraction is the execution of the "extract" step in a traditional ETL pipeline, tailored to the characteristics of sensor networks. Its primary objective is to capture all required measurements from the physical environment and reliably transfer them into the pipeline's digital domain. Successful completion of this stage results in the generation of raw sensor datasets that are prepared for subsequent processing.

Archival Metadata (A):
At the fifth step, beyond raw values, contextual metadata is systematically captured to ensure traceability. Each extraction event is accompanied by descriptive attributes, including sensor identifiers, units, sampling rates, firmware versions, and extraction times. Metadata are maintained in a structured catalog to support discoverability and to provide essential documentation for downstream users.

The data collection and acquisition pipeline ensures that, along with the raw data, all the contextual information about the data is captured and preserved in a structured way. This step focuses on capturing metadata associated with sensor data and maintaining metadata in a structured catalog or repository for future reference. Metadata here includes descriptive information such as the sensor that produced the data, the collection location and time, units of measurement, calibration details, and any transformations applied during extraction. A metadata repository or data catalog is often used to store and organize such information, as it allows project participants to document and share data, effectively keeping a record of the data's origin, structure, and meaning. Maintaining this metadata in a centralized, structured catalog enables data engineers and analysts to easily query and retrieve context for any dataset, thereby enabling future users to understand the data's provenance and utility. The outcome of this step is a well-curated metadata archive accompanying the sensor data, which is as important as the data itself for enabling meaningful analysis. Table 6.2 showcases an example of indicator entries in a metadata catalog.

Table 6.2 Example of indicator entries in a metadata catalog

Indicator	Definition
dataset_id	Unique ID of the dataset
description	Short purpose statement of the dataset
sensor_id	Device ID of the physical sensor
asset_id	ID of machine or line the sensor belongs to
measure	Quantity measured, e.g., electricity consumption
unit	SI unit, e.g., kWh
range_min	Minimum operating range
range_max	Maximum operating range
value	An example of recorded data instance
precision	Device precision or resolution
interval	Recording interval, e.g., 1 s, 10 s
device_version	Version of device
install_date	Date of installing the device
notes	Optional comments

Migration to Database (M):

The sixth step completes the pipeline by transferring the collected sensor data, along with its metadata, to a permanent storage system for ready access for analysis and integration. Once registered in the catalog, datasets are made available for subsequent modules of data preparation and profiling.

In this stage, the pipeline performs data ingestion into a database. Data ingestion represents the culmination of the collection process, in which incoming measurements are transferred to a persistent storage system for efficient access and analysis. In the present study, a relational database is employed, as the structured representation of data is required to support immediate querying in subsequent modules. This stage encompasses the structuring of ingested data to meet analytical needs, for example, by organizing records into tables indexed by timestamp, sensor identifier, or operational batch, and by providing mechanisms that ensure reliable and consistent transfer, such as batch loading or streaming inserts with integrated error checking. Once migrated, the sensor data becomes part of the project's broader data platform, ready to feed analytics dashboards, machine learning models, and other downstream applications. The migration to the database stage thus signifies the transition from data acquisition to data utilization: sensor observations, having been systematically collected and documented, are integrated into an accessible repository that completes the STREAM pipeline. At this point, the pipeline formally hands off to data analysts and decision support, which build on the robust, traceable foundation established by the preceding stages.

6.2.2 Evaluation and Benchmarking against State of the Art

The effectiveness of the proposed STREAM pipeline is evaluated against three SotA approaches for data collection and acquisition. The comparison considers four critical dimensions that together capture both technical and practical aspects of data acquisition: the number of stages (Sta.), the extent to which organizational objectives are integrated (Obj.), the involvement of metadata to ensure traceability and reproducibility (Meta.), and the capability to directly collect physical-sensor data from real-world environments (Phy.).

The results are summarized in Table 6.3, where "Y" and "N" denote "Yes" and "No," respectively.

Table 6.3 Comparative evaluation of data collection and acquisition methods

Ref.	Sta.	Obj.	Meta.	Phy.
[241]	4	N	N	Y
[242]	9	N	Y	Y
[243]	9	N	Y	Y
STREAM pipeline	7	Y	Y	Y

The comparison shows that the method [241], with only four stages, provides insufficient coverage of essential processes, while STREAM adopts a seven-stage structure that balances comprehensiveness with operational efficiency. Existing methods [241–243] do not explicitly integrate organizational objectives, creating a gap between technical implementation and decision-making requirements. STREAM addresses this gap by embedding business objectives into pipeline design to ensure decision relevance. Metadata involvement is absent in [241] and only partially addressed in other approaches, whereas STREAM systematically integrates metadata recording, enhancing transparency and reproducibility. Finally, although the method [242] supports physical-sensor acquisition, its focus is primarily on image data collection, which lies outside the scope of this study. In contrast, STREAM is specifically designed for physical-sensor data contexts, offering both scientific rigor and practical applicability.

In summary, the evaluation demonstrates that the STREAM pipeline offers a more holistic, practically deployable framework than existing methods. By balancing structural efficiency, embedding organizational objectives, ensuring metadata transparency, and enabling real-world sensor integration, STREAM advances the state of the art and establishes a robust foundation for data acquisition. Its objective-driven design and systematic metadata integration ensure adaptability to evolving data governance requirements and applicability across diverse domains.

6.3 Module 2—Framework for Data Characteristic Understanding and Preprocessing

Note: Parts of this section are based on the author's first-author journal article: *"A systematic data characteristic understanding framework towards physical-sensor big data challenges"* [115].

This section proposes a systematic data characteristic understanding framework to analyze physical-sensor big data challenges. It aims to quantify the characteristics of data recorded through physical sensors and understand potential challenges before undertaking data preprocessing strategies. Its principal contributions and novelty pertain to the following aspects:

1. To address the limitations of quantifying the data characteristic model, this study develops a quantitative 6Vs model and each dimension involves a set of data-driven statistical indicators, replacing subjective appraisal with objective measurement.
2. To cope with the drawbacks of applying the general data characteristic model in physical-sensor big data, the study integrates time-series-specific indicators into the data characteristic model, capturing temporal dynamics that generic data-characteristic schemes overlook.
3. To enable quantitative diagnosis of data issues, Common physical-sensor big-data challenges and integrated evaluation metrics are systematically linked to individual 6Vs dimensions
4. To visualize the application of the proposed framework, a pipeline to utilize the data characteristic understanding framework is developed.

This section is organized as follows. Section 6.3.1 presents an overview of the developed data characteristic understanding framework. Section 6.3.2 elaborates on the data-characteristic indicators and evaluation metrics. Section 6.3.3 discusses the key challenges in big data associated with physical-sensor datasets. Section 6.3.4 presents the details of the pipeline for implementing the proposed framework. Finally, Sect. 6.3.5 provides a comparative analysis between the proposed model and SotA approaches, highlighting its methodological novelty and advancements.

6.3.1 Proposed Data Characteristic Understanding Framework

The characteristics and challenges of big data are often conceptualized through the "Vs" framework, which encapsulates key dimensions for understanding and managing complex data environments. Based on the literature study in Sect. 3.2, this study adopts the 6Vs framework, including volume, variety, velocity, veracity, value, and variability, as shown in Fig. 6.1.

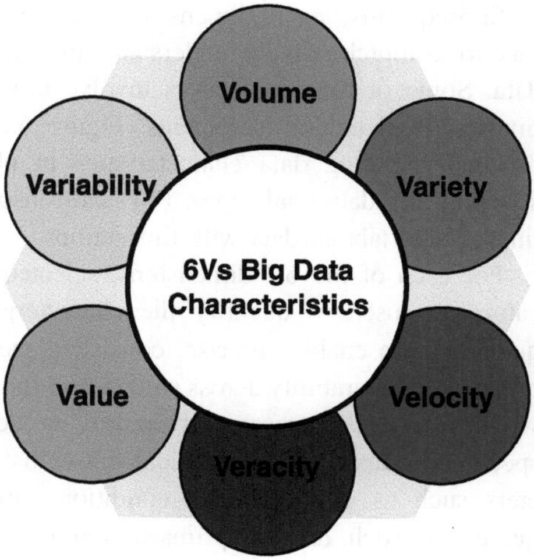

Fig. 6.1 6Vs big data characteristics

This 6Vs model comprises three conventional dimensions (Volume, Variety, and Velocity) and three novel and widely used dimensions (Veracity, Value, and Variability), with mutually defined terms in the literature study.

Volume is the most prominent characteristic of big data, referring to the size and scale of datasets [244]. However, assessing data volume remains relative, making it challenging to establish a definitive threshold for categorizing data in the context of big data. Variety underscores the heterogeneity of data types, encompassing structured, semi-structured, and unstructured formats, thereby highlighting the diversity inherent in big data sources [133]. Velocity refers to the speed at which data is received, stored, and processed, often in real-time or near-real-time systems [119]. Veracity reflects the degree of trustworthiness, reliability, and accuracy of data, shaped by collection processes, processing methodologies, and the integrity of underlying infrastructures [133]. In the context of scientific data, veracity has additionally been characterized as data consistency, which can be quantitatively assessed through statistical measures of reliability [244]. Value emphasizes the importance of extracting actionable insights from large datasets. The notion of "low-value density" illustrates that while the intrinsic value of big data is not directly proportional to its volume, substantial value can nonetheless be realized through sophisticated analysis of high-volume datasets [119]. Finally, variability captures the dynamic and inconsistent nature of data, arising from the integration of multiple sources with diverse formats and structures [130].

Subsequently, each dimension is mapped with multiple statistical indicators to comprehensively understand the characteristics of physical-sensor big data. Some of these indicators involve time-related statistical metrics, such as timestamp-related measurements. Figure 6.2 illustrates the general framework for understanding data characteristics in physical-sensor data and the corresponding big-data challenges. Physical-sensor data in this PhD study represents time-related tabular data with timestamps.

For each of the 6V dimensions, selected or newly proposed statistical indicators are used to quantify the characteristics of physical-sensor data. This quantification enables precise, consistent measurement of each data dimension, ensuring comparability across studies and the applicability of the proposed framework to diverse datasets for improving decision-making. The indicators are specifically designed for physical-sensor data, which capture real-world parameters such as environmental conditions, machine operations, and production quality. As such, data are primarily temporal and numerical; indicators related to timestamps, probability distributions, and other statistical properties are essential for characterizing their behavior. Detailed descriptions of the indicators, including abbreviations, definitions, and calculation formulas, are provided in Sect. 6.3.2.

The third part introduces the evaluation metrics for each dimension. Each metric synthesizes information from the respective indicators to assess the overall data quality within that dimension. While the metrics provide an aggregate quality assessment, the indicators offer detailed characteristics that substantiate and contextualize this evaluation. A comprehensive understanding of data characteristics, therefore, requires consideration of both indicators and metrics. Definitions and calculation formulas for all metrics are described in Sect. 6.3.2, following the presentation of each metric in its dimension.

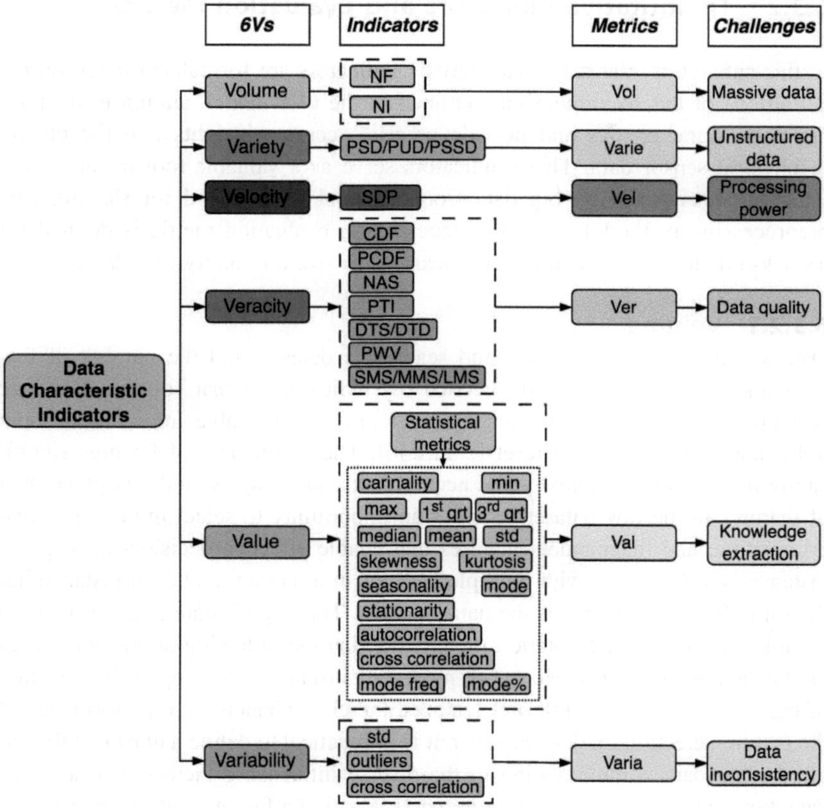

Fig. 6.2 Data characteristic framework addressing big data challenges. Each dimension of the 6Vs model is associated with multiple indicators, which are subsequently mapped to a unified evaluation metric and a corresponding big data challenge

The fourth part addresses the big data challenges associated with physical-sensor data. These challenges are identified through the analysis of characteristic indicators and the definitions of the 6 V dimensions. They directly influence data quality and offer practical insights for designing effective preprocessing strategies. A detailed discussion of these challenges and potential solutions is presented in Sect. 6.3.3.

6.3.2 Quantitative Indicators and Evaluation Metrics

In this subsection, the data characteristic indicators are formulated based on the definitions of the six dimensions outlined in the 6Vs model, aiming to quantify big data characteristics and provide precise, accurate insights into the quality of physical-sensor data. These indicators serve as a valuable tool for analyzing the challenges posed by big data from physical sensors and for shaping data preprocessing methodologies. Subsequently, an evaluation metric is defined for each V-dimension to quantitatively measure the overall quality of a dataset.

6.3.2.1 Volume

Data volume refers to the size and scale of a dataset, and the number of features and instances (NF & NI) are two key indicators of that volume. A feature is a unique characteristic or attribute that provides valuable information about individual instances in a dataset [245, 246]. The uniqueness of features significantly impacts the complexity and accuracy of data analysis, and a large number of features in the raw dataset provides an opportunity to select informative, discriminating, and independent features that enable effective decision-making. An instance is a data point with multiple features in a dataset, and each instance has the same feature structure as the dataset [247]. The large instance size provides a reliable statistical representation of data distribution, allowing strong inferences on the data quality [248]. Moreover, more data instances can support the selection of more informative and relevant features, thereby enhancing the performance of the feature-selection model. However, it is impractical to define a universal threshold for big data volume, owing to the diverse influencing factors such as time, data type, and specific task requirements [119]. Different contexts necessitate distinct data volumes, reflecting the unique demands of various tasks.

The evaluation metric of the volume of a dataset *DS* is defined as Equation 6.1 shows:

$$Vol(DS) = NF(DS) \times NI(DS) \tag{6.1}$$

where $Vol(DS)$ represents the score of the volume of the dataset *DS*, while $NF(DS)$. and $NI(DS)$ denote the two indicators NF and NI of the dataset *DS*.

A higher value of *Vol* indicates a larger data volume, enabling the comparison of the data-processing task's demand to ascertain whether the data volume is adequate for the task.

6.3.2.2 Variety

Variety refers to the data forms in a dataset, including structured data, semi-structured data, and unstructured data [133]. Structured data is highly organized and easily decipherable by machine learning algorithms, stored in relational databases [119, 247]. In real-world applications, structured data includes sensor, market, and consumption data, among others [249]. Unstructured data are difficult to analyze by conventional data processing tools and methods, which typically include text and social media data [250, 251]. Semi-structured data does not follow the tabular format and cannot be stored in relational databases; however, it contains several structural elements, such as tags and metadata, that facilitate data understanding [119, 247]. The most typical semi-structured data in physical-sensor systems are IoT data [249].

The distribution of data forms is the indicator to represent the variety dimension of characteristics as Table 6.4 demonstrates, including the percentages of structured data (PSD), unstructured data (PUD), and semi-structured data (PSSD). Each indicator represents the percentage of the volume of a particular data form, and the sum of these three indicators should equal one.

Table 6.4 Proportion of data forms

Percentage of structured data (PSD)	Percentage of unstructured data (PUD)	Percentage of semi-structured data (PSSD)

(PSD+PUD+PSSD = 1)

Equations 6.2–6.4 show the calculation of each indicator of data variety.

$$PSD = \frac{volume\ of\ structured\ data}{volume\ of\ all\ data} \times 100\% \tag{6.2}$$

$$PUD = \frac{volume\ of\ unstructured\ data}{volume\ of\ all\ data} \times 100\% \tag{6.3}$$

$$PSSD = \frac{volume\ of\ semi-structured\ data}{volume\ of\ all\ data} \times 100\% \tag{6.4}$$

Equation 6.5 demonstrates the evaluation metric of the variety of a dataset DS.

$$Varie(DS) = \frac{PSD(DS)}{PUD(DS) + PSSD(DS)} \tag{6.5}$$

where $Varie(DS)$ represents the score of the variety of the dataset DS, while the elements on the right side of the equation denote the data-variety indicators of the dataset DS.

This metric represents the ratio of structured to non-structured data. A value greater than 1 suggests that most of the data is structured, while a value less than 1 indicates that strategies should be implemented to convert the remaining data into structured formats. If all data instances in the dataset are structured data, the $Varie(DS)$ is recorded as "$+\infty$" to represent the best performance in data variety.

The classification of data forms can guide further data processing. While ML algorithms can be directly applied to analyze structured data, it is challenging to analyze unstructured and semi-structured data efficiently. This is due to the heterogeneous nature of the data sources, which present a variety of data types and representations. Therefore, it is necessary to convert them into structured data with data preprocessing techniques, including data cleaning, data integration, and data transformation [252–254].

6.3.2.3 Velocity

Velocity comprises the speed of data production and data processing [247]. Big data does not always require immediate use; however, in certain domains, there is a substantial advantage to acquiring up-to-the-second information and responding accordingly. For example, devices in the cyber-physical system usually rely on a real-time operating system that enforces strict timing standards for execution [247]. As a result, they may encounter issues when data from a big data application is not delivered on time. The speed of data production (SDP) is used as an indicator of velocity, as this study primarily focuses on data characteristics before processing. SDP denotes the frequency at which data are updated in a data storage platform, such as an IoT system. In numerous domains such as cyber-physical systems and real-time applications, data is continuously generated and ingested by storage platforms. This constant stream of data imposes unique demands on data storage, retrieval, and transmission systems, which should keep pace with the SDP to ensure timely and accurate data processing.

Equation 6.6 defines the evaluation metric $Vel(DS)$ of the velocity of a dataset DS. Since only one indicator is defined in this dimension, it naturally serves as the metric for assessing data velocity.

$$Vel(DS) = SDP(DS) \tag{6.6}$$

6.3.2.4 Veracity

Veracity represents the accuracy and reliability of big data, which is most relevant to the data quality and trustworthiness [133, 247]. Because of the increasing diversity of data sources and variety of big data, data can be incomplete, inconsistent, and noisy, negatively impacting big data analytics [126, 131]. In this study, several quantitative indicators, serving as measures of data quality and trustworthiness, are chosen or developed to illustrate data veracity in multiple dimensions.

The correctness of data formats (CDF) denotes the extent to which each feature's data format matches the data processing requirements. For example, the correct data format of the feature "the number of the productions" should be an integer. The CDF is recorded as "YES" or "NO", representing the correctness or not. For multi-feature datasets, the percentage of the correctness of data formats (PCDF) can be utilized as the assessment criterion, as shown in Equation 6.7.

$$PCDF = \frac{number\ of\ features\ with\ correct\ data\ format}{number\ of\ features} \times 100\% \tag{6.7}$$

The abnormal spikes represent the anomalous data points or subsequences in the time series, indicating the important abnormal events, such as production faults, system defects, and so on, which reflect the reliability of physical-sensor data collection [236, 248]. Data spikes are detected by rule-based strategies [255] or machine learning algorithms [256], and then the abnormal spikes are selected based on the real-world system properties. The number of abnormal spikes (NAS) is used to demonstrate data reliability, and the spike occurrence times and values are also recorded to analyze abnormal spikes more comprehensively and systematically.

A time interval represents the amount of time between two given time points in the time series, and it should be constant in a stable system [5, 257]. However, due to data communication delays in IoT systems or missing values, time intervals in real-world datasets may vary across positions. This variability creates challenges for time series analysis, as many strategies, such as first-order differencing and sliding windows, assume a fixed time interval. In this research, the percentage of normal time intervals (PTI) serves as the chosen evaluation criterion displayed in Equation 6.8. A normal time interval is defined by the system settings.

$$PTI = \frac{number\ of\ normal\ time\ intervals}{number\ of\ time\ intervals} \times 100\% \tag{6.8}$$

In a time series, each timestamp should record only one value, whether in a single dimension or multiple dimensions. Duplicate timestamps indicate that multiple values are associated with the same timestamp, typically due to recording errors. Therefore, duplicate timestamps should be recorded as abnormal data. The duplicate timestamps are classified into two categories: duplicate timestamps with the same value (DTS) and duplicate timestamps with different values (DTD). In further processing, DTS can be easily integrated into one data instance by removing repeated records, whereas in DTD some advanced methods should be developed to find out the most trustworthy value among the records.

The presence of missing values degrades the data quality and adds complications and uncertainty to big data processing [139, 258]. The missing data are categorized into three types, including missing completely at random (MCAR), missing at random (MAR), and missing not at random (MNAR) [258, 259]. The majority of the missing physical-sensor data are assumed to be MAR, where there exist differences between missing and observed values, but these differences can be explained by other observed data [260, 261]. The percentage of missing values for each feature (PMV) can be utilized to assess the data complementation shown in Equation 6.9.

$$PMV = \frac{number\ of\ missing\ values\ in\ a\ certain feature}{number\ of\ values\ in\ this feature} \times 100\% \tag{6.9}$$

Except for the PMV, the missing time span is another important index that indicates the period during which all values are missing. Different time spans require distinct imputation methods. For example, in the short span, some statistical values based on the distribution, such as mean, median, and mode [258] can be used to impute the missing values. However, in the long span, the data distribution is unclear, and the advanced deep-learning algorithms should be used to estimate the missing values [260]. In this study, the missing time spans are classified into three groups based on their length, including short-term missing span (SMS), medium-term missing span (MMS), and long-term missing span (LMS). The classification threshold is determined by the application requirements and constraints.

Equation 6.10 demonstrates the evaluation metric $Ver(DS)$ of the veracity of a dataset DS.

$$\begin{aligned} Ver(DS) =& (1 - PCDF(DS)) \times W_{41} + \frac{NAS(DS)}{NI(DS) - 2} \times W_{42} \\ &+ (1 - PTI(DS)) \times W_{43} + PMV(DS) \times W_{44} \end{aligned} \tag{6.10}$$

Ver(*DS*) consists of four components associated with the weights W_{41}–W_{44} respectively. Each component is represented by a percentage derived from the veracity indicators, ranging from 0 to 1. The indicators "NAS" and "PMV" are computed for each feature, and the average values of these two indicators across all features are utilized as the values in Equation 6.10. The values of all five weights are set at $\frac{1}{4}$ by default and can be further adjusted based on application requirements. The sum of the four weight values should equal 1. Therefore, the value of *Ver* ranges from 0 to 1, with higher values indicating lower veracity.

6.3.2.5 Value

Value represents the context and usefulness of data for deriving insights and facilitating informed decision-making, which is the ultimate goal of working with data [133, 262]. It is essential to identify how data can contribute to achieving application objectives and create a positive impact. Deriving value from big data varies across projects and is intricately tied to the techniques used for data processing. To investigate the potential value of big data, the statistical metrics about data distribution can be calculated and analyzed. Table 6.5 lists the definitions of the 16 factors of data values.

Table 6.5 Definitions of the factors of data values [144, 263–265]

Factors	Definitions
cardinality	The number of unique values
min	The minimum value of the data
1st qrt	The value located at the first quarter of the values in ascending order
mean	The average value of the data
median	The median value of the data
3rd qrt	The value located at the third quarter of the values in ascending order
max	The maximum value of the data
std	The standard deviation of the data
skewness	Skewness is a measure of the asymmetrical probability distribution of a real-valued random variable about its mean value. The negative skew indicates that the tail is on the left side of the distribution, and the positive skew indicates that the tail is on the right.

(continued)

Table 6.5 (continued)

Factors	Definitions
kurtosis	Kurtosis is a measure of the "tailedness" of the probability distribution of a real-valued random variable. The kurtosis for a standard normal distribution is 3. Kurtosis more than 3 indicates a "peaked" distribution, and kurtosis less than 3 indicates a "flat" distribution.
seasonality	Repeating cycle in the series with fixed frequencies (hour of the day, week, month, year, etc.). A seasonal pattern exists in a fixed, known period.
stationarity	Stationarity refers to a statistical property of a time series where its statistical characteristics, such as mean and variance, do not change over time.
autocorrelation	The correlation of a signal with a delayed copy of itself
mode	The most frequent value in the feature
mode freq	The frequency of the mode value in the feature
%mode	The percentage of the mode value

Continuous features and categorical features are two distinct types of variables. Continuous features are numeric variables with an infinite number of values between any two data points, whereas categorical features represent characteristics that can be divided into distinct categories without inherent order or priority. Consequently, because of their distinct data properties, the factors that reveal their data values differ as well. Table 6.6 and Table 6.7 show the statistical data characteristics of a continuous feature and a categorical feature, respectively. The factors associated with continuous features reveal the distribution's characteristics. However, unlike continuous data, categorical data does not adhere to a mathematical distribution of values. Therefore, the factors revealing the percentage and distribution of each category are employed.

Table 6.6 Statistical data characteristic factors of a continuous feature

cardinality	min	1st qrt	mean	median	3rd qrt	max	std
skewness	kurtosis	seasonality	stationarity	autocorrelation			

Table 6.7 Statistical data characteristic factors of a categorical feature

cardinality	mode	mode freq	mode%	seasonality	stationarity	autocorrelation

Equation 6.11 displays the evaluation metric $Var(DS)$ of the value of a dataset DS.

$$Var(DS) = \frac{number\ of\ invalid\ indicators}{number\ of\ all\ potential\ indicators} \tag{6.11}$$

$Var(DS)$ indicates the percentage of invalid indicators in the data values, with a value range of 0 to 1. A higher Var value indicates a less comprehensive data value representation.

6.3.2.6 Variability

Variability signifies the inconsistency in data flows, measuring the spread or dispersion of data values and providing insights into the extent to which individual data points diverge from the central or mean value [130]. Data patterns and characteristics are subject to change over time or in response to different scenarios and operations. Variability provides users with a tool to quantify the extent of variation in datasets, thereby aiding in assessing uncertainty or unpredictability. The standard deviation (std) in Sect. 6.3.2.5 quantifies the dispersion of values and can thus serve as an index of variability.

An outlier is a data instance that significantly differs from the other observations, representing the abnormal variability of the dataset [266, 267]. Outliers can be detected using the IQR rule and graphically illustrated with a boxplot. Equations 6.12–6.14 outline the formulas to identify outliers.

$$upper\ boundary = Q3 + 1.5 \times IQR \tag{6.12}$$

where Q3 represents the 75th percentile of the data and IQR is the interquartile range shown in Equation 6.14.

$$lower\ boundary = Q1 - 1.5 \times IQR \tag{6.13}$$

where Q1 denotes the 25th percentile of the data.

$$IQR = Q3 - Q1 \tag{6.14}$$

Values that exceed the upper boundary or fall below the lower boundary are considered outliers. In practical applications, the quartile values Q1 and Q3, as well as the coefficient 1.5, can be adjusted to meet specific requirements. In physical-sensor systems, it is advisable to incorporate additional constraints, derived from established rules of thumb or system settings, to effectively limit outlier detection.

$$outlier\ rate = \frac{number\ of\ outliers\ in\ a\ certain\ feature}{number\ of\ values\ in\ this\ feature} \tag{6.15}$$

The outlier rate in Equation 6.15 is calculated as an indicator to represent the overall outliers in each feature.

Correlation measures the variability between features, referring to the degree to which a pair of features is related [144, 268]. Cross-correlation is an established and reliable measure of the correlation between two univariate time series that accounts for time delay. For two time series $X = \{X_1, \ldots, X_n\}$ and $Y = \{Y_1, \ldots, Y_n\}$, the cross-correlation with time delay k $R_k(X, Y)$ is

$$R_k(X, Y) = \frac{\sum(X_t - \overline{X})(Y_t - \overline{Y})}{\sqrt{\sum(X_t - \overline{X})^2}\sqrt{\sum(Y_t - \overline{Y})^2}} \tag{6.16}$$

where $\overline{X}, \overline{Y}$ denote the mean of X and Y respectively.

Equation 6.17 demonstrates the evaluation metric $Varia(DS)$ of the variability of a dataset DS.

$$Varia(DS) = Nstd(DS) \times W_{51} + PO(DS) \times W_{52} + (1 - VC(DS)) \times W_{53} \tag{6.17}$$

where $Varia(DS)$ denotes the score of the variability of DS, $Nstd(DS)$ represents the normalized standard deviation defined in Equation 6.18, $PO(DS)$ stands for the percentage of outliers defined in Equation 6.19, and $VC(DS)$ signifies the validity of cross-correlation defined in Equation 6.20.

The indicator "std" represents the standard deviations of each feature in a dataset. In Equation 6.18, to calculate the $Nstd$ and ensure that its value falls in the range [0, 1], the "std" values are transformed to the range [0, 1] via min-max scaling. Subsequently, the average value of the transformed "std" values is computed to obtain $Nstd$.

$$Nstd(DS) = Ave(Scaling(std)) \tag{6.18}$$

The "outlier rate" denotes the percentage of outliers in a feature, as Equation 6.15 shows. The *PO* in Equation 6.19 computes the average of all values regarding "outlier rate" in the dataset to show the dataset-level percentage of outliers.

$$PO(DS) = Ave(outlierrate) \tag{6.19}$$

The *VC* stands for the validity of cross-correlation, indicating the percentage of high correlation values. A high correlation value is defined as greater than 0.7 in this study.

$$VC(DS) = \frac{number\ of\ high\ correlation\ values}{number\ of\ correlation\ values} \tag{6.20}$$

$Varia(DS)$ is composed of three components associated with the weights W_{51}–W_{53} respectively. Each component is represented by a percentage derived from the veracity indicators, ranging from 0 to 1. The values of all three weights are set at $\frac{1}{3}$ by default and can be further adjusted based on application requirements. The sum of the three weight values should equal 1. Therefore, the value of *Varia* ranges from 0 to 1, with higher values indicating greater data variability and inconsistency.

6.3.3 Big Data Challenges in Physical-Sensor Environments

The big data challenges are generated from a literature review and mapped to distinct dimensions of the 6Vs model based on their definitions. The objective is to propose a framework that guides future research in addressing these challenges effectively. The data preprocessing recommendations to address the challenges are formulated based on the characteristic indicators outlined in Sect. 6.3.2.

6.3.3.1 Volume

The challenge in data volume is to develop adequate techniques to effectively handle massive data [269]. Managing, storing, and processing datasets with a substantial number of instances and features poses significant difficulties. For instance, large-scale datasets might not be processed rapidly due to the limited computational ability of processors. Moreover, high-dimensional data suffer from the "curse of dimensionality" due to sparse data distributions, less reliable nearest neighbors, and so on. The characteristic indicators of data volume are NF and NI, which represent the number of features and instances, respectively. This dimension serves as the general representation of the size of a dataset. Consequently, methods to mitigate the negative impacts of large data size, such as feature selection, dimensionality reduction, and data splitting, should be selected by combining information from other data characteristics.

6.3.3.2 Variety

Handling data heterogeneity is a challenge in data variety because traditional tools like SQL do not perform well in storing semi-structured or unstructured data [270]. In physical-sensor data, there exists some semi-structured and unstructured data. Semi-structured physical-sensor data are text-based representations of structured data, stored as key-value pairs and ordered lists, such as JSON and XML. Unstructured physical sensor data is stored in log files on IoT devices. Because most popular AI algorithms perform well only on structured data, it is essential to transform all unstructured and semi-structured data into structured data. ML and AI techniques can be employed to extract relevant information from unstructured data and map it to the defined schema for structured data. For example, information in the text data is extracted using natural language processing methods, and the necessary entities, such as dates, names, and locations, are mapped to a predefined structure. Semi-structured data are easier to transform, as specific transformation tools have been developed and can be used directly to convert them into the desired structured format.

6.3.3.3 Velocity

The traditional algorithms and systems cannot provide sufficient data processing power, while the business partners require real-time response and in-time predictive maintenance of the system [271]. The scope of this study does not encompass data processing velocity, as the primary focus is on examining raw data before preprocessing. Data velocity in this study refers to SDP (speed of data production), i.e., the frequency of data updates on the data storage platform. Data should be updated at a short interval to avoid significant information loss; however, the hardware might pose a challenge in achieving the required update velocity. The challenge in data update velocity stems from the time required for sensors to record data, coupled with the inherent time delay in communication between the sensors and the storage platform. Therefore, high-quality sensors and communication devices should be implemented in the data processing systems to improve the velocity.

6.3.3.4 Veracity

The challenges associated with data veracity highlight issues in big data quality, including incorrect data formats, abnormal spikes, inconsistent time intervals, duplicate timestamps, and missing values. Despite large-scale data being available for use, low-quality data can lead to inaccurate and unreliable decision-making [272].

Incorrect data formats can lead to computing errors and system failures. For instance, recording an integer value as a string can cause calculation failures, since a string lacks the inherent ability to participate in mathematical operations. Therefore, all data formats should be assessed, and any found to be improper should be corrected.

The abnormal spikes represent the anomalous data points or subsequences in the time series, indicating the important abnormal events detected by sensors. The abnormal spikes can be detected by rule-based strategies [249] or machine learning algorithms [250]. Next, the extracted abnormal spikes can be analyzed to identify potential system faults, enhancing the overall diagnostic capabilities. Moreover, the values of abnormal spikes should be replaced with reasonable alternatives to improve the reliability of analysis across the entire sequence. The missing-data imputation methods introduced at the end of this section can be used to estimate alternatives.

Due to data communication delays in IoT systems or missing values, time intervals in physical-sensor datasets may vary across positions, even when default settings require constant time intervals. This variability poses challenges for time series analysis, as many strategies, such as first-order differencing and sliding windows, assume a fixed time interval. The irregular time intervals can be adjusted by considering the underlying reasons for the inconsistency. If the inconsistency is due to time delays, the timestamps can be adjusted directly according to the default settings. When missing values contribute to variability, imputing missing data can effectively address this challenge.

The duplicate timestamps result from recording errors and are categorized into DTS (duplicate timestamps with the same value) and DTD (duplicate timestamps with different values) in this study. In further processing, DTS can be straightforwardly integrated into one data instance by removing repeated records, whereas in DTD some advanced methods, including statistical analysis and AI algorithms, should be developed to determine the most reliable value among the records.

The prevalence of missing data not only diminishes performance in monitoring decisions but also influences the immediate utilization of data analytics applications that rely on reliable access to accurate data in the system. The simplest strategy for handling missing values is to delete the corresponding data points. However, this method yields inconsistent time intervals in time series analysis, as removing values creates gaps in the temporal sequence, thereby affecting the overall integrity of the analysis. As an alternative solution, one can select a continuous subsequence without any missing values for further analysis. This method is effective for time series data with a small number of missing values, particularly when they are concentrated within limited periods. However, when numerous missing values are distributed throughout the dataset, the selected subset may be small and fail to adequately capture the dataset's characteristics. In such scenarios, missing data imputation methods, such as regression models [273] and GANs [274] can be employed to estimate and fill in the gaps in the dataset.

6.3.3.5 Value

The challenge in the data value dimension lies in the inability to extract useful information from numerous data sources and to uncover the hidden value in recorded data [269, 272]. The data characteristics introduced in Sect. 6.3.2.5 are statistical metrics pertaining to data distribution. To extract valuable insights from the data, it is imperative to conduct further analysis of the statistical values. The preprocessing steps, including data cleaning and transformation, heavily depend on the information derived from the data distribution. For instance, decisions on how to handle missing values rely on a thorough understanding of the distribution of gaps in the sequence. Therefore, the computed statistical values should be linked to calculations across other characteristic dimensions to obtain a more comprehensive and accurate understanding of the collected physical-sensor big data. This approach helps make more reliable recommendations for data preprocessing.

6.3.3.6 Variability

Data variability refers to the inconsistency of data points and features, as measured by outliers and cross-correlation between features. Outliers can introduce noise during model training, distorting the outcomes of data analytics. Additionally, interpreting cross-correlation results in time-series analysis is challenging due to time lags. To mitigate bias in datasets and uncover variables associated with target features, it is imperative to employ strategies that address the challenges posed by data inconsistency.

Detected outliers should be replaced with reasonable values, and models for imputing missing values can be used to estimate the missing data points. Furthermore, it is crucial to analyze the factors contributing to the outliers, such as potential sensor recording errors or operational faults.

Cross-correlation stands out as an easy-implemented method for examining the relationship between features utilizing a coefficient. However, for a more comprehensive analysis of feature relationships, it is advisable to incorporate additional techniques such as feature engineering [275] and causal inference [181] in the data preprocessing stage.

6.3.4 Implementation Pipeline for Data Characteristic Understanding

Figure 6.3 demonstrates the data characteristic understanding pipeline. Data characteristic understanding in this pipeline includes timestamp understanding, value understanding, and feature understanding.

In the first stage, DTS and DTD are calculated to identify duplicate timestamps. If duplicate timestamps share the same value, it is easy to select one and remove the other records. If a timestamp matches multiple values, the most trustworthy value should be selected or computed based on the system property, expert recommendation, or statistical distributions. After removing duplications, PTI is computed to detect irregular time intervals. The standard time interval is a fixed value set in the system settings during the data acquisition stage. When consolidating all features into a dataset, irregular time intervals can lead to issues with value mapping. For instance, if it is assumed that values in the same row correspond to the same time, discrepancies in time intervals across features can result in values in the same row being recorded at different times. This discrepancy can subsequently disrupt the seamless processing of data. Therefore, the PTI computed at the stage will be used in feature understanding to reset timestamps.

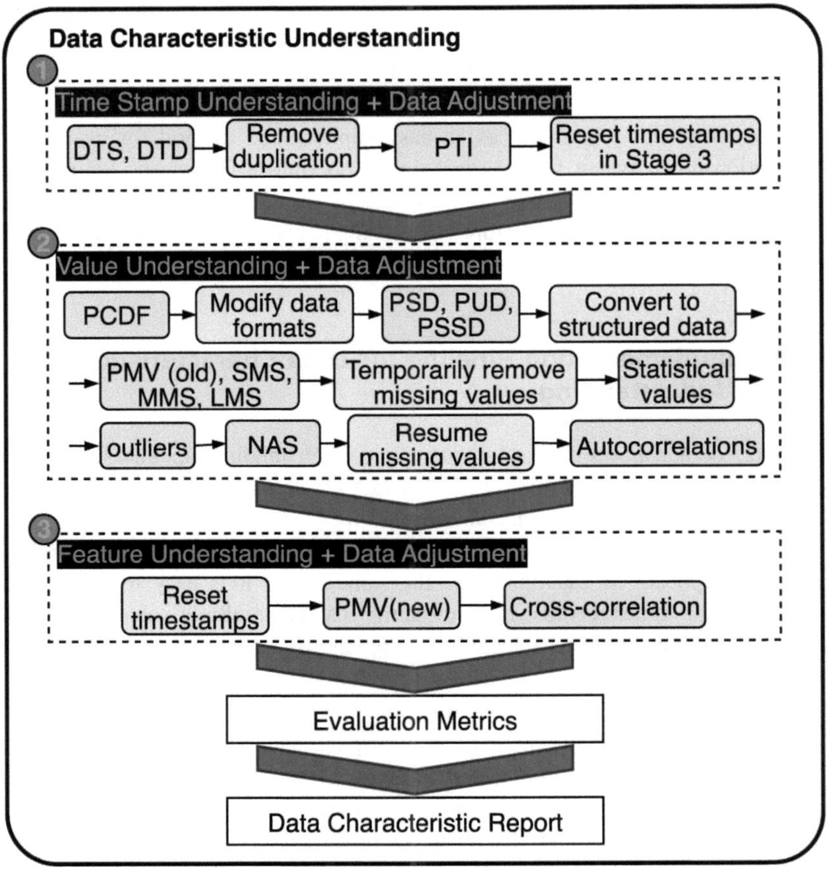

Fig. 6.3 The pipeline of data characteristic understanding. The three dashed rectangle blocks represent the three stages of data characterization, where the light-blue blocks indicate the computation of data-characteristic indicators, and the light-orange blocks denote necessary data adjustments

Following timestamp understanding, value understanding is employed. This begins by calculating PCDF to verify the data format, as an incorrect format may lead to calculation errors. For instance, when a floating-point number is mistakenly recorded as an integer, it results in the loss of decimal information. After modifying the data formats, the data forms are analyzed by computing PSD,

PUD, and PSSD. The semi-structured and unstructured data should be converted into structured data as only structured data can be easily processed by most present machine learning algorithms and other data analytic approaches. Next, missing values are systematically analyzed by calculating PMV, SMS, MMS, and LMS. Missing values negatively affect the calculation of statistical values, as they occupy positions in the dataset but do not contribute to the computation. Although missing-value imputation is a significant research topic in data preprocessing, it is outside the scope of this study, which aims to analyze data characteristics and make recommendations for data preprocessing to address big data challenges. Therefore, this study employs a straightforward approach: simply removing missing values. Then, statistical values, outliers, and NAS are computed or detected to identify the characteristics of the time series' statistical distribution. Subsequently, the previously removed missing values are reinstated for calculating autocorrelation. Autocorrelation relies on the time lag, and the removal of missing values disrupts the continuity of the time series.

The third stage is the understanding of the feature characteristic. To address timestamp inconsistencies, the PTI detects irregular timestamps across all features in the first stage. New timestamps are established with proper intervals in the dataset. Values associated with irregular timestamps are then allocated to the nearest proper timestamp. In cases where multiple values need to be assigned to the same position, the appropriate value should be selected based on system characteristics or computed using statistical measures such as the mean and median. The new data instances without associated values are marked as missing. Subsequently, changes in data volumes lead to an increased occurrence of missing values; therefore, the PMV indicator is recalculated to monitor the current state of missing values. The adjustment of timestamps does not affect outliers or abnormal spikes, and they can be combined and used directly in this stage. Next, cross-correlations between features are computed to detect and analyze potential feature relationships.

After computing all characteristic indicators, evaluation metrics are calculated to demonstrate the overall quality of the dataset. These metrics provide valuable insights into the suitability of this pipeline for facilitating further decision-making regarding data preprocessing.

6.3.5 Comparative Evaluation with State-of-the-Art Approaches

The results of the proposed data characteristic understanding model are compared with those of seven existing models to verify the contributions of this study. The evaluation and comparison of data characteristic understanding models encompass five dimensions: the number of Vs dimensions (Dim.), the number of indicators (Indi.), quantitative ability (Quanti.), capacity for processing panel data (Panel), and capability for processing time series (Time). The results are presented in Table 6.8. In Table 6.8, "n/a" denotes no applicable data, while "Y" and "N" represent yes and no, respectively.

Table 6.8 Model comparison across five dimensions for understanding data characteristics

Ref.	Dim.	Indi.	Quanti.	Panel	Time
[121]	4	4	Y	Y	N
[122]	6	13	Y	Y	Y
[123]	5	n/a	N	Y	Y
[126]	6	n/a	N	Y	N
[127]	6	n/a	N	Y	N
[128]	6	n/a	N	Y	N
[144]	n/a	26	Y	N	Y
Proposed framework	6	31	Y	Y	Y

Based on the comparison in Table 6.8, the three limitations of the existing models introduced in Sect. 3.2 have been addressed by the proposed framework.

Firstly, the selected dimensions of the proposed 6Vs model have mutual and unique definitions and there is no overlap among them. The proposed framework exhibits the highest number of dimensions and the most clearly defined mutual understanding of these dimensions among the other seven models. Moreover, it encompasses the largest array of indicators, thereby effectively quantifying the Vs dimensions. For example, The data quality evaluation framework developed in [121] employs volume, velocity, variety, and veracity to assess data quality. However, the model presented in this study incorporates two additional dimensions, namely value and variability, offering more comprehensive and valuable information. The model in [122] introduces the concept of vincularity into its 6Vs model and quantifies this dimension using an indicator called traceability. However, the popularity of this dimension is limited in the literature discussed in Sect. 3.2, rendering its definition less convincing. In contrast, the dimension "Variability" is widely used, with its definition consistently defined similarly across many scholarly works.

Secondly, the existing 6Vs models in [123, 126–128] only provide qualitative definitions and analyses, lacking quantitative metrics. This limitation restricts a thorough assessment of data characteristics. In contrast, the proposed framework assigns statistical indicators to each dimension and unveils the big data challenges. Additionally, data preprocessing recommendations are derived from these indicators to improve the data quality.

Lastly, no data characteristic understanding models are developed specifically for the physical-sensor datasets in the literature study. Many models [121, 123, 126–128] can be employed to analyze all types of big data and do not involve time-related characteristic indicators. The study in [144] analyzes diverse, controllable time-series characteristics to generate new high-quality time series. However, this framework lacks a systematic analysis of data characteristics and does not examine timestamps. The proposed framework incorporates a comprehensive set of characteristic indicators for physical-sensor data. This includes indicators for panel data, time series, and timestamps.

6.4 Module 3—Clustering Approaches for Pattern Discovery in Energy KPIs

This section establishes a comprehensive and systematic foundation for pattern discovery across both static and dynamic data contexts. It introduces clustering algorithms designed to reveal patterns within KPIs related to energy consumption. Because the KPI under study is univariate and may be observed either as time-series trajectories or as static snapshots, two complementary clustering methodologies are proposed, each calibrated to the statistical and temporal characteristics of its respective data modality. Section 6.4.1 presents the GMM selected for clustering static data, detailing its methodological rationale, algorithmic procedures, and the internal evaluation approach for assessing clustering performance and determining the optimal number of clusters. Section 6.4.2 further discusses the suitability and advantages of GMM clustering, as well as the proposed internal evaluation strategy. Section 6.4.3 describes the novel time-series clustering algorithm and composite internal evaluation method developed in this study, outlining their methodological innovations. Finally, Sect. 6.4.4 details the experimental framework used to validate, evaluate, and benchmark the proposed time-series clustering approach and the composite internal evaluation strategy.

6.4.1 Gaussian Mixture Model Clustering for Static Data: Method and Evaluation

Note: Parts of this section are based on the author's first-author conference paper: *"Fuel Efficiency Analysis of the Public Transportation System Based on the Gaussian Mixture Model Clustering"* [276].

6.4.1.1 GMM Clustering Algorithm

The Gaussian Mixture Models offer a probabilistic soft-clustering mechanism, assigning each data point a probability of membership to each cluster [152]. Unlike hard clustering approaches, such as K-means, GMMs inherently account for uncertainty and allow for overlapping clusters [277], a critical advantage when cluster boundaries are ambiguous or when natural variation leads to intertwined data groupings [278]. Furthermore, GMMs support flexible modeling of cluster shapes and variances. Each cluster is parameterized by its own mean and variance, enabling the representation of data distributions with heterogeneous scales and densities. In contrast, K-means assumes clusters to be equally sized and spherical, which can oversimplify the inherent structure of univariate datasets and lead to suboptimal clustering results. Another notable advantage of GMMs lies in their density estimation capability, which facilitates the identification of outliers [278]. Data points with low likelihood under the fitted mixture model are naturally flagged as anomalies, a feature particularly valuable in the context of energy-efficiency KPIs, where such anomalies may reflect sensor errors, faulty measurements, or abnormal system behaviors. Finally, GMMs provide interpretable model parameters, including cluster means, variances, and mixing coefficients. These parameters not only describe the clustering structure in a transparent, statistically meaningful way but also provide insights into the central tendencies, dispersion, and relative sizes of the identified clusters. Such interpretability enhances the analytical utility of GMMs for scientific reporting and domain-specific decision support.

The following presents the mathematical formulation of the GMM clustering algorithm.

The probability density function of the multivariate GMM is:

$$p(x) = \sum_{i=1}^{K} \pi_i \mathcal{N}(x|\boldsymbol{\mu}_i, \boldsymbol{\Sigma}_i) \tag{6.21}$$

where K refers to the number of mixture components, π_i represents the weight of the i-th Gaussian component, and $\mathcal{N}(x|\boldsymbol{\mu}_i, \boldsymbol{\Sigma}_i)$ denotes the i-th Gaussian distribution with the mean $\boldsymbol{\mu}_i$ and the covariance $\boldsymbol{\Sigma}_i$.

Parameters of the Gaussian process, such as the mean and covariance, are estimated using the EM algorithm, which iteratively adjusts the parameters in an E-step by calculating the expected log-likelihood and an M-step by maximizing this expectation. In a GMM with K components and N observations, the E-step assigns each sample to a component with a soft assignment.

$$\gamma_j(\mathrm{x}_n) \leftarrow \frac{\pi_j \mathcal{N}\left(\mathrm{x}_n \middle| \boldsymbol{\mu}_j, \boldsymbol{\Sigma}_j\right)}{\sum_{k=1}^{K} \pi_k \mathcal{N}(\mathrm{x}_n|\boldsymbol{\mu}_k, \boldsymbol{\Sigma}_k)} \forall j = 1, \ldots K; n = 1, \ldots, N \tag{6.22}$$

where $\gamma_j(\mathrm{x}_n)$ refers to the probability that the n-th data point is generated by the j-th Gaussian component and π_j denotes the weight of the j-th component, where $0 \leq \pi_j \leq 1$ for each $j \in \{1, \ldots K\}$ and $\sum_{k=1}^{K} = 1$.

In the M-step, the parameters π_j, $\boldsymbol{\mu}_j$ and $\boldsymbol{\Sigma}_j$ are re-estimated and updated separately for each mixture component based on the soft assignments in the E-step, following the order of Equations 6.23–6.26.

$$\hat{N}_j \leftarrow \sum_{n=1}^{N} \gamma_j(\mathrm{x}_n) \tag{6.23}$$

$$\hat{\pi}_j^{\mathrm{new}} \leftarrow \frac{\hat{N}_j}{N} \tag{6.24}$$

$$\hat{\boldsymbol{\mu}}_j^{\mathrm{new}} \leftarrow \frac{1}{\hat{N}_j} \sum_{n=1}^{N} \gamma_j(\mathrm{x}_n)\mathrm{x}_n \tag{6.25}$$

$$\hat{\Sigma}_j^{\mathrm{new}} \leftarrow \frac{1}{\hat{N}_j} \sum_{n=1}^{N} \gamma_j(\mathrm{x}_n)(\mathrm{x}_n - \hat{\boldsymbol{\mu}}_j^{\mathrm{new}})(\mathrm{x}_n - \hat{\boldsymbol{\mu}}_j^{\mathrm{new}})^{\mathrm{T}} \tag{6.26}$$

6.4.1.2 Internal Evaluation Method

The initial determination of the number of clusters is crucial when applying the GMM clustering algorithm, as it directly influences the quality and interpretability of the clustering outcomes. Both cohesion and separation metrics need to be considered to select the optimal number of clusters [279]. Cohesion denotes the degree of proximity among data points within a cluster, while separation signifies the distinctiveness between clusters. In this case, three clustering evaluation indices, including the Silhouette (SIL) index [280], the Calinski-Harabasz (CH) index [281], and the Davies-Bouldin (DB) index [282], are employed to assess clustering performance across varying numbers of clusters. Subsequently, by aggregating the rankings derived from these indices and computing their average, a robust and objective criterion is established for selecting the optimal number of clusters. This multi-metric approach mitigates the limitations of relying on a single index and enhances the reliability of cluster number determination within the GMM framework.

The Silhouette Index

The SIL index considers the pairwise distance between clusters. It ranges from -1 to 1, and an SIL close to 1 indicates a good partition of the data points.

For the i-th sample in the I-th cluster C_I, $I = 1, \ldots, K$, the silhouette width is:

$$s_i = \frac{b_i - a_i}{\max(a_i, b_i)} \tag{6.27}$$

where a_i refers to the mean distance between the i-th instance and all other samples in C_I, and b_i denotes the smallest mean distance between the i-th instance in C_I and all samples outside C_I.

Assuming the number of data points in the cluster C_I is M, the SIL index for C_I is:

$$SIL_I = \frac{1}{M} \sum\nolimits_{i=1}^{M} s_i \tag{6.28}$$

The SIL index for the entire dataset with K clusters is:

$$SIL = \max\nolimits_K SIL_I \tag{6.29}$$

The Calinski-Harabasz Index

The CH index calculates the sum of squares of the values within and between the clusters. A higher value of the CH index indicates better clustering performance. Assuming a dataset with N observations is clustered into K clusters, the CH index is:

$$CH = \frac{BC}{WC}\frac{N-K}{K-1} \tag{6.30}$$

where BC represents the weighted sum of squared Euclidean distances between each cluster centroid and the overall centroid of the dataset, and WC refers to the sum of squared Euclidean distances between data points and their respective cluster centroids.

The Davies-Bouldin Index

The DB index computes the average similarity between each cluster and its most similar cluster, where the similarity signifies the ratio of the within-cluster scatter to the between-cluster distance. A lower DB value indicates better clustering performance. Assuming a dataset with N observations is clustered into K clusters, the DB index is:

$$DB = \frac{1}{K}\sum_{i=1}^{K}\max_{j\neq i}\left(\frac{d_i + d_j}{d(c_i + c_j)}\right) \tag{6.31}$$

where c_i and c_j are the centroids of clusters i and j, d_i and d_j denote the average Euclidean distances from c_i to the data points in the cluster i and c_j to the data points in the cluster j respectively, and $d(c_i + c_j)$ refers to the Euclidean distance between c_i and c_j.

Integrated Evaluation Index

Let K be the number of evaluated clusters and let $M = \{m_1, m_2, m_3\}$ denote the set of clustering evaluation metrics, where m_1 refers to the SIL index, m_2 represents the CH index, and m_3 denotes the DB index. For each metric $m_i(i = 1, 2or3)$, assign a rank $R_i(k)(k = 1, \ldots, K)$ to the clustering result with K clusters based on the metric's performance (higher values for SIL and CH indices are better; lower values for DB index are better).

The integrated evaluation index EVA_{int} is then defined as follows. Lower EVA_{int} values indicate a higher overall ranking across all metrics.

$$EVA_{int}(k) = \frac{1}{|M|}\sum\nolimits_{i=1}^{|M|} R_i(k) \tag{6.32}$$

where $|M|$ is the number of base metrics (here, $|M| = 3$).

The optimal number of clusters K^* is selected as follows.

$$K^* = \arg\min\nolimits_k EVA_{int}(k) \tag{6.33}$$

6.4.2 Discussion and Justification of Clustering Choices for Static Data

This section presents the GMM clustering algorithm implemented for analyzing static, univariate KPI data on energy consumption. Recognizing the importance of determining the optimal number of clusters, a multi-metric evaluation strategy is developed that integrates the SIL, CH, and DB indices. By averaging metric rankings, this approach provides a balanced and objective criterion for cluster selection, effectively overcoming the limitations of relying on a single validation metric.

The GMM algorithm exhibits several methodological strengths. Its capacity to model clusters with varying means and variances allows it to effectively capture complex, heterogeneous patterns in real-world KPI datasets. Furthermore, its density-estimation capability enables robust outlier detection, which is beneficial for identifying anomalies indicative of sensor inaccuracies or unusual energy consumption.

The integrated multi-metric approach used to determine the optimal number of clusters further reinforces the methodological rigor of the GMM clustering framework. Combining cohesion- and separation-based metrics mitigates biases or shortcomings inherent to any single metric, yielding a reliable and comprehensive assessment of clustering quality.

In summary, the GMM clustering algorithm, augmented by the proposed evaluation strategy, provides a robust, interpretable, and methodologically sound solution for uncovering patterns in static energy-consumption KPIs. This framework effectively addresses key challenges in clustering univariate static data and provides a solid foundation for subsequent analytical stages. Its application is further demonstrated in the case study presented in Sect. 8.2 of this thesis.

6.4.3 TS-IDEC: A Novel Time-Series Clustering Algorithm and Evaluation Framework

Note: Parts of this section are based on the author's first-author journal article: *"Discovering Operational Patterns Using Image-Based Convolutional Clustering and Composite Evaluation: A Case Study in Foundry Melting Processes"* [145].

The literature study in Sect. 3.3 has discussed the challenges in existing time-series clustering algorithms, particularly their limitations in handling real-world industrial environments characterized by noisy, unlabeled, and variable-length sequences. To address these gaps, this study develops a novel deep clustering framework, TS-IDEC (Time-Series Image-based Deep Embedded Clustering), designed to analyze complex industrial time-series data.

TS-IDEC introduces a hybrid pipeline that first transforms univariate time-series sequences into grayscale images using an overlapping sliding window. This transformation enables the application of convolutional feature extraction techniques, effectively bridging the gap between temporal and spatial data representations. A deep convolutional autoencoder (DCAE) is then employed to learn latent representations that capture both localized and global structural patterns. Building on the IDEC model [160], TS-IDEC integrates both soft probabilistic clustering and hard centroid-based clustering in a unified dual-mode strategy. This integration enhances clustering robustness and reliability, particularly in the face of noisy and heterogeneous data.

To facilitate unsupervised model selection and evaluation, this study further proposes a composite internal evaluation metric, S_{eva}. Although Sect. 6.4.1.2 has introduced the EVA_{int}, and it works well on simple, well-separated datasets, but its effectiveness diminishes when applied to complex datasets. Specifically, during experimental analysis of complex datasets, EVA_{int} often fails to differentiate between clustering solutions of varying quality. This limitation arises because EVA_{int} relies on averaging the rankings of evaluation scores across multiple criteria. In challenging and complex datasets, individual scores within a given criterion tend to be very similar, reducing sensitivity to subtle differences in clustering performance. Furthermore, discrepancies between criteria can lead to diverging score rankings, thereby undermining the reliability of the averaged result. To overcome these issues, S_{eva} combines normalization and ranking strategies to enhance discriminative power and provide a more robust assessment of clustering quality in complex real-world data environments.

The dual-mode clustering outputs (soft and hard) are compared and evaluated using the metric S_{eva}, and the better result is selected through a two-stage evaluation process. Moreover, S_{eva} is also employed in empirical analysis to assess the overall performance of the proposed clustering algorithm and determine the optimal number of clusters.

The scientific contributions of this work are as follows:

1. The development of a novel deep unsupervised clustering architecture that combines image-based sequence transformation with convolutional representation learning;
2. The integration of soft and hard clustering mechanisms into a unified dual-mode strategy, improving clustering robustness in real-world scenarios;
3. The design of a composite internal evaluation metric for reliable model validation and evaluation in the absence of ground truth labels.

6.4.3.1 TS-IDEC Algorithm

TS-IDEC Architecture and Design Principles

The proposed TS-IDEC framework is designed to address three core challenges in clustering industrial time-series data: (i) capturing localized temporal patterns within noisy sequences, (ii) improving clustering robustness in the absence of ground truth, and (iii) integrating explainable model evaluation and selection into the unsupervised learning pipeline. TS-IDEC builds upon the IDEC algorithm developed by [160], but extends it in multiple critical ways to support its application to real-world contexts.

First, to better preserve temporal structure and local pattern continuity, each univariate time series is transformed into a two-dimensional grayscale image using an overlapping sliding window approach. This transformation enables the use of convolutional operations sensitive to spatial and temporal locality, thereby enhancing the network's ability to extract meaningful sequence features.

Second, the fully connected layers in the original IDEC architecture are replaced with the DCAE layers. The encoder component is composed of convolutional and pooling layers, while the decoder consists of deconvolutional and upsampling layers. This architectural shift enables the network to leverage local translation-invariant features and scale more effectively with larger datasets, both of which are essential for analyzing long-duration operational sequences from industrial processes.

Third, TS-IDEC introduces a dual-mode clustering strategy. A soft clustering layer, based on the Student's t-distribution kernel, is used during training to refine latent representations while preserving cluster structure [283]. In parallel, a hard clustering approach, based on the K-means algorithm, is applied to the same latent space after training to improve cluster separation. These two outputs: denoted as C_1 (soft) and C_2 (hard), are subsequently evaluated using a two-stage evaluation approach, and the better-performing result is selected as the final clustering solution.

After defining the architectural components, it is important to clarify how the training and clustering outputs are selected. TS-IDEC is optimized by minimizing a joint loss function composed of a reconstruction loss, denoted as L_{rec}, and a clustering loss, denoted as L_{cl}. The reconstruction loss ensures that the autoencoder learns structure-preserving latent representations from the grayscale image input, while the clustering loss refines those representations to improve cluster compactness and separation. The combined loss function is optimized using stochastic gradient descent. Upon convergence, the model produces two candidate clustering results: a soft assignment output C_1 derived from the probabilistic clustering layer, and a hard clustering output C_2 generated by applying the K-means algorithm to the latent space. A two-stage evaluation procedure, based on qualitative consistency and a composite internal metric detailed in Sect. 6.4.3.2, is used to select the better-performing result. The final output is denoted as C_{best}, representing the clustering result that balances accuracy and reliability.

The complete architecture of TS-IDEC is illustrated in Fig. 6.4. The input time series x_0 is first transformed into a grayscale image x_1, which serves as the input to the convolutional encoder. The encoder maps this input to a latent representation $\boldsymbol{Z} \in \mathrm{R}^{128}$, which is used simultaneously for reconstruction via the decoder and for clustering via both soft and hard assignment pathways. The reconstructed image is denoted as $\widehat{x_1}$. The training process jointly minimizes a reconstruction loss and a clustering loss, ensuring that latent representations are both compact and cluster discriminative.

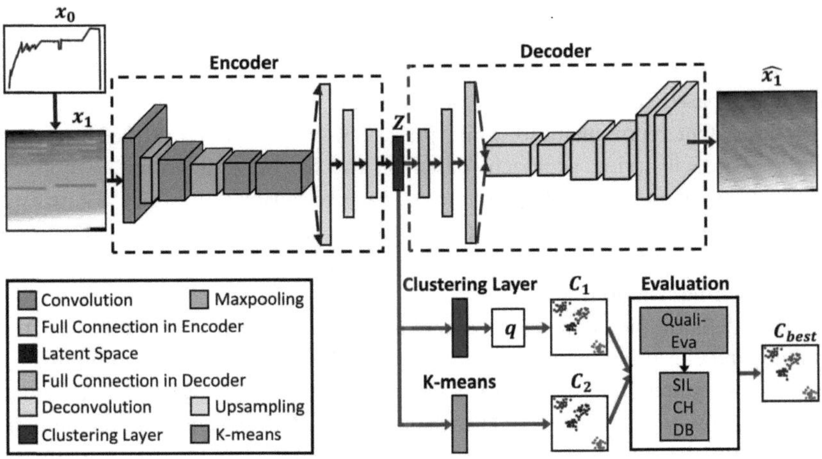

Fig. 6.4 Architecture of the TS-IDEC algorithm. Legends in the bottom-left corner show the component categories in the architecture

This architectural design makes TS-IDEC suitable for real-world time-series clustering, where data are often unlabeled, irregular, and sensitive to operational variations. The integration of time-series-aware input transformation, deep spatial-temporal feature learning, and dual clustering selection ensures the framework provides a robust and scalable solution for process pattern discovery.

Temporal Transformation via Overlapping Sliding Windows

Time-series data from real-world operations often exhibit variable sequence lengths, local fluctuations, and nonstationary behavior, making direct clustering difficult. To enhance pattern recognition and preserve temporal dependencies, TS-IDEC first transforms each univariate time series into a structured, image-like representation using an overlapping sliding window approach. This preprocessing step enhances spatial coherence, facilitates localized feature extraction through convolution, and improves robustness to noise.

Let the original univariate time series be denoted as $x_0 \in \mathbb{R}^{\mathrm{N}}$, where N is the number of time points. The overlapping sliding window segments x_0 into n_s-length windows with an overlap of n_o, where $(n_o < n_s)$. These windows are stacked as rows to form a two-dimensional matrix $\boldsymbol{x}_1 \in \mathbb{R}^{n_s \times n_s}$, where both the number of rows and columns are equal to the window size. This results in a grayscale image-like structure suitable for convolutional processing.

The total number of values N_1 required to construct this matrix is given by:

$$N_1 = n_s + (n_s - 1)(n_s - n_o) \tag{6.34}$$

To ensure that all N values in the time series are utilized, appropriate values for n_s and n_o should be selected to satisfy the condition $N_1 \geq N$. If $N_1 > N$, padding of $N_1 - N$ values can be applied as a preprocessing step for the time series.

An illustration of this transformation process is shown in Fig. 6.5. The original time series x_0 is segmented into overlapping chunks, each contributing a row to the matrix $\boldsymbol{x}_1$. Colored boxes in the left-hand plot represent individual sliding windows, while their corresponding rows are mapped to the grayscale image on the right. The transformation preserves both short-term temporal patterns within windows (horizontal axis) and transitions across windows (vertical axis), thus enabling dual-perspective feature extraction during learning.

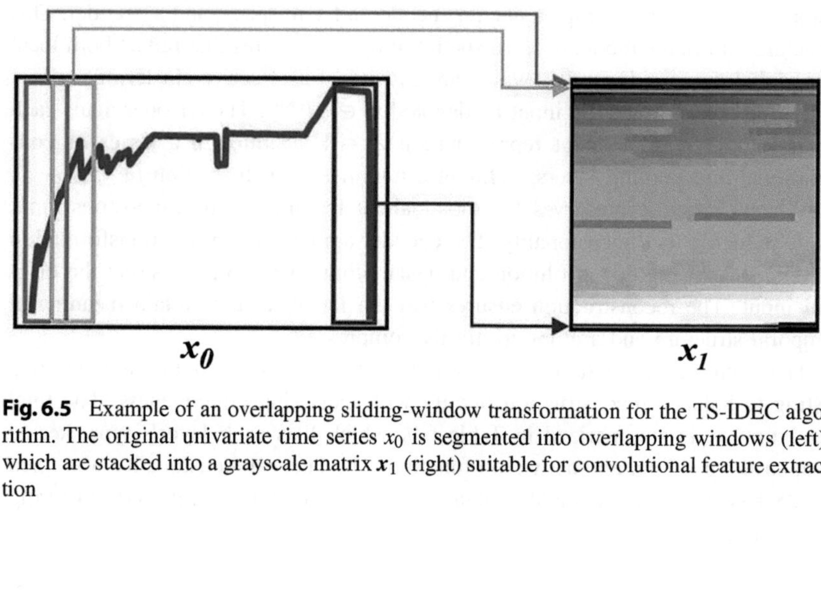

Fig. 6.5 Example of an overlapping sliding-window transformation for the TS-IDEC algorithm. The original univariate time series x_0 is segmented into overlapping windows (left), which are stacked into a grayscale matrix $\boldsymbol{x}_1$ (right) suitable for convolutional feature extraction

This encoding of temporal structure helps capture fine-grained operational transitions and long-range dependencies, two common challenges in real-world process monitoring [284, 285]. Moreover, overlapping improves generalization by generating multiple slightly varied training instances from the same base sequence, while minimizing the risk of omitting important transitions between operational states.

By converting time-domain signals into structured spatial representations, this transformation bridges the gap between time-series modeling and image-based convolutional learning. The resulting matrices serve as input to the encoder in TS-IDEC, enabling the downstream architecture to exploit spatial locality and structural regularities that are difficult to learn directly from raw sequences.

Deep Convolutional Autoencoder and Clustering Mechanism

The core of the TS-IDEC framework is a deep convolutional autoencoder (DCAE) that learns compact, informative latent representations of time-series inputs, which are transformed into grayscale matrices. As shown in Fig. 6.4, the DCAE comprises three main components: an encoder, a latent space, and a decoder. This structure allows the model to learn spatial-temporal features that reflect both local and global process dynamics, which are essential for effective clustering.

Let the transformed 2D input be denoted $\boldsymbol{x}_i \in \mathbb{R}^{n_s \times n_s}$. The encoder maps each input sample $\boldsymbol{x}_i$ to a latent representation $Z \in \mathbb{R}^{128}$ through a series of convolutional and pooling layers, defining a nonlinear transformation $f_W\colon \boldsymbol{x}_i \rightarrow z_i$. This latent space Z preserves the most salient features of the time-series input while reducing its dimensionality. The decoder applies the inverse transformation $g_{W'}\colon z_i \rightarrow \hat{\boldsymbol{x}}_i$ using deconvolution and upsampling layers to reconstruct the original input. The reconstruction ensures that the latent features retain meaningful temporal structure and are not arbitrarily compressed.

The architectural parameters of the DCAE were selected through iterative testing to balance reconstruction fidelity with clustering effectiveness. The final configuration is summarized in Table 6.9, which lists each layer's type, kernel size, stride, padding, and activation function. The latent dimensionality was fixed at 128 based on experimental evaluation of compression quality and clustering performance.

Table 6.9 Parameter settings of the DCAE architecture used in the TS-IDEC algorithm

Block name	Layer type	Kerner size	Stride	Padding	Filters /Neurons	Activation
Encoder						
conv1	convolutional layer	3 × 3	1	2	16	ReLU
maxpool1	maxpooling layer	2 × 2	2	0	N/A	N/A
conv2	convolutional layer	5 × 5	1	0	32	ReLU
maxpool2	maxpooling layer	2 × 2	2	0	N/A	N/A
conv3	convolutional layer	3 × 3	1	1	32	ReLU
conv4	convolutional layer	3 × 3	1	1	64	ReLU
fc1-en	fully connected layer	N/A	N/A	N/A	2304	ReLU
fc2-en	fully connected layer	N/A	N/A	N/A	1028	ReLU
fc3-en	fully connected layer	N/A	N/A	N/A	512	ReLU
Latent space						
fc-latent	fully connected layer	N/A	N/A	N/A	128	ReLU
Decoder						
fc3-de	fully connected layer	N/A	N/A	N/A	512	ReLU
fc2-de	fully connected layer	N/A	N/A	N/A	1028	ReLU
fc1-de	fully connected layer	N/A	N/A	N/A	2304	ReLU
deconv4	deconvolutional layer	3 × 3	1	1	32	ReLU
deconv3	deconvolutional layer	3 × 3	1	1	32	ReLU

(continued)

Table 6.9 (continued)

Block name	Layer type	Kerner size	Stride	Padding	Filters /Neurons	Activation
upsample2	upsampling layer	2 × 2	2	0	N/A	N/A
deconv2	deconvolutional layer	5 × 5	1	0	16	ReLU
upsample1	upsampling layer	2 × 2	2	0	N/A	N/A
deconv1	deconvolutional layer	3 × 3	1	2	1	N/A

Once the latent space Z is learned, clustering is performed using a dual-mode strategy. The first mode is a soft clustering mechanism, implemented through a Student's t-distribution kernel as proposed by [283]. Given the initial K cluster centroids $\{\mu_j(j = 1, \ldots K)\}$ obtained through a simple clustering algorithm, such as K-means clustering, and the data points z_i from the latent space Z, the probability of assigning a sample z_i to cluster j, with centroid μ_j, is computed as:

$$q_{i,j} = \frac{\left(1 + \|z_i - \mu_j\|^2/\alpha\right)^{-\frac{\alpha+1}{2}}}{\sum_{j'}\left(1 + \|z_i - \mu_{j'}\|^2/\alpha\right)^{-\frac{\alpha+1}{2}}} \tag{6.35}$$

where α refers to the degree-of-freedom parameter of the t-distribution, $q_{i,j}$ denotes the probability of assigning a sample i to cluster j, and $\|\cdot\|$ denotes the Euclidean norm.

This soft assignment matrix is used to refine cluster assignments during training and contributes directly to the clustering loss in Equation 6.38. The assignment of z_i to cluster j is determined by $\arg\max_j q_{i,j}$, with the resulting soft clustering outcome denoted as C_1.

The second mode is hard clustering, performed by applying the standard K-means algorithm directly to the latent space Z after training. This produces a second candidate output C_2, which is typically more stable for deployment in industrial decision systems.

Next, to evaluate the clustering quality of C_1 and C_2, a two-step evaluation approach is employed as demonstrated in Fig. 6.4. The first stage involves qualitative assessment. In some experiments with complex datasets, the data points may not be well separated. For example, the soft clustering result C_1 may consist of only one cluster, or the hard clustering result C_2 may contain clusters with extremely few data points. If one of these results is suboptimal based on the predefined clustering settings and requirements, the other is directly selected as the superior clustering result, denoted as C_{best}. If both exhibit similar performance in the qualitative assessment, a subsequent quantitative evaluation is performed. In this step, to determine the most appropriate final clustering output, both C_1 and C_2 are evaluated using S_{eva}. The better-performing output is selected as C_{best}. This two-stage evaluation ensures that the final clustering solution is both quantitatively sound and domain-explainable, which is essential for decision support in industrial applications.

Loss Function and Optimization

The TS-IDEC framework is trained through a joint optimization of two objective functions: the reconstruction loss L_{rec} and the clustering loss L_{cl}. This approach ensures that the learned latent representations not only reconstruct the input data accurately but are also discriminative for clustering. This dual-objective formulation enables the latent space to reflect both the structure of the time-series inputs and the underlying grouping patterns.

The total loss function L is defined as a weighted sum of the reconstruction loss L_{rec} and the clustering loss L_{cl}, following the formulation in [160]:

$$L = L_{rec} + \gamma L_{cl} \tag{6.36}$$

where $\gamma > 0$ is a hyperparameter that balances the relative importance of clustering against reconstruction during training.

The reconstruction loss L_{rec} is measured using the mean squared error (MSE) between the input matrix x_i and its reconstructed counterpart $\widehat{x_i}$:

$$L_{rec} = \sum\nolimits_{i=1}^{n} \|x_i - \widehat{x_i}\|^2 \tag{6.37}$$

This loss ensures that the latent representation retains enough temporal and structural information to reconstruct the original sequence with minimal distortion.

The clustering loss, first introduced in [283], is defined as the Kullback-Leibler (KL) divergence between the soft assignment distribution $Q = [q_{i,j}]$ and the target distribution $P = [p_{i,j}]$, which is constructed to sharpen the cluster assignments and emphasize points with high-confidence predictions:

$$L_{cl} = \mathrm{KL}(P\|Q) = \sum\nolimits_i \sum\nolimits_j p_{i,j} \log \frac{p_{i,j}}{q_{i,j}} \quad (6.38)$$

where $q_{i,j}$ is defined in Equation 6.35 as the probability of assigning a sample i to cluster j, and $p_{i,j}$ is the auxiliary distribution presented in Equation 6.39:

$$p_{i,j} = \frac{q_{i,j}^2/f_j}{\sum_{j'} q_{i,j'}^2/f_{j'}} \quad (6.39)$$

where $f_j = \sum_i q_{i,j}$ denotes the frequency of samples assigned to the cluster j.

This target distribution serves three purposes: it enhances cluster purity by emphasizing confident assignments, balances cluster influence by normalizing frequencies, and helps refine cluster boundaries during optimization [283].

The loss is jointly optimized using the Adam optimizer [286], which updates both the model weights and the cluster centroids. The gradients of L_{cl} with respect to the latent vectors z_i and the centroids μ_j are computed as follows:

$$\frac{\partial L_{cl}}{\partial z_i} = \frac{\alpha+1}{\alpha} \sum\nolimits_j \left(1 + \frac{\|z_i - \mu_j\|^2}{\alpha}\right)^{-1} \times \left(p_{i,j} - q_{i,j}\right)\left(z_i - \mu_j\right) \quad (6.40)$$

$$\frac{\partial L_{cl}}{\partial \mu_j} = -\frac{\alpha+1}{\alpha} \sum\nolimits_j \left(1 + \frac{\|z_i - \mu_j\|^2}{\alpha}\right)^{-1} \times \left(p_{i,j} - q_{i,j}\right)\left(z_i - \mu_j\right) \quad (6.41)$$

Given a mini-batch with m samples and the learning rate λ, each μ_j is updated as follows:

$$\mu_j = \mu_j - \frac{\lambda}{m} \sum\nolimits_{i=1}^{m} \frac{\partial L_{cl}}{\partial \mu_j} \quad (6.42)$$

The decoder weights W' are updated as follows:

$$W' = W' - \frac{\lambda}{m} \sum\nolimits_{i=1}^{m} \frac{\partial L_{rec}}{\partial W'} \quad (6.43)$$

The encoder weights W are updated as follows:

$$W = W - \frac{\lambda}{m}\sum_{i=1}^{m}\left(\frac{\partial L_{rec}}{\partial W} + \gamma\frac{\partial L_{cl}}{\partial W}\right) \tag{6.44}$$

This optimization strategy ensures that the encoder's latent representations are both reconstructive and conducive to effective clustering. The balance coefficient γ is chosen empirically to avoid overfitting to either objective.

6.4.3.2 Composite Internal Evaluation Method

In the absence of labeled data, evaluating clustering performance relies on internal validation metrics that assess the compactness and separation of clusters solely from the input data structure. While widely used, individual internal metrics often yield conflicting or unstable results, particularly when applied to high-dimensional, noisy, and irregular time-series data, which is typical in real-world operational contexts. To overcome this limitation, this study proposes a composite internal evaluation strategy that integrates multiple standard metrics into a unified, normalized score, enabling robust and interpretable model selection.

This study focuses on three widely used internal clustering indices: SIL [280], CH [281] and DB [282]. The definition and formulas of these three evaluation metrics have been described in Sect. 6.4.1.2. These metrics capture complementary aspects of clustering quality, including cohesion and separation, but differ in scale, sensitivity to outliers, and response to cluster shape and density. As shown in earlier studies [163], no single metric performs consistently across all datasets, and metric-specific biases can distort evaluation outcomes in unsupervised settings.

To construct a robust evaluation score, this study applies a normalization and aggregation procedure. First, each metric is rescaled using min-max normalization, with outliers mitigated using interquartile range (IQR) filtering. Then, rank normalization is incorporated, replacing numerical values with their ranks in a sorted order. Rank normalization is robust to outliers while preserving the relative ordering of the data. The final normalized score for each metric $i \in \{SIL, CH, DB\}$ is computed as the average of its min-max scaled and rank-normalized forms:

$$S^i_{norm} = \left(S^i_{minmax} + S^i_{rank}\right)/2 \tag{6.45}$$

where S^i_{minmax} denotes the scores obtained after applying min-max scaling to the values with outliers removed, and S^i_{rank} refers to the scores after applying rank normalization to the original evaluation scores, where i corresponding to the three base evaluation metrics.

Let X denote the original vector of scores and X' the same vector with outliers removed using IQR filtering. The min-max normalized score S^i_{minmax} is computed differently depending on whether higher or lower values indicate better clustering:

$$S^i_{minmax} = \begin{cases} \frac{X'-\min(X')}{\max(X')-\min(X')} i = SIL\ or\ CH \\ 1 - \frac{X'-\min(X')}{\max(X')-\min(X')} i = DB \end{cases} \tag{6.46}$$

The rank-normalized score S^i_{rank} is defined as:

$$S^i_{rank} = \frac{\text{rank}(X) - 1}{N - 1} \tag{6.47}$$

where rank$(\cdot)$ is the rank of X in a sorted order and N refers to the number of values in the dataset. If $i = SIL$ or CH, rank$(\cdot)$ is computed in ascending order, whereas if $i = DB$, rank$(\cdot)$ is computed in descending order.

Finally, the composite evaluation score S_{eva} is calculated by averaging the normalized scores across all three metrics:

$$S_{eva} = \left(\sum\nolimits_i S^i_{norm}\right)/3 \tag{6.48}$$

Based on the calculation in Equations 6.45–6.47, S_{eva} is in the range [0, 1], and a higher value indicates a better clustering performance.

This composite score has multiple functions in this study. First, it is used to select the final clustering result C_{best} from the two candidate outputs produced by TS-IDEC. Specifically, if the soft clustering result C_1 and the hard clustering result C_2 yield distinct scores, the result with the higher S_{eva} is selected. Additionally, this composite score is also employed to compare the performance of the TS-IDEC algorithm with the baseline methods and determine the optimal number of clusters in the absence of ground truth in Sect. 6.4.4.

6.4.4 Empirical Benchmarking and Evaluation of Time-Series Clustering

Note: Parts of this section are based on the author's first-author journal article: *"Discovering Operational Patterns Using Image-Based Convolutional Clustering and Composite Evaluation: A Case Study in Foundry Melting Processes"* [145].

This section presents a comprehensive evaluation of the proposed TS-IDEC framework through benchmark comparisons, robustness testing, and ablation studies. The experiments aim to (i) assess TS-IDEC's performance relative to classical and deep clustering methods, (ii) validate the framework's stability under parameter variation, and (iii) justify the architectural and evaluation design choices through controlled ablations. All experiments are conducted on real-world univariate temperature time-series data collected from an industrial foundry, as described in Sect. 7.2.

6.4.4.1 Experimental Setup and Baselines

To evaluate the performance of the proposed TS-IDEC algorithm, this study conducts a series of comparative experiments against classical and deep learning-based time-series clustering methods. The dataset is the real-world dataset from the foundry processes, which will be introduced in Sect. 7.2. The dataset comprises 3,927 univariate temperature time series, each representing a complete melting operation.

All time-series instances are initially of variable length due to differing melting durations. To ensure consistency and compatibility with all clustering models, each sequence is resampled to a fixed length of 497 time steps using linear interpolation and aggregation. This length corresponds approximately to the median duration across all melting operations, enabling batch processing without excessive truncation or padding. The pre-processed sequences serve as the input to both classical and deep clustering baselines.

The proposed TS-IDEC is compared against seven clustering methods, as shown in Table 6.10. The K-shape, K-means-DTW, and K-means-SoftDTW methods are implemented using the *tslearn* library (*version 0.6.3*) [287], while all deep clustering models, including TS-IDEC, are implemented in *PyTorch 2.3.1* [288].

Table 6.10 Overview of time series clustering algorithms used for benchmarking

Algorithm	Reference	Description
K-shape	[158]	A shape-based clustering algorithm using normalized cross-correlation.
K-means-DTW	[157]	Classical K-means applied with Dynamic Time Warping (DTW) distance.
K-means-SoftDTW	[156]	A differentiable version of DTW that allows smooth optimization.
IDEC	[160]	A deep-embedded clustering method using fully connected autoencoders and soft assignment.
IDEC-conv1D	Adapted from [160]	A modified version of IDEC using a 1D convolutional encoder to better capture temporal patterns.
DTC	[289]	Deep Temporal Clustering that integrates sequential feature learning and clustering in an end-to-end framework.
EDESC	[290]	A deep subspace clustering model designed for high-dimensional data.

For TS-IDEC, the input sequences are first transformed into 32×32 grayscale matrices using the overlapping sliding window method described in Sect. 6.4.3.1. The convolutional autoencoder architecture follows the configuration shown in Table 6.9. Key hyperparameters are tuned based on a series of preliminary experiments:

- **Learning rate**: Chosen from {0.05, 0.01, 0.001, 0.0005}, with 0.001 yielding stable convergence.
- **Batch size**: Tested from {8, 16, 32, 64}; 32 is selected for its balance of efficiency and performance.
- **Weighting coefficient λ**: Set to 0.5 to balance reconstruction and clustering losses.
- **Epochs**: Set to 1,000 to ensure convergence without overfitting.

All experiments are conducted on an *NVIDIA GeForce RTX 3060 GPU* using *Python 3.11.7*. Each model was trained five times with different random seeds, and results are reported as mean values with standard error.

The IDEC model used a traditional fully connected autoencoder with an encoder layer configuration of 256–128-64 neurons. Training was performed with a batch size of 8. To enhance temporal feature extraction, IDEC-conv1D replaced the encoder with a 1D convolutional architecture, detailed in Table 6.11 below.

Table 6.11 Parameter setting of the DCAE architecture of the IDEC-conv1d algorithm

Block name	Layer type	Kerner size	Stride	Padding	Filters /Neurons	Activation
Encoder						
conv1	convolutional layer	5	3	2	8	ReLU
avgpool1	average pooling layer	2	2	0	N/A	N/A
conv2	convolutional layer	3	1	1	16	ReLU
avgpool2	average pooling layer	2	2	0	N/A	N/A
conv3	convolutional layer	3	1	1	16	ReLU
fc1-en	fully connected layer	N/A	N/A	N/A	672	ReLU
fc2-en	fully connected layer	N/A	N/A	N/A	512	ReLU
fc3-en	fully connected layer	N/A	N/A	N/A	256	ReLU
Latent space						
fc-latent	fully connected layer	N/A	N/A	N/A	64	ReLU
Decoder						
fc3-de	fully connected layer	N/A	N/A	N/A	256	ReLU
fc2-de	fully connected layer	N/A	N/A	N/A	512	ReLU
fc1-de	fully connected layer	N/A	N/A	N/A	672	ReLU

(continued)

Table 6.11 (continued)

Block name	Layer type	Kerner size	Stride	Padding	Filters /Neurons	Activation
deconv3	deconvolutional layer	3	1	1	16	ReLU
upsample2	upsampling layer	2	2	0	N/A	N/A
deconv2	deconvolutional layer	3	1	1	8	ReLU
upsample1	upsampling layer	2	2	0	N/A	N/A
deconv1	deconvolutional layer	5	3	2	1	N/A

This setup ensures a fair comparison between TS-IDEC and relevant baselines under consistent experimental conditions, allowing for rigorous assessment of clustering effectiveness, model robustness, and architectural design choices.

6.4.4.2 Benchmark Comparison: TS-IDEC vs. Baselines

To assess the clustering performance of TS-IDEC, this study conducts a comparative evaluation against seven baseline algorithms introduced in Sect. 6.4.4.1. All methods are tested on the standardized furnace-melting dataset under the same experimental conditions. Their performance is evaluated using the proposed composite metric S_{eva} introduced in Sect. 6.4.3.2.

Each algorithm is allowed to search for the optimal number of clusters within the range representation $k \in [3, 16]$, and the best performing result based on S_{eva} is reported. The evaluation scores are summarized in Table 6.12 and visualized in Fig. 6.6, where "KM" denotes K-means. In Table 6.12, the values preceding the "±" symbol indicate the evaluation scores, while the values following it denote the standard errors of repetitions.

The results in Table 6.12 and Fig. 6.6 indicate that TS-IDEC achieves the highest overall performance based on the composite evaluation score $S_{eva} = 0.7523$, outperforming all baselines, including SotA deep clustering methods such as IDEC and EDESC.

Table 6.12 Normalized evaluation scores of different algorithms for time-series clustering

Methods	n_ clusters	S_{norm}^{SIL}	S_{norm}^{CH}	S_{norm}^{DB}	S_{eva}
K-shape	3	**0.988 ± 0.0**	0.082 ± 0.0	**0.971 ± 0.0**	0.685 ± 0.0
KM-DTW	3	0.709 ± 0.0371	0.503 ± 0.0312	0.459 ± 0.0297	0.557 ± 0.0305
KM-SoftDTW	4	0.648 ± 0.0365	0.442 ± 0.0256	0.473 ± 0.0197	0.521 ± 0.0094
IDEC	3	0.621 ± 0.0545	0.903 ± 0.0587	0.688 ± 0.0385	0.737 ± 0.0428
IDEC-conv1d	3	0.612 ± 0.0191	**0.917 ± 0.0244**	0.542 ± 0.0547	0.690 ± 0.0220
DTC	3	0.532 ± 0.0307	0.750 ± 0.0529	0.508 ± 0.0371	0.597 ± 0.0323
EDESC	3	0.692 ± 0.0040	0.878 ± 0.0035	0.682 ± 0.0040	0.750 ± 0.0015
TS-IDEC	4	0.649 ± 0.0274	0.825 ± 0.0551	0.783 ± 0.0361	**0.752 ± 0.0072**

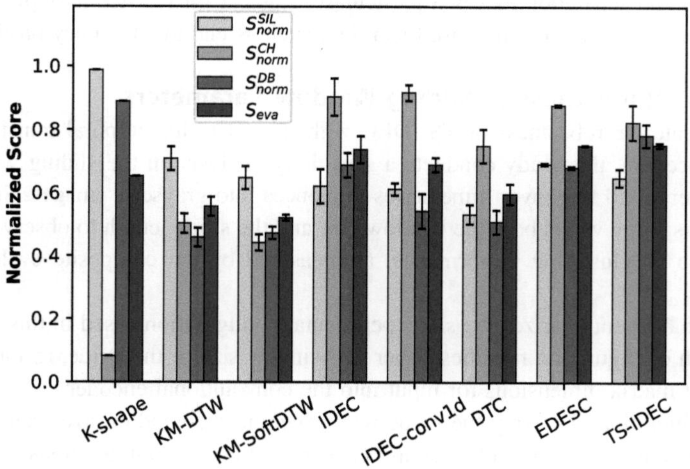

Fig. 6.6 Normalized evaluation scores of different time-series clustering algorithms. The x-axis represents the names of algorithms, where "KM" denotes K-means. The y-axis shows the normalized scores ranging from 0 to 1. Each group of four bars corresponds to distinct evaluation metrics, as indicated in the legend, with error bars representing the standard error of repetitions

While TS-IDEC does not rank first in any of the individual normalized metrics, including S_{norm}^{SIL}, S_{norm}^{CH} and S_{norm}^{DB}, it consistently ranks second or third across all three, highlighting its robustness and stability across diverse evaluation dimensions. In contrast, methods like K-shape exhibit strong performance in SIL and DB but perform poorly in CH, revealing limitations in cluster separation despite good cohesion.

Among deep baselines, IDEC and EDESC show competitive performance, with EDESC scoring slightly higher in S_{eva} than IDEC. However, both are outperformed by TS-IDEC, which integrates convolutional feature extraction, dual-mode clustering, and composite evaluation into a unified pipeline. The superior DB score of TS-IDEC suggests that its clusters are not only compact but also well-separated, even in the presence of overlapping operational modes and nonstationary behavior.

Importantly, the optimal cluster number selected for TS-IDEC is four, as determined by maximizing S_{eva}, while other methods tend to prefer fewer clusters. This indicates that TS-IDEC is capable of capturing finer operational distinctions that may be missed by more rigid or assumption-heavy algorithms.

Overall, these findings validate the effectiveness and generalizability of TS-IDEC in real-world, label-free industrial settings. Its balanced performance across cohesion and separation makes it particularly suitable for real-world applications that require effective unsupervised learning, such as energy-efficiency profiling.

6.4.4.3 Robustness to Sliding Window Parameters

To evaluate the robustness of TS-IDEC with respect to its temporal transformation procedure, this study conducts a sensitivity analysis on the sliding window parameters used to convert time-series sequences into grayscale images. Specifically, this study varies both the window size and the stride length to observe their influence on clustering performance, as measured by the composite evaluation score S_{eva}.

Table 6.13 summarizes the six experimental configurations used in this analysis. Each configuration modifies either the window size or the stride, resulting in different matrix dimensions for input into the convolutional encoder.

Configurations 1–4 vary the stride while keeping the window size fixed at 32, thus adjusting the degree of overlap between segments. Configurations 5 and 6 investigate the impact of varying the window size, which represents shorter or longer temporal patterns, respectively.

Table 6.13 Sliding window parameter settings for the TS-IDEC algorithm

Config ID	Window size	Stride	Resulting matrix shape
1 (default)	32	15	32×32
2	32	10	48×32
3	32	20	25×32
4	32	32	16×32
5	24	21	24×24
6	40	12	40×40

Fig. 6.7 illustrates the S_{eva} scores achieved by TS-IDEC under each configuration. The light blue bar indicates the default setting, while green and orange bars represent variations in stride and window size, respectively.

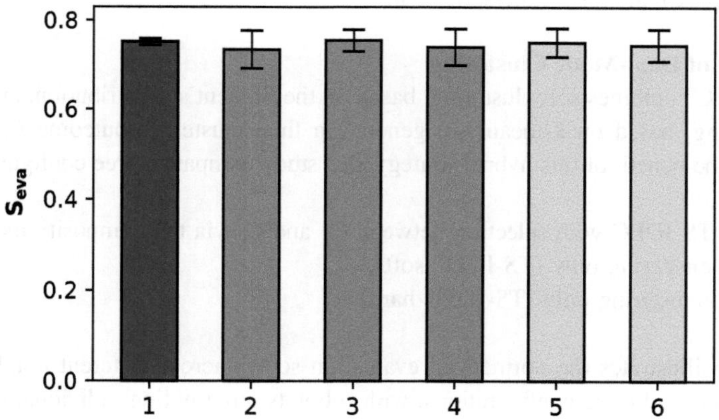

Fig. 6.7 Evaluation scores of different experimental configurations for sensitivity analysis of developing the TS-IDEC algorithm. The x-axis corresponds to the config ID as presented in Table 6.13, while the y-axis indicates the evaluation score S_{eva}. The light blue bars represent the default configuration, the light green bars illustrate experiments analyzing the impact of stride, and the light orange bars depict experiments assessing the effect of varying the window size. The error bars represent the standard error of repetitions

Across all six configurations, the model achieves consistently strong clustering performance, with only minor fluctuations in S_{eva}. The default setting (config 1) yields slightly better average performance, but no statistically significant degradation is observed in any alternative configuration. In particular, the model remains stable even with minimal overlap (config 4) or highly extended windows (config 6), demonstrating robust generalization to variations in the temporal resolution of input data.

6.4.4.4 Design Justification through Ablation Analysis

To validate the architectural and methodological choices in TS-IDEC, this study conducted two ablation studies: (i) evaluating the contribution of the dual-mode clustering strategy, and (ii) assessing the effectiveness and the trustworthiness of the composite internal evaluation metric S_{eva}. These studies isolate the effects of key components and confirm their necessity for robust and high-quality clustering of complex real-world time-series data.

Impact of Dual-Mode Clustering

TS-IDEC combines soft clustering, based on the Student's t-distribution, and hard clustering, based on k-means, to generate a final clustering outcome C_{best}. To assess the benefit of this hybrid strategy, this study compares three configurations:

- Full TS-IDEC with selection between C_1 and C_2 via the composite metric,
- Soft clustering only (TS-IDEC-soft),
- Hard clustering only (TS-IDEC-hard).

Fig. 6.8 illustrates the normalized evaluation scores across different numbers of clusters for all three configurations, with subplots representing individual internal metrics and the final S_{eva}.

The results indicate that hard clustering alone provides stable performance but struggles with soft transitions and noisy boundaries, which are common in real-world furnace operations. In contrast, soft clustering alone shows greater sensitivity and can capture nuanced behavior, but it suffers from convergence issues in some runs, sometimes collapsing into a single dominant cluster and significantly degrading performance. The full TS-IDEC model, which integrates both hard and soft clustering, consistently achieves the best overall performance. By combining the stability of hard assignments with the flexibility of soft probability distributions, TS-IDEC delivers more reliable and higher-quality clustering results across diverse experimental settings.

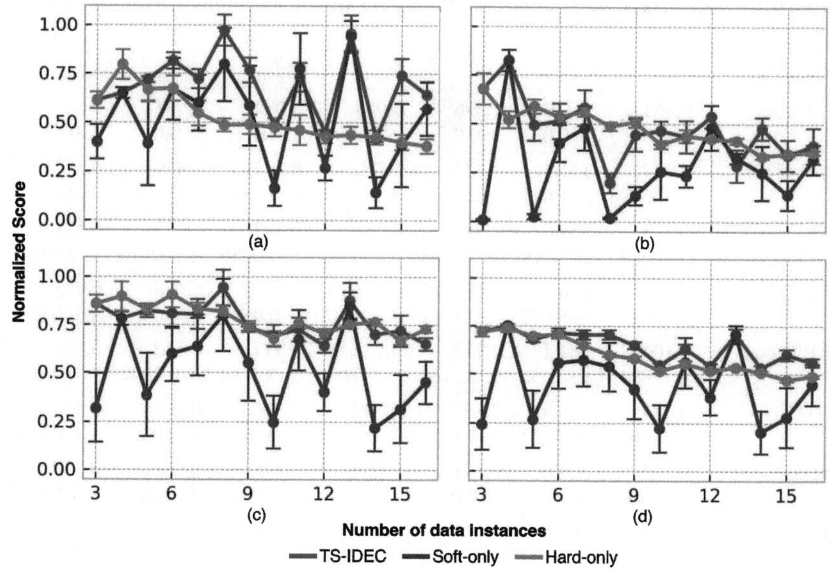

Fig. 6.8 Evaluation scores of the ablation study for developing the TS-IDEC algorithm. X-axes denote the number of clusters, and y-axes refer to the normalized evaluation scores. Sub-figures (a)-(d) represents the four evaluation scores S_{norm}^{SIL}, S_{norm}^{CH}, S_{norm}^{DB} and S_{eva} respectively. Three lines stand for the methods shown in the legend, respectively, and error bars represent the standard deviation of repetitions

Importance of Composite Evaluation Metric

To justify the use of the composite evaluation score S_{eva} for model selection, this study compares it against:

- Individual raw metrics: SIL, CH, and DB,
- Individual normalized metrics: S_{norm}^{SIL}, S_{norm}^{CH}, and S_{norm}^{DB}.

Table 6.14 summarizes the evaluation scores of all methods under these seven metrics, using the same optimal clustering result from each algorithm's best run. The values preceding the "±" symbol indicate the evaluation scores, while the values following it denote the standard errors of repetitions.

Table 6.14 Comparison of time-series clustering algorithms under different evaluation metrics

Methods	SIL	CH	DB	S_{norm}^{SIL}	S_{norm}^{CH}	S_{norm}^{DB}	S_{eva}
K-shape	0.464 ± 0.0	60.06 ± 0.0	1.596 ± 0.0	0.988 ± 0.0	0.082 ± 0.0	0.971 ± 0.0	0.685 ± 0.0
KM-DTW	0.044 ± 0.0108	111.4 ± 14.41	3.444 ± 0.1437	0.709 ± 0.0371	0.503 ± 0.0312	0.459 ± 0.0296	0.557 ± 0.0305
KM-softDTW	0.113 ± 0.0197	239.0 ± 22.79	2.945 ± 0.2428	0.648 ± 0.0365	0.442 ± 0.0256	0.473 ± 0.0197	0.521 ± 0.0094
IDEC	0.110 ± 0.0187	576.9 ± 54.27	2.184 ± 0.1101	0.621 ± 0.0545	0.903 ± 0.0587	0.688 ± 0.0385	0.737 ± 0.0428
IDEC-conv1d	0.106 ± 0.0045	584.1 ± 21.55	2.717 ± 0.2762	0.612 ± 0.0191	0.917 ± 0.0244	0.542 ± 0.0547	0.690 ± 0.0220
DTC	0.089 ± 0.0063	475.8 ± 36.11	2.862 ± 0.1276	0.532 ± 0.0307	0.750 ± 0.0529	0.508 ± 0.0371	0.597 ± 0.0323
EDESC	0.123 ± 0.0007	554.6 ± 3.68	2.171 ± 0.0163	0.692 ± 0.0040	0.878 ± 0.0035	0.682 ± 0.0040	0.750 ± 0.0015
TS-IDEC	0.114 ± 0.0068	501.5 ± 48.37	1.918 ± 0.0929	0.649 ± 0.0274	0.825 ± 0.0551	0.783 ± 0.0361	0.752 ± 0.0072

The raw metrics provide inconsistent guidance. For example, K-shape achieves the highest SIL and DB values but ranks among the lowest in CH values. This inconsistency arises because each internal clustering metric emphasizes different, often complementary, aspects of clustering quality. Consequently, reliance on any single metric provides an incomplete and potentially biased evaluation, as individual metrics may favor specific cluster shapes, sizes, or distributions while neglecting others.

Normalizing each metric improves the comparability across methods. For instance, while the normalized SIL score for K-shape remains high, the normalized CH score is significantly lower, correctly revealing its poor separation quality. Moreover, normalization balances the evaluation scale, making individual metrics more stable, interpretable, and directly comparable.

The composite metric S_{eva}, by contrast, provides a more balanced and stable signal. TS-IDEC's leading score in S_{eva}, despite not ranking first in every individual metric, confirms its robust all-around performance. This result justifies the use of S_{eva} as a selection criterion for final clustering output and demonstrates the advantage of multi-perspective internal validation in unsupervised industrial contexts.

6.5 Module 4—Causal Reasoning and Inference: Pipeline and Algorithms

Note: this section are based on the author's first-author publications: *"Data-Driven Causal Reasoning for Eco-Driving Behavior Analysis in Public Transportation Systems" [165], and "Uncovering Causal Drivers of Energy Efficiency for Industrial Process in Foundry via Time-Series Causal Inference"* [166].

This section establishes a comprehensive, systematic foundation for causal inference across static and dynamic contexts. It introduces a causal reasoning pipeline designed to address the challenge of understanding and interpreting complex relationships within data, particularly in scenarios where identifying the root causes of key variables is essential for informed decision-making. Understanding causality is crucial for not only explaining observed phenomena but also for making accurate predictions, guiding interventions, and informing policy decisions.

The key contributions and novelty of this study are outlined as follows:

1. A novel causal reasoning pipeline, inspired by [291], is proposed to:
    a) Learn quantitative causal mechanisms from observational data;
    b) Evaluate the inferred causal structures in the absence of ground truth;
    c) Identify the root causes of variations in target variables.
2. A split-and-ensemble approach for the DAGMA-DCE algorithm is introduced to advance static causal discovery. This Approach:
    a) Enhances computational efficiency by reducing the effective training set size;
    b) Preserves the accuracy of base learners through a hybrid data-splitting scheme;
    c) Mitigates the dataset bias by a rule-based ensemble mechanism;
    d) Offers generalizability and can be adapted for use with other static causal discovery methods.
3. A hybrid and integrated approach is developed to improve the PCMCI+ algorithm, aiming to enhance causal discovery in time-series data. This methodology:
    a) Improves the accuracy of time-series causal discovery by integrating multiple conditional independent (CI) tests in the PCMCI+ algorithm;
    b) Maintains a low FDR in causal discovery.

The remainder of this section is structured as follows. Section 6.5.1 provides an overview of the entire causal reasoning pipeline, outlining its core stages and underlying rationale. Section 6.5.2 introduces the causal discovery algorithm designed for static data, while Sect. 6.5.3 offers an empirical evaluation of its performance using synthetic benchmark datasets and relevant metrics. Section 6.5.4 then details the causal discovery approach to time-series data, followed by Sect. 6.5.5, which presents empirical analyses and comparative evaluations specific to the temporal datasets. Recognizing the challenges posed by the lack of ground truth in real-world settings, Sect. 6.5.6 introduces an approach for evaluating causal graphs without reference structures. Finally, Sect. 6.5.7 introduces a method for conducting root cause analysis to identify the key drivers of observed system behavior.

6.5.1 Overview of Causal Reasoning Pipeline

6.5.1.1 Pipeline Description

This section provides an overview of the causal reasoning pipeline developed in this study. The proposed causal reasoning pipeline demonstrated in Fig. 6.9 aims to estimate causal graphs, which represent the directional relationships between variables, thereby providing a clear map of how different factors influence one another. By focusing on the estimation and evaluation of causal graphs, this pipeline enables researchers to pinpoint the root causes of key variables within a system. This ability to trace effects back to their origins offers a significant advantage in understanding complex phenomena, enabling the design of more effective interventions and anticipating the consequences of changes within the system. This pipeline offers a robust tool for uncovering and understanding the underlying causal structures that drive observed behaviors.

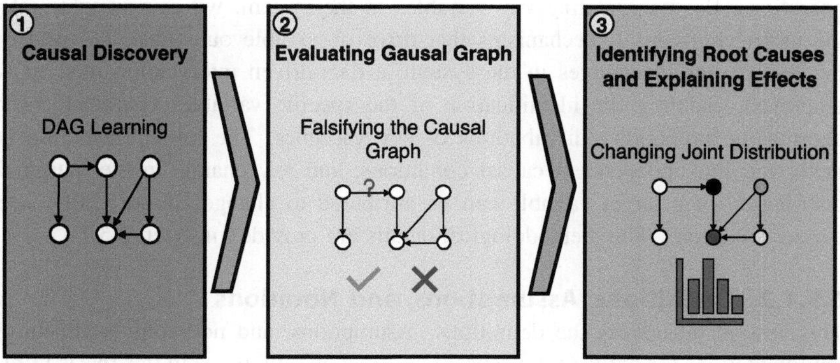

Fig. 6.9 Proposed causal reasoning pipeline. The pipeline consists of three stages: causal discovery, causal graph evaluation without ground truth, and identification of the root causes of key variables

The proposed pipeline starts with causal discovery, learning both the causal graph (DAG) and the causal strengths, which quantify the strength of causal relationships. Because static and time-series data exhibit different statistical structures, distinct algorithms are employed to learn the causal graph. For static data, a DAG with edge weights that quantify direct causal effects among contemporaneous variables is estimated. For time-series data, a lagged causal graph is learned, with coefficients that encode the strength of temporal dependencies. Section 6.5.2 details the causal discovery algorithm for static data and Sect. 6.5.4 presents the time-series causal discovery algorithm.

In the next stage, the faithfulness of the causal graph should be evaluated. However, causal inference lacks ground truth, making it difficult to assess the quality of the causal graph. While domain experts can describe known dependencies within a system, this approach is prone to human error and incomplete knowledge. To quantitatively evaluate the consistency and faithfulness of a DAG using observational data alone, this study employs an interpretable metric that determines whether the DAG fits significantly better than a random baseline. To assess whether the number of violations in a causal graph identified by the causal discovery algorithm is high or low, it is compared to a baseline constructed by randomly permuting its nodes. The employed metric is described in Sect. 6.5.6.

The final stage focuses on performing causal inference using the fitted DAG. Understanding causality through intervention is essential for developing effective strategies across domains such as healthcare, transportation, and industrial operations. By manipulating key variables in the system, we gain insights into the underlying causal mechanisms that drive observable outcomes. To identify the root causes of changes in the system, a data-driven intervention method is employed, enabling the identification of the specific variables responsible for altering the probability distributions of key variables. The joint distribution is factorized into independent causal conditions, and any change in the marginal distribution of a target variable can be attributed to changes in some of those causal conditions. The methodological details are provided in Sect. 6.5.7.

6.5.1.2 Definitions, Assumptions, and Notations

This section introduces the definitions, assumptions, and notations establishing the foundations for multivariate causal reasoning and inference in this thesis [199, 292], with a focus on graphical terminology as well as the underlying statistical definitions and assumptions.

First of all, consider finitely many random variables $\mathbf{X} = (X_1, \ldots, X_d) \in \mathbb{R}^d$ with index set $\mathbf{V} := \{1, \ldots, d\}$, whose i-th component X_i is a random variable, with i.i.d. observations $\mathcal{D} = \{x^{(n)}{}_{n=1}^{N}\}$, noises $N_i (i = 1, \ldots, d)$ associated with X_i and N_i is independent with N_j for all $i \neq j$, joint distribution $P_{\mathbf{X}}$, and probability density $p(\mathbf{x})$. The definitions regarding causal graphs, d-separation and SCMs are as follows. In Pearl's theory [199, 200, 239], SEMs and SCMs are interchangeable, so SEMs in this PhD thesis share the same definition as SCMs.

Definition 6.1 (Causal Graph): A causal graph $\mathcal{G} = (V, E)$ consists of nodes or vertices V and edges $E \subseteq V^2$ with $(v, v) \notin E$ for any $v \in V$. A node i is called a parent of j if $(i, j) \in E$ and $(j, i) \notin E$, and a child if $(j, i) \in E$ and $(i, j) \notin E$. The set of parents of j is denoted by $\mathbf{PA}_j^{\mathcal{G}}$, and the set of its children is denoted by $\mathbf{CH}_j^{\mathcal{G}}$. If there is no pair (j, k) with directed paths from j to k and from k to j, and all edges are directed, $\mathcal{G}$ is called a directed acyclic graph (DAG).

Definition 6.2 (*d*-separation): ***d*** In a DAG $\mathcal{G}$, a path between nodes i_l and i_m is blocked by a set $\mathbf{S}$, with neither i_l nor i_m in $\mathbf{S}$, whenever there is a node i_k, such that one of the following two possibilities holds:

(i) $i_k \in \mathbf{S} \wedge ((i_{k-1} \rightarrow i_k \rightarrow i_{k+1}) \vee (i_{k-1} \leftarrow i_k \leftarrow i_{k+1}) \vee (i_{k-1} \leftarrow i_k \rightarrow i_{k+1}))$;
(ii) neither i_k nor any of its descendants is in $\mathbf{S}$ and $i_{k-1} \rightarrow i_k \leftarrow i_{k+1}$.

Furthermore, in a DAG $\mathcal{G}$, we say that two disjoint subsets of vertices $\mathbf{A}$ and $\mathbf{B}$ are by a third disjoint subset $\mathbf{S}$ if every path between nodes in $\mathbf{A}$ and $\mathbf{B}$ is blocked by $\mathbf{S}$.

Definition 6.3 (Structural Causal Models (SCMs)): An SCM $\mathfrak{S} := (\mathbf{S}, P_{\mathbf{N}})$ consists of a collection $\mathbf{S}$ of d structural assignments

$$X_j := f_j(\mathbf{PA}_j, N_j), j = 1, \ldots, d \tag{6.49}$$

where $\mathbf{PA}_j$ refers to the parents of X_j, and $P_{\mathbf{N}}$ represents the joint distribution of noise variables.

The causal graph $\mathcal{G}$ of an SCM is obtained by creating one vertex for each X_j and drawing directed edges from each parent in $\mathbf{PA}_j$ to X_j. $\mathcal{G}$ is assumed to be acyclic. The elements of $\mathbf{PA}_j$ is also defined as the direct causes of X_j and X_j is called a direct effect of each of its direct causes.

Afterward, to establish the theoretical foundations of causal inference, a set of assumptions is introduced, which applies to all causality-related analyses in this thesis.

Assumption 6.1 (Causal Sufficiency): Assume that all common causes (confounders) of $\mathbf{X}$ are observed and included in the SCM. Under causal sufficiency, there are no hidden confounders. With causal sufficiency, the graph $\mathcal{G}$ provides a complete representation of causal dependencies.

Assumption 6.2 (Causal Markov Condition): Assume that the distribution $P_{\mathbf{X}}$ is induced by an SCM with a graph $\mathcal{G}$. Then, $P_{\mathbf{X}}$ is Markovian with respect to $\mathcal{G}$. Every variable X_j is independent of its non-descendants, given its direct parents in $\mathbf{PA}_j$ in $\mathcal{G}$. The Markov assumption enables us to read off independence from the graph structure.

Assumption 6.3 (Causal Faithfulness): Assume that $P_{\mathbf{X}}$ exhibits no conditional independence except that implied by $\mathcal{G}$. $\mathcal{G}$ explains all observed independence.

Assumption 6.4 (Causal Minimality): Assume $P_{\mathbf{X}}$ is Markovian with respect to $\mathcal{G}$, but not to any proper subgraph of $\mathcal{G}$. Causal faithfulness and minimality allow us to infer dependences from the graph structure.

Based on the Definitions 6.1–6.3 and Assumptions 6.1–6.4, causal reasoning and inference investigation is conducted, which is described as a hierarchy of three levels in Pearl's theory [199, 200, 239], including association, intervention, and counterfactuals.

Association:
The first level is defined as reasoning about cause-effect associations in observed data. At this level, the central question is *"What do we see or expect?"* Answers are obtained directly from observational data through probabilistic relationships, and statistical and machine learning models are employed to estimate the SCM and $\mathcal{G}$. This stage is referred to as causal discovery in this thesis.

Intervention:
The second level is defined as reasoning about the effects of deliberate manipulations within a system. At this level, the central question is *"What happens if we intervene?"* Answers require modifying the underlying structural causal model by setting variables to specific values, commonly represented using Pearl's do-operator [199, 200, 239], in order to estimate the causal effect of interventions. An intervention induces a new distribution over the system, which generally differs from the observational distribution. If interventions are allowed to arbitrarily alter the system, the two distributions will become unrelated. In such cases, rather than studying them jointly, the observational and interventional systems may be treated as independent [292].

Counterfactuals:
The third level is defined as reasoning about hypothetical alternatives to observed outcomes. At this level, the central question is *"What would have happened if circumstances had been different?"* Answers rely on modeling individual-level causal mechanisms within the SCM to compare observed outcomes with their unobserved counterfactual counterparts. Formally, counterfactual queries can be addressed by modifying an SCM through changes in its noise distributions, which may be induced by conditioning on observations, thereby enabling the evaluation of counterfactual outcomes [292].

To conduct the systematic experiments of an intervention study, do-calculus [199, 200, 239] is introduced, providing the formal basis for identifying and transforming causal effects expressed with the intervention operator $do(\cdot)$.

Do-Calculus:
Do-calculus is a set of three inference rules, allowing the systematic reduction of interventional distributions $p^{\mathfrak{S};do(X:=x)}$, into expressions that depend only on observational distributions, under appropriate graphical conditions defined by a causal model. Given the graph $\mathcal{G}$ and disjoint subsets $\mathbf{X}$, $\mathbf{Y}$, $\mathbf{Z}$ and $\mathbf{W}$, the three rules are as follows:

(i) "Insertion or deletion of observations":

$$p^{\mathfrak{S};do(\mathbf{X}:=\mathbf{x})}(\mathbf{y}|\mathbf{z},\mathbf{w}) = p^{\mathfrak{S};do(\mathbf{X}:=\mathbf{x})}(\mathbf{y}|\mathbf{w})$$

if **Y** and **Z** are d-separated by **X** and **W** in a graph where incoming edges in **X** have been removed.

(ii) "Action or observation exchange":

$$p^{\mathfrak{S};do(\mathbf{X}:=\mathbf{x},\mathbf{Z}:=\mathbf{z})}(\mathbf{y}|\mathbf{w}) = p^{\mathfrak{S};do(\mathbf{X}:=\mathbf{x})}(\mathbf{y}|\mathbf{z},\mathbf{w})$$

if **Y** and **Z** are d-separated by **X** and **W** in a graph where incoming edges in **X** and outgoing edges from **Z** have been removed have been removed.

(iii) "Insertion or deletion of actions":

$$p^{\mathfrak{S};do(\mathbf{X}:=\mathbf{x},\mathbf{Z}:=\mathbf{z})}(\mathbf{y}|\mathbf{w}) = p^{\mathfrak{S};do(\mathbf{X}:=\mathbf{x})}(\mathbf{y}|\mathbf{w})$$

if **Y** and **Z** are d-separated by **X** and **W** in a graph where incoming edges in **X** and **Z(W)** have been removed. **Z(W)** refers to the subset of nodes in **Z** that are not ancestors of any node in **W** in a graph that is obtained from $\mathcal{G}$ after removing all edges into **X**.

So far, the necessary definitions, assumptions, and terminologies have been introduced to establish the theoretical foundation of multivariate causal inference and reasoning. These foundations apply to both static data and time-series analysis. However, the notational conventions in time-series causal inference differ from those commonly used in static causal inference. In the following, the theoretical foundation is extended to the time-series setting [180].

When discussing causal inference in time series, consider a d-variate time series $(\mathbf{X}_t)_{t\in\mathbb{Z}}$, where each $\mathbf{X}_t$ for fixed time step t is the vector $(X_t^1, \ldots, X_t^d)$. Because causal influence can never go from the future to the past, there are two types of causal relations in multivariate time series: time-lagged effects and instantaneous effects.

First, for time-lagged effects, $\mathcal{G}$ with nodes X_t^j for $(j, t) \in \{1, \dots, d\} \times \mathbb{Z}$ contains only arrows from X_t^j to X_s^k for $t < s$ but not for $t = s$. Second, for instantaneous effects, $\mathcal{G}$ contains arrows from X_t^j to X_s^k for some j and k in addition to arrows going from X_t^m to X_s^l for $t < s$ and some m and l.

6.5.2 Static Causal Discovery Using Bagging DAGMA-DCE

The objective of the causal discovery algorithm is to learn the DAGs to represent SCMs. The weighted adjacency matrix of a DAG can be interpreted as a causal strength matrix that quantifies the magnitude of causal influence between variables. Based on the literature study in Sect. 3.4.1, score-based approaches, which evaluate candidate causal graphs using global optimization guided by a scoring function, offer an accurate, efficient, and consistent means of learning graph structures. This study adopts the DAGMA-DCE algorithm [178] as the base learner for estimating the causal structure, as it has demonstrated SotA performance and interpretability in prior experiments. To further enhance efficiency and accuracy, a split-and-ensemble strategy is introduced, leading to the development of the Bagging-DAGMA-DCE algorithm.

6.5.2.1 DAGMA-DCE

DAGMA-DCE [178] represents the differentiable causal discovery with differential causal effects. It augments the paradigm of score-based DAG learning with an interpretable, model-agnostic notion of edge weight: each directed edge $i \to j$ is scored by the root-mean-square (RMS) differential causal effect of X_i on X_j under the empirical data distribution. In DAGMA-DCE, the entries of the weighted adjacency matrix are the RMS entries of the Jacobian matrix [178]. Although backward passing through the Jacobian is computationally expensive, it is straightforward to compute the elements for any differentiable model, such as a Monte Carlo approximation of the empirical Jacobian matrices.

Based on the definitions in Sect. 6.5.1.2, $\mathcal{M}_\theta = \{f_{j,\theta}{}_{j=1}^{d}\}$ is defined as a differentiable causal model parameterized by θ, and each component $f_{j,\theta}$ denotes the function $\boldsymbol{x} \mapsto$ of an SCM.

The adjacent matrix $\mathbf{W}$, composed of the RMS differential causal effect of X_i on X_j, is defined as the L^2 norm of the derivative $\partial_i f_j$ with respect to the probability distribution of $\mathbf{X}$, denoted by $\mathbb{P}^{\mathbf{X}}$. In this study, the causal effects are computed using the Monte Carlo approximation as follows.

$$\mathbf{W}_{i,j} \triangleq \partial_i f_j \|(\mathbf{X})\|_{L^2(\mathbb{P}^{\mathbf{X}})} = \sqrt{\int_{\mathbb{R}^d} \left(\partial_i f_j(\mathbf{X})\right)^2 p_{\mathbf{X}}(\mathbf{X}) d\mathbf{X}}$$
$$\approx \sqrt{\frac{1}{N} \sum\nolimits_{n=1}^{N} \left(\partial_i f_j(x_n)\right)^2} \tag{6.50}$$

where $p_{\mathbf{X}}(\mathbf{X})$ refers to the density of $\mathbb{P}^{\mathbf{X}}$ with respect to the Lebesgue measure, and $x_n \sim p_{\mathbf{X}}(\mathbf{X})$. As the entries of $\mathbf{W}$ are the RMS entries of the Jacobian matrix, it is then straightforward to calculate $\mathbf{W}_{i,j}$ for any differentiable model, with the above being a Monte Carlo approximation over empirical Jacobian matrices.

The above definition of $\mathbf{W}$ allows for a principled sparsity penalty. Indeed, if $\partial_i f_j$ is square-integrable with respect to $\mathbb{P}^{\mathbf{X}}$, then Jensen's inequality implies that it is also integrable, which allows the sparsity penalty to be defined and approximated as follows.

$$g(\mathcal{M}_\theta) = \|\partial_i f_j(\mathbf{X})\|_{L^1(\mathbb{P}^{\mathbf{X}})} \approx \sqrt{\frac{1}{N} \sum_{n=1}^{N} |\partial_i f_j(x_n)|} \tag{6.51}$$

Next, the constraint function is defined as follows. The DAGMA algorithm [177] introduces a novel acyclicity characterization based on the log-determinant (log-det) function and M-matrices. This formulation offers improved accuracy and runtime performance due to smoother and better-behaved gradients [177]. This constraint is motivated by the fact that a matrix $\mathbf{W}$ represents a DAG iff it is nilpotent, which corresponds to the condition $h^s_{\text{ldet}}(\mathbf{W}) = 0$. The characterization function h^s_{ldet}: $\mathbb{W}^s \to \mathbb{R}$ is calculated as:

$$h^s_{\text{ldet}}(\mathbf{W}) = -logdet(sI - \mathbf{W} \circ \mathbf{W}) + d\log s \tag{6.52}$$

where $\mathbf{W}$ refers to the weighted adjacency matrix, $s > 0$ is a parameter in M-matrices, and d represents the number of variables.

Combining the Equations 6.50–6.52, the optimization problem defined in DAGMA-DCE is as follows.

$$\min_\theta \text{MSE}(\mathcal{M}_\theta; \mathcal{D}) + \lambda_1 g(\mathcal{M}_\theta)$$

$$\text{s.t.} h^s_{\text{ldet}}(\mathbf{W}) = 0 \tag{6.53}$$

where MSE(·) denotes the calculation of mean square errors, and λ_1 is the coefficient of the regularizer $g(\mathcal{M}_\theta)$.

6.5.2.2 Bagging DAGMA-DCE

Figure 6.10 showcases the Bagging DAGMA-DCE algorithm, especially the split-and-ensemble procedure. The split-and-ensemble approach mitigates the negative effects of the noise in the datasets and accelerates computation by employing parallel processing, as each base learner operates on a smaller subset of data [181].

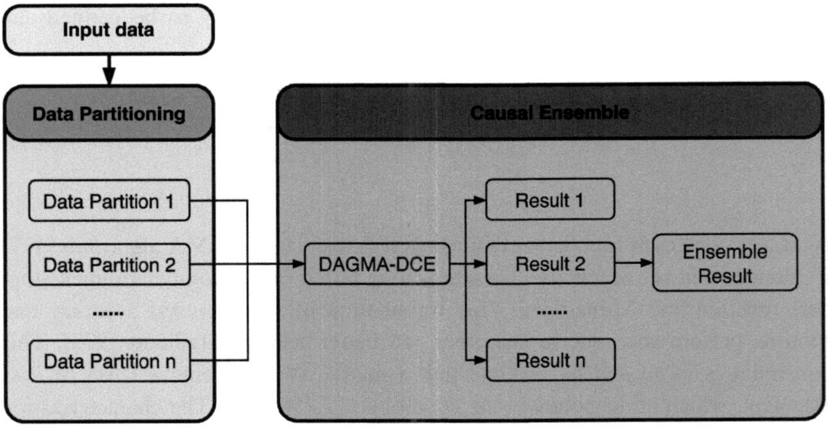

Fig. 6.10 The split-and-ensemble procedure of the Bagging DAGMA-DCE algorithm. The "Data Partitioning" stage represents the split component, while the "Causal Ensemble" stage corresponds to the ensemble component

In the data partitioning stage, the input dataset S is split into K partitions $S^1, \ldots, S^K$ following the rule shown in Equation 6.54.

$$S^i = S^i_{\text{fix}} + S^i_{\text{rand}} \quad i = 1, \ldots, K \tag{6.54}$$

where S^i denotes the i-th subset, consisting of the fixed partition S^i_{fix} and the random partition S^i_{rand}. S^i_{fix} ensures that each data point is utilized at least once by base learners, while S^i_{rand} enhances the robustness of the ensemble procedure by ensuring that several data points are included multiple times at random. S^i_{fix} represents the average assignment of all data points across the base learners. For instance, if the dataset S with N data points $\{d_1, \ldots, d_N\}$ is split into K partitions, S^1_{fix} is set as $\left\{d_1, \ldots, d_{\left\lfloor \frac{N}{K} \right\rfloor}\right\}$ and S^2_{fix} is set as $\left\{d_{\left\lfloor \frac{N}{K} \right\rfloor+1}, \ldots, d_{\left\lfloor \frac{2N}{K} \right\rfloor}\right\}$, where $\lfloor\cdot\rfloor$ denotes the floor function, rounding a real number down to the nearest integer. S^i_{rand} is the set of data points picked without replacement from the dataset S/S^i_{fix}. The number of elements in S^i_{rand} depends on the task requirements.

Each subset S^i is trained by the DAGMA-DCE algorithm [178] separately and in parallel, whose principle has been introduced in Sect. 6.5.2.1. The outputs are K weighted adjacency matrices $W^1, \ldots, W^K$ associated with the K subsets, the value of the element $W^m_{i,j}$ denotes the strength of the variable i causes the variable j in subset m. Afterward, the K matrices whose sizes are all $n \times n$ are ensembled through a rule-based ensemble strategy. The developed rule-based ensemble approach is more accurate than majority voting, which is proved by experiments in Sect. 6.5.3. In this step, the K weighted adjacency matrices are ensembled into one matrix WE based on three rules as follows. To determine the element $WE_{i,j}(i, j = 1, \ldots, n)$, the set $V_{i,j} = \left\{W^1_{i,j}, \ldots, W^K_{i,j}\right\}$ is defined to represent values from all base learners in the same position, and $z_{i,j}$ is denoted as the number of zero elements in $V_{i,j}$. Four ensemble rules are developed to combine the K base-learner result. The formal definition is as follows. Rules 1 and 2 implement enhanced majority-voting strategies, whereas Rules 3 and 4 utilize rule-based ensemble methods. The parameters α_1, β_1, α_2 and β_2 are flexibly selected in experiments to optimize system performance. Additionally, Rules 3 and 4 can be repeatedly applied in implementation by further subdividing the range of $z_{i,j}$, thus enabling finer granularity and increased adaptability. For example, the range of $z_{i,j}$ can be partitioned into two segments: $[0.4K, 0.5K)$ and $[0.5K, 0.6K]$, and each of these subgroups can then independently apply Rules 3 and 4.

- **Rule 1:** *When* $z_{i,j} > 0.6K$, *set* $WE_{i,j}$ *at* 0.
- **Rule 2:** *When* $z_{i,j} < 0.4K$, *set* $WE_{i,j}$ *at* $(\sum_{t=1}^{K} W^t_{i,j})/(K - z_{i,j})$.
- **Rule 3:** *When* $0.4K \leq z_{i,j} \leq 0.6K$, *set* $WE_{i,j}$ *at* 0 *if* $z_{i,j} = \alpha_1$ *and* $(\sum_{t=1}^{K} W^t_{i,j})/(K - z_{i,j}) \leq \beta_1$.
- **Rule 4:** *When* $0.4K \leq z_{i,j} \leq 0.6K$, *set* $WE_{i,j}$ *at* $(\sum_{t=1}^{K} W^t_{i,j})/(K - z_{i,j})$ *if* $z_{i,j} = \alpha_2$ *and* $(\sum_{t=1}^{K} W^t_{i,j})/(K - z_{i,j}) \geq \beta_2$.

The developed rule-based ensemble strategy outperforms majority voting due to its flexibility and adaptability. Rules 1 and 2 improve accuracy by assigning different weights to individual votes. Rules 3 and 4 allow finer control and capture complex decision boundaries more flexibly and efficiently than traditional majority voting.

6.5.3 Empirical Evaluation of Static Causal Discovery

In this section, several experiments are performed to compare the proposed ensemble DAGMA-DCE algorithm to the DAGMA-DCE, DAGMA, and NOTEARS algorithms. The proposed rule ensemble strategy is also compared to majority voting. The synthetic datasets are designed to emulate the uncertainty and complexity of real-world scenarios. They include both linear and nonlinear SEMs with varying degrees of sparsity and density in the causal graphs, ensuring the evaluation spans a wide range of structural complexities representative of real-world causal relationships. Furthermore, to simulate real-world conditions, the datasets incorporate noise at varying levels, including both Gaussian and non-Gaussian distributions. This design enables a thorough assessment to evaluate the robustness of the proposed algorithm under diverse conditions of uncertainty and variability.

Section 6.5.3.1 introduces the details of parameter settings, synthetic datasets, and evaluation metrics. Section 6.5.3.2 discusses the experimental results.

6.5.3.1 Experimental Settings

In the following experiments, both linear and nonlinear SEMs are generated to create synthetic datasets. These settings are commonly used in tests of DAG-learning algorithms [174, 177, 178]. The linear SEMs incorporate mixture noises, including Gaussian, exponential, Gumbel, uniform, and binomial noises, to simulate complex linear systems. The nonlinear SEMs are modeled using a multilayer perceptron with similar mixture noises. The causal graphs are simulated through scale-free graph models, where “SF1” represents sparse graphs with an expected d edges for d nodes, and “ER4” represents dense graphs with an expected $4d$ edges. d is chosen from $\{20, 30, 40, 50, 60\}$. Crucially, all weights are sampled from $U((-1.1, -0.1) \cup (0.1, 1.1))$. All datasets contain 2,000 data instances.

All hyperparameters in NOTEARS, DAGMA, and DAGMA-DCE follow the default setting in [174, 177, 178]. The Bagging DAGMA-DCE involves DAGMA-DCE-EN (naïve ensemble, or majority voting) and DAGMA-DCE-ER (rule-based ensemble, the proposed method). The baser learners in both ensemble algorithms follow the settings in DAGMA-DCE. The experiments consist of two parts. The first part involves comparison experiments that evaluate the accuracy of the five algorithms mentioned. The second part focuses on parameter-tuning experiments, examining the impact of varying the number of base learners and the subset length for each base learner on performance. d is set to 50 in this part, since the real-world dataset in the case study contains 50 features. In the comparison experiments, the number of base learners is set at 5, with each subset containing 500 instances. Thresholds are determined by Rules 3 and 4, defined in Sect. 6.5.2.2. When $\alpha_1, \alpha_2 = 2$, we set $\beta_1, \beta_2 = 0.45$. When $\alpha_1, \alpha_2 = 3$, we set $\beta_1, \beta_2 = 0.7$. In the parameter-tuning experiments, the number of base learners is initially set to 5, while the subset size varies to 500, 800, 1,100, and 1,400 instances. Since 800 instances yield the best performance, the subset size is then fixed at 800, and the number of base learners is set at 5, 10, and 15, respectively. The threshold settings are illustrated in Table 6.15.

Table 6.15 Thresholds of rule-based ensemble strategy for the Bagging DAGMA-DCE algorithm

Number of base learners: 5		
No.	α_1, α_2	β_1, β_2
5.1	2	0.45
5.2	3	0.7
Number of base learners: 10		
No.	α_1, α_2	β_1, β_2
10.1	4	0.4
10.2	5	0.5
10.3	6	0.7
Number of base learners: 15		
No.	α_1, α_2	β_1, β_2
15.1	7	0.4
15.2	8	0.65

The evaluation metrics for assessing results in causal discovery experiments are the structural Hamming distance (SHD) and the false discovery rate (FDR). SHD calculates the number of incorrect edges in a learned DAG as shown in Equation 6.55, and FDR measures the metric to control the expected proportion of false positives among all discoveries, as demonstrated in Equation 6.56. Lower scores for both SHD and FDR indicate better performance.

$$SHD(\mathcal{G}, \mathcal{G}_0) = Additions + Deletions + Reversals \tag{6.55}$$

where $\mathcal{G}$ denotes the learned DAG, $\mathcal{G}_0$ is the ground truth, *Additions* counts the edges that are present in $\mathcal{G}$ but not in $\mathcal{G}_0$, *Deletions* stands for the edges that are present in $\mathcal{G}_0$ but not in $\mathcal{G}$, and *Reversals* represents the edges that are present in both $\mathcal{G}$ and $\mathcal{G}_0$, but with opposite directions.

$$FDR = \frac{FP}{FP + TP} \tag{6.56}$$

where *FP* stands for the number of false positives, and *TP* represents the number of true positives.

All experiments are run on an *NVIDIA GeForce RTX 3060* GPU, and the programming environment is Python (*version 3.11.7*).

6.5.3.2 Experimental Results and Discussions

Comparative Evaluation

The results show that the Bagging DAGMA-DCE with the rule-based ensemble approach achieves state of the art in most experiments. Figure 6.11 shows the SHD and FDR of experiments on linear SEMs, and Fig. 6.12 illustrates results on nonlinear experiments. Figure 6.13 demonstrates that the split-and-ensemble approach improves computational efficiency compared to the original DAGMA-DCE algorithm.

In Fig. 6.11, the proposed DAGMA-DCE-ER achieves the best FDR score in all experiments on the SF1 datasets. Additionally, it demonstrates a comparable SHD score to DAGMA and DAGMA-DCE-EN on the same datasets. On the SF4 datasets, DAGMA-DCE-ER performs similarly to DAGMA in both FDR and SHD across node counts from 20 to 50. Across all experiments, DAGMA-DCE-ER outperforms DAGMA-DCE-EN, highlighting the superiority of the rule-based ensemble method over majority voting.

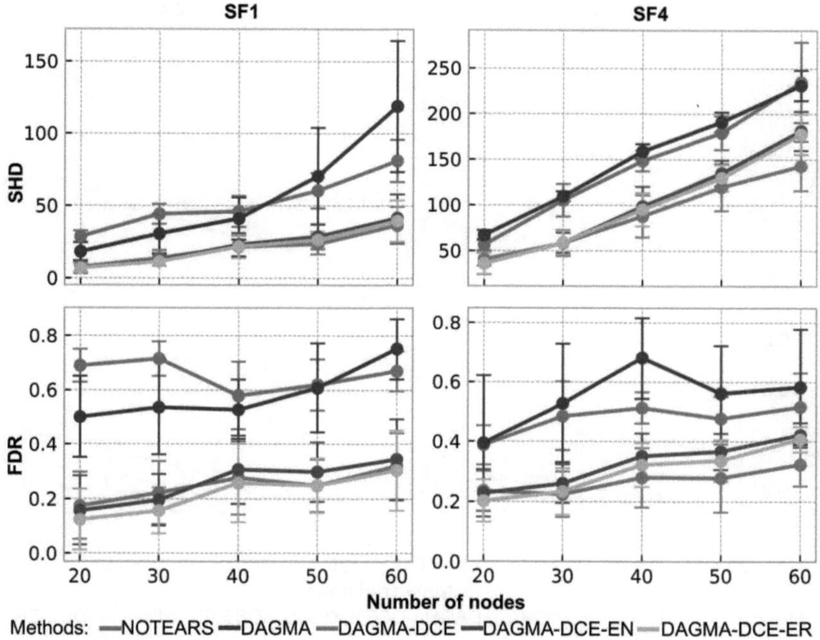

Fig. 6.11 Experiments on linear SEMs for static causal discovery. It includes results for SHD (top) and FDR (bottom) for synthetic datasets generated by the SF1 (left) and SF4 (right) models, as detailed in Sect. 4.1. X-axes denote the number of nodes of DAGs. Five lines stand for the methods shown in the legend, respectively, and error bars represent the standard deviation of repetitions

Figure 6.12 indicates that DAGMA-DCE-ER consistently achieves the best score in all experiments on the SF1 datasets. On the SF4 datasets, DAGMA-DCE-ER demonstrates superior FDR performance when the number of nodes ranges from 20 to 50, while achieving similar scores to DAGMA and DAGMA-DCE-EN in other experiments on the same datasets. In all experiments, except for the SHD score on the SF4 data, DAGMA-DCE-ER outperforms DAGMA-DCE-EN, underscoring the superiority of the rule-based ensemble method over majority voting.

The experimental results indicate that the proposed DAGMA-DCE-ER achieves SotA performance in most cases and performs comparably to the state of the art in others. Additionally, each base learner is trained on only 25%

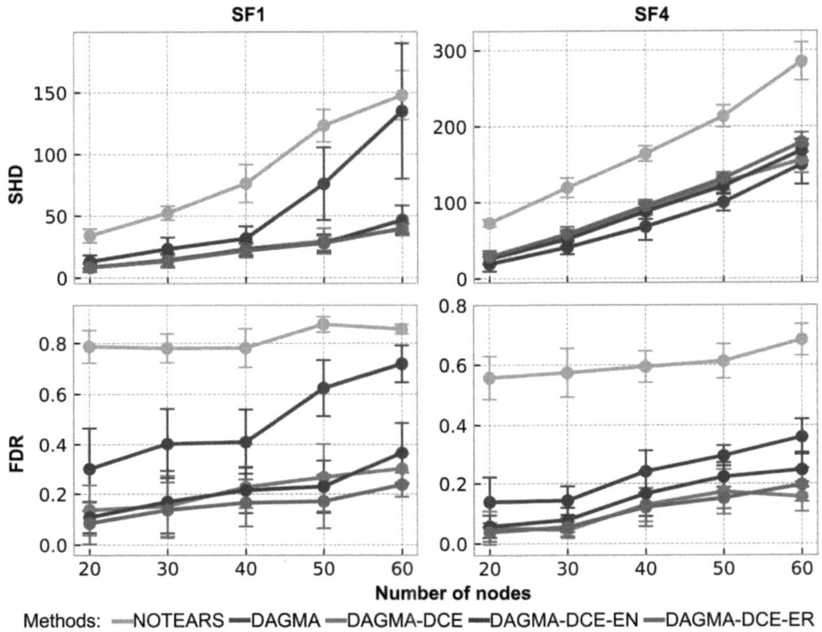

Fig. 6.12 Experiments on Nonlinear SEMs for static causal discovery. It includes results for SHD (top) and FDR (bottom) on synthetic datasets generated by the SF1 (left) and SF4 (right) models. X-axes denote the number of nodes of DAGs. Five lines stand for the methods shown in the legend, respectively, and error bars represent the standard deviation of repetitions

of randomly selected data instances from the entire dataset, suggesting that DAGMA-DCE-ER can run significantly faster than DAGMA-DCE when utilizing parallel computing. Furthermore, DAGMA-DCE-ER outperforms DAGMA-DCE-EN in most experiments, highlighting the superiority of the rule-based ensemble method over majority voting.

Figure 6.13 illustrates the computational time for synthetic dataset experiments, demonstrating that the split-and-ensemble method significantly reduces the computational time of DAGMA-DCE. The results show that DAGMA-DCE-EN and DAGMA-DCE-ER exhibit nearly identical computational times, as they share the same base learner and parameter settings. Additionally, the short error bars indicate that all algorithms perform consistently across multiple experiments, highlighting their stability.

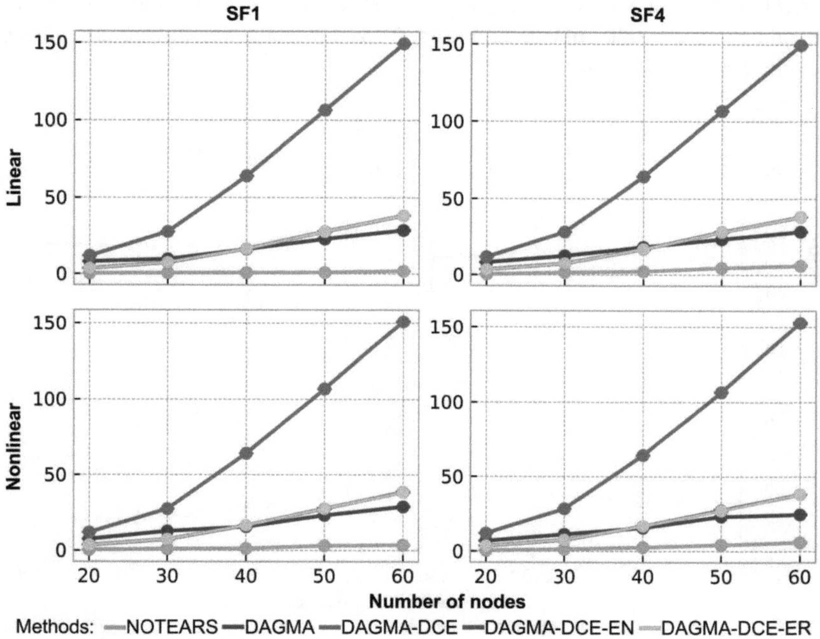

Fig. 6.13 Computational time of all experiments for static causal discovery. It includes results of linear (top) and nonlinear (bottom) synthetic datasets generated from SF1 (left) and SF4 (right) models. X-axes denote the number of nodes of DAGs. Five lines stand for the methods shown in the legend, respectively, and error bars represent the standard deviation of repetitions

The experimental results in Figs. 6.11–6.13 demonstrate the notable performance of the proposed Bagging DAGMA-DCE algorithm compared to SotA causal inference methods based on the evaluation metrics SHD and FDR. The rule-based ensemble strategy effectively mitigates noise, improves accuracy, and increases computation speed.

Sensitivity Analysis of Bagging Parameters

In the following experiments, the number of data instances and base learners is optimized by fixing the number of nodes to 50, matching the 50 features present in the real-world data used in the case study. Initially, the number of data instances is tested at 500, 800, 1,100, and 1,400. As shown in Fig. 6.6.14, 800 data instances yield the optimal result. Subsequently, the number of data instances is held constant at 800 while varying the number of base learners to values of 5, 10, and 15. The results, illustrated in Fig. 6.15, indicate no significant differences among these configurations.

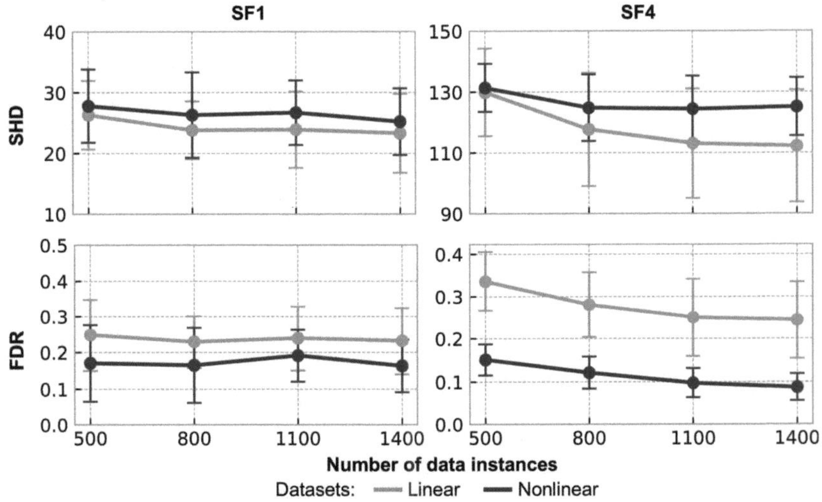

Fig. 6.14 Experiments on the selection of the number of data instances on the Bagging DAGMA-DCE algorithm. It includes results for SHD (top) and FDR (bottom) on synthetic datasets generated by the SF1 (left) and SF4 (right) models. The number of nodes is fixed at 50. X-axes denote the number of data instances. Two lines represent results on linear and nonlinear datasets, as shown in the legend, and error bars indicate the standard deviation of repetitions

Figure 6.14 shows that accuracy generally increases with the number of data instances, except for the FDR of the SF1 dataset at 1,100 instances. Both SHD and FDR decrease sharply between 500 and 800 instances, after which improvement becomes marginal. Considering the computational cost associated with larger sample sizes, 800 instances represent the optimal balance between accuracy and efficiency.

Figure 6.15 shows no significant improvement in accuracy with an increasing number of base learners. Given that a larger number of base learners increases computational time, setting it to 5 is recommended.

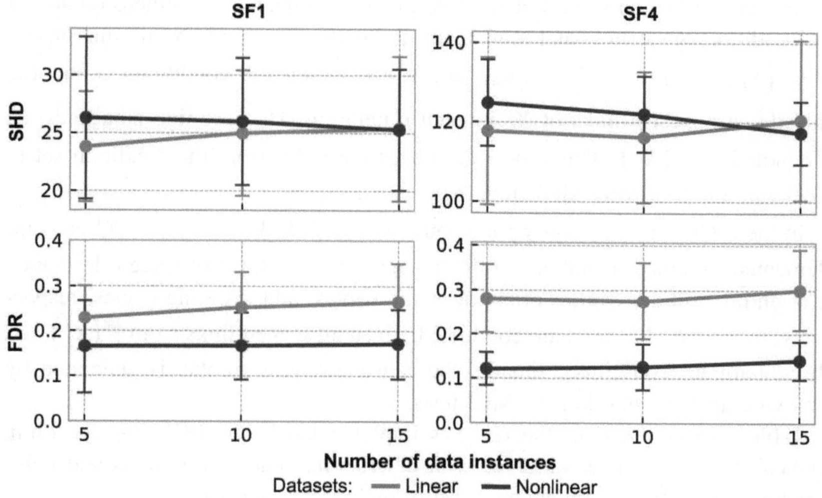

Fig. 6.15 Experiments on the selection of the number of base learners on the Bagging DAGMA-DCE algorithm. It includes results for SHD (top) and FDR (bottom) on synthetic datasets generated by the SF1 (left) and SF4 (right) models. The number of nodes is fixed at 50. X-axes denote the number of base learners. Two lines represent results on linear and nonlinear datasets, as shown in the legend, and error bars indicate the standard deviation of repetitions

6.5.4 Time-Series Causal Discovery Using Integrated PCMCI+

The PCMCI algorithm [197] quantifies causal relationships in large-scale nonlinear time-series data using CI tests, and its extension, PCMCI+ [198] includes the discovery of instantaneous (contemporaneous) relationships to improve the reliability of causal detection. Compared to generic PC/FCI-style approaches, PCMCI+ [198] optimizes conditioning sets and employs momentary conditional independence (MCI) tests, thereby improving recall and reducing false positives in the presence of strong autocorrelation, a common feature of real-world time series. Therefore, this study adopts PCMCI+ as the time-series causal discovery algorithm due to its superior performance in complex nonlinear systems and its unique optimization of instantaneous links.

The PCMCI+ algorithm comprises two main steps: condition selection using the PC algorithm and MCI testing. In the first stage, the goal of the PC phase is to remove conditions on irrelevant variables, thereby reducing the dimensionality of the conditioning sets for MCI tests. Considering the time series **X**, all time-lagged pairs $\left(X_{t-\tau}^{i}, X_{t}^{j}\right), \tau = 1, \ldots, \tau_{\max}$ are tested, given the conditions containing only the strongest p links of X_t^j in each p-iteration. The resulting adjacency set is denoted as $\hat{\mathcal{P}}\left(X_t^j\right)$. This process removes the noise from the condition set to accelerate the following MCI step.

In the MCI step, the contemporaneous links $\left(X_t^i, X_t^j\right)$ for all $X_t^i \neq X_t^j$ are supplemented, and the orientations of the linkage are determined by three rules aimed at orienting collider triples, orienting chain triples, and avoiding cycles, respectively. Next, the MCI tests are conducted, given all lagged links from $\hat{\mathcal{P}}\left(X_t^j\right)$ and all contemporaneous links. Finally, the causal strength graphic is generated by removing all links that fail the MCI tests.

Table 6.16 summarizes the CI tests implemented in the PCMCI+ algorithm, applicable to continuous variables with diverse marginal distributions and noise structures, as is frequently encountered in real-world datasets.

Table 6.16 Assumptions and applicability for different CI tests in the PCMCI+ algorithm [293]

No.	CI test	Assumptions and applicability
1	RobustParCorr	Suitable for univariate, continuous variables with linear relationships, robust to varying marginal distributions
2	ParCorrWLS	Suitable for univariate, continuous variables with linear relationships, can handle heteroskedasticity using weighted least squares
3	GPDC	Suitable for univariate, continuous variables with additive (including nonlinear) dependencies
4	CMIknn	Suitable for multivariate, continuous variables with more general dependencies via a permutation-based test

The experiments presented in Sect. 6.5.5 demonstrates that, in complex systems, PCMCI+ combined with CMIknn outperforms the other three CI tests in both SHD and FDR, achieving an FDR close to zero. However, despite its low FDR, this method still fails to identify certain true causal links. In contrast, the other three CI tests, although they yield more false positives, detect more causal relationships overall. To enhance the overall accuracy of PCMCI+, a hybrid approach integrating all four CI tests is designed.

This integration methodology is designed to enhance the accuracy of causal discovery by supplementing PCMCI+results with the CMIknn test, while preserving its low FDR. The approach begins by computing four causal adjacency matrices using the four distinct CI tests listed in Table 6.16. These matrices are denoted as $\mathbf{W}_i$, where $i = 1,2,3,4$, corresponding to the order of CI tests in Table 6.16. The final integrated causal matrix $\mathbf{W}_{hybrid}$ is obtained through the following set-based operation:

$$\mathbf{W}_{hybrid} = (\mathbf{W}_1 \cap \mathbf{W}_2 \cap \mathbf{W}_3) \cup \mathbf{W}_4 \tag{6.57}$$

This formulation retains the high-confidence causal links agreed upon by the first three tests while incorporating additional links identified by the fourth test (CMIknn), which is known for its low FDR. $\mathbf{W}_{hybrid}$ is further refined by resolving bidirectional links. Specifically, if both $X^i \rightarrow X^j$ and $X^j \rightarrow X^i$ are present, the direction included in $\mathbf{W}_4$ is retained, and the other is removed. The result is a balanced integration that improves overall detection of true causal relationships without substantially increasing false positives. The effectiveness of this approach is evaluated and discussed in detail in Sect. 6.5.5.

6.5.5 Empirical Evaluation of Time-Series Causal Discovery

In this section, several experiments are conducted to compare the proposed integrated PCMCI+ method with four baseline PCMCI+variants, each using a different CI test as listed in Table 6.16. Afterward, an ablation study is designed to assess the necessity of incorporating all three causal matrices $\mathbf{W}_1$, $\mathbf{W}_2$ and $\mathbf{W}_3$ in the integration scheme. To ensure that the evaluation reflects the uncertainty and complexity typical of real-world scenarios, synthetic datasets are carefully constructed. They include both linear and nonlinear SEMs with varying time lags, capturing a broad spectrum of causal structures. Furthermore, to simulate real-world conditions, the datasets incorporate noise at varying levels, including both Gaussian and non-Gaussian distributions. This design enables a thorough assessment to evaluate the robustness of the proposed algorithm under diverse conditions of uncertainty and variability.

Section 6.5.5.1 introduces the synthetic datasets and experimental settings, and Sect. 6.5.5.2 discusses the experimental results.

6.5.5.1 Synthetic Datasets Description and Experimental Settings

In the following experiments, both linear and nonlinear SEMs are generated to create synthetic datasets. These settings are commonly used in tests of time-series causal inference algorithms [181, 294, 295]. To emulate the characteristics of complex time-dependent systems, the SEMs incorporate mixture noises, including Gaussian, uniform, and Weibull noises. Three distinct causal structures are designed as presented in Equations 6.58–6.60, where ϵ refers to random noises. For each causal structure, three datasets with distinct numbers of observations are generated: 500, 2,000, and 5,000, respectively.

The first causal structure, defined in Equation 6.58, corresponds to three datasets: DS11 (500 observations), DS12 (2,000 observations), and DS13 (5,000 observations). Variables X^1 and X^2 are root variables and independent of each other. X^3, X^4 and X^5 are computed based on Equation 6.58.

$$\begin{cases} X_t^1 = 0.9X_{t-1}^1 + \epsilon_{11} \\ X_t^2 = \sin 0.1t + \epsilon_{12} \\ X_t^3 = 0.78X_{t-1}^1 + 0.84X_{t-4}^2 + \epsilon_{13} \\ X_t^4 = 0.2\left(X_{t-1}^1\right)^2 + 0.62X_{t-2}^1 + \epsilon_{14} \\ X_t^5 = 1.86\exp\left(0.15X_{t-1}^3\right) + \epsilon_{15} \\ X_t^6 = 1.28\sin\left(X_{t-2}^2\right) + 0.55X_t^4X_{t-3}^2 + \epsilon_{16} \end{cases} \tag{6.58}$$

The second causal structure, defined in Equation 6.59, corresponds to three datasets: DS21 (500 observations), DS22 (2,000 observations), and DS23 (5,000 observations). Variables X^1–X^4 are root variables and independent of each other. X^5–X^9 are computed based on Equation 6.59.

$$\begin{cases} X_t^1 = 0.94X_{t-1}^1 + \epsilon_{21} \\ X_t^2 = \cos 0.06t + \epsilon_{22} \\ X_t^3 = 0.88X_{t-1}^3 + \epsilon_{23} \\ X_t^4 = \sin 0.2t + \epsilon_{24} \\ X_t^5 = 0.64X_{t-1}^1 - 0.23X_{t-3}^3 X_{t-2}^1 + \epsilon_{25} \\ X_t^6 = 0.49\left(X_{t-1}^2\right)^2 + \epsilon_{26} \\ X_t^7 = 1.01\sin(0.8X_{t-2}^5) + 0.35X_{t-1}^3 + \epsilon_{27} \\ X_t^8 = 0.88X_{t-1}^3 X_{t-1}^4 + 0.78X_{t-2}^3 X_t^4 + \epsilon_{28} \\ X_t^9 = 0.75X_{t-4}^5 + 0.75\cos X_{t-1}^6 + 0.35X_{t-1}^7 + \epsilon_{29} \end{cases} \tag{6.59}$$

The third causal structure, defined in Equation 6.60, corresponds to three datasets: DS31 (500 observations), DS32 (2,000 observations), and DS33 (5,000 observations). Variables X^1–X^3 are root variables and independent of each other. X^4–X^{12} are computed based on Equation 6.60.

$$\begin{cases} X_t^1 = 0.9X_{t-1}^1 + \epsilon_{31} \\ X_t^2 = \cos 0.07t + \epsilon_{32} \\ X_t^3 = 0.85X_{t-1}^3 + \epsilon_{33} \\ X_t^4 = 0.57X_{t-1}^1 + 0.76X_{t-2}^2 + \epsilon_{34} \\ X_t^5 = X_{t-1}^1 X_{t-1}^3 + 0.45X_t^1 + \epsilon_{35} \\ X_t^6 = 1.2\exp(0.3X_{t-1}^3) + \epsilon_{36} \\ X_t^7 = 0.96\sin(X_{t-1}^4) + 0.44X_{t-2}^6 X_{t-1}^4 + \epsilon_{37} \\ X_t^8 = 0.02\left(X_{t-1}^5\right)^2 + 0.015\left(X_{t-2}^5\right)^2 + \epsilon_{38} \\ X_t^9 = 0.68X_{t-4}^3 + 0.56\cos(X_{t-1}^7)X_{t-1}^7 + \epsilon_{39} \\ X_t^{10} = 0.78X_{t-1}^7 + 0.95X_{t-2}^8 + 0.45X_{t-1}^7 X_{t-2}^8 + \epsilon_{310} \\ X_t^{11} = \exp(0.35X_{t-1}^9) + 0.4X_t^9 + \epsilon_{311} \\ X_t^{12} = 1.2\sin(X_{t-1}^9) + 0.8X_{t-1}^{11} + 0.6X_{t-3}^8 + \epsilon_{312} \end{cases} \tag{6.60}$$

In the first experiment, the proposed integration method, PCMCI+_hybrid, is evaluated in comparison to four individual CI test variants of PCMCI+: PCMCI+_rpc, PCMCI+_pcw, PCMCI+_gpdc, and PCMCI+_cmiknn, following the order presented in Table 6.16. The evaluation consists of two parts: (1) considering only the presence of causal links, and (2) considering causal links along with their time delays. In the first case, only the existence of a causal relationship between variables (e.g.$X^i \rightarrow X^j$), is assessed, regardless of the lag. In the second case, lag-specific causal links (e.g., $X^i_{t-1} \rightarrow X^j_t$ and$X^i_{t-2} \rightarrow X^j_t$) are treated as distinct. The evaluation metrics used are SHD and FDR.

Next, in the second experiment, the ablation study is conducted to evaluate the effectiveness of the integration method in Equation 6.57. All possible combinations of the causal matrices $\mathbf{W}_1, \mathbf{W}_2$ and $\mathbf{W}_3$ are systematically tested. Table 6.17 summarizes the six experimental configurations used in this analysis. The evaluation procedure and metrics are the same as in the first experiment.

Table 6.17 Explanation of experimental configurations in the ablation study of the Integrated PCMCI+ algorithm

No.	Name	Explanation
1 (default)	PCMCI+_hybrid	$(\mathbf{W}_1 \cap \mathbf{W}_2 \cap \mathbf{W}_3) \cup \mathbf{W}_4$
2	PCMCI+_hybrid-1	$(\mathbf{W}_2 \cap \mathbf{W}_3) \cup \mathbf{W}_4$
3	PCMCI+_hybrid-2	$(\mathbf{W}_1 \cap \mathbf{W}_3) \cup \mathbf{W}_4$
4	PCMCI+_hybrid-3	$(\mathbf{W}_1 \cap \mathbf{W}_2) \cup \mathbf{W}_4$
5	PCMCI+_hybrid-12	$\mathbf{W}_3 \cup \mathbf{W}_4$
6	PCMCI+_hybrid-23	$\mathbf{W}_1 \cup \mathbf{W}_4$
7	PCMCI+_hybrid-13	$\mathbf{W}_2 \cup \mathbf{W}_4$

6.5.5.2 Results and Discussion

Tables 6.18–6.21 present the results of the comparative evaluation. Tables 6.18 and 6.19 showcase the SHD and FDR of the presence of causal links. Across all nine datasets, PCMCI+_hybrid achieves the lowest or equal-lowest SHD, as shown in Table 6.18. This indicates that the hybrid integration adds correct edges without introducing structural noise. The FDR results in Table 6.19 complement this observation. PCMCI+_hybrid ties the CMIknn variant at 0 % FDR across eight datasets and never exceeds 0.14, confirming that the additional edges are statistically trustworthy.

Tables 6.20 and 6.21 present the SHD and FDR of the causal links with time delay. When lags are distinguished, the integrated method again achieves the lowest SHD in all nine datasets. The FDR profile is similar to that observed for link presence, confirming that no additional false positives are introduced.

Tables 6.22–6.25 present the results of the ablation study, which evaluates seven variants obtained by selectively removing one or two of the consensus matrices $\mathbf{W}_1$, $\mathbf{W}_2$ and $\mathbf{W}_3$ while always retaining the low-FDR matrix $\mathbf{W}_4$. Tables 6.22 and 6.23 showcase the SHD and FDR of the presence of causal links.

Table 6.18 SHD of the presence of causal links in comparative evaluation for time-series causal discovery

Alg.	DS11	DS12	DS13	DS21	DS22	DS23	DS31	DS32	DS33
PCMCI+_rpc	4	6	4	6	8	9	11	13	19
PCMCI+_pcw	4	4	4	6	4	7	8	13	20
PCMCI+_gpdc	2	2	0	2	3	1	3	4	1
PCMCI+_cmiknn	1	1	0	1	0	0	3	2	2
PCMCI+_hybrid	1	0	0	0	0	0	3	1	1

Table 6.19 FDR of the presence of causal links in comparative evaluation for time-series causal discovery

Alg.	DS11	DS12	DS13	DS21	DS22	DS23	DS31	DS32	DS33
PCMCI+_rpc	0.44	0.50	0.38	0.30	0.42	0.46	0.39	0.44	0.56
PCMCI+_pcw	0.38	0.38	0.38	0.33	0.2	0.33	0.28	0.44	0.57
PCMCI+_gpdc	0.17	0.25	0.0	0.10	0.23	0.0	0.0	0.17	0.0
PCMCI+_cmiknn	0.14	0.0	0.0	0.0	0.0	0.0	0.0	0.0	0.0
PCMCI+_hybrid	0.14	0.0	0.0	0.0	0.0	0.0	0.0	0.0	0.0

Table 6.20 SHD of causal links with time delay in comparative evaluation for time-series causal discovery

Alg.	DS11	DS12	DS13	DS21	DS22	DS23	DS31	DS32	DS33
PCMCI+_rpc	7	9	6	9	14	15	15	20	31
PCMCI+_pcw	6	6	4	12	10	16	13	24	32
PCMCI+_gpdc	3	3	0	5	4	5	5	8	2
PCMCI+_cmiknn	1	1	0	3	3	1	4	3	3
PCMCI+_hybrid	1	0	0	2	3	1	4	2	2

Across all nine datasets, the complete PCMCI+_hybrid configuration attains the minimum SHD; in no case is it outperformed by any ablated variant. Its median SHD is 0, whereas the best competitor (-1 or -2) rises to a median of 1, and variants excluding $\mathbf{W}_3$ (-3, -23, -13) deteriorate sharply. A similar pattern holds for FDR: PCMCI+_hybrid maintains an FDR of 0% on eight datasets and never exceeds 14%, while the worst ablated setting (-23) reaches 50% on DS33.

Table 6.21 FDR of causal links with time delay in comparative evaluation for time-series causal discovery

Alg.	DS11	DS12	DS13	DS21	DS22	DS23	DS31	DS32	DS33
PCMCI+_rpc	0.46	0.53	0.42	0.33	0.53	0.56	0.42	0.52	0.66
PCMCI+_pcw	0.40	0.40	0.30	0.45	0.40	0.60	0.35	0.58	0.66
PCMCI+_gpdc	0.22	0.27	0.0	0.10	0.20	0.10	0.0	0.24	0.0
PCMCI+_cmiknn	0.11	0.0	0.0	0.0	0.0	0.0	0.0	0.0	0.0
PCMCI+_hybrid	0.11	0.0	0.0	0.0	0.0	0.0	0.0	0.0	0.0

Table 6.22 SHD of the presence of causal links in the ablation study of the Integrated PCMCI+ algorithm

Alg.	DS11	DS12	DS13	DS21	DS22	DS23	DS31	DS32	DS33
PCMCI+_hybrid	1	0	0	0	0	0	3	1	1
PCMCI+_hybrid-1	1	1	0	0	0	0	3	2	1
PCMCI+_hybrid-2	1	1	0	0	0	0	3	1	1
PCMCI+_hybrid-3	1	0	1	0	2	1	4	4	7
PCMCI+_hybrid-12	1	2	1	1	2	0	3	4	1
PCMCI+_hybrid-23	3	4	3	1	4	4	6	12	13
PCMCI+_hybrid-13	3	2	1	2	2	2	7	11	16

Table 6.23 FDR of the presence of causal links in the ablation study of the Integrated PCMCI+ algorithm

Alg.	DS11	DS12	DS13	DS21	DS22	DS23	DS31	DS32	DS33
PCMCI+_hybrid	0.14	0.0	0.0	0.0	0.0	0.0	0.0	0.0	0.0
PCMCI+_hybrid-1	0.14	0.14	0.0	0.0	0.0	0.0	0.0	0.06	0.0
PCMCI+_hybrid-2	0.14	0.14	0.0	0.0	0.0	0.0	0.0	0.0	0.0
PCMCI+_hybrid-3	0.14	0.0	0.14	0.0	0.17	0.09	0.13	0.17	0.29
PCMCI+_hybrid-12	0.14	0.25	0.0	0.09	0.17	0.0	0.0	0.17	0.0
PCMCI+_hybrid-23	0.33	0.38	0.33	0.09	0.29	0.29	0.25	0.42	0.44
PCMCI+_hybrid-13	0.33	0.25	0.14	0.17	0.17	0.17	0.26	0.41	0.50

Tables 6.24 and 6.25 present the SHD and FDR of the causal links with time delay. The default method again dominates, achieving the lowest SHD across all nine datasets. Removing $\mathbf{W}_3$ inflates both SHD and FDR significantly, while excluding only $\mathbf{W}_1$ or $\mathbf{W}_2$ has milder effects but still yields consistent losses of several correctly identified edges and sporadic FDR increases.

Table 6.24 SHD of causal links with time delay in the ablation study of the Integrated PCMCI+ algorithm

Alg.	DS11	DS12	DS13	DS21	DS22	DS23	DS31	DS32	DS33
PCMCI+_hybrid	1	0	0	2	3	1	4	2	2
PCMCI+_hybrid-1	1	1	0	2	3	1	4	2	2
PCMCI+_hybrid-2	1	1	0	2	3	1	4	2	2
PCMCI+_hybrid-3	1	0	1	2	4	2	5	7	10
PCMCI+_hybrid-12	1	2	0	3	5	1	4	5	2
PCMCI+_hybrid-23	3	6	4	3	7	5	7	16	19
PCMCI+_hybrid-13	3	2	1	4	5	4	8	15	23

Table 6.25 FDR of causal links with time delay in the ablation study of the Integrated PCMCI+ algorithm

Alg.	DS11	DS12	DS13	DS21	DS22	DS23	DS31	DS32	DS33
PCMCI+_hybrid	0.11	0.0	0.0	0.0	0.0	0.0	0.0	0.0	0.0
PCMCI+_hybrid-1	0.11	0.11	0.0	0.0	0.0	0.0	0.0	0.0	0.0
PCMCI+_hybrid-2	0.11	0.11	0.0	0.0	0.0	0.0	0.0	0.0	0.0
PCMCI+_hybrid-3	0.11	0.0	0.11	0.0	0.09	0.08	0.11	0.23	0.32
PCMCI+_hybrid-12	0.11	0.20	0.0	0.08	0.17	0.0	0.0	0.15	0.0
PCMCI+_hybrid-23	0.27	0.42	0.33	0.08	0.29	0.25	0.23	0.45	0.50
PCMCI+_hybrid-13	0.27	0.20	0.11	0.15	0.17	0.20	0.24	0.44	0.55

The experiments verify that the PCMCI+_hybrid algorithm consistently delivers the lowest SHD while maintaining an effectively zero FDR. Its advantage is robust to changes in sample size, causal density, and temporal lag. The ablation results validate the design choice of intersecting $\mathbf{W}_1$, $\mathbf{W}_2$ and $\mathbf{W}_3$ before uniting with the low-FDR $\mathbf{W}_4$, omitting any component demonstrably degrades performance. The integration strategy simultaneously maximizes recall and minimizes the type-I error. Consequently, the hybrid formulation constitutes a SotA solution for causal discovery in noisy, nonlinear, and lagged time-series systems.

6.5.6 Evaluating Causal Graphs without Ground Truth

In real-world systems, true causal relationships are often unknown, leaving researchers without a definitive ground truth to evaluate inferred causality. Consequently, metrics that quantitatively assess the quality of a causal graph serve as valuable tools for validation prior to its application in downstream tasks. This paper employs the interpretable metrics developed in [202] to determine whether the DAG exhibits a statistically significant improvement in fit compared to a random model. This metric is based on sampling node permutations of the given graph and examines several of its properties using group theory and hypothesis testing. This approach has been evaluated on both simulated and real-world datasets from various domains under different noise levels in [202]. This permutation-based test [202] supplies the evaluation module for causal graphs when no ground truth is available. It complements the causal discovery algorithms in Sects. 6.5.2 and 6.5.4 by providing a principled, distribution-free yardstick for judging whether a proposed DAG merits further consideration.

The principle of this method is a statistical hypothesis test that can falsify a user-supplied causal graph by asking whether it is significantly more consistent with the data than a randomly permuted version of itself. It consists of three steps: (i) Count the graph's CI violations; (ii) Create a baseline by permuting node labels; (iii) Permutation test.

One common approach to evaluate a DAG using observed data is by means of statistical testing of independence relations implied by the estimated causal DAG $\widehat{\mathcal{G}}$. One of the standard assumptions in causal inference is the causal Markov condition, which is equivalently formulated as the local Markov condition (LMC) [199]. To test whether a distribution satisfies the LMC relative to a DAG, the study in [202] thus list the CIs entailed by the DAG via the graphical d-separation criterion [296] and test whether those are satisfied or violated by the distribution at hand.

Definition 6.4 (Parental Triples): For a certain DAG $\mathcal{G}$, we refer to the ordered triple $(i, j \in \mathrm{ND}_i^{\mathcal{G}} \setminus \mathrm{Pa}_i^{\mathcal{G}}, Z = \mathrm{Pa}_i^{\mathcal{G}})$ as a parental triple and denote the set of all such triples implied by $\mathcal{G}$ as $\mathrm{T}_{\mathrm{Pa}}^{\mathcal{G}}$, where $\mathrm{Pa}_i^{\mathcal{G}}$ refers to the set of all parents of $i \in \mathcal{G}$ ($\mathrm{Pa}_i^{\mathcal{G}} \in \varnothing$ iff j is a root node), and $\mathrm{ND}_i^{\mathcal{G}}$ denotes the set of all non-descendants of $i \in \mathcal{G}$.

According to the theory of LMC, every parental triple $(i, j, Z) \in \mathrm{T}_{\mathrm{Pa}}^{\mathcal{G}}$ implies the CI $\cdot$ $X_i \perp\!\!\!\perp_P X_j | Z$. Afterward, the notion of the violations of LMC is defined as follows.

Definition 6.5 (Violations of LMCs): $V_{\mathrm{LMC}}^{\hat{\mathcal{G}},\mathcal{D}}$ is denoted as the set of triples $(i, j, Z) \in \mathrm{T}_{\mathrm{Pa}}^{\mathcal{G}}$, for which (i, j) is an ordered pair, and LMC violations are observed on the data $\mathcal{D}$, i.e.

$$V_{\mathrm{LMC}}^{\hat{\mathcal{G}},\mathcal{D}} = \left\{(i, j, Z) \in \mathrm{T}_{\mathrm{Pa}}^{\mathcal{G}}: X_i \perp\!\!\!\perp_{\mathcal{D}} X_j \,|Z\right\} \tag{6.61}$$

Furthermore, the fraction of LMC violations is denoted as

$$\phi_{\mathrm{LMC}}^{\widehat{\mathcal{G}},\mathcal{D}} = \frac{\left|V_{\mathrm{LMC}}^{\widehat{\mathcal{G}},\mathcal{D}}\right|}{\left|\mathrm{T}_{\mathrm{Pa}}^{\widehat{\mathcal{G}}}\right|} \tag{6.62}$$

However, the metrics in Equations 6.61 and 6.62 are insufficient to measure the consistency of a DAG as the probability of type I errors remains unknown in practice [297]. Therefore, a baseline is derived to compare the number of LMC violations $V_{\mathrm{LMC}}^{\widehat{\mathcal{G}},\mathcal{D}}$ to [202].

The baseline is a random draw from a set of conditional independence statements, and the following is a set of requirements that a random draw from the baseline should satisfy.

- They should infer the same number m of conditional independences as the given graph $\widehat{\mathcal{G}}$.
- They should partition m into m_r conditional independences with conditioning sets of size r with the same numbers m_r as $\widehat{\mathcal{G}}$ does.
- Conditional independences inferred by draws from the baseline should be closed under the semi-graphoid axioms.

The first requirement ensures that the number of observed LMC violations on the baseline is comparable to those observed on $\widehat{\mathcal{G}}$. The second requirement ensures that type I and type II errors, when testing implied CIs on the baseline, are comparable to those on $\widehat{\mathcal{G}}$. Lastly, the third requirement ensures that the CI statements from the baseline do not imply additional CIs (which are not already in the set) via the semi-graphoid axioms.

To satisfy all the requirements, a baseline can be constructed by sampling node permutations of $\widehat{\mathcal{G}}$. More formally, let S_n stand for the set of permutations π on the vertices $\{1, \ldots n\}$ of $\mathcal{G}$, and $\sigma_\pi(\mathcal{G})$ denotes the graph for which the edge $i \rightarrow j$ exists iff $\pi(i) \rightarrow \pi(j)$. exists in $\mathcal{G}$ for any permutation $\pi \in S_n$. Due to the one-to-one correspondence between π and σ, $\sigma \in S_{\mathcal{G}}$ is referred to as one node-permutation of $\mathcal{G}$.

Next, the null hypothesis H_0 is designed to formalize the skepticism about whether the DAG $\hat{\mathcal{G}}$ captures any information about the true causal DAG $\mathcal{G}$. The hypothesis states:

Hypothesis H_0: The DAG $\hat{\mathcal{G}}$ is drawn uniformly at random from a distribution Q on the set of DAGs that remains invariant under permutations of nodes, that is $Q(\mathcal{G}) = Q(\sigma(\mathcal{G}))$ for all $\sigma \in S_{\mathcal{G}}$.

Based on the defined hypothesis, the number of violations $\left|V_{\mathrm{LMC}}^{\hat{\mathcal{G}},\mathcal{D}}\right|$ is defined as test statistics and the null is built via $\left|V_{\mathrm{LMC}}^{\sigma(\hat{\mathcal{G}}),\mathcal{D}}\right|$. The first evaluation metric is designed in Equation 6.63.

$$p_{LMC}^{\hat{G},\mathcal{D}} = \Pr(\left|V_{LMC}^{\sigma(\hat{\mathcal{G}}),\mathcal{D}}\right| < \left|V_{LMC}^{\mathcal{G},\mathcal{D}}\right|) \tag{6.63}$$

Afterward, $V_{TPa}^{\sigma(\hat{\mathcal{G}}),\hat{\mathcal{G}}}$ is defined as the set of all ordered triples that are parentally d-separated in $\sigma(\hat{\mathcal{G}})$ but not d-separated in $\hat{G}$. Then the second metric is designed in Equation 6.64.

$$p_{TPa}^{\hat{\mathcal{G}}} = \Pr(\left|V_{TPa}^{\sigma(\hat{\mathcal{G}}),\mathcal{G}}\right| < \left|V_{TPa}^{\mathcal{G},\hat{\mathcal{G}}}\right|) \tag{6.64}$$

The two proposed metrics are interpreted as follows [202]. p_{LMC} measures how the count of identified violations for $\hat{\mathcal{G}}$ compares to a baseline of node-permuted DAGs, while p_{TPa} stands for a measure of its falsifiability. By defining a threshold α for the p-values, these metrics help determine the significance of the results. If $p_{TPa}^{\hat{\mathcal{G}}} \leq \alpha$, this suggests that the independence entailed by $\hat{\mathcal{G}}$ are meaningful and that $\hat{\mathcal{G}}$ is falsifiable through testing its implied CIs. Furthermore, if $p_{TPa}^{\hat{\mathcal{G}}} \leq \alpha$ and $p_{LMC}^{\hat{\mathcal{G}},\mathcal{D}} \leq \alpha$, this indicates no evidence of CI violations against $\hat{\mathcal{G}}$, and that $\hat{\mathcal{G}}$ is significantly better than randomly generated DAGs in terms of preserving CIs.

6.5.7 Root Cause Analysis for Key Variables

Changes in empirical distributions across time, environments, or sub-populations are common in many real-world applications. To identify the root causes of specific variables, it is essential to understand the factors driving distribution changes, so as to take corrective action, update models, or design interventions. These drivers can be pinpointed in the causal mechanisms responsible for changes in the distribution. This study employs the method proposed in [201] to factorize the joint distribution into independent causal conditionals. Any shift in the joint or marginal distribution of a target variable can thus be attributed to changes in one or more of these causal conditionals. Specifically, the Shapley value [298] is utilized to manage the interdependence of changes in mechanisms, as the impact of altering one mechanism is influenced by which others have already been changed. This approach has been evaluated on both simulated and real-world datasets from various domains under different noise levels in [201].

This method is based on the theory of probabilistic causal models, which use probability to infer causal relationships between variables. The causal Markov assumption allows us to factorize the joint distribution $P_{\mathbf{X}}$ into causal mechanisms $P_{X_j|PA_j}$ at each node X_j. Each causal mechanism $P_{X_j|PA_j}$ remains invariant to interventions in other variables.

Based on the derivation and proof in [201], the KL divergence can be a measure that quantifies the change in the joint distribution, as it measures the "distance" between two probability distributions. The KL divergence from the joint distribution of the old causal mechanism $P_{\mathbf{X}}$ to that of the new one $\tilde{P}_{\mathbf{X}}$ is defined as follows [299]. Equation 6.65 shows the definition of the KL divergence and Equation 6.66 represents the application of KL divergence in this study.

$$KL(P\|Q) := \sum\nolimits_{x\in\mathfrak{X}} P(x)\log\left(\frac{P(x)}{Q(x)}\right) \tag{6.65}$$

where P and Q are two probability distributions of a discrete random variable defined on the same probability space $\mathfrak{X}$, and $KL(P\|Q)$ is their KL divergence.

$$KL\left(\tilde{P}_{\mathbf{X}}\|P_{\mathbf{X}}\right) = \sum\nolimits_{j=1}^{d} KL\left(\tilde{P}_{X_j|PA_j}\|P_{X_j|PA_j}\right) \tag{6.66}$$

The KL divergence is always non-negative. Therefore, the contribution of a node X_j to the change in the joint distribution, measured in terms of the KL divergence, cannot be negative. If the causal mechanism of a variable does not change, then its contribution will be zero.

Estimating the KL divergence in high dimensions is a challenging problem. In practice, it is often of interest to understand why the marginal distribution of a target variable changed, rather than the change in the joint distribution of all variables. In the following part, using a concept from game theory, the Shapley value [298], the study in [201] formalizes how to attribute changes in the marginal distribution of a target variable to each node in the causal graph. The attribution process involves replacing the causal mechanisms one at a time, considering all possible orders in which they could be replaced. For each ordering, the marginal distribution of the target variable is updated after each substitution, and the incremental effect attributable to each mechanism is recorded. These marginal contributions are then averaged over all possible permutations, resulting in a Shapley value for each mechanism that quantifies its overall contribution to the observed shift in the target distribution.

Based on the derivation and proof in [201], suppose that the marginal distribution of a target variable X_k changes from P_{X_k} to $\tilde{P}_{X_k}$, Shapley values of all variables will sum up to the KL divergence of the marginal distribution from P_{X_k} to $\tilde{P}_{X_k}$, i.e.

$$\sum\nolimits_{j=1}^{d} \phi_j(KL) = KL\left(\tilde{P}_{X_k} \| P_{X_k}\right) \tag{6.67}$$

where $\phi_j(KL)$ refers to the Shapley value contribution of X_j to the change in the marginal distribution of the target variable X_k.

To apply the attribution method to real-world data, a causal graph and its causal conditionals are required. Given two samples, for each node X_j, the causal condition $P_{X_j|PA_j}$ is estimated from the first sample and $\tilde{P}_{X_j|PA_j}$ is estimated from the second sample. Suppose that $P_{X_j|PA_j}$ can be expressed as a function $g(A)$ of the domain index A shown in Fig. 6.16. If the causal graph is induced by a functional causal model, then the quantities, such as functional models and noise levels, that may change over time or across domains can be written as functions of A. Under these assumptions, if the causal mechanism $P_{X_j|PA_j}$ remains consistent across various values of A, then conducting the conditional independence test $X_j \perp\!\!\!\perp A|PA_j$ is sufficient to identify any changes in $P_{X_j|PA_j}$.

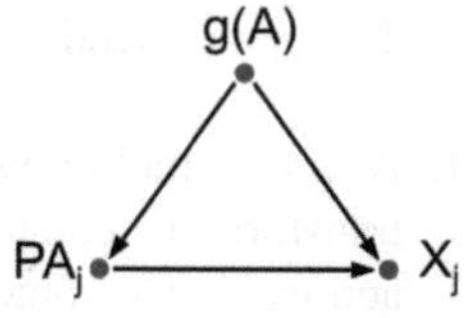

Fig. 6.16 The assumed causal graph to detect causal mechanism change [201]

Note that the functional relationships between variables X_j and time (or domain) index A is unknown. It is therefore important to use a non-parametric conditional independence test. This work uses a kernel-based conditional independence test developed in [300].

6.6 Module 5—Multimodal LLM-Based Framework for Data Narration and Insight Generation

Note: Parts of this section are based on the author's first-author journal article: *"Multi-Agent Multimodal Large Language Model Framework for Automated Interpretation of Fuel Efficiency Analytics in Public Transportation"* [203].

This Section presents an intelligent multi-agent framework that integrates multimodal LLMs to support scientific data narration and industrial insight generation. First, scientific data narration transforms multimodal scientific data, such as charts and tables, into clear, interpretable narratives. Second, industrial insight generation produces practical, actionable recommendations grounded in the global knowledge encoded within the LLM. By combining the narrative generation capabilities of multimodal LLMs with the coordination strengths of agent-based systems, the proposed framework effectively bridges the gap between complex data analytics and stakeholder-oriented decision support.

The main scientific contributions of this study are as follows.

1. A novel multimodal LLM-based multi-agent framework is proposed for transforming complex scientific data analytics into coherent narratives and actionable recommendations. The framework processes multimodal inputs and enhances the accessibility of analytical results for stakeholders.
2. A comprehensive comparison of SotA LLMs and prompting strategies is conducted to identify optimal configurations for data narration.
3. The framework is validated through extensive experiments on real-world datasets, demonstrating its practical applicability and effectiveness.

Section 6.6.1 presents the proposed multi-agent framework in detail, and Sect. 6.6.2 reports the experimental setup and results of comparative evaluation and empirical analysis.

6.6.1 Multi-Agent Framework Design for LLM-Based Narration

The objective of this study is to develop a novel multi-agent-based approach capable of generating coherent data story narration from scientific data analytics and producing actionable recommendations for stakeholders. At its core, this approach distributes complex reasoning and evaluation tasks across specialized agents, enabling iterative and intelligent refinement. To ensure the accuracy and clarity of the generated narratives, a multi-agent architecture, referred to as a *block*, is designed. This architecture is illustrated in Fig. 6.17.

This architecture comprises three specialized agents, each fulfilling a distinct role within the data-to-insight workflow. The process begins with the *data narration agent*, which serves as the initial storyteller. Its role is to bridge the gap between raw multimodal inputs, such as charts, tables, and numerical results, and human-understandable narratives, leveraging the LLM's global knowledge to generate context-aware textual outputs. Next, the *LLM-as-a-judge agent* acts as an automated reviewer, providing critical reasoning and iterative evaluation to assess narrative quality, internal consistency, and alignment with analytical objectives. Finally, the *human-in-the-loop evaluator* provides expert oversight, refining and validating machine-generated outputs in domain-specific applications as needed. Together, these agents create a dynamic workflow that advances from data interpretation to actionable insights, supporting real-world decision-making processes.

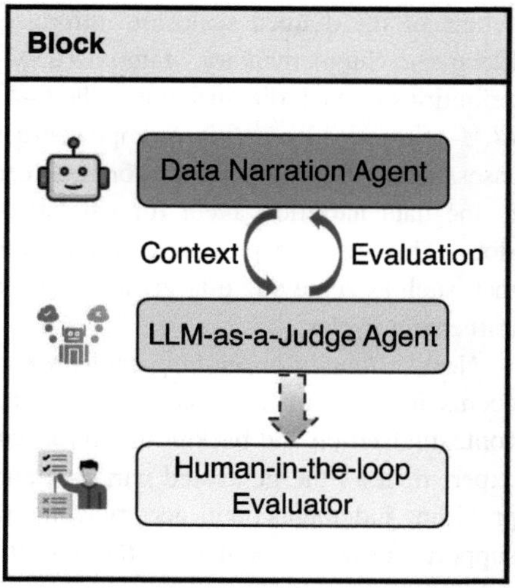

Fig. 6.17 The multi-agent architecture for data narration. This architecture includes three agents: a *data narration agent,* an *LLM-as-a-judge agent,* and an optional *human-in-the-loop evaluator*

The *data narration agent* is responsible for processing multimodal inputs such as charts, tables, and numerical results, and transforming them into coherent, context-aware textual narratives with an LLM. The *LLM-as-a-judge agent* then assesses the generated narratives for quality, internal consistency, and alignment with the intended analytical objectives. To enhance the reliability and domain relevance of the outputs, an optional *human-in-the-loop evaluator* is included. This agent provides expert oversight and enables the validation or refinement of the machine-generated narratives in applications that require domain-specific sensitivity.

Within the block, the *data narration agent* is automatically triggered upon a user uploading a dataset. It then interprets multimodal inputs derived from data analytics tasks, generating corresponding textual explanations and descriptive narratives. These outputs are then passed to the *LLM-as-a-judge agent*, which systematically assesses the generated narratives across four key dimensions: clarity, relevance, insightfulness, and contextualization. These dimensions are derived from a review of the literature, as discussed in [205, 210, 301]. Each evaluation dimension is scored on a scale from 0 to 4, with higher scores indicating better performance. To ensure reliability, the agent's stability is assessed by running repeated evaluations on identical narratives. When setting the hyperparameter "temperature = 0.1", the agent consistently produced identical scores and comments across runs, confirming its deterministic behavior and robustness. The details of the defined scale are introduced in Listing A.4 in Appendix A.1 in Electronic Supplementary Material (ESM). This evaluation basis, including the definitions of each dimension and the 0–4 scoring criteria, is also provided to the *LLM-as-a-judge agent* via prompt instructions to ensure consistent and aligned assessments. Based on these scores, a feedback report is generated and returned to the data narration agent for validation and potential refinement of the data story. This iterative process continues until a predefined stopping condition is met, such as achieving a target average score or reaching a maximum number of refinement cycles.

Next, a *human-in-the-loop evaluator* can be engaged when a domain expert deems intervention necessary, such as for complex inputs or when additional contextualization and background information are required. In such instances, the expert reviews the generated narrative and issues explicit validation commands, providing judgments on its accuracy, interpretability, and overall utility. This input supports further refinement of the narrative and helps ensure its alignment with domain-specific expectations.

After designing the multi-agent architecture, a structured multi-agent framework is developed. The overall workflow of the framework is illustrated in Fig. 6.18.

The framework distributes analytical interpretation across modular stages, where each stage builds upon the cumulative knowledge and narratives of preceding stages. This design enables iterative refinement through the *block* designed in Fig. 6.17, and supports seamless integration of machine-generated insights into human-centered decision-making processes. By maintaining interconnected streams of contextual background and narrative outputs, the system ensures transparency and traceability throughout the workflow. The overall architecture systematically converts multimodal artefacts into coherent, context-rich reports aligned with the needs of diverse industrial stakeholders.

As illustrated in Fig. 6.18, the framework proceeds through four connected stages: raw-data description, data modeling, post-hoc analytics, and integration and narration. Contextual knowledge in each subsequent stage builds cumulatively, incorporating both background from preceding stages and the narrative outputs generated at those stages. For instance, the "Background+" in Stage 2 integrates the "Background" in Stage 1 along with Narrative 1.1–1.x.

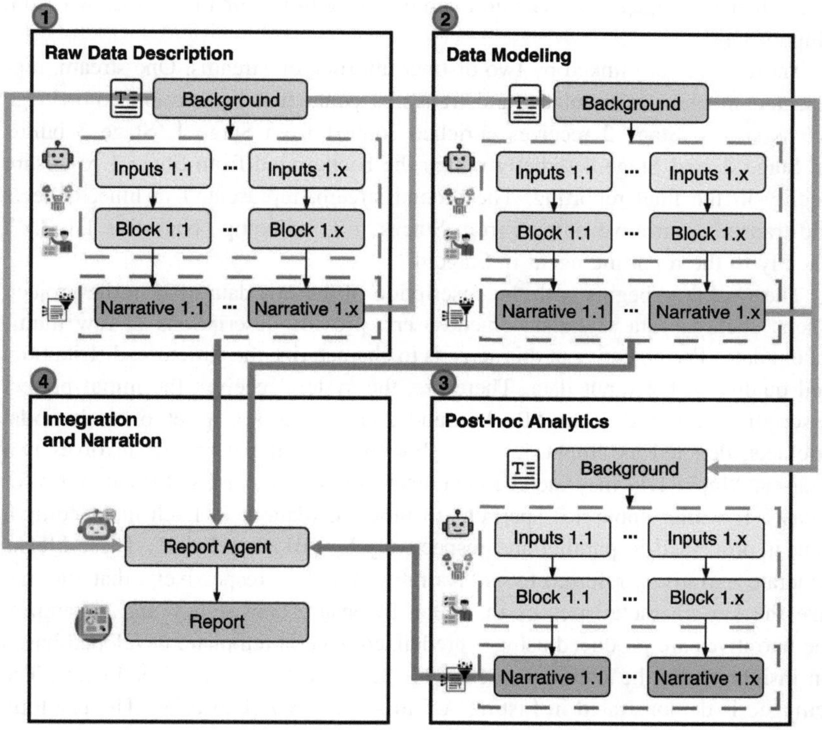

Fig. 6.18 The workflow of the proposed LLM-agent framework for data narration and reporting. This framework consists of four connected stages: raw-data description, data modeling, post-hoc analytics, and integration and narration. The grey information stream aggregates and transmits contextual background knowledge across stages, while the blue stream collects and delivers narrative outputs

Each of the first three stages also includes a series of modular processing units. The yellow boxes labeled "Input x.y" denote the multimodal data elements provided for interpretation, such as figures, charts, or tables. These are processed by the orange boxes labeled "Block x.y", which correspond to the multi-agent architecture outlined in Fig. 6.17. Each block takes a specific input to produce a textual output, represented by the green boxes labeled "Narrative x.y". For example, "Inputs 1.1" consists of a combination of figures and tables, then "Block 1.1" processes these using the multi-agent approach in Fig. 6.17, yielding Narrative

1.1, a natural language explanation summarizing trends or insights drawn from "Inputs 1.1".

These stages are linked by two distinct information streams. One stream, represented in grey, accumulates and transmits contextual background knowledge across stages: Stage 2 receives enriched context from Stage 1, Stage 3 builds on Stage 2, and Stage 4 directly reuses the background from Stage 1 to ensure fidelity in the final reporting. The second stream, represented in blue, collects and transmits narrative outputs from Stages 1–3, including "Narrative 1.1–3.x", directly to the reporting agent in Stage 4.

The workflow begins with the description of the raw data used in the project. Users, such as data scientists or end-users, provide descriptions of raw multimodal data. The objective at this stage is to characterize the structure, distribution, and quality of the input data. Therefore, the system receives the initial project description, referred to as "Background", and processes a set of multimodal artefacts, denoted as "Input 1.1–1.x". For instance, if the project involves two datasets, "Input 1.1" may include data distribution charts and statistical tables for dataset 1, while "Input 1.2" pertains to those for dataset 2. Each input component is processed in parallel and respectively by "Block 1.1–1.x". These blocks generate narratives, referred to as "Narrative 1.1–1.x" respectively, that summarize the key characteristics of the data. To ensure consistency and coherence, the narratives are produced using a predefined general template, developed based on insights from the literature [210, 221, 222] and the needs of end-users. The template is demonstrated in Listing A.5 in Appendix A.1 in ESM. The resulting narratives "Narrative 1.1–1.x" are preserved in the narrative stream, while the combination of the original project description "Background" and the generated descriptions are compiled into an enriched contextual file, referred to as "Background+". This enhanced background is then forwarded to support the subsequent stage of the workflow.

The second stage, *Data Modeling*, centers on the modeling aspect of data analytics. The objective of this stage is to explain the analytical results using statistical or machine learning models. The enriched background, "Background+", provides the necessary context for each multimodal modeling artefact, denoted as "Input 2.1–2.x". For example, if the project employs two analytical methods, such as clustering and causal inference, then "Input 2.1" may consist of charts, figures, or tables showcasing clustering results, while "Input 2.2" corresponds to the outputs of the causal inference analysis. Each input component is processed in parallel and independently by modules referred to as "Block 2.1–2.x". These blocks generate narratives, "Narrative 2.1–2.x", which summarize and interpret the modeling results using the same general template introduced in Listing A.5

in Appendix A.1 in ESM. The newly generated narratives are appended to the existing narrative stream. Additionally, a further enriched contextual file, denoted as "Background++", is created by combining "Background+" with the modeling narratives to support Stage 3.

In the third stage, the system explains post-hoc analytics to further interpret model outputs. Leveraging the comprehensive background "Background++" that now includes the project context, data summaries, and modeling explanations, the system processes a range of multimodal post-hoc artefacts. These may include SHAP value distributions, counterfactual explanations, and statistical evaluations of model residuals. For instance, "Input 3.1" might consist of multimodal representations of SHAP value distributions, "Input 3.2" of counterfactual explanations, and "Input 3.3" of residual diagnostics. Each input component is handled in parallel by corresponding modules, labeled "Block 3.1–3.x", which generate explanatory narratives, "Narrative 3.1–3.x", according to the template introduced in Listing A.5 in Appendix A.1 in ESM. The system itself does not autonomously select or suggest post-hoc analysis methods; it relies entirely on artefacts provided by data scientists or domain experts. Following this stage, all relevant contextual information is consolidated and ready for the final stage, *Integration and Narration.*

The final stage of the workflow integrates all previously generated narratives ("Narrative 3.1–3.x") and the background context ("Background") into a cohesive technical report. A dedicated agent, denoted as the *reporting agent*, receives the complete set of narratives "Narrative 3.1–3.x" along with the original project description "Background". Without altering the factual content, this agent standardizes terminology, eliminates redundancies, and organizes the material into a logically structured, coherent document. The final output report includes an executive summary, a methodological exposition, analytical findings, and actionable recommendations derived from the multimodal scientific data narratives. The report is formatted to facilitate interpretation by industrial stakeholders with diverse levels of technical expertise. The level of technical detail and complexity can be adjusted by modifying the corresponding prompts.

Overall, the proposed framework offers a principled approach to transforming complex, multimodal analytical results into high-quality documentation. By maintaining a strict separation between cumulative context and interpretive content, supporting parallel processing through modular blocks, and preserving an auditable flow of information across all stages, the system enables transparent, reliable, and stakeholder-aligned reporting in data-intensive industrial environments.

It is important to note that the number of narratives generated in each stage depends entirely on the multimodal artifacts produced by the data analytics project. The system processes each artifact as input and does not intervene in determining its quantity or content. Hyperparameters such as temperature and token limits are configured to ensure consistent narrative generation, but do not affect the number of narratives.

6.6.2 Comparative Evaluation and Empirical Analysis

6.6.2.1 Experimental Design and Settings

A series of experiments is conducted to evaluate the effectiveness of the proposed framework and validate its components.

The first set of experiments assesses the performance of different prompting strategies and LLMs in the data narration task. The datasets used in this set of experiments comprise 20 charts and 5 tables, encompassing data analysis tasks related to data characteristic understanding, clustering, and causal inference.

Three prompting strategies are selected as candidates: CoT [64], CCoT [222], and DataNarrative (DN) [210]. CoT is widely used as a prompting technique and a standard benchmark for eliciting step-by-step reasoning in LLMs. CCoT extends CoT by first generating structured contextual representations, making it suitable for multimodal reasoning tasks. DN is the most relevant published approach to this study. All three approaches are implemented in a zero-shot setting, chosen for their speed and efficiency in real-world applications.

In zero-shot scenarios, where no task-specific examples are provided, prompting strategies can enhance LLM performance by guiding inference. The CoT uses simple cues like "Let's think step by step" in a zero-shot context to elicit multi-step reasoning [64]. The CCoT first generates a structured scene graph from an image, then reasons over it alongside the original prompt, enabling compositional understanding without fine-tuning or annotations [222]. The DN prompting operates on structured inputs such as tables and charts, prompting the model to produce coherent narratives that highlight trends, anomalies, and relationships directly from the raw data [210].

Five LLMs are evaluated, including GPT-4.1 mini [61], o4-mini [217], Claude 3.5 Haiku [62], Gemini 2.5 flash [63], and LLama 4 maverick [302]. These models represent the latest lightweight versions developed by leading LLM providers. They offer a practical balance between performance and cost, with LLama 4 maverick being open-source and freely available for public use. The experimental design evaluates all 15 combinations of the selected prompting strategies and LLMs. Performance is assessed using five criteria:

- Execution time, measured in seconds, quantifies the time required to generate each narrative;
- Cost, measured in cents (0.01 USD), reflects the expense of using the model based on its API pricing;
- Narrative length, defined as the total word count of the generated output;
- Informativeness, measured as the number of distinct information points extracted from the visual input;
- Accuracy, calculated as the percentage of correct information points relative to the total number of points generated.
- Accurate Narrative Information Density (ANID), defined as the number of correct distinct information points per 100 words in a generated narrative.

In this study, an information point is defined as a single word or short phrase that conveys a discrete piece of meaning relevant to the content of the input being narrated. For example, in the sentence "The x-axis denotes fuel efficiency measured in liters per 100 kilometers", the term "fuel efficiency" forms one information point by identifying the variable on the x-axis, whereas "liters per 100 kilometers" forms a second information point by specifying that variable's unit. The correctness of each information point is assessed by cross-checking it against domain-specific ground truth, common-sense knowledge, and the original inputs.

Together, these metrics provide a comprehensive basis for evaluating the prompt's efficiency, precision, and overall quality in automated data narration.

The second set of experiments focuses on selecting the most suitable LLM for Stage 4 of the framework, which generates the final report. The datasets used in this set of experiments comprise three reports, each focusing on tasks related to data characteristic analysis, clustering, and causal inference.

Based on the results of the first experiment demonstrated in Table 6.26 in Sect. 6.6.2.2, which indicates that OpenAI models outperform others in data narration, three OpenAI models are selected as candidates: GPT-4.1 mini, GPT-4.1, and o4-mini. The quality and utility of the reports generated are evaluated using the following criteria:

- Flesch Reading Ease (FRE) [303]: A readability score that indicates how easy a text is to read, with higher values corresponding to easier reading (typically ranging from 0 to 100).

- Flesch-Kincaid Grade Level (FKGL) [303]: A metric that estimates the U.S. school grade level required to understand the text, with lower values indicating greater accessibility.
- Automated Readability Index (ARI) [304]: Another readability measure based on word and sentence length, providing a numeric grade level; lower values reflect simpler language.
- Cost: The monetary cost of generating each report, measured in cents (USD 0.01), based on API pricing for each model.
- Report length (RL): The total word count of the generated report, reflecting the amount of explanatory content produced.
- Number of recommendations with data support (NRDS): The subset of recommendations explicitly grounded in the data narratives.
- Percentage of recommendations with data support (PRDS): The percentage of recommendations explicitly grounded in the data narratives relative to the total number of actionable suggestions included in the report.

Together, these metrics offer a comprehensive basis for comparing the readability, efficiency, and practical utility of each model in producing stakeholder-ready reports.

The third set of experiments consists of ablation studies designed to evaluate the contribution of each agent in the framework to the quality of the final report. This set of experiments includes eleven repetitions using distinct multimodal inputs to ensure the reliability and consistency of the results. Specifically, the study examines the effectiveness of the background description, the *LLM-as-a-judge agent*, and the *human-in-the-loop evaluator* by analyzing the impact of their removal. The experiments assess how each agent influences key aspects of the data narrative, including coherence, informativeness, and reliability.

The experimental results are presented in Sect. 6.6.2.2. The representative examples of data narration are provided in Appendix A.2 in ESM. The key prompts and their associated contextual inputs are illustrated in Listings A.1-A.3 in Appendix A.2 in ESM.

6.6.2.2 Results and Discussion

Table 6.26 presents the evaluation metrics and corresponding scores for various combinations of LLMs and prompting strategies applied to scientific data narration. The values preceding the "$\pm$" symbol indicate the evaluation scores introduced in Sect. 6.6.2.1, while the values following it denote the standard errors of repetitions. In the context of method selection, accuracy is prioritized, while narrative length, informativeness, and ANID are secondary criteria, as they directly reflect the quantity and accuracy of the information conveyed. Execution time and cost are ranked third in priority, but remain important considerations for practical deployment.

Table 6.26 Evaluation results for LLM and prompt strategy combinations in scientific data narration

LLM	Prompting	Time (s)	Cost (cent)	Narrative length	Informativeness	Accuracy (%)	ANID
GPT-4.1 mini	CoT	10.93 ± 0.726	0.20 ± 0.009	274.5 ± 9.37	20.14 ± 0.523	97.39 ± 0.901	7.26 ± 0.242
	CCoT	33.25 ± 2.597	0.53 ± 0.030	268.6 ± 10.60	19.91 ± 0.674	96.45 ± 1.486	7.34 ± 0.272
	DN	9.43 ± 0.501	0.20 ± 0.008	287.3 ± 10.45	24.00 ± 0.874	94.83 ± 1.201	8.15 ± 0.193
o4-mini	CoT	19.03 ± 1.560	0.94 ± 0.032	258.8 ± 8.91	20.27 ± 0.693	93.47 ± 2.818	7.42 ± 0.348
	CCoT	53.64 ± 4.396	2.59 ± 0.205	242.0 ± 9.28	19.45 ± 0.812	87.52 ± 4.055	7.30 ± 0.417
	DN	23.14 ± 1.386	1.12 ± 0.044	297.2 ± 13.53	24.95 ± 1.051	89.75 ± 3.124	7.87 ± 0.371
Claude 3.5 Haiku	CoT	9.12 ± 0.369	0.34 ± 0.017	187.5 ± 5.84	16.35 ± 0.641	82.83 ± 3.294	7.25 ± 0.338
	CCoT	20.26 ± 0.555	0.87 ± 0.046	182.3 ± 4.58	16.30 ± 0.625	86.84 ± 3.929	8.21 ± 0.447
	DN	10.84 ± 0.955	0.37 ± 0.016	223.4 ± 4.35	19.35 ± 0.63	88.31 ± 2.863	7.97 ± 0.278
Gemini 2.5 Flash	CoT	7.24 ± 0.496	0.17 ± 0.016	305.5 ± 11.28	21.59 ± 0.792	88.76 ± 2.755	6.32 ± 0.267
	CCoT	20.43 ± 1.083	0.56 ± 0.065	262.9 ± 18.37	18.68 ± 1.011	89.85 ± 2.515	7.00 ± 0.326
	DN	5.99 ± 0.366	0.17 ± 0.022	347.6 ± 24.98	25.27 ± 1.677	83.60 ± 3.594	6.55 ± 0.369
Llama 4 Maverick	CoT	17.31 ± 2.380	N/A	208.5 ± 10.06	16.81 ± 0.787	87.84 ± 2.754	7.11 ± 0.349
	CCoT	39.32 ± 5.007	N/A	212.2 ± 7.63	16.5 ± 0.683	86.37 ± 4.432	7.12 ± 0.400
	DN	18.78 ± 3.012	N/A	222.5 ± 10.16	18.64 ± 0.746	85.87 ± 4.694	7.28 ± 0.441

For LLM selection, the candidate LLMs are first evaluated based on accuracy, ANID, narrative length, and informativeness. Among the candidates, GPT-4.1 mini and o4-mini consistently outperform the others, especially in accuracy and narrative length, suggesting that OpenAI's models are particularly effective for this task. Although Gemini 2.5 Flash generates longer narratives, these outputs contain fewer distinct information points and exhibit lower accuracy, indicating a tendency to include excessive non-informative content and occasional fabricated information. While o4-mini incurs the highest cost, it remains within an acceptable range. GPT-4.1 mini, in contrast, is more cost-efficient and produces narratives that are both longer and more accurate. Although o4-mini achieves a higher informativeness score in CoT and DN prompting strategies, it also generates a higher proportion of incorrect information. Given its superior balance between performance and cost, GPT-4.1 mini is selected for the subsequent experiments.

The prompting strategies are then compared. CoT achieves the highest accuracy, producing the most precise narratives. While CCoT generates more information points, its advantage over CoT is relatively small and comes at a substantially higher computational cost, approximately three times the execution time and 2.5 times the cost. DN generates the most extensive and concise descriptions but exhibits the lowest accuracy. In contrast, CoT demonstrates the most balanced performance across all evaluation dimensions, delivering competitive accuracy, more informative narratives, and significantly lower computational demands. Based on this comprehensive assessment, CoT is identified as the most effective and efficient prompting strategy for the task.

Table 6.27 presents the evaluation metrics for three LLMs, including GPT-4.1, GPT-4.1 mini, and o4-mini, applied to the task of report generation. The metrics include readability scores (FRE, FKGL, and ARI), computational cost (in USD cents), report length (RL, in words), number of recommendations with data support (NRDS), and percentage of recommendations with data support (PRDS) as introduced in Sect. 6.6.2.1. The values preceding the "±" symbol indicate the evaluation scores, while the values following it denote the standard errors of repetitions.

Table 6.27 Evaluation metrics for different LLMs applied to report generation

LLM	FRE	FKGL	ARI	Cost	RL	NRDS	PRDS
GPT-4.1	21.0 ± 3.70	14.0 ± 0.44	14.5 ± 0.86	2.39 ± 0.052	1029.7 ± 30.39	4.33 ± 0.272	79.1 ± 10.11
GPT-4.1 mini	27.9 ± 3.46	14.1 ± 0.37	15.0 ± 0.55	0.48 ± 0.018	1029.0 ± 40.48	5.0 ± 0.0	84.9 ± 6.77
o4-mini	23.8 ± 2.14	13.9 ± 0.39	15.4 ± 0.36	1.61 ± 0.045	909.3 ± 30.04	4.0 ± 0.471	82.1 ± 7.34

Among these metrics, NRDS and PRDS are the most important, as they indicate the model's ability to generate actionable insights grounded in analytical results. GPT-4.1 mini achieves the best overall performance, producing an average of five supported recommendations, about 85% of which are directly grounded in the multimodal analytical results. It also attains the highest FRE readability score, while FKGL and ARI remain comparable across all models. In contrast, GPT-4.1 and o4-mini incur substantially higher computational costs without clear performance gains. Considering all evaluation dimensions, GPT-4.1 mini achieves the most favorable balance between effectiveness and efficiency. It combines the highest analytical grounding (NRDS and PRDS) with the best readability score (FRE) and the lowest computational cost, while maintaining comparable text complexity to the other models. Therefore, GPT-4.1 mini is selected as the most suitable model for report generation in this framework.

Next, to systematically evaluate the contributions of the individual components within the proposed multi-agent architecture presented in Fig. 6.17, an ablation study is conducted. This study aims to discern the relative impacts of the CoT prompting approach, contextual background propagation (B), the LLM-as-a-judge agent (E), and optional human oversight on the quality of generated scientific narratives. Four distinct configurations were analyzed: CoT-only, CoT combined with contextual background (CoT+B), CoT with contextual background and the LLM-as-a-judge agent (CoT+B+E), and the full baseline comprising CoT, background, LLM-as-a-judge, and human-in-the-loop evaluator as detailed in Fig. 6.17. As in the baseline experiments, all cases pass the LLM-as-a-judge evaluation without requiring validation. To demonstrate the functionality of the LLM-as-a-judge agent, the CoT+B+E experiment is designed to explicitly invoke the agent by forcing it to revise the narrative context once.

Each configuration is rigorously tested on the same set of eleven data narration scenarios in Sect. 6.6.2.1, employing three primary metrics: narrative length, informativeness, and accuracy, as detailed previously in Sect. 6.6.2.1. Figure 6.19

illustrates these results by depicting comparative performance across these metrics for all configurations tested.

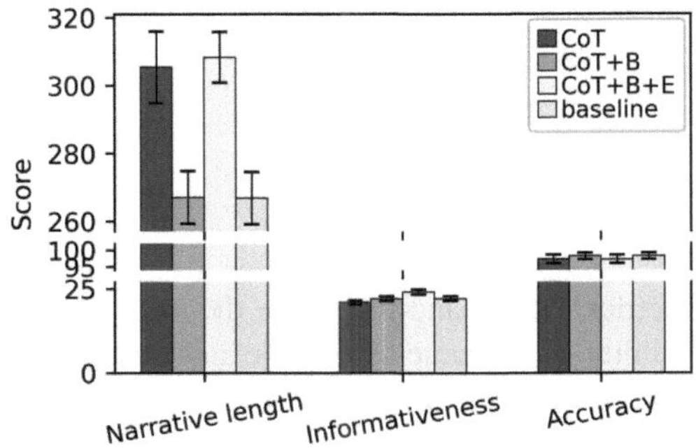

Fig. 6.19 Evaluation scores for ablation studies in data narration scenarios. The x-axis indicates the evaluation criteria. The y-axis reflects the corresponding scores. Each group of four bars corresponds to distinct experimental configurations, as indicated in the legend, with error bars representing the standard error of repetitions. The short black lines and the white gaps on the y-axis indicate axis breaks, which are used to conserve space and enable clearer visual comparison

The results in Fig. 6.19 suggest that the baseline method performs best overall across key evaluation dimensions. In the accuracy category, the baseline outperforms all other prompting strategies, indicating that it generates the most correct and reliable output. While CoT+B exhibits performance that appears comparable across three evaluation criteria, this similarity is superficial. In the baseline, the E stage does not perform additional validation because all narratives successfully pass automated evaluation. Crucially, 10 of the 11 narratives in the baseline require no human intervention, underscoring their inherent robustness and reduced reliance on downstream adjustments. It makes the overall procedure nearly identical to that of CoT+B. The single case involving human intervention in the baseline shows an improvement in narrative quality. This highlights its strength in producing factually accurate, relevant content, which is critical for tasks requiring precision.

Although the baseline narrative is the shortest among the four methods, this should not be interpreted as a limitation. On the contrary, the shorter narrative length reflects the baseline's efficiency in communication, achieving similar levels of informativeness with significantly fewer words. This suggests that the baseline can deliver concise yet meaningful responses, avoiding redundancy or unnecessary elaboration that may be present in longer narratives generated by other methods.

Furthermore, the informativeness score of the baseline remains competitive. Despite its brevity, it successfully conveys the essential information needed to understand the data, comparable to or slightly below that of the CoT+B+E method. This reinforces the idea that longer responses do not necessarily translate to more informative content. Instead, the baseline achieves a more optimal balance between clarity, informativeness, and brevity.

In contrast, while methods such as CoT and CoT+B+E produce longer narratives, their higher word counts do not correspond to improved accuracy. Their performance in accuracy falls behind the baseline. Although CoT+B+E achieves a slightly higher informativeness score compared to the baseline, likely due to the inclusion of more contextual and descriptive details. However, this added detail introduces a greater risk of irrelevant or inaccurate statements, which ultimately undermines factual precision. The results indicate that unnecessary validation in LLM-based data narration tasks may introduce irrelevant or inaccurate content, ultimately reducing the narrative's overall factual precision.

In summary, the baseline configuration proves to be the most effective approach overall, achieving the highest accuracy while maintaining strong informativeness and generating the most concise narratives. These results underscore its capacity to produce high-quality, precise, and communication-efficient outputs. The framework is intentionally designed to minimize, though not eliminate, human intervention. While most narratives are generated autonomously, selective expert input is incorporated in exceptional cases where refinement or domain-specific correction is required. This hybrid setup strikes a deliberate balance between automation and human oversight, supporting both the scalability and reliability of the system in real-world data analytics workflows.

6.7 Summary and Transition to Case Studies

This chapter has presented the implementation and verification of the proposed AI-driven decision support framework. For each of the five modules designed in Chap. 5, including data collection and acquisition, data profiling and preprocessing, pattern clustering and behavioral analysis, causal reasoning and inference, and multimodal narration and decision support, SotA methods have been either adopted from the literature or newly developed to address the research gaps identified in Chap. 3. These implemented algorithms and sub-frameworks ensure the framework's operational feasibility, methodological rigor, and originality.

Each module has been rigorously evaluated through comparative benchmarking, parameter sensitivity analysis, and ablation studies. In addition, the developed methods are compared against SotA baselines to ensure scientific novelty and demonstrate substantive contributions. This evaluation approach aligns with established verification practices in the data science domain. The evaluations have confirmed the correctness, robustness, and efficiency of the developed algorithms and sub-frameworks, demonstrating clear advantages over baseline and SotA approaches. These verified methods enable the proposed framework to integrate descriptive, diagnostic, explanatory, and interpretative components within a unified architecture.

Importantly, this chapter demonstrates how the modular architecture functions as a coherent end-to-end pipeline: raw sensor data progress through profiling, clustering, and causal reasoning stages before being automatically translated into multimodal narratives and actionable recommendations. This transformation from raw data to decision-ready insights highlights both the framework's originality and its practical value.

The following chapters extend this validation to real-world contexts through two case studies. Chapter 7 applies the framework to improving energy efficiency in the foundry industry, while Chap. 8 demonstrates its application to enhancing fuel efficiency in public transportation systems. Together, these studies provide empirical evidence of the framework's applicability, scalability, and effectiveness in delivering decision support for energy-intensive domains.

7 Case Study 1: Improving Energy Efficiency in the Foundry Industry

This chapter presents a case study that develops, demonstrates, and evaluates an AI-driven decision support framework to improve energy efficiency in the foundry industry. The iron and steel sector, which emitted approximately 2.6 Gt CO_2 in 2022 and accounted for about 29% of global industrial emissions, is one of the largest contributors to climate change [3, 305]. Despite numerous proposed strategies to meet the Net Zero Emissions by 2050 targets [306], a systematic and explainable AI-driven decision support framework remains absent in this domain. Many foundries still lack integrated pipelines that can transform raw sensor data into actionable insights. Significant gaps also remain in extracting causal insights from time-series process data and in presenting analytical results in a transparent, interpretable, and directly useful form for decision-makers.

To address these challenges, this study applies the conceptual framework introduced in Chap. 5 and operationalizes it using the algorithms and sub-frameworks described in Chap. 6. By tailoring these methods to the context of foundry operations, the case study demonstrates how advanced data-driven analytics can generate actionable insights for improving energy efficiency.

Supplementary Information The online version contains supplementary material available at https://doi.org/10.1007/978-3-658-51965-0_7.

Z. Ma, *Artificial Intelligence-Driven Decision Support Framework for Improving Energy Efficiency in Industry and Transportation*,
https://doi.org/10.1007/978-3-658-51965-0_7

The remainder of this chapter is structured as follows. Section 7.1 introduces the foundry sector and the selected case study facility. Section 7.2 defines the research problem, translates business requirements into technical formulations, and outlines methodological boundaries. Section 7.3 presents the dataset and demonstrates how the AI-driven framework is applied in the foundry context. Section 7.4 reports the outcomes of data preparation, clustering, causal inference, and multimodal decision-support generation. Section 7.5 evaluates the performance, robustness, and practical relevance of the framework. Finally, Sect. 7.6 summarizes this chapter.

7.1 Industrial Context and Case Study Overview

The foundry industry plays a central role in manufacturing by supplying metal castings used across sectors such as transportation, construction, and consumer goods. Driven by rising demand, global crude steel output nearly doubled between 2000 and 2024 [307, 308]. At the same time, the iron and steel industry has emerged as one of the hard-to-abate sectors, facing major technological, financial, and infrastructural barriers to decarbonization [309]. It is responsible for about 6% of global CO_2 emissions and roughly 8% of energy-related emissions [309, 310].

Although practices differ among facilities, the casting process generally follows a shared sequence [311]. Casting can be defined as the transformation of liquid metal into a solid object that conforms to a mold [311]. The process starts with melting and pouring the liquid metal into a mold, which determines the geometry of the final workpiece. Depending on requirements, additional operations may be introduced, such as inserting cores to create hollow sections or applying post-casting treatments. Casting methods vary in whether gravity or external pressure is used to fill the mold, which directly affects cycle time. Molds are typically grouped into two categories: disposable molds, which are broken after each use, and permanent molds, which can be reused.

The melting process accounts for approximately 55% of the foundry's total energy consumption, making it a primary target for energy efficiency gains [8, 312]. Melting is typically carried out in furnaces such as induction, electric arc, or blast furnaces, selected according to their operational characteristics. The input, usually a mix of pig iron, scrap, and alloying additions, is melted, after which the molten metal may be held temporarily or fed directly to casting. The subsequent casting stage produces the primary shape of the workpiece, which solidifies during cooling and is released from the mold. While the general workflow is comparable across foundries, the specific steps are product- and facility-dependent. Figure 7.1 illustrates the melting stage in detail, based on the case study foundry selected for this research.

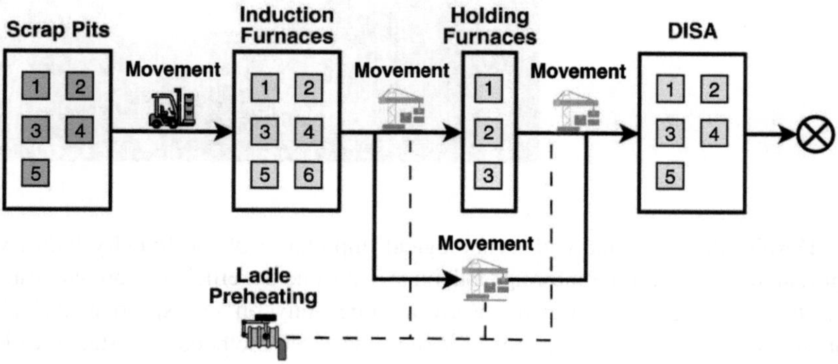

Fig. 7.1 An example of the foundry melting process

In this example shown in Fig. 7.1, the process begins with sorting and preparing the melting materials by scraping metal collected from scrap pits. These inputs are introduced into an induction furnace and heated to the target temperature, taking ferromagnetic losses into account. Once the melt reaches the specified temperature, it is transferred into a pre-heated ladle, where doping may be performed to fine-tune material properties before the melt is transferred into a holding furnace. The transfer marks the conclusion of the melting stage.

The forming stage is then carried out in DISA machines. The melt is withdrawn from the holding furnace into a pre-heated ladle, where further alloying can be performed to meet customer-specific requirements. It is subsequently poured into molding equipment, typically sand molds, to produce the primary casting. The castings then pass through a controlled cooling line, completing the primary forming process. Figure 7.2 illustrates the picture of the induction furnace used in the case study foundry.

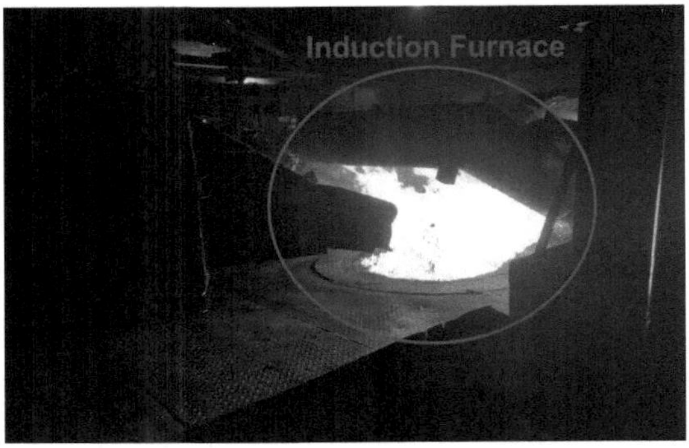

Fig. 7.2 An example of the open induction furnace at the case study facility. The machine within the red circle is the open induction furnace

Despite the economic and technological importance of the foundry industry, current practices for monitoring and improving energy efficiency remain fragmented and largely descriptive. Many facilities rely on retrospective analysis of isolated performance indicators, lacking integrated methods to systematically process sensor data, uncover operational patterns, and establish causal drivers of efficiency. As a result, decision-makers often receive information that is either too granular to support strategic improvements or too aggregated to guide operational interventions. What is missing is a systematic, explainable, and adaptive pipeline that can transform heterogeneous furnace data into actionable knowledge. This gap directly motivates the application of the proposed AI-driven decision support framework, which integrates five key modules (data acquisition, preprocessing, clustering, causal reasoning, and multimodal decision support) to address the limitations of existing approaches and provide a structured pathway from raw data to informed decision-making.

7.2 Research Problem and Case Constraints

Defining the research problem and its constraints is a critical step in framing the case study within both the domain context and the methodological design. This case study focuses on the foundry industry, where the energy-intensive melting process offers significant potential for efficiency improvement. This section formalizes the overarching objective of enhancing energy efficiency in foundry operations into a concrete research problem. The defined constraints establish the scientific boundaries of the study, ensuring transparency, reproducibility, and analytical rigor. By translating foundry-specific operational knowledge into technical formulations, this section lays the foundation for subsequent experimentation and evaluation. The scope of the case study follows the first two stages of the DataPro pipeline [234], as outlined in Sect. 5.3.

7.2.1 Business Context and Objectives

The business understanding phase aims to identify the objectives of industrial stakeholders by situating the research within the industrial context. It involves analyzing the current business situation, clarifying specific objectives, and outlining success criteria from an industry perspective. To support this process, the BMC [234, 238] is applied as a structured tool for systematically capturing business context and end-user requirements. The BMC provides a comprehensive representation of stakeholder needs, value propositions, and operational conditions, thereby ensuring that the subsequent technical formulation is firmly grounded in the domain. An example of this analysis is presented in Table 7.1.

Table 7.1 The BMC of the foundry case study

BMC components	Details
Key partners	• Data scientists and AI researchers • Foundry operators and managers (end-users) • IoT and sensor technology providers • Energy utilities and regulators • Maintenance and service providers
Key activities	• Big data analysis and AI-driven pattern discovery • Causal inference for identifying efficiency drivers • Integration with IIoT and production management systems • Operator training and knowledge transfer • Continuous monitoring, validation, and model updates
Key resources	• Skilled professionals (AI engineers, domain experts, operators) • Historical and real-time sensor data • IoT infrastructure, physical sensors, and data storage platforms • Software platforms and computational infrastructure • Domain expertise in foundry operations

(continued)

Table 7.1 (continued)

BMC components	Details
Value propositions	• Improving energy efficiency of melting processes • Identifying and standardizing efficient operational practices • Providing explainable insights into factors influencing energy consumption • Supporting predictive maintenance and operational reliability • Enabling data-driven decision making for cost reduction and sustainability
Customer relationships	• Collaborative co-design with operators and engineers • Continuous feedback loops for improving recommendations • Technical consultation and training support • Maintenance and update services for AI models and dashboards
Channels	• Integration into existing IIoT dashboards and production control systems • Digital service delivery via cloud or on-premise solutions • Reports and decision-support interfaces tailored for operators and managers
Customer segments	• Foundry production operations (day-to-day users) • Research and development (R&D) units within foundries • Management teams seeking energy-cost reductions • External stakeholders (regulators, sustainability auditors)
Cost structure	• Investment in IoT infrastructure and sensor maintenance • Software development, deployment, and updates • Personnel and training costs • Ongoing operational and maintenance costs
Revenue streams	• Internal cost savings from improved energy efficiency • Productivity gains from reduced downtime and optimized operations • Potential licensing of AI framework/software to other foundries • Consulting or service contracts for customization and support

Within the BMC, the top four components are particularly relevant to the development and implementation of the decision support framework in the foundry industry. Key partners comprise data scientists, foundry operators, and IoT solution providers, who collectively contribute complementary expertise in data analytics, process understanding, and technological infrastructure. Key activities center on large-scale data analysis and the deployment of advanced

AI techniques to extract actionable insights and facilitate data-driven decision-making. Key resources include skilled professionals, comprehensive datasets from thermal, electrical, and cooling systems, and computational infrastructures capable of supporting industrial-scale data processing. Value propositions emphasize enhanced energy efficiency, identification and standardization of efficient operational practices, and the provision of explainable insights into the causal factors influencing energy consumption.

Together, these components establish the business context that anchors the subsequent technical development of the framework. In particular, the value propositions define the domain objectives, which are then translated into the research directions and scientific problems addressed in this study. The key activities indicate the scope of the technical methods employed.

7.2.2 Technical Formulation and Constraints

The technical understanding of this study involves defining input data, expected outputs, evaluation metrics, and operational constraints. The key elements of technical understanding are summarized in Table 7.2.

Table 7.2 Elements of technical understanding in the foundry case study

Categories	Elements
Input	• Sensor data from a foundry • Foundry operational diagram and description
Output	• Interpretable insights into energy efficiency • Efficient operational patterns • Factors influencing energy efficiency • Data-driven recommendations for improving energy efficiency
Evaluation metrics	• Evaluation metrics defined in Sect. 4.3.2
Constraints (detailed in Table 7.3)	• Domain constraints • Operational constraints • Data constraints • Methodological constraints

The input data consists of historical process records from the foundry, including time-series sensor data (e.g., energy consumption, temperature, and material loads) as well as operational diagrams and process descriptions. These sources provide the data foundation for characterizing the operational states of the melting process. The expected outputs are interpretable insights into energy efficiency, including the identification of efficient operational patterns, the determination of factors influencing energy consumption, and the generation of data-driven recommendations to improve foundry operations.

The evaluation metrics adopted in this case study follow the definitions in Sect. 4.3.2, including capabilities, robustness, explainability, domain integrity, and potential for iterative validation.

The study is also bound by a set of research constraints that delineate its scope and define the conditions under which results should be interpreted. These constraints are categorized into four dimensions: domain, operational, data, and methodological, as presented in Table 7.3.

Table 7.3 Research constraints in the foundry case study

Categories	Context
Domain constraints	• This study is restricted to the foundry industry, with emphasis on melting processes. • The case study reflects the operational characteristics of a single foundry site.
Operational constraints	• The primary performance criterion is energy efficiency. • The scope is limited to technical feasibility, focusing on industrial process operations.
Data constraints	• Analysis is based on historical physical-sensor data collected from the case study foundry. • Data quality issues are mitigated during preprocessing, but residual uncertainties may remain. • The temporal resolution and coverage are limited to the available archival records, without a controlled experimental design.
Methodological constraints	• The research applies statistical analysis and machine learning algorithms for data-driven analytics. • Decision-support outputs are derived from retrospective data analysis and automated recommendations.

While these constraints ensure transparency and reproducibility, they also limit the generalizability of the findings. The focus on a single foundry site restricts cross-industry applicability, and reliance on retrospective sensor data means that recommendations are validated historically rather than in real-time operations. Furthermore, methodological choices, such as the use of machine learning and causal inference algorithms, are constrained by the quality and scope of available data. These limitations highlight the need for future work to extend the framework across multiple industrial sites, incorporate prospective validation under live operating conditions, and explore complementary methods for causal validation. Such efforts would improve scalability and external validity, thereby strengthening the framework's broader applicability.

Within the defined constraints, the study on developing an AI-driven decision support framework for improving energy efficiency in the foundry industry advances the following five research problems:

- **Data preprocessing:** understanding data characteristics and addressing data quality issues.
- **Pattern discovery:** applying clustering techniques to segment operational patterns and classify energy efficiency profiles.
- **Process characterization:** developing systematic methods to describe the statistical and operational properties of heterogeneous foundry process data.
- **Causal analysis:** employing causal inference and reasoning to identify and validate factors that influence energy-related operations.
- **Decision support:** designing an LLM-based recommendation module to translate analytical outputs into actionable, domain-specific insights.

7.3 Data Foundation and Framework Implementation

This section presents the case-specific foundation for implementing the AI-driven decision support framework in the foundry context. It begins with an overview of the dataset and the operational characteristics of the selected furnace, which serve as the empirical basis for the analysis. Building on this foundation, the section integrates the algorithms and sub-frameworks introduced in Chap. 6 into a unified decision support pipeline. The aim is to demonstrate how the conceptual model developed in Chap. 5 can be concretely realized and adapted to the industrial conditions of foundry operations.

7.3.1 Data Sources and Variables

As introduced in Sect. 7.1, induction furnaces were chosen as the research focus because the melting process occurs in these units and accounts for the majority of electricity consumption. As shown in Fig. 7.1, the case study foundry operates six induction furnaces. Given their similar operational characteristics, this study focuses on one representative furnace for detailed analysis.

All data are stored in an Industrial Internet of Things (IIoT) system and collected from physical sensors installed in the selected induction furnace during the period from *"2022–10-12 11.08:50"* to *"2024–04-30 22:00:00" (yyyy-mm-dd hh:mm:ss)*. Table 7.4 provides an overview and description of the variables in the dataset. Each variable has its own timestamps.

Table 7.4 Variables and description of induction furnace operation

No.	Variable	Unit	Description	Resolution
1	Weight	kg	The weight of materials added to the furnace	10 seconds
2	State	bit	Array of bits, each indicates the current operational state of the furnace	Event-based
3	Furnace temperature	°C	Temperature of the melt in the furnace	10 seconds
4	Frequency	Hz	Operating frequency of the furnace	10 seconds
5	Voltage	Volt	Operating voltage of the furnace	10 seconds
6	Current	Ampere	Operating current of the furnace	10 seconds
7	Isolation resistance	kOmh	Electrical isolation resistance of the furnace	10 seconds
8	Energy act	kWh	Total energy consumed by each melting cycle	10 seconds
9	Energy specific	kWh/tonne	Specific energy consumption per tonne of the manufactured metal	10 seconds
10	Power	kW	Instantaneous electrical power usage of the furnace	10 seconds
11	CWTemperature	°C	Cooling water temperature, measured at ten different locations around the furnace	10 seconds
12	CWQuantity	L/min	Cooling water flow rate, measured at ten different locations around the furnace	10 seconds

Each variable listed in Table 7.4 captures a critical dimension of furnace operation and its relationship to energy efficiency. For example, furnace temperature directly reflects the thermal conditions governing melting efficiency, while voltage, current, and power capture the electrical load driving energy consumption. The weight of charged material determines the energy demand per batch and interacts with specific energy consumption (kWh/tonne) as a key efficiency indicator. Cooling water temperature and flow rate provide insight into heat transfer losses and the stability of auxiliary systems, while isolation resistance signals potential electrical inefficiencies or equipment wear. Together, these variables form a comprehensive dataset that not only records operational states but also captures the causal mechanisms that influence overall energy performance.

7.3.2 Framework Overview

Figure 7.3 provides an overview of the AI-driven decision support framework for enhancing energy efficiency in the foundry industry.

Building on the conceptual foundation in Fig. 5.1(Sect. 5.2), the framework is adapted to the specific demands of foundry operations. It addresses the absence of an integrated AI pipeline capable of transforming raw sensor data into actionable knowledge, with particular emphasis on deriving causal insights from time-series data and presenting results in a decision-oriented form. The framework comprises five interconnected modules that progress from data acquisition and preprocessing to pattern discovery, causal inference, and decision support.

Module 1 focuses on data collection and acquisition. Foundry data are dispersed across multiple systems, including sensor readings, batch records, and contextual notes. This module establishes a robust pipeline to continuously capture and consolidate heterogeneous data, aligning real-time sensor measurements such as furnace temperatures and power consumption with production metadata. Securing the breadth and integrity of the data foundation enables comprehensive and reliable downstream analysis.

Once collected, the data should be transformed into a form suitable for analysis. Industrial sensor data are noisy and prone to gaps, outliers, and inconsistencies that obscure true process behavior. This module evaluates the statistical properties and quality of raw data, identifies anomalies, and applies cleaning and transformations. Time synchronization, contextual annotation, and feature selection ensure retention of the most relevant variables. The outcome is a structured, high-quality dataset that overcomes one of the main bottlenecks in applying AI methods to industrial operations.

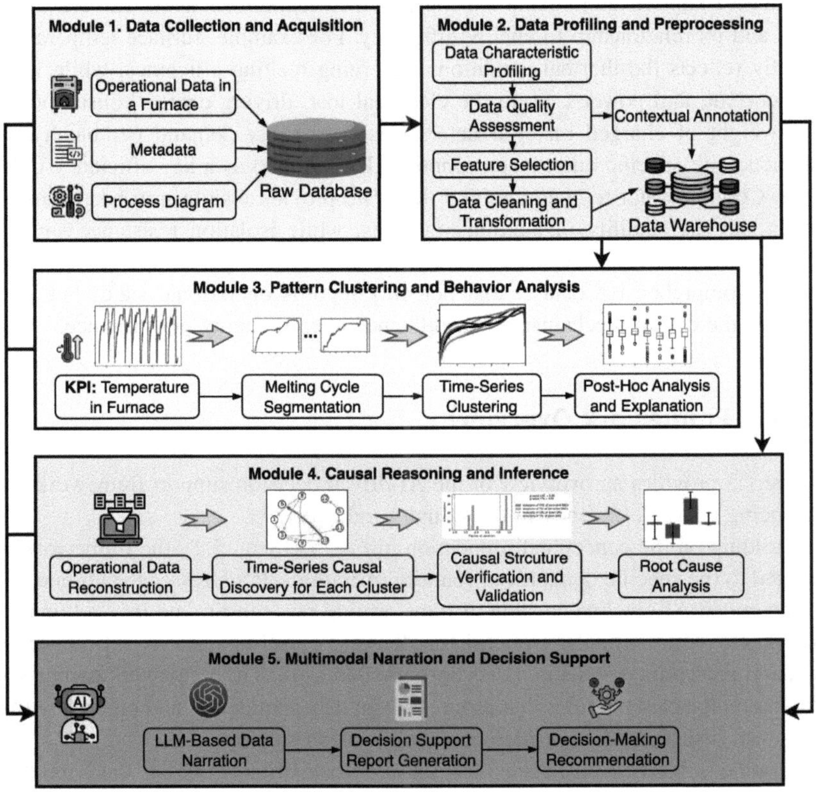

Fig. 7.3 Decision support framework for improving energy efficiency in the foundry industry. It is a realization based on the conceptual framework in Fig. 5.1

With the data prepared, the framework proceeds to pattern clustering and behavior analysis. Foundry melting cycles vary substantially, making it difficult to separate efficient from inefficient practices. Furnace temperature is used as the key performance indicator to characterize each cycle. Data are segmented into melting cycles, which are then clustered based on similarity. Comparative analysis of cluster-level energy performance highlights both best practices and inefficient operating modes, providing an initial layer of insight into operational variability and consistency.

While pattern discovery provides valuable insights, it does not explain why certain operational modes lead to higher energy consumption. To address this limitation, this module applies causal inference to uncover underlying cause-effect relationships within and across clusters. Intervention-based root-cause analysis isolates the drivers of critical variables influencing energy performance. By moving from correlation to causation, this stage identifies actionable levers for achieving measurable efficiency improvements.

The final stage translates the analytical findings into decision support. Analytical outputs such as clusters, charts, or causal graphs are often inaccessible to practitioners without advanced data expertise. This module employs multimodal LLMs to generate clear, evidence-based narratives supported by visualizations. The reports contextualize findings, prioritize key insights, and provide practical recommendations directly applicable to foundry operations. By ensuring transparency and interpretability, the framework transforms complex analyses into actionable knowledge.

Collectively, the five modules form an integrated pipeline that directly addresses industrial and technical challenges in the foundry sector. They enable systematic progression from fragmented process data to validated causal knowledge and, ultimately, to decision support outputs that are transparent, interpretable, and actionable for practitioners.

Table 7.5 demonstrates the selection of algorithms and sub-frameworks from Chap. 6 that are employed to implement the decision support framework.

Table 7.5 The algorithms or sub-frameworks to implement the framework in the foundry case study

Module	Algorithm or sub-framework
1	• The STREAM pipeline (Sect. 6.2)
2	• Data characteristic understanding framework (Sect. 6.3)
3	• TS-IDEC algorithm for time-series clustering (Sect. 6.4.3)
4	• Integrated PCMCI + algorithm for time-series causal discovery (Sect. 6.5.4) • Method for evaluating causal graphs without ground truth (Sect. 6.5.6) • Method for root cause analysis (Sect. 6.5.7)
5	• LLM-based data narration and insight generation framework (Sect. 6.6)

Most experimental stages of this case study draw directly on the algorithms and sub-frameworks validated in Chap. 6, while only a small subset required domain-specific adaptation. In the foundry context, several specialized algorithms are developed, including physical-sensor data preparation (Sect. 7.3.3), melting cycle segmentation (Sect. 7.3.4), and data selection for time-series causal inference (Sect. 7.3.5).

7.3.3 Sensor Data Preparation and Feature Engineering

The raw sensor signals obtained from the induction furnace contain redundancies, inconsistencies, and missing values that should be systematically addressed before advanced modeling can be performed. The generic data characteristic understanding framework has been developed and introduced in Sect. 6.3. However, it should be extended with domain-specific adaptations tailored to the foundry context. Accordingly, two preprocessing algorithms are developed. Algorithm 7.1 (Listing 7.1) reduces redundancy in the cooling water measurements by reconstructing correlated signals into concise yet informative representations. Building upon this, Algorithm 7.2 (Listing 7.2) applies the framework of Sect. 6.3 to complete the data preparation process.

Listing 7.1 Pseudocode of cooling water feature engineering

Algorithm 7.1: Cooling Water Data Reconstruction

Input:
Raw cooling water data: $F_{11} = \{F_{11-1}, \dots, F_{11-10}\}, F_{12} = \{F_{12-1}, \dots, F_{12-10}\}$.
Output:
Reconstructed cooling water data: F_{11}, F_{12}.
Procedure:
for each $k \in \{11,12\}$ do
  Compute the correlation matrix C_k for F_k.
  if all entries of $C_k \geq \tau$ then
    Replace $F_k \leftarrow \frac{1}{10}\sum_i F_{k-i}$
  else
    Select a subset $R_k \subseteq \{F_{k-1}, \dots, F_{k-10}\}, |R_k| \geq 1$,
    based on statistical or domain-specific criteria.
    Replace $F_k \leftarrow \{F_{k-j}\}$.
  end if
end for
Return reconstructed F_{11}, F_{12}.

Algorithm 7.1 in Listing 7.1 addresses the reconstruction of cooling-water measurements collected from multiple physical sensors installed around the induction furnace. In the raw dataset, the cooling water temperature F_{11} and the cooling water flow rate F_{12} are measured at ten locations. Since these measurements often exhibit high redundancy due to strong correlations, directly including all sensor signals may introduce noise and unnecessary dimensionality.

The reconstruction procedure is based on correlation analysis of the sensor subsets. For each measurement group (F_{11} and F_{12}), the pairwise correlation matrix is computed. If the correlations among all sensors within a group exceed a predefined threshold τ (set at 0.7 in this study), the group is considered redundant, and the signals are aggregated by averaging to produce a single representative feature. Conversely, if correlations are low, one or more representative variables are retained, selected according to statistical significance (e.g., variance contribution) or domain-specific criteria (e.g., location relevance for process monitoring). This reconstruction ensures that F_{11} and F_{12} are represented by concise but informative signals, reducing redundancy while preserving meaningful variation.

Listing 7.2 Pseudocode of induction furnace data preparation

Algorithm 7.2: Induction Furnace Data Preparation

Input:
Raw physical sensor data: $\{F_1, \ldots, F_{12}\}$,
where $F_{11} = \{F_{11-1}, \ldots, F_{11-10}\}, F_{12} = \{F_{12-1}, \ldots, F_{12-10}\}$.
Output:
Cleaned dataset $\boldsymbol{S}$.
Procedure:
Reconstruct F_{11} and F_{12} using Algorithm 7.1.
⊳ *follows the data characteristic understanding framework in Section 6.2*
for each $k \in \{1, \ldots, 12\}$ do
    Perform feature-level data understanding on F_k.
    Reconstruct timestamps for F_k.
end for
Remove features with large proportions of missing values.
Align and combine variables under unified timestamps.
Perform dataset-level data understanding.
Apply necessary data preprocessing (e.g., cleaning, normalization, filtering).
Return Cleaned dataset $\boldsymbol{S}$.

Algorithm 7.2 in Listing 7.2 provides a systematic workflow for preparing the induction furnace dataset for analysis. It integrates feature-level and dataset-level data understanding in accordance with the framework in Sect. 6.3. The algorithm takes as input the raw physical sensor dataset, consisting of twelve variables ($F_1 - F_{12}$), including reconstructed cooling water variables from Algorithm 1.

The preparation process begins by reconstructing the cooling water variables. Each variable is then examined individually through feature-level data understanding, including reconstructing and aligning timestamps, detecting anomalies, and validating the signal's statistical properties. Particular attention is given to timestamp reconstruction. Although the nominal resolution of the dataset is 10 seconds, each sensor operates independently, and communication delays between the physical sensors and the data storage system can lead to minor temporal misalignments. As a result, simultaneous events may be recorded with slightly different timestamps. For example, one sensor may record a measurement at *"17:10:12,"* while another records the same event at *"17:10:13."* To ensure consistency across variables, such discrepancies are resolved by rounding timestamps to the nearest 10-second mark (e.g., *"17:10:10"*). This procedure guarantees that all time-series signals are coherent, synchronized, and aligned for subsequent analysis.

Next, variables with large proportions of missing values are removed to improve dataset reliability. The remaining variables are aligned under unified timestamps, enabling consistent cross-variable comparisons and joint analysis. Following this, dataset-level data understanding is conducted to evaluate statistical distributions, correlations, and overall integrity across the entire dataset. Finally, necessary preprocessing operations, such as cleaning, normalization, and filtering, are applied to prepare the data for subsequent modeling and algorithmic analysis.

The result of Algorithm 7.2 is a cleaned and well-structured dataset that preserves essential operational information while ensuring quality, consistency, and analytical readiness. This dataset serves as the foundation for clustering, causality analysis, and decision-support tasks presented in later sections.

7.3.4 Melting Cycle Identification and Segmentation

Operational segmentation plays a critical role in the data analysis procedure and is inherently domain-specific. To address this requirement in the foundry context, a melting cycle segmentation algorithm is proposed, as demonstrated in Listing 7.3.

Listing 7.3 Pseudocode of melting cycle segmentation

```
Algorithm 7.3: Melting Cycle Segmentation
Input:
  Operation temperature time series: Temp = {Temp[1], ..., Temp[n]}.
  Energy consumption time series: E = {E[1], ..., E[n]}.
Output:
  Set of melting cycles: M = {m_1, ..., m_k},
  where each cycle m_k = [T_start[k], T_end[k]].
Procedure:
  Initialize k ← 0, M ← ∅
  for i = 1 to n − 1 do
     ▷ Detect start of a new melting cycle
     if E[i] = 0 ∧ E[i + 1] > 0 then
        k ← k + 1
        T_start[k] ← i + 1
     end if
     ▷ Detect end of the current melting cycle
     if E[i] > 0 ∧ E[i + 1] = 0 then
        Let j ≥ 1 be the smallest index such that:
           Temp[i + j] = min{Temp[t]: t ∈ [i: i + J]} for predefined J ≥ 2
        T_end[k] ← i + j
        m_k ← [T_start[k], T_end[k]
        M ← M ∪ {m_k}
     end if
  end for
  Return M
```

Algorithm 7.3 in Listing 7.3 formalizes the procedure of segmenting melting cycles. The algorithm takes as input the operation temperature data and the corresponding energy consumption profile over n time steps. The output is a set of melting cycles M, each defined by a start and end timestamp T_{start} and T_{end}. A cycle begins when the furnace energy consumption transitions from zero to a positive value, indicating that a new melting operation has started.

The cycle end is initially indicated by a return to zero energy consumption, suggesting that the melting process has been completed. However, using this point directly as the cycle end can be misleading. After heating ceases, the furnace exhibits thermal inertia: the melt temperature remains high for a short duration before entering a cooling phase. To capture this physical behavior, the algorithm does not immediately assign the zero-energy timestamp as the cycle ending. Instead, it searches within a forward-looking interval to identify the minimum recorded temperature, reflecting the onset of the cooling stage. This minimum temperature point is then designated as the end time of the melting cycle.

By combining these start and end markers, the algorithm segments the continuous sensor data into distinct melting cycles. Each cycle is represented as an interval $[T_{start}, T_{end}]$., and the collection of all such intervals constitutes the set of melting cycles. The result is a structured representation of furnace operations that provides a reliable foundation for downstream analyses, such as clustering, causal modeling, and decision-support system development.

7.3.5 Data Selection for Causal Inference

A data selection step is required before conducting time-series causal inference because the full dataset is too large to be processed efficiently with available computational resources. Although all variables and observations are potentially useful for understanding the process, applying causal inference directly to the complete dataset would be prohibitively time-consuming and memory-intensive. By selecting a representative subset of the data, the framework makes the analysis computationally feasible while preserving the system's essential dynamics.

Figure 7.4 demonstrates the flowchart of data selection for time-series causal inference.

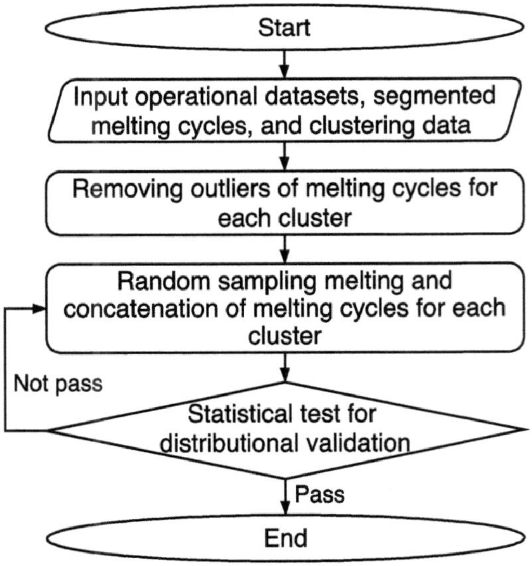

Fig. 7.4 Flowchart of data selection for time-series causal inference in the foundry case study

The procedure begins with outlier removal. Cycle-level variables, such as production duration, total energy consumption, and specific energy consumption per tonne, may contain extreme values due to operational anomalies or sensor errors. Their removal ensures that the dataset reflects typical operational behavior and that subsequent steps are not dominated by atypical cycles.

Following this, a random subset of melting cycles is drawn from each cluster. Sampling without replacement prevents duplication and preserves diversity while reducing the dataset to a tractable size. Random selection mitigates systematic sampling bias, but it is not sufficient on its own: the resulting subset should be validated to confirm that it adequately represents the statistical properties of the original cluster.

To this end, two complementary validation metrics are applied: the Earth Mover's Distance (EMD) [313] and the Maximum Mean Discrepancy (MMD) [314]. EMD provides an interpretable measure of the minimal work required to transform one distribution into another, thereby capturing shifts in the marginal distributions of individual features. MMD, in contrast, evaluates the similarity of multivariate time-series distributions in a reproducing kernel Hilbert space, making it sensitive to higher-order statistical differences and more subtle deviations in temporal dynamics. By enforcing thresholds on both metrics, the algorithm ensures that the selected subsets are statistically consistent with the original data while avoiding redundancy.

The final output is a collection of validated subsets—one for each cluster—concatenated to form the dataset used for causal reasoning and inference. This approach strikes a balance between two competing requirements: preserving the statistical fidelity of the original dataset and reducing its scale to enable computationally feasible causal analysis. The resulting dataset provides a reliable foundation for uncovering causal relationships in melting operations, ensuring that the conclusions drawn are both interpretable and robust.

The step-by-step procedure of Algorithm 7.4 (Listing 7.4) operationalizes the conceptual workflow in Fig. 7.4.

Listing 7.4 Pseudocode of data selection for time-series causal inference

Algorithm 7.4: Data Selection for Time-Series Causal Inference

Input:

Dataset $\boldsymbol{S}$ with features $\{F_1, \ldots, F_k\}$ (output of Algorithm 7.2).
Melting cycles M from Algorithm 7.3.
Dataset $\mathcal{D} = \{x_1, \ldots, x_N\}$,
where each melting cycle $\boldsymbol{x} \in \mathcal{D}$ is represented as
$x = (id, c, d, e, u)$, with $\boldsymbol{id}$ is the melting cycle identifier, $\boldsymbol{c}$ is the cluster identifier,
$\boldsymbol{d}$ is the production duration, $\boldsymbol{e}$ is the energy consumption,
and $\boldsymbol{u}$ is energy consumption per unit.

Output:

Subset $\mathcal{D}' \subset \mathcal{D}$, consisting of selected melting cycles for each cluster.
Concatenated dataset $\boldsymbol{S}'$

Procedure:

1: for each cluster $c \in C$ do
2: Define $\mathcal{D}_c = \{x \in \mathcal{D} | x.c = c\}$.
3: ▷ *Step 1: Outlier removal*
4: for each feature $f \in \{d, e, u\}$, remove $\boldsymbol{x} \in \mathcal{D}_c$ if
5: $(x.f < Q_1(f) - \alpha \cdot IQR(f)) \vee (x.f > Q_3(f) + \alpha \cdot IQR(f))$,
6: where Q_1, Q_3 are the first and third quartiles, α is the predefined coefficient,
7: and $IQR(f) = Q_3(f) - Q_1(f)$.
8: end for
9: ▷ *Step 2: Random Sampling and data reconstruction*
10: Initialize $\boldsymbol{S}_c \leftarrow \boldsymbol{empty\ dataset}$
11: for each $x \in \mathcal{D}_c$ do
12: $[t_s, t_e] \leftarrow [T_{start}[x.id], T_{end}[x.id]]$ ▷ *from Algorithm 7.3*
13: $S_x^f \leftarrow \boldsymbol{S}[t_s, t_e]$
14: $\boldsymbol{S}_c \leftarrow \boldsymbol{S}_c \oplus S_x^f$ ▷ *$\oplus$ denotes concatenation*
15: end for
16: Select candidate subset $\mathcal{D}'_c \subset \mathcal{D}_c$ randomly without replacement.
17: Initialize $\boldsymbol{S}'_c \leftarrow \boldsymbol{empty\ dataset}$
18: for each $x' \in \mathcal{D}'_c$ do
19: $[t_s, t_e] \leftarrow [T_{start}[x'.id], T_{end}[x'.id]]$ ▷ *from Algorithm 7.3*
20: $S_x^f \leftarrow \boldsymbol{S}[t_s, t_e]$
21: $\boldsymbol{S}'_c \leftarrow \boldsymbol{S}'_c \oplus S_x^f$
22: end for
23: ▷ *Step 3: Distributional validation*
24: $EMD \leftarrow \emptyset$
25: for each feature $f \in \{F_1, \ldots, F_k\}$ do
26: $emd(f) \leftarrow EarthMover(\boldsymbol{S}'_c(f), \boldsymbol{S}_c(f))$
27: $emd_{std}(f) \leftarrow emd(f)/\sigma(\boldsymbol{S}_c(f))$
28: $EMD \leftarrow EMD \cup emd_{std}(f)$
29: end for
30: $MMD \leftarrow MaximumMeanDiscrepancy(\boldsymbol{S}'_c, \boldsymbol{S}_c)$
31: if $(|\{f: emd_{std}(f) < \beta\}| / |\{F_1, \ldots, F_k\}| \geq \gamma) \wedge (MMD < \delta)$ then
32: Accept $\mathcal{D}'_c$ and $\boldsymbol{S}'_c$.
33: else
34: Repeat step 16-22.
35: end if
36: end for
37: Return $\mathcal{D}' = \bigcup_{c \in C} \mathcal{D}'_c$, $\boldsymbol{S}' = \bigcup_{c \in C} \boldsymbol{S}'_c$

7.4 Results and Analysis

This section presents the results and analysis of implementing the AI-driven decision support framework for improving energy efficiency in the foundry industry. The results are organized into four main components, including exploratory data understanding and preparation (Sect. 7.4.1), time-series clustering and pattern analysis (Sect. 7.4.2), time-series causality analysis (Sect. 7.4.3), and generation of a decision support report using multimodal LLMs (Sect. 7.4.4). Together, these components demonstrate the framework's capability to process raw furnace data, uncover operational patterns, identify causal relationships, and translate analytical findings into actionable recommendations.

7.4.1 Exploratory Data Understanding and Preparation Results

Note: Parts of this section are based on the author's first-author journal article: *"A systematic data characteristic understanding framework towards physical-sensor big data challenges"* [115].

This section showcases the results of data characteristic understanding and data preparation in the foundry case study.

First of all, the Pearson correlation of cooling water systems variables is calculated based on Algorithm 7.1 (Listing 7.1), and the correlation is visualized in Fig. 7.5.

Figure 7.5 shows that all ten measurement points exhibit strong correlations. In sub-figure 7.5(a), temperature measurements 1–8 are correlated at approximately 0.98, while measurement 9 shows correlations of around 0.90 with the others, and measurement 10 shows correlations of about 0.95. Sub-figure 7.5(b) demonstrates that all water flow measurements are highly correlated, with values above 0.97. These results suggest a high degree of redundancy among the measurement points and indicate that the system exhibits consistent thermal and flow behavior. Based on Algorithm 7.1 in Listing 7.1, the cooling water temperature and flow are aggregated, respectively, by averaging to produce single representative features.

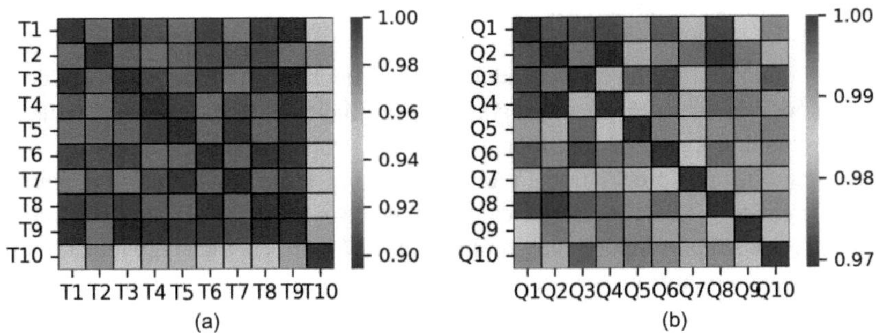

Fig. 7.5 Correlation of cooling water data: (a) correlations among cooling water temperatures at ten measurement points; (b) correlations among cooling water flow quantities at ten measurement points. The color scale indicates the Pearson correlation values

Next, systematic data characteristic understanding is conducted to analyze the data quality based on the 6 V's model and defined data characteristic indicators and evaluation metrics in Sect. 6.3. Table 7.6 displays the evaluation scores of the 6 Vs data characteristics quantified by the metrics defined in Sect. 6.3. The findings reveal a large data volume and good data variety, but limited data velocity. The low data veracity score underscores the dataset's commendable accuracy and reliability. Moreover, the score for data value indicates a comprehensive representation of data values, while the score for data variability indicates medium data variability and medium informativeness.

Table 7.6 Evaluation scores of data characteristic understanding of the furnace dataset

6 Vs	Volume	Variety	Velocity	Veracity	Value	Variability
Evaluation metrics	Vol	Varie	Vel	Ver	Val	Varia
Scores	53,965,188	$+\infty$	10 s	0.0503	0.0763	0.3608

Table 7.7 shows the results of the data characteristic understanding of the furnace dataset, which is generalized based on the data characteristic indicators under the 6 Vs illustrated in Fig. 6.2. The features "F1"-"F12" refer to the variables in Table 7.4.

Table 7.7 Indicators of data characteristic understanding of the furnace dataset

Volume	**NF**	12	**NI**	4,497,099									
Variety	**PSD/PUD/PSSD**	**F1**	**F2**	**F3**	**F4**	**F5**	**F6**	**F7**	**F8**	**F9**	**F10**	**F11**	**F12**
		100%/0/0	100%/0/0	100%/0/0	100%/0/0	100%/0/0	100%/0/0	100%/0/0	100%/0/0	100%/0/0	100%/0/0	100%/0/0	100%/0/0
Velocity	**SDP**	10s											
Veracity	**Features**	**F1**	**F2**	**F3**	**F4**	**F5**	**F6**	**F7**	**F8**	**F9**	**F10**	**F11**	**F12**
	CDF	Yes	Yes	Yes	Yes	Yes	Yes	Yes	Yes	Yes	Yes	Yes	Yes
	PCDF	100%											
	NAS	2	N/A	44	1070	90	86	7489	0	0	109	0	0
	PTI	99.09%	N/A	99.09%	99.09%	99.09%	99.09%	99.09%	99.09%	99.09%	99.09%	99.09%	99.09%
	DTS/DTD	282/0	N/A	212/0	212/0	212/0	212/0	212/0	212/0	212/0	212/0	282/0	282/0
	PMV old	0.027%	99.99%	15.95%	15.95%	15.95%	15.95%	15.93%	15.95%	15.95%	15.95%	0%	0%
	PMV new	8.849%	99.99%	24.78%	24.78%	24.78%	24.78%	24.76%	24.78%	24.78%	24.78%	8.832%	8.832%
	SMS/MMS/LMS	8339/5/5	N/A	8328/5/4	8329/5/4	8328/5/4	8328/5/4	8329/5/4	8328/5/4	8328/5/4	8328/5/4	8340/5/4	8340/5/4
Value	**Statistical metrics**	See Table 7.8											
Variability	**std**	See Table 7.8		**cross correlation**		See Figure 7.7							
	outlier rate	**F1**	**F2**	**F3**	**F4**	**F5**	**F6**	**F7**	**F8**	**F9**	**F10**	**F11**	**F12**
		0%	N/A	0%	2.929%	0%	0%	1.898%	0%	3.627%	0%	0%	0%

The data volume includes indicators NF and NI, which represent the number of features and instances in the dataset, respectively. The results in the data variety indicate that all records in this dataset are structured. Data velocity indicates an update interval of 10 seconds due to the IoT system's default settings.

Data veracity comprises metrics on data formats, time intervals, duplicate times, abnormal spikes, and missing values. The results show that all data formats in this dataset are correct, and 99.09% of time intervals in all features follow the default settings. In all cases, duplicate timestamps are associated with identical values, indicating that the data has been recorded erroneously on more than one occasion. "F4" and "F7" contain more abnormal spikes than other features, which might be false temperature and power readings due to sensor errors at high temperatures.

Due to limited domain knowledge at this stage and because the identified abnormal spikes do not compromise subsequent analysis of data characteristics and quality, these spikes are retained to preserve data integrity and avoid premature exclusion.

The rate of missing values is evaluated in two datasets. The PMV (old) metric calculates the proportion of missing values in the raw dataset, whereas the PMV (new) metric measures the proportion of missing values in the adjusted dataset, where timestamps are realigned according to the pipeline introduced in Fig. 6.3. The adjusted dataset shows a higher proportion of missing values because some timestamps are missing in the raw data. This arises primarily from sensors being deactivated under specific operational conditions. In this case study, missing spans are categorized as follows: short-term ($\leq$30 minutes), medium-term (30 minutes–6 hours), and long-term (>6 hours). Notably, the variable "F2" (State) has nearly 100% missing values. Figure 7.6 demonstrates the completeness of the adjusted furnace dataset.

To address the missing data, the variable "F2" is removed because it has almost no records. For the remaining 11 features, timestamps with medium- and long-term gaps are excluded, as the study focuses on melting cycles, and such gaps typically correspond to periods when the furnace is not operating. Their removal, therefore, does not interfere with the analysis. For short-term missing values, if one or two consecutive records are absent, the gaps are imputed using the average of the preceding and following values, since these cases are mainly due to recording delays or rounding. Longer short-term gaps are removed.

Next, the metrics in the data value dimension are recorded in Table 7.8. The data validity dimension involves the standard deviation in Table 7.8, cross-correlation in Fig. 7.7, and outlier rate. The results show that "F1" has 1.282%

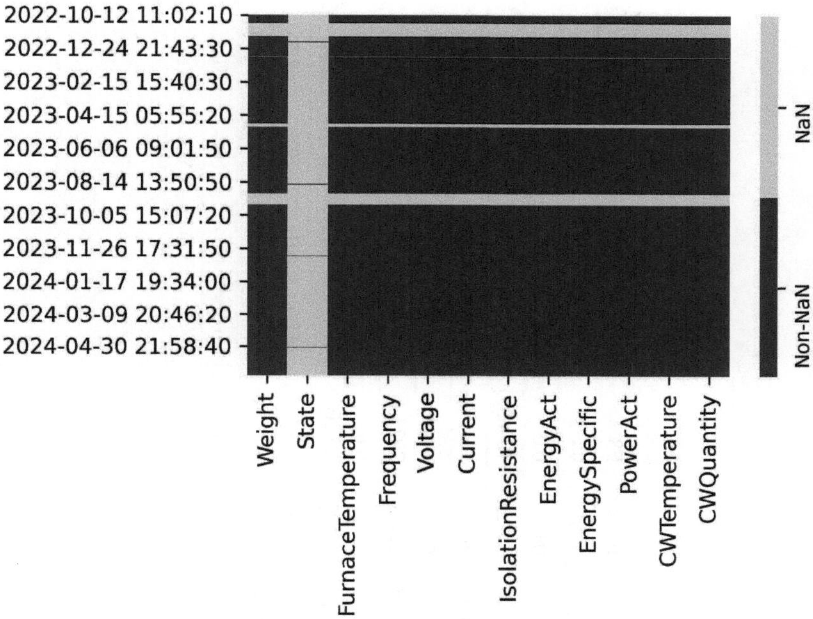

Fig. 7.6 Data completeness of the adjusted furnace dataset, where blue denotes available data and yellow indicates missing values

outliers, "F4" contains 0.01% outliers, and others have no outliers. In the data preprocessing phase, it is imperative to replace these outlier values with appropriate and reasonable substitutes.

Table 7.8 shows the statistical values of each feature in the furnace dataset as the results of the data value dimension. The minimum values for all features, except "F12", are zero, reflecting the default setting of the IoT system when the furnace is in standby mode. The median values of "F4", "F5", "F6", and "F10" are also zero, indicating that the electricity system is inactive for more than half of the recorded time. This suggests that the electrical components are not continuously in operation during melting cycles. Furthermore, the first quartile of "F3" (Furnace temperature) is zero, implying that a substantial portion of the collected data corresponds to periods when the furnace was in standby status. Moreover, the maximum value of "F4" (Frequency) is abnormally high, indicating a faulty record; such outliers are corrected by replacing them with the upper bound of the interquartile range (IQR).

Table 7.8 Statistical values of each feature in the furnace dataset

	F1	F3	F4	F5	F6	F7	F8	F9	F10	F11	F12
cardinality	12820	1621	1944	3003	3003	3561	9455	3276	6255	695	1310
min	0.0	0.0	0.0	0.0	0.0	0.0	0.0	0.0	0.0	6.0	0.0
max	42079.0	1620.0	181222.0	3744.0	3027.0	3023.0	16003.0	9893.0	6422.0	75.4	142.1
mean	4292.0	579.6	69.3	853.4	774.3	26.1	1799.5	492.8	1675.6	33.4	104.2
median	3469.0	229.0	0.0	0.0	0.0	6.3	762.0	508.0	0.0	26.6	124.5
std	3516.9	619.3	208.9	1298.6	1172.8	224.8	2023.4	338.1	2571.4	18.0	35.0
skewness	0.39	0.35	310.6	0.90	0.93	11.24	0.61	4.33	0.95	0.67	−1.16
excess kurtosis	−0.91	−1.58	256031.9	−1.16	−1.02	126.8	−1.07	36.5	−1.01	−1.18	0.22
1st qrt	756.0	0.0	0.0	0.0	0.0	3.9	0.0	341.0	0.0	19.6	62.5
3rd qrt	7460.0	1173.0	150.0	2749.0	2105.0	8.65	3934.0	567.0	4657.0	56.1	127.3
seasonality	No	No	No	No	No	No	No	No	No	No	No
stationary	Yes	Yes	Yes	Yes	Yes	Yes	Yes	Yes	Yes	Yes	Yes

Figure 7.7 illustrates the cross-correlation among different features in the dataset. As no prior domain knowledge is available regarding appropriate time lags, a lag of 6 is selected, corresponding to a delay of one minute. The results show that some features are strongly correlated, while others exhibit weaker associations. Cross-correlation thus provides a useful means of exploring relationships between features and serves as a basis for comparison with the subsequent causality analysis.

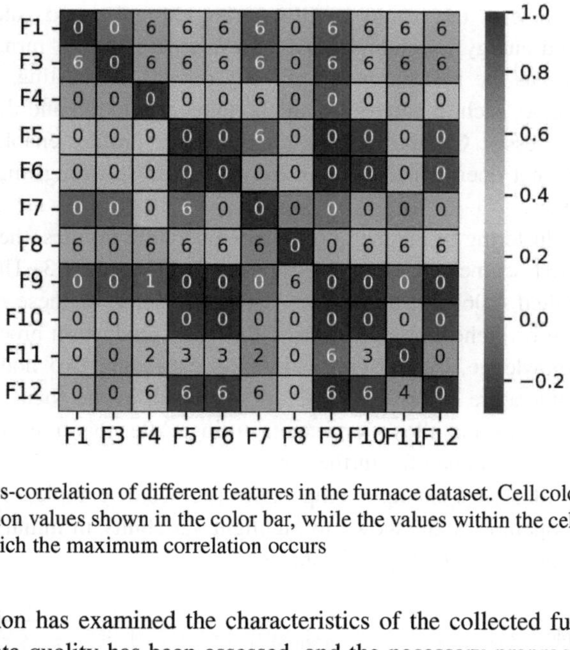

Fig. 7.7 Cross-correlation of different features in the furnace dataset. Cell colors correspond to the correlation values shown in the color bar, while the values within the cells indicate the time lag at which the maximum correlation occurs

This section has examined the characteristics of the collected furnace operation data. Data quality has been assessed, and the necessary preprocessing steps, including missing value treatment and feature selection, have been performed. As a result, a high-quality dataset is now available for subsequent analysis. From an industrial perspective, this stage demonstrates that sensor data in foundry operations can be systematically cleaned and aligned to provide a reliable foundation for decision support. For operators and managers, this means that noisy or inconsistent raw signals, which often hinder day-to-day monitoring, can be transformed into coherent and trustworthy datasets. In practice, such preprocessing allows engineers to make confident judgments about furnace performance trends without being misled by faulty sensors, redundant measurements, or missing values.

7.4.2 Clustering and Operational Pattern Analysis

Note: Parts of this chapter are based on the author's first-author journal article: *"Discovering Operational Patterns Using Image-Based Convolutional Clustering and Composite Evaluation: A Case Study in Foundry Melting Processes"* [145].

This section presents the results of time-series clustering and pattern analysis for the selected energy consumption KPI. In this case study, "furnace temperature" is chosen as the KPI because it directly reflects the heating, melting, and cooling stages. As such, it captures both energy consumption and the underlying operational processes. Clustering furnace temperature profiles enables the identification of distinct operational patterns and their corresponding implications for energy efficiency.

To enable clustering of the melting cycle temperature profiles, the temperature sequence is first segmented using Algorithm 7.3 in Listing 7.3. This procedure initially identified 4,067 melting cycles. However, some of these corresponded to maintenance or preheating operations rather than production processes. Based on domain knowledge, cycles with a duration exceeding two hours or with a maximum temperature below 1,400 °C are excluded, as the focus of this study is on melting metals and alloys for manufacturing. After this filtering step, 3,927 melting cycles are retained for further analysis.

Figure 7.8 illustrates example temperature profiles of complete melting operations. Three operations are shown to highlight variability in initial temperature, process duration, and overall profile shape.

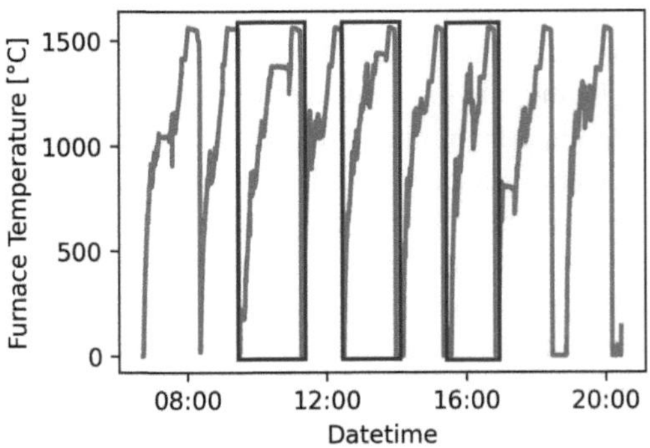

Fig. 7.8 Sample temperature profile of complete melting operations. The blue curve represents the melting operation over time, while the red boxes highlight individual melting cycles

Next, the proposed TS-IDEC algorithm is employed to cluster the melting cycles. The theory and implementation details have been explained in detail in Sect. 6.3.2 and the publication [145]. In this section, the optimal number of clusters is selected, and the final clustering results are presented. Fig. 7.9 presents the composite evaluation scores S_{eva} achieved by TS-IDEC across different numbers of clusters. While the optimal result is observed at four clusters, local maxima at seven and twelve clusters suggest the presence of meaningful substructure in the data as well.

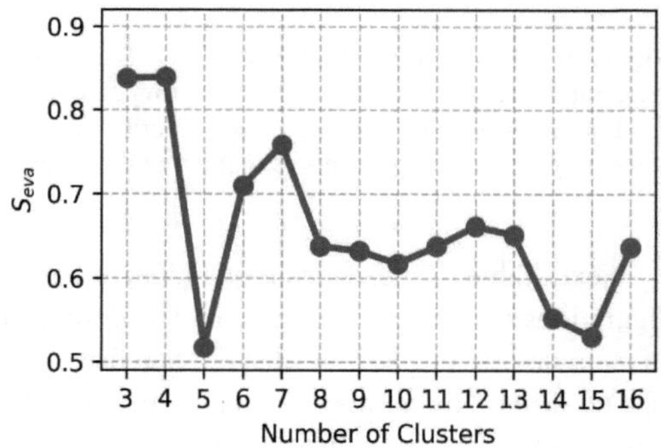

Fig. 7.9 Normalized evaluation scores of different numbers of clusters for the TS-IDEC algorithm

To further explore cluster explainability, this research examines three configurations—four, seven, and twelve clusters—using both low-dimensional visualization and statistical summaries.

The t-SNE plots in Fig. 7.10 show the latent representations of the time-series data projected into two dimensions for each cluster configuration. Each dot represents a single melting operation, and colors denote cluster membership.

The four-cluster solution (Fig. 7.10(a)) produces relatively well-separated groups, although some overlap remains, suggesting the presence of soft transitions or outliers. The seven-cluster solution (Fig. 7.10(b)) provides finer granularity, with improved intra-cluster cohesion and clearer inter-cluster separation. This configuration represents an appropriate balance between cluster resolution and interpretability. In contrast, the twelve-cluster result (Fig. 7.10(c)) leads to excessive fragmentation and greater overlap, thereby reducing both separation and interpretability.

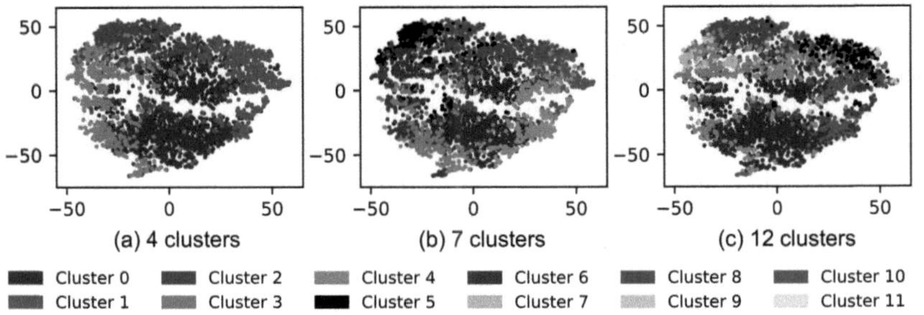

Fig. 7.10 The t-SNE illustration of TS-IDEC clustering results in different numbers of clusters. Subfigures (a)—(c) depict the clustering outcomes for 4, 7, and 12 clusters, respectively. Each solid data point represents a time series projected into the t-SNE space, with colors indicating cluster assignments as defined in the legend

Next, Table 7.9 provides a quantitative comparison of distinct clustering configurations for objective judgment. The dominant cluster ratio measures the share of samples in the largest cluster. Standard deviation reflects imbalance across cluster sizes. The number of small clusters indicates over-fragmentation, defined here as clusters containing less than 1% of the data.

Table 7.9 Comparison of distinct clustering solutions in the foundry case study

Cluster number k	Dominant cluster ratio (%)	Standard deviation of cluster sizes	Number of small clusters (<1%)
4	53.6	650.1	0
7	39.8	414.3	0
12	47.2	490.8	4

The results in Table 7.9 highlight clear trade-offs across the three candidate solutions. At k = 4, more than half of all samples (53.6%) fall into a single dominant cluster, with the highest standard deviation (650.1), indicating strong imbalance and loss of granularity. At the other extreme, k = 12 produces four very small clusters (<1% of data each), suggesting over-fragmentation and reduced stability. The intermediate solution, k = 7, achieves the lowest dominant cluster ratio (39.8%) and the lowest standard deviation (414.3), reflecting a more balanced distribution of samples across clusters without introducing spurious minor groups. These results support k = 7 as the most robust clustering solution, offering a compromise between compactness and granularity.

Figure 7.11 demonstrates the results of TS-IDEC clustering with seven clusters.

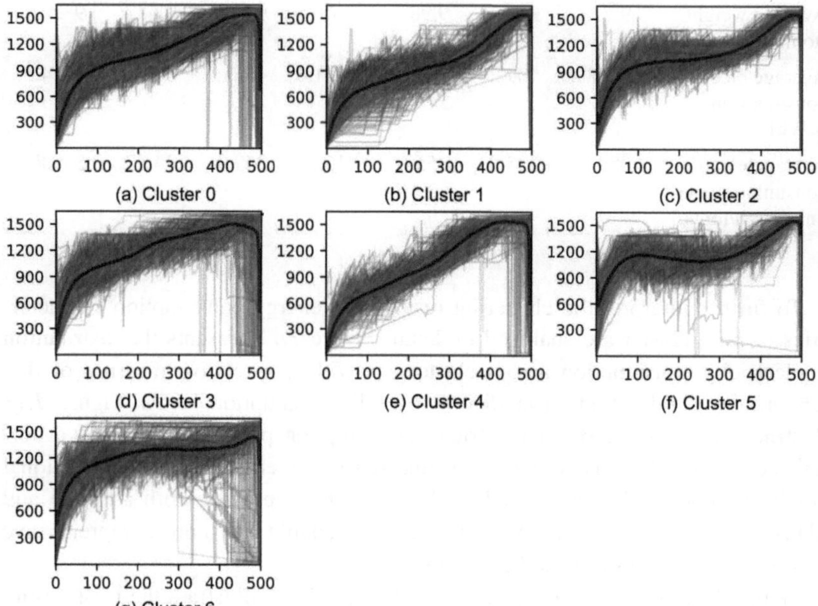

Fig. 7.11 Illustration of TS-IDEC clustering results with 7 clusters. Subfigures (a)-(g) display the time-series data corresponding to Clusters 0–6, respectively. In each subfigure, the bold red curve represents the cluster center, while the remaining curves depict individual time series within the cluster. The x-axis refers to the sequential data points, and the y-axis denotes furnace temperature in degrees Celsius (°C)

Table 7.10 summarizes key operational statistics for the seven-cluster configuration, which was selected for in-depth explainability based on the trade-off between granularity and clarity.

Table 7.10 Statistical characteristics of the seven clusters in the foundry case study

Attributes	Cluster 0	Cluster 1	Cluster 2	Cluster 3	Cluster 4	Cluster 5	Cluster 6
Cardinality	1562	488	466	440	353	313	305
Average production time [s]	4882.7	4340.5	4500.3	6043.2	4641.2	4963.7	7481.9
Average weight [tonne]	9.7	9.98	9.98	9.73	9.5	9.64	9.25
Average electricity consumption [kWh]	5068.4	5093.0	5260.1	5041.6	4853.6	5031.6	5054.5
Average electricity consumption per unit [kWh/tonne]	389.2	325.0	355.6	415.2	359.9	341.7	389.8

To further interpret the clustering results, the energy consumption characteristics of each cluster are analyzed in detail. Figure 7.12 presents the distribution of electricity consumption across clusters, providing a relative measure of dispersion and highlighting variability in overall consumption levels. Figure 7.13 illustrates the distribution of electricity consumption per tonne, offering a normalized perspective that emphasizes differences in efficiency and operational variability among clusters. Together, the two figures provide both absolute and relative insights into electricity usage patterns, enabling a more comprehensive understanding of cluster-specific performance.

Figure 7.12 and Fig. 7.13, together with Table 7.10, illustrate the relationship between electricity consumption, production characteristics, and energy efficiency across Clusters 0–6. While absolute electricity consumption per melting cycle (Fig. 7.12) shows broadly similar medians of around 5000 kWh across clusters, the per-unit consumption normalized by weight (Fig. 7.13) provides a clearer differentiation of energy efficiency.

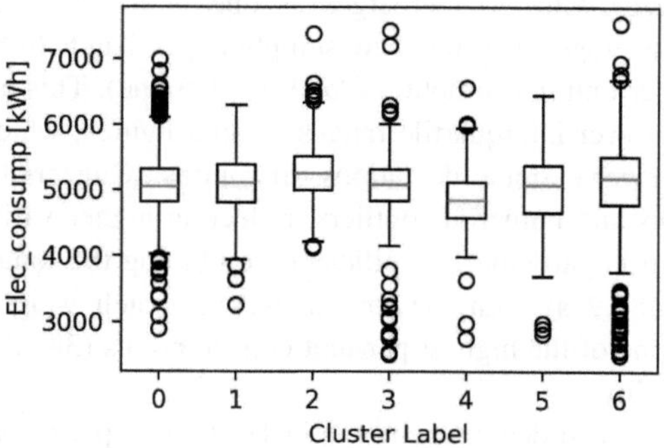

Fig. 7.12 Distribution of electricity consumption across Clusters 0–6 in the foundry case study. The x-axis represents cluster labels, and the y-axis indicates electricity consumption (kWh). The boxplots display the median, interquartile range, and overall variability within each cluster. Outliers are indicated by black circular markers. Box widths are scaled according to the coefficient of the interquartile range

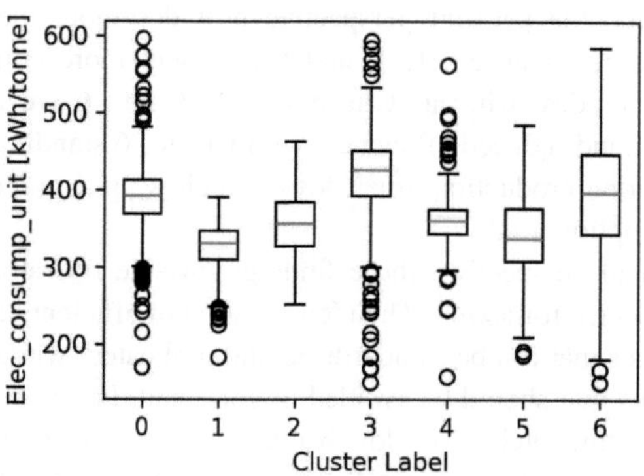

Fig. 7.13 Distribution of electricity consumption per unit across Clusters 0–6 in the foundry case study. The x-axis represents cluster labels, and the y-axis indicates electricity consumption per unit (kWh/tonne). The boxplots display the median, interquartile range, and overall variability within each cluster. Outliers are indicated by black circular markers. Box widths are scaled according to the coefficient of the interquartile range

From Table 7.10, Cluster 4 emerges as one of the most efficient groups, with the lowest average electricity consumption per batch (4,853.6 kWh) and a relatively low per-unit consumption (359.9 kWh/tonne). This efficiency is reinforced by the narrower interquartile ranges in both figures, which suggest stable operations with fewer extreme deviations. In contrast, Clusters 0, 2, and 6 show wider distributions and numerous outliers, reflecting higher variability in energy demand. Cluster 6 is particularly inefficient, combining the longest average production time (7,481.9 s) with the lowest average batch weight (9.25 tonnes), which results in one of the highest per-unit consumptions (389.8 kWh/tonne) and substantial variability.

Clusters 1 and 5 also demonstrate relatively efficient performance, with lower per-unit consumptions (325.0 and 341.7 kWh/tonne, respectively). Their compact boxplot distributions confirm this stability, as fewer extreme outliers are observed. Cluster 3, however, performs poorly, with both an extended production time (6,043.2 s) and the highest per-unit consumption (415.2 kWh/tonne), making it the least energy-efficient cluster overall.

These results show that while absolute cycle-level consumption remains similar across clusters, the per-unit perspective provides more meaningful insight into energy efficiency. Clusters 1, 4, and 5 represent more consistent and efficient operational modes, whereas Clusters 0, 2, 3, and 6 are characterized by greater variability and reduced efficiency, with Cluster 6 standing out as the least favorable due to long production times, lower batch weight, and elevated per-unit electricity consumption.

From a practical perspective, these findings provide operators with concrete benchmarks for decision-making. The identification of efficient clusters highlights operational regimes that can be standardized and replicated, while inefficient clusters reveal patterns that should be avoided or corrected. For example, recognizing that prolonged melting cycles with low batch weights consistently fall into inefficient clusters suggests that adjusting production scheduling and charging practices could directly improve energy performance. In this way, the clustering analysis not only characterizes operational variability but also translates into actionable guidance for managing furnace operations.

7.4.3 Causality Analysis of Furnace Operations

Note: Parts of this section are based on the author's first-author journal article: *"Uncovering Causal Drivers of Energy Efficiency for Industrial Process in Foundry via Time-Series Causal Inference"* [166].

This section investigates the causal structure of furnace melting processes, focusing on both the variable-level causal relationships within clusters and the root causes across clusters. The analysis follows the causal inference pipeline introduced in Fig. 6.9 (Sect. 6.5.1). Cluster-specific datasets are first selected, reconstructed, and validated using Algorithm 7.4 (Listing 7.4). The detailed results of statistical tests for subset selection and validation are shown in Appendix B in ESM. The Integrated PCMCI + method (Sect. 6.5.4) is then applied to uncover causal dependencies among the 11 variables within each cluster. The resulting directed acyclic graphs (DAGs) are evaluated through a permutation-based falsification test [202] (Sect. 6.5.6) and revised according to the test outcomes. Finally, targeted interventions are conducted to identify the root causes of variables related to energy efficiency, as described in Sect. 6.5.7 [201]. Together, these steps ensure that the framework moves beyond correlation analysis to uncover the underlying mechanisms governing energy consumption and efficiency in furnace operations. The falsification test and root cause analysis are conducted using the Python library *DoWhy-GCM* [291], an extension of the *DoWhy* [315, 316] library (*version 0.8.1*).

Table 7.11 summarizes the assessment results and corresponding validation recommendations for the seven DAGs. The number of permutations is set to 100 for the falsification test.

Table 7.11 Assessment results and validation suggestions for each of the seven DAGs in the foundry case study

Cluster	p-value LMC	p-value TPa	Suggestions
0	0.02	0.0	N/A
1	1.0	0.0	N/A
2	0.28	0.0	Remove edge 5 → 11
3	0.37	0.0	Remove edge 4 → 11
4	1.0	0.0	N/A
5	0.38	0.0	N/A
6	0.22	0.0	Remove edge 10 → 11

The p-value of LMC indicates the informativeness of the given DAG, with lower values indicating greater informativeness. The p-value of TPa reflects the trustworthiness of the DAG, where lower values are preferable. As an example, the output from the *DoWhy-GCM* tool for Cluster 0 states:

> *"The given DAG is informative because 0 / 100 of the permutations lie in the Markov equivalence class of the given DAG (p-value: 0.00). The given DAG violates 38/41 LMCs and is better than 98.0% of the permuted DAGs (p-value: 0.02)."*

As shown in Table 7.11, all DAGs yield a TPa p-value of 0.0, indicating that they are highly informative. The DAG in Cluster 0 has a low LMC p-value of 0.02, suggesting strong trustworthiness and reliability. By contrast, the DAGs in Clusters 1 and 4 yield LMC p-values of 1.0, reflecting very low reliability. The remaining DAGs (Clusters 2, 3, 5, and 6) have LMC p-values around 0.3, which suggests moderate but acceptable reliability. Additionally, Clusters 2, 3, and 6 provide concrete recommendations for edge removal, thereby further enhancing the validity of the learned DAGs.

Next, Fig. 7.14 illustrates the causal graphs within each cluster after the validation.

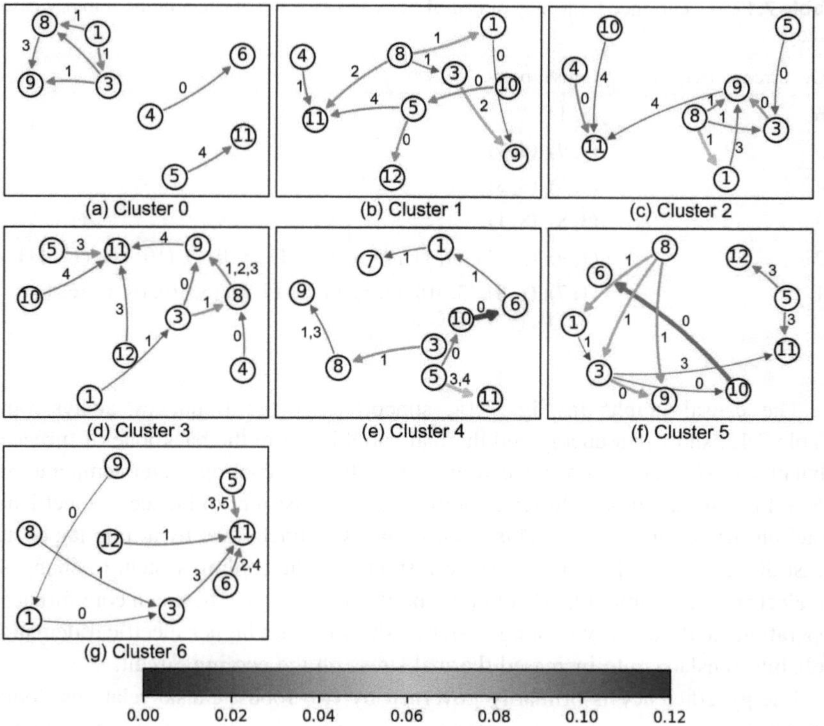

Fig. 7.14 Causal graphs for Clusters 0–6 in the foundry case study. Subfigures (a)-(g) correspond to DAGs for Clusters 0–6, respectively. Each node (black circle with a number) represents a variable listed in Table 7.4. Directed edges denote causal relationships (e.g., $a \to b$ indicates a causes b). The values along the edges represent the time lag, with "1" denoting 10 seconds. The color of each edge reflects causal strength according to the color bar, while edge width also encodes strength, with wider edges indicating stronger relationships

Table 7.12 introduces the occurrence frequency of discovered causal pairs across the seven clusters. Each pair (i, j) denotes a directed causal relation from variable i to variable j, as defined in Table 7.4.

Table 7.12 Occurrence frequency of causal pairs across seven clusters in the foundry case study

Occurrence frequency	Causal pairs
6	(5, 11)
5	(3, 9), (8, 9)
4	(1, 3), (8, 3)
3	(3, 8), (8, 1)
2	(1, 9), (3, 11), (4, 11), (5, 12), (9, 11), (10, 6), (10, 11), (12, 11)
1	(1, 7), (1, 8), (3, 10), (4, 6), (4, 8), (5, 3), (5, 10), (6, 1), (6, 11), (8, 11), (9, 1), (10, 5)

The causal graphs in Fig. 7.14, supported by the frequency analysis in Table 7.12, show that energy and thermal variables form the backbone of furnace dynamics. The most frequent causal pair, voltage → cooling water temperature (5 → 11), appears in six clusters, confirming the consistent influence of electrical load on the cooling system. This relationship is characterized by a time lag of at least 30 seconds, indicating a delayed response of the cooling system to changes in electricity consumption. This link highlights the interplay between core furnace operations and auxiliary cooling systems, showing that higher electrical demand reliably translates into increased thermal stress on the cooling circuit.

Energy efficiency is primarily governed by two robust causal relations: total energy consumption → specific energy consumption (8 → 9) and furnace temperature → specific energy consumption (3 → 9), each of which recurs in five clusters. These links indicate that efficiency depends jointly on the amount of energy supplied and the thermal state of the melt. Two additional high-frequency relations, weight → furnace temperature (1 → 3) and total energy consumption → furnace temperature (8 → 3), occur in four clusters each. Notably, while four clusters support 8 → 3, three clusters display the reverse, 3 → 8, suggesting bidirectional interactions between temperature and total energy. This interplay among energy consumption, temperature dynamics, and material input defines a stable causal core that underpins furnace performance across operational regimes.

The causal graphs demonstrate that causal relationships differ across clusters. Cluster 0, which contains the most melting cycles, exhibits the following causal structures. Furnace temperature (3) drives both total energy consumption (8) and specific energy consumption (9), underlining the role of thermal conditions in shaping energy use and efficiency. Interestingly, weight (1) influences furnace temperature (3), likely reflecting the alignment of temperature changes with material charging or melting progression in this regime.

Clusters 1, 4, and 5 are associated with higher efficiency. However, the DAGs for Clusters 1 and 4 are unreliable, so emphasis is placed on Cluster 5. In this cluster, Furnace temperature (3) causally affects specific energy consumption (9), power (10), and cooling water temperature (11), showing its broad influence on both electricity consumption and cooling systems. At the same time, total energy consumption (8) drives weight (1), furnace temperature (3), and specific energy consumption (9). The joint effect of weight (1) and total energy consumption (8) causing furnace temperature (3) suggests that material load and cumulative energy input together determine thermal operation state.

In contrast, Cluster 6 represents the least efficient regime. Here, both weight (1) and total energy (8) causally determine furnace temperature (3), creating reinforcing dependencies. Additionally, specific energy consumption (9) causes weight (1), an atypical reversal that implies efficiency metrics might be entangled with material variables in non-productive ways. Such feedback loops indicate unstable or inefficient dynamics, where energy use is not effectively translated into productive melting.

After identifying the causal relationships within each cluster, the root causes of key variables related to energy efficiency are further examined [165, 201]. Three representative clusters are selected for analysis based on the clustering analysis in Sect. 7.4.2 and the verification of causal graphs: Cluster 5, the most energy-efficient cluster; Cluster 6, the least energy-efficient cluster; and cluster 0, which contains the largest number of melting cycles and thus represents the most general operational conditions. Four variables central to furnace energy performance are targeted: variable 3 (furnace temperature), variable 8 (total energy consumption), variable 9 (specific energy consumption), and variable 10 (power). For each cluster, the main drivers of these variables are identified by perturbing their distributions using the mean values of the same variable in the intervention dataset. The results of these intervention analyses are presented in Figs. 7.15–7.20.

Figure 7.15 illustrates the contribution of each variable arising from differences in its causal mechanism to the change in mean values between Cluster 5 (baseline) and Cluster 0 (intervention). The analysis focuses on the causal drivers of furnace temperature (3), specific energy consumption (9), and power (10), while total energy consumption (8) shows no direct causal links in the DAG of Cluster 5.

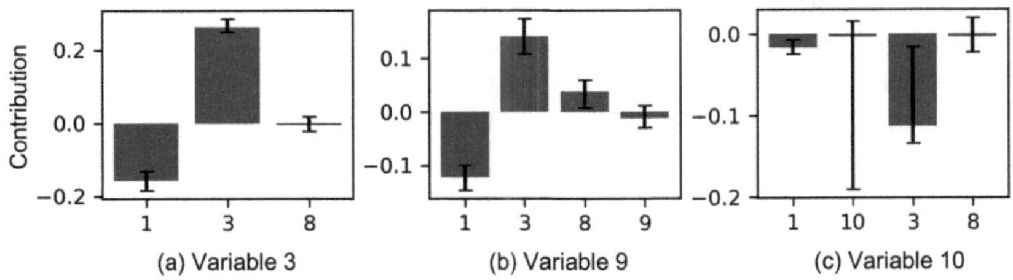

Fig. 7.15 Contribution of each variable arising from differences in its causal mechanism to the change in mean values between Cluster 5 (baseline) and Cluster 0 (intervention) in the foundry case study. Subfigures (a)-(c) correspond to different target variables in the DAG. Each bar represents the mean contribution score, while each error bar denotes the uncertainty of the contribution estimate

The results indicate that furnace temperature (3) is a dominant driver not only of itself but also of specific energy consumption (9) and power (10). This highlights the central role of thermal conditions in shaping both efficiency and real-time energy demand. In practice, this means that stable control of furnace temperature is critical: fluctuations directly translate into increased energy consumption per tonne and variations in instantaneous power use. For both furnace temperature (3) and specific energy consumption (9), weight of input material (1) emerges as an additional important driver. This finding reflects the operational reality that introducing cold material consistently disrupts the melt temperature, leading to higher energy demand and reduced efficiency.

Figure 7.16 illustrates the contribution of each variable arising from differences in its causal mechanism to the change in mean values between Cluster 5 (baseline) and Cluster 6 (intervention). The analysis focuses on the target variables furnace temperature (3), specific energy consumption (9), and power (10).

All three target variables exhibit strong self-dependence, indicating that their current states heavily influence their future behavior. Beyond this persistence, furnace temperature (3) is additionally driven by weight (1), reflecting the impact of metal addition on thermal dynamics. Specific energy (9) is further influenced by temperature (3) and total energy (8), linking efficiency to both thermal and cumulative energy conditions. Power (10) is influenced by temperature (3) and total energy (8), indicating how fluctuations in thermal control and cumulative input propagate into power demand. Together, these results suggest that inefficiency in Cluster 6 arises from unstable interactions among metal weight, furnace temperature, and energy use.

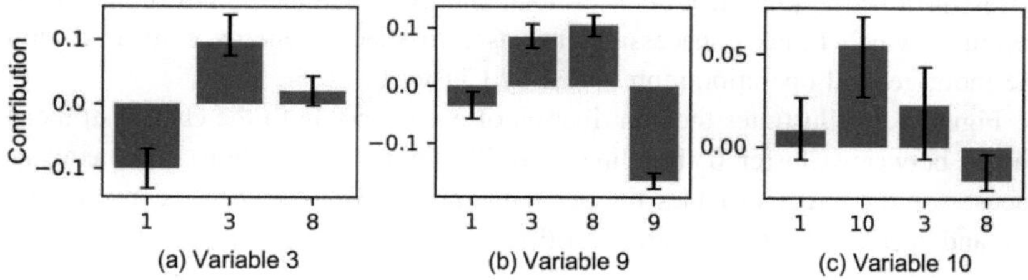

Fig. 7.16 Contribution of each variable arising from differences in its causal mechanism to the change in mean values between Cluster 5 (baseline) and Cluster 6 (intervention) in the foundry case study. Subfigures (a)-(c) correspond to different target variables in the DAG. Each bar represents the mean contribution score, while each error bar denotes the uncertainty of the contribution estimate

Figure 7.17 illustrates the contribution of each variable to the change in mean values between Cluster 0 (baseline) and Cluster 5 (intervention). The analysis focuses on the target variables furnace temperature (3), total energy consumption (8), and specific energy consumption (9).

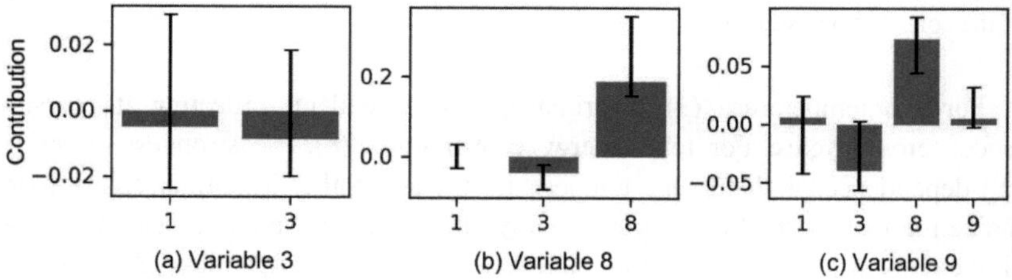

Fig. 7.17 Contribution of each variable arising from differences in its causal mechanism to the change in mean values between Cluster 0 (baseline) and Cluster 5 (intervention) in the foundry case study. Subfigures (a)-(c) correspond to different target variables in the DAG. Each bar represents the mean contribution score, while each error bar denotes the uncertainty of the contribution estimate

For total energy consumption (8), the main driver is self-dependence, reflecting persistence of cumulative energy across cycles. For specific energy consumption (9), the strongest driver is total energy (8), followed by furnace temperature (3), indicating that efficiency is jointly shaped by cumulative energy input and thermal conditions. This comparison highlights that the superior efficiency of Cluster 5 arises from better alignment between total energy consumption and furnace temperature, which limits unnecessary increases in specific energy compared with the more general operation represented by Cluster 0.

Figure 7.18 illustrates the contribution of each variable to the change in mean values between Cluster 0 (baseline) and Cluster 6 (intervention). The analysis focuses on the target variables furnace temperature (3), total energy consumption (8), and specific energy consumption (9).

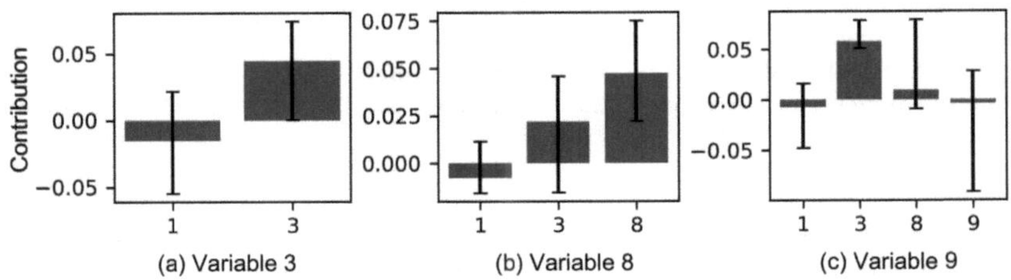

Fig. 7.18 Contribution of each variable arising from differences in its causal mechanism to the change in mean values between Cluster 0 (baseline) and Cluster 6 (intervention) in the foundry case study. Subfigures (a)-(c) correspond to different target variables in the DAG. Each bar represents the mean contribution score, while each error bar denotes the uncertainty of the contribution estimate

Furnace temperature (3) is primarily self-dependent, reflecting its persistence across cycles. For total energy consumption (8), the strongest driver is self-dependence, with furnace temperature (3) as another important contributor, indicating that thermal conditions directly affect cumulative energy use. For specific energy consumption (9), the main driver is furnace temperature (3), showing that inefficiency in Cluster 6 is strongly tied to unstable temperature dynamics. These results suggest that the inefficiency of Cluster 6 arises from poor thermal control: furnace temperature fluctuations not only increase total energy use but also directly worsen specific energy consumption.

Figure 7.19 illustrates the contribution of each variable to the change in mean values between Cluster 6 (baseline) and Cluster 0 (intervention). The analysis focuses on the target variables furnace temperature (3), total energy consumption (8), and specific energy consumption (9).

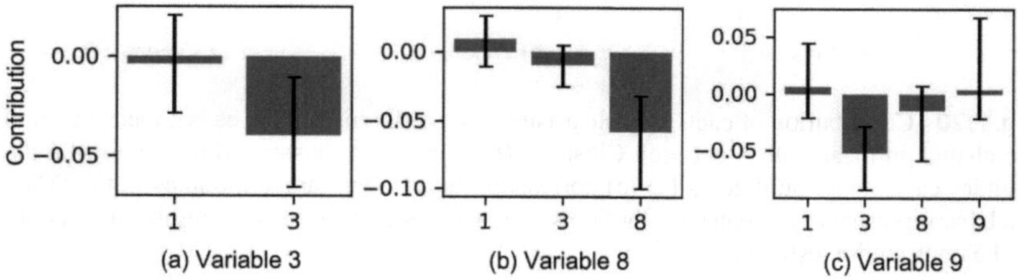

Fig. 7.19 Contribution of each variable arising from differences in its causal mechanism to the change in mean values between Cluster 6 (baseline) and Cluster 0 (intervention) in the foundry case study. Subfigures (a)-(c) correspond to different target variables in the DAG. Each bar represents the mean contribution score, while each error bar denotes the uncertainty of the contribution estimate

Both furnace temperature (3) and total energy consumption (8) are primarily self-dependent, indicating that their states persist across cycles. By contrast, specific energy consumption (9) is mainly driven by furnace temperature (3), emphasizing that efficiency differences between these clusters are largely explained by variations in thermal control. In practical terms, this suggests that moving from the inefficient regime of Cluster 6 to the more general operations of Cluster 0 is achieved by stabilizing furnace temperature, which in turn improves specific energy performance.

Figure 7.20 illustrates the contribution of each variable to the change in mean values between Cluster 6 (baseline) and Cluster 5 (intervention). The analysis focuses on the target variables furnace temperature (3), total energy consumption (8), and specific energy consumption (9).

All three variables show strong self-dependence, reflecting persistence across cycles. In addition, both total energy consumption (8) and specific energy consumption (9) are influenced by furnace temperature (3), confirming that thermal conditions remain the key driver of energy performance. This indicates that the transition from the inefficient regime of Cluster 6 to the efficient regime of Cluster 5 is achieved by stabilizing furnace temperature, thereby reducing total energy use and improving efficiency per tonne.

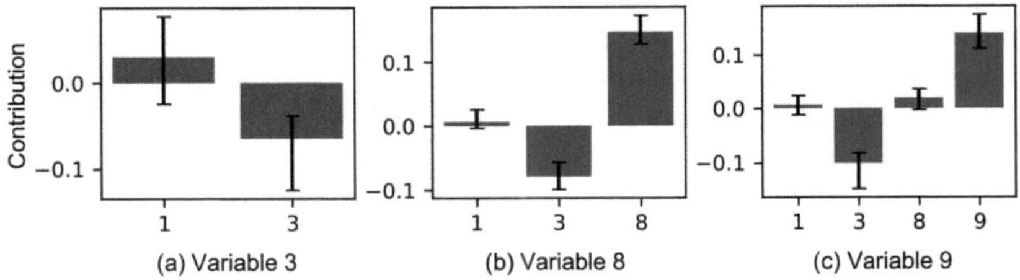

Fig. 7.20 Contribution of each variable arising from differences in its causal mechanism to the change in mean values between Cluster 6 (baseline) and Cluster 5 (intervention) in the foundry case study. Subfigures (a)-(c) correspond to different target variables in the DAG. Each bar represents the mean contribution score, while each error bar denotes the uncertainty of the contribution estimate

From a practical standpoint, these causal findings highlight concrete intervention targets. For example, the strong dependence on furnace temperature suggests that advanced thermal control systems and improved charging practices could directly improve efficiency. Operators can interpret this as a clear priority for monitoring and adjustment, while managers can use causal maps to justify investment in better control techniques. In this way, causal analysis not only explains why inefficiencies occur but also provides a decision-oriented pathway to more efficient operational modes.

7.4.4 LLM-Based Decision Support Outputs

This section presents the multimodal LLM-based decision support mechanism. While Sects. 7.4.1–7.4.3 reported the results of Modules 2–4 in Fig. 7.3, the focus here is on Module 5, which leverages the multimodal LLM multi-agent framework developed in Sect. 6.6 to automatically interpret inputs from the preceding data analytics.

In this module, multimodal inputs, such as background context, charts, and tables, are first transformed into textual explanations through an LLM-based data narration process. Building on these narratives, the system then generates recommendations for decision-making. In the present case study, three categories of recommendations are produced: (i) recommendations for improving data quality, (ii) energy-efficiency recommendations derived from clustering analysis, and (iii) energy-efficiency recommendations based on causal analysis.

The first stage, multimodal data narration, is applied to a large set of inputs, the majority of which have already been presented in Sects. 7.4.1–7.4.3. To avoid redundancy, this section concentrates on the subsequent stage, namely the LLM-generated recommendations. A representative subset of the multimodal data narration results is provided in Listing A.6 in Appendix A.2 in ESM.

Listing 7.5 presents the LLM-generated recommendations aimed at improving the quality of foundry operation data. These recommendations are derived from the multimodal results in Module 2 (Sect. 7.4.1).

Listing 7.5 LLM-generated recommendations for improving the quality of foundry operational data

Based on the comprehensive data analysis, the following recommendations are proposed to enhance data quality and support effective decision-making in foundry operations:

1. Sensor Calibration and Maintenance

The presence of abnormal spikes and outliers, particularly in frequency and isolation resistance measurements, indicates potential sensor malfunctions or calibration drift. Regular sensor calibration and preventive maintenance schedules should be implemented to minimize erroneous readings and improve data veracity.

2. Data Redundancy Reduction

Given the high correlation among cooling water sensors, consolidating these measurements into aggregated features reduces data dimensionality and storage requirements without sacrificing informational content. This approach simplifies data processing pipelines and enhances computational efficiency.

3. Enhanced Data Logging for Operational States

The near-complete absence of data for the furnace operational state variable (F2) limits the ability to contextualize sensor readings. Improving the reliability and completeness of operational state logging, possibly through redundant sensors or alternative data sources, will enrich the dataset and enable more nuanced analyses.

4. Missing Data Management

Short-term missing data imputation using interpolation is effective for minor gaps; however, longer gaps should be investigated to identify root causes such as sensor downtime or communication failures. Implementing real-time monitoring and alert systems can proactively address data loss and maintain dataset continuity.

5. Data Segmentation by Operational Phases

The dataset contains substantial standby period data, which may dilute analysis focused on active melting cycles. Segmenting data by operational phases and focusing analyses on active periods will improve the relevance and accuracy of insights derived.

6. Integration of Domain Knowledge

Incorporating domain expertise into data preprocessing, such as defining acceptable operational ranges and expected sensor behaviors, will enhance anomaly detection and data cleaning processes. This integration supports more informed decision-making and process optimization.

Listing 7.6 presents the LLM-generated recommendations for improving energy efficiency in the foundry industry, derived from the clustering analysis results in Module 3 (Sect. 7.4.2). These recommendations translate the identified operational patterns into actionable guidance.

Listing 7.6 LLM-generated recommendations for improving energy efficiency in the foundry industry based on clustering analysis

```
Based on the clustering analysis and operational data, the following recommendations are proposed to stakeholders for enhancing energy efficiency in foundry melting processes:
1. Optimize Batch Weight and Production Time
- Clusters with higher batch weights and shorter production times tend to be more energy-efficient per tonne.
- Strategies to increase batch size without compromising quality can reduce specific energy consumption.
- Reducing prolonged melting cycles, especially those resembling cluster 6 profiles, will improve throughput and energy use.
2. Standardize Operational Procedures
- Clusters with stable and consistent temperature profiles (clusters 1, 4, 5) correlate with better energy performance.
- Implementing standardized operating procedures and training to replicate these efficient profiles can reduce variability and energy waste.
3. Monitor and Control Furnace Temperature Profiles
- Continuous monitoring of furnace temperature allows early detection of deviations leading to inefficiency.
- Advanced control systems can adjust power input and cooling dynamically to maintain optimal melting conditions.
4. Enhance Cooling System Efficiency
- Cooling water temperature and flow impact furnace operation and energy consumption.
- Regular maintenance and optimization of cooling circuits can prevent overheating and reduce energy losses.
5. Leverage IIoT Data for Predictive Maintenance
- The IIoT system provides rich data for identifying maintenance needs before failures occur.
- Preventing unplanned downtime and maintaining furnace insulation and electrical isolation can sustain energy efficiency.
6. Investigate Alloying and Material Preparation
- Variations in input materials and alloying steps affect melting behavior.
- Optimizing scrap sorting and doping processes may reduce melting time and energy demand.
```

Listing 7.7 presents the LLM-generated recommendations for improving energy efficiency in the foundry industry, derived from the causality analysis results in Module 4 (Sect. 7.4.3). These recommendations emphasize the key causal drivers of efficiency, such as stabilizing furnace temperature, managing charging operations, and controlling cumulative energy use.

Listing 7.7 LLM-generated recommendations for improving energy efficiency in the foundry industry based on causality analysis

```
Based on the causal analysis and operational data, the following recommendations are proposed to improve energy efficiency in foundry induction furnaces:
1. Enhance Thermal Stability Control: Since furnace temperature is a key driver of energy consumption and efficiency, implementing advanced temperature control systems can minimize fluctuations. This may include real-time monitoring and automated adjustments to heating power and material charging schedules.
2. Optimize Material Charging Practices: The causal impact of material weight on furnace temperature suggests that managing the timing and quantity of metal additions can reduce thermal shocks. Gradual or staged charging strategies could help maintain stable melt temperatures and improve energy efficiency.
3. Integrate Electrical and Cooling System Management: The delayed causal effect of voltage on cooling water temperature highlights the need for coordinated control. Enhancing cooling system responsiveness and capacity can mitigate thermal stress, preventing energy losses and equipment wear.
4. Target Inefficient Operational Regimes: Identifying and minimizing time spent in inefficient clusters (e.g., Cluster 6) through operational adjustments can yield significant energy savings. Training operators to recognize and respond to signs of unstable furnace behavior is essential.
5. Leverage IIoT Data for Continuous Improvement: The rich sensor data and causal models provide a foundation for predictive maintenance and process optimization. Stakeholders should invest in data analytics capabilities to monitor furnace performance and implement evidence-based interventions.
```

These LLM-generated recommendations in Listings 7.5–7.7 demonstrate the framework's ability to translate complex analytical results into transparent, context-aware, and operationally meaningful guidance. For practitioners, the outputs illustrate how data-driven insights can be embedded into daily workflows, spanning sensor maintenance, production scheduling, and thermal control. Although the recommendations presented here have not yet been validated in live collaboration with operators, they show the potential of explainable AI to bridge the gap between advanced analytics and real-world decision-making.

7.5 Framework Evaluation and Discussion

This section evaluates the implemented AI-driven decision support framework for improving energy efficiency in the foundry industry. The evaluation follows the criteria defined in Sect. 4.3.2, which together provide a balanced assessment of methodological soundness and practical relevance. The five criteria are capabilities, robustness, explainability, domain integrity, and iterative validation potential.

Table 7.13 summarizes the quantitative metrics. The following subsections expand on the qualitative evaluation of each dimension, highlighting both strengths and limitations observed in the case study.

Table 7.13 Integrated qualitative and quantitative evaluation results for the foundry case study

Criterion	Quantitative metrics	Results
Capabilities	1) Decision-task coverage rate 2) Customization rate	1) 100% 2) 100%
Robustness	1) Unexpected condition solving rate	1) > 90%
Explainability	1) Rate of recommendations with traceable rationale	1) 100%
Domain Integrity	1) Rate of compliance with domain rules	1) 100%
Iterative Validation Potential	1) Iterative validation rate	1) 100%

Capabilities

The framework provides a comprehensive suite of decision-support functions tailored to energy-efficiency challenges in foundry operations. It achieves full task coverage by addressing data preparation, pattern discovery, causal analysis, and recommendation generation. A key strength is its adaptability to stakeholder needs. Operators, engineers, and managers can tailor the system by selecting alternative KPIs for clustering, adjusting root-cause analysis variables, or refining LLM-generated prompts. This adaptability ensures relevance across diverse decision contexts while maintaining methodological rigor.

However, a limitation is that the current evaluation focuses on a single foundry site with induction furnaces. To strengthen generalizability, the framework should be validated across multiple foundries with different furnace technologies and operational environments.

Robustness

The framework demonstrates reliable performance under varied operating conditions, successfully resolving more than 90% of unexpected data quality and process challenges. Robustness is supported by structured approaches: systematic data characterization, cycle segmentation, and subset selection for causal inference.

One limitation is that several causal graphs (DAGs) proved unreliable after validation. At present, no definitive method is included to resolve this issue. Future work could explore ensemble causal inference methods or hybrid validation strategies combining algorithmic outputs with expert feedback. Despite this shortcoming, the framework provides a strong methodological foundation for deployment in real-world industrial contexts, where reliability is critical for user trust.

Explainability

Explainability is a defining strength of the framework. Unlike many black-box AI applications in industrial analytics, this framework integrates multiple layers of interpretability:

- Data characterization clarifies input reliability.
- Post-hoc clustering analysis explains operational groupings.
- Causal inference identifies true efficiency drivers.
- LLM-generated narratives translate results into stakeholder-friendly insights.

All recommendations are traceable to analytical evidence, achieving 100% explainability. This transparency fosters trust among practitioners, enabling them to evaluate and act on recommendations with confidence. The approach also advances academic contributions by demonstrating how multimodal narration can bridge the gap between technical AI outputs and practical decision-making.

Domain Integrity

The framework demonstrates strong domain integrity, embedding foundry-specific rules, terminology, and operational constraints into its analyses and outputs. Recommendations align with established industrial practices, such as monitoring furnace temperature stability, optimizing charging, and maintaining cooling systems.

A limitation is the potential for overfitting to the specific case study environment. While domain expertise has been successfully incorporated, further validation across other foundries and process settings is needed to ensure broader industrial applicability. Nevertheless, aligning AI-driven insights with real-world practices increases the credibility and practical adoption potential of the framework.

Iterative Validation Potential

A major strength of the framework is its ability to support continuous validation and learning. The system enables iterative improvement through operator feedback, repeated model retraining, and ongoing integration of new data. This aligns with agile AI deployment practices, ensuring that the framework is not static but evolves alongside operational conditions.

For example, recommendations can be tested in practice, evaluated for energy savings, and adjusted over multiple rounds of validation. Such iterative feedback loops not only enhance accuracy but also promote stakeholder engagement by allowing practitioners to co-shape the system. This adaptability positions the framework as a dynamic decision support tool capable of sustaining long-term effectiveness.

In summary, the proposed AI-driven decision support framework demonstrates strong performance across all five evaluation criteria, thereby fulfilling the research objectives of developing a robust, explainable, and domain-adaptive system to enhance energy efficiency in the foundry industry. It achieves comprehensive decision-task coverage, adaptability to stakeholder needs, robustness under varying operating conditions, and full traceability of recommendations through multi-layered explainability. The framework also embeds foundry-specific knowledge and supports iterative validation, ensuring continuous learning and sustained performance. Limitations include instability in causal graphs across specific data clusters, single-site evaluation, and limited cross-domain validation. Overall, it provides a rigorous, transparent, and scalable foundation for AI-driven decision support in energy-intensive manufacturing.

7.6 Summary and Key Contributions

This chapter has presented a comprehensive case study that applies the AI-driven decision-support framework to the foundry industry, focusing on improving energy efficiency in induction furnace operations. The study addresses one of the most energy-intensive stages of foundry production and demonstrates how advanced data-driven methods can be transformed into actionable insights for industrial decision-making.

The key contributions are as follows:

- Data foundation and preprocessing: A systematic approach has been established for preparing heterogeneous furnace sensor data. Novel preprocessing methods, including cooling-water feature reconstruction and melting-cycle segmentation, ensure data quality and interpretability while effectively handling redundancy, noise, and missing values.
- Pattern discovery: Through the proposed TS-IDEC clustering algorithm, the framework identifies distinct operational modes of melting cycles and quantifies their efficiency. This enables the recognition of best-practice operations and inefficient regimes, forming a foundation for performance benchmarking and process analysis.

- Causal analysis: The integration of Integrated PCMCI + with root-cause analysis allows the framework to progress beyond correlation-based insights, revealing causal drivers of energy consumption and efficiency. This capability enhances the explanatory power of industrial AI applications.
- Decision support: The multimodal LLM-based narration module translates complex analytical outputs into stakeholder-oriented recommendations. This component bridges the gap between technical AI insights and practical industrial decision-making, ensuring transparency, interpretability, and user engagement.
- Evaluation and validation: The framework is rigorously evaluated against five criteria, including capabilities, robustness, explainability, domain integrity, and iterative validation. Results confirmed its methodological soundness, adaptability, and relevance for real-world application, while also highlighting areas for future improvement.

Despite these contributions, certain limitations remain. The analysis is limited to a single foundry site and primarily relies on historical data, limiting its generalizability to other industrial contexts. Moreover, while causal inference techniques provide valuable explanatory insights, their reliability varies across clusters and requires reinforcement through hybrid validation methods combining algorithmic inference with expert knowledge. Future work should extend the framework to additional industrial sectors, incorporate real-time decision support capabilities, and strengthen causal verification mechanisms.

In summary, this chapter demonstrates the feasibility and value of the proposed AI-driven decision support framework in an industrial context. It establishes an end-to-end pipeline that transforms raw sensor data into interpretable, actionable recommendations, thereby advancing both the theoretical development of AI-based decision-support methodologies and their practical application in energy-intensive industries. The next chapter builds upon this foundation by applying the framework to a second case study in the transportation sector, thereby examining its adaptability and transferability across domains.

Case Study 2: Improving Fuel Efficiency in Public Transportation Systems

8

This chapter presents a case study that develops, demonstrates, and evaluates an AI-driven decision support framework for enhancing fuel efficiency in public transportation systems. The transportation sector emitted approximately 8.0 Gt CO_2 in 2022, making it the second-largest source of carbon emissions among energy end-use sectors [1]. Within transportation, road activities account for about 73 % of total emissions [2]. Public transportation, particularly bus networks, plays a vital role in sustainable mobility by reducing the dependence on private vehicles, yet it remains a significant contributor to energy consumption and GHG emissions. Improving fuel efficiency in bus operations, therefore, represents a major opportunity to mitigate environmental impacts and advance city sustainability [317, 318].

Although research on AI-based approaches to transport efficiency has expanded rapidly, most existing studies focus on vehicle-level control systems or fuel-consumption prediction models [319, 320]. Few have developed systematic, explainable frameworks that integrate data analytics, causal reasoning, and decision support for fleet-level optimization. In practice, transportation operators still lack integrated tools that can convert heterogeneous sensor data into transparent, actionable insights to support eco-driving, route planning, and operational decision-making.

To address these limitations, this case study applies the AI-driven decision support framework introduced conceptually in Chap. 5 and operationalized through the algorithms and sub-frameworks described in Chap. 6. The framework is

Supplementary Information The online version contains supplementary material available at https://doi.org/10.1007/978-3-658-51965-0_8.

Z. Ma, *Artificial Intelligence-Driven Decision Support Framework for Improving Energy Efficiency in Industry and Transportation*,
https://doi.org/10.1007/978-3-658-51965-0_8

adapted to the transportation context to transform multi-source bus data into interpretable knowledge, identify causal drivers of fuel efficiency, and generate stakeholder-oriented recommendations for improved driving practices and route management.

The remainder of this chapter is structured as follows. Section 8.1 introduces the public transportation domain and provides an overview of the case study system. Section 8.2 defines the research problem, translates business requirements into technical formulations, and establishes methodological boundaries. Section 8.3 presents the dataset and details how the AI-driven framework is implemented in the transportation context. Section 8.4 reports the outcomes of data preparation, clustering, causal inference, and multimodal decision-support generation. Section 8.5 assesses the methodological soundness and practical relevance of the framework. Finally, Sect. 8.6 synthesizes the key findings, highlights limitations, and outlines directions for future research and application.

8.1 Industrial Context and Case Study Overview

Public transport refers to high-capacity vehicles operating on fixed routes and schedules, serving as the backbone of urban mobility in cities worldwide [321]. As a critical component of modern urban infrastructure, public transportation systems facilitate large-scale mobility while reducing reliance on private vehicles. However, they contribute substantially to fuel consumption and GHG emissions [322]. According to recent statistics, buses account for a significant fraction of road transport emissions, making them a key target for energy efficiency improvements [323, 324].

Bus operations are influenced by highly dynamic factors, including driving behavior, traffic flow, road conditions, and scheduling policies. These factors interact in complex and often nonlinear ways, resulting in substantial variability in fuel consumption across different driving strategies, route profiles, and operational practices. At the same time, the growing availability of digital data from vehicle sensors and traffic monitoring systems provides a valuable foundation for data-driven analysis and the development of decision-support tools.

This case study focuses on a bus system in Aalborg, Denmark. It encompasses a fleet of buses for which operational data were collected through the installation of physical sensors, meters, CAN bus systems, and GPS devices. These instruments provide detailed information on driver behavior, vehicle performance, and route characteristics. The corresponding bus routes are illustrated in Fig. 8.1.

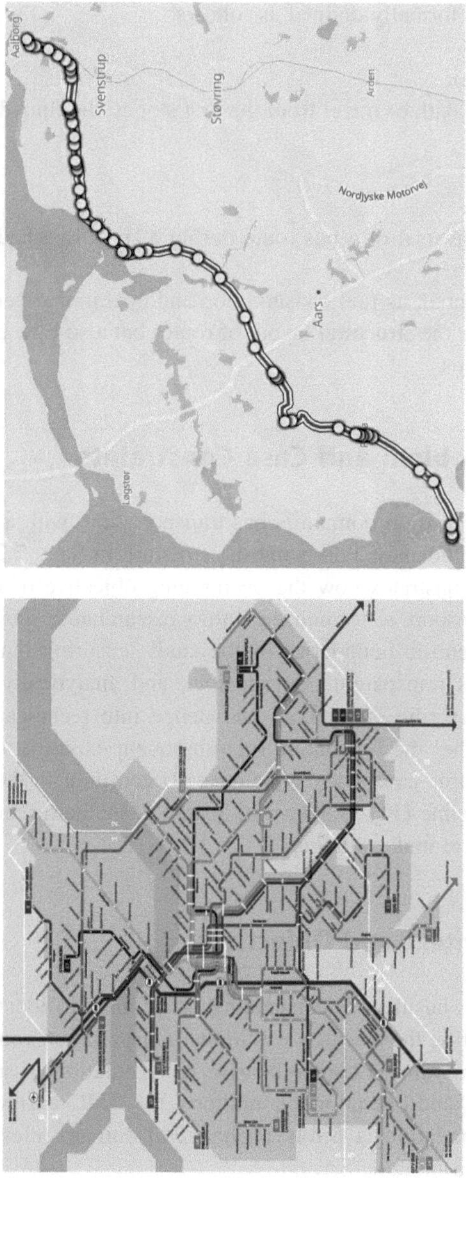

Fig. 8.1 The public transportation system in the case study: (a) a complete set of bus routes, with each color representing a route [325]; (b) an example of an individual bus route, where white circles denote bus stops and green lines indicate the route [276]

To enable systematic analysis, the study distinguishes between bus routes and bus trips [276], which are formally defined as follows:

Definition 8.1 (Bus Route):
A bus route is the planned path of travel from the first stop to the final destination within a bus service plan.

Definition 8.2 (Bus Trip):
A bus trip is the actual traversal of a bus route during a specific scheduled time interval.

This distinction is essential, as fuel consumption and operational performance are not only determined by the structural layout of routes but also by the temporal dynamics of individual trips.

8.2 Research Problem and Case Constraints

In this case study, the application domain is bus transportation, with a particular focus on improving fuel efficiency. Following the structure in Sect. 7.2 for Case Study 1, this section demonstrates how the overarching objective of enhancing fuel efficiency in bus transport is formalized into a researchable scenario. The constraints define the scientific boundaries of the study, ensuring that the proposed framework remains transparent, reproducible, and analytically rigorous. By translating transport-specific operational knowledge into technical formulations, this section establishes the foundation for subsequent experimentation and evaluation. The scope of this case study is delineated according to the first two stages of the DataPro pipeline [11] as shown in Sect. 5.2, including the business understanding and technical understanding.

8.2.1 Business Context and Objectives

Similar to Sect. 7.2.1, the business understanding phase aims to identify stakeholder objectives by situating the research within the transportation context using the BMC [11, 12]. By providing a comprehensive representation of stakeholder needs, value propositions, and operational conditions, the BMC ensures that the subsequent technical formulation is firmly anchored in domain relevance. The BMA analysis is presented in Table 8.1.

Table 8.1 The BMC of the transportation case study

BMC components	Details
Key partners	• Data scientists and AI researchers • Public transport operators and fleet managers (end-users) • IoT, GPS, and telematics technology providers • Municipal transport authorities and policymakers • Energy and environmental regulators
Key activities	• Data integration and analysis of heterogeneous bus sensor data • Application of AI techniques for pattern discovery and causal reasoning • Development of fuel-efficiency and eco-driving models • Integration of decision-support outputs into fleet management dashboards • Continuous monitoring, model refinement, and training for drivers
Key resources	• Skilled professionals (data scientists, transport engineers, and IT staff) • Historical and real-time telematics data (speed, acceleration, fuel rate, GPS, CAN bus signals) • IoT infrastructure and data storage platforms • Computational infrastructure and software tools • Domain expertise in bus operations and eco-driving practices
Value propositions	• Improving fleet-wide fuel efficiency and reducing operational costs • Identifying and promoting efficient driving behaviors • Providing explainable insights into factors influencing fuel consumption • Supporting eco-driving training, route optimization, and predictive maintenance • Enabling data-driven decision making for sustainable mobility
Customer relationships	• Collaboration with fleet operators and drivers for feedback and validation • Continuous improvement of recommendations through operational feedback loops • Technical consultation and support services for framework implementation • Training and knowledge-sharing programs for drivers and dispatchers

(continued)

Table 8.1 (continued)

BMC components	Details
Channels	• Integration into existing fleet management and IIoT dashboards • Cloud-based digital service delivery • Customized reports and visual decision-support tools for managers and drivers • Periodic analytics updates and performance summaries
Customer segments	• Public transport operators (primary users) • Bus drivers • Municipal transport authorities and policymakers (strategic users) • Research and development (R&D) units focused on sustainable mobility
Cost structure	• Investment in telematics infrastructure and data storage • AI framework development and software maintenance • Personnel and training costs for drivers and engineers • Continuous system updates and operational maintenance
Revenue streams	• Operational cost savings through fuel-efficiency improvements • Increased service reliability and reduced downtime • Potential licensing of the AI framework to other transport operators • Consulting services and support contracts for customized deployment

Within the BMC, the top four components (key partners, activities, resources, and value propositions) are particularly relevant to the development and implementation of the decision support framework. The key partners bring together domain expertise, technological infrastructure, and regulatory alignment. The key activities focus on applying advanced AI methods to derive actionable insights from large-scale transportation data. The key resources highlight the combination of skilled professionals, robust digital infrastructure, and domain-specific operational knowledge required for deployment. Finally, the value propositions aim to improve fuel efficiency, promote sustainable transport operations, and provide explainable insights into the causal factors influencing fuel consumption.

Collectively, these components establish a clear business context that anchors the subsequent technical development of the framework. The value propositions define the domain objectives, such as fuel efficiency, behavioral optimization, and sustainable operation, which are subsequently translated into the scientific problems and technical methods addressed in this study.

8.2.2 Technical Formulation and Constraints

The technical understanding of this study involves defining input data, expected outputs, evaluation metrics, and operational constraints. The key elements of technical understanding are summarized in Table 8.2.

Table 8.2 Elements of technical understanding in the transportation case study

Categories	Elements
Input	• Sensor data from multiple buses
Output	• Interpretable insights into fuel efficiency • Efficient bus trips • Factors influencing fuel efficiency • Data-driven recommendations for improving fuel efficiency
Evaluation metrics	• Evaluation metrics defined in Sect. 4.3.2
Constraints (detailed in Table 8.3)	• Domain constraints • Operational constraints • Data constraints • Methodological constraints

The input data comprise driving records from the bus fleet, including meter readings (e.g., speed, acceleration, gear position, and fuel consumption), CAN bus signals (e.g., engine parameters), GPS data (e.g., location and route), and additional sensor measurements (e.g., ambient temperature). Together, these sources provide a comprehensive foundation for analyzing fuel efficiency and its influencing factors. The expected outputs are interpretable insights into fuel efficiency, including the identification of efficient operational patterns, the determination of key factors affecting fuel consumption, and the generation of data-driven recommendations to improve fuel efficiency.

The evaluation metrics adopted in this case study follow the definitions in Sect. 4.3.2, including capabilities, robustness, explainability, domain integrity, and iterative validation potential.

The study is also bound by a set of research constraints that delineate its scope and define the conditions under which results should be interpreted. These constraints are categorized into four dimensions: domain, operational, data, and methodological, as presented in Table 8.3.

Table 8.3 Research constraints in the transportation case study

Categories	Context
Domain constraints	• This study is restricted to bus transportation. • The case study analyzes bus trips across multiple buses, drivers, and routes.
Operational constraints	• The primary performance criterion is fuel efficiency. • The scope is limited to technical feasibility, focusing on operations in bus trips.
Data constraints	• Analysis is based on historical physical sensor data collected from the bus transportation system case. • Data quality issues are mitigated during preprocessing, but residual uncertainties may remain. • The temporal resolution and coverage are limited to the available archival records, without a controlled experimental design.
Methodological constraints	• The research applies statistical analysis and machine learning algorithms for data-driven analytics. • Decision-support outputs are derived from retrospective data analysis and automated recommendations.

Within the defined constraints, the study on developing an AI-driven decision support framework for improving fuel efficiency in the public transportation systems advances the following five research problems:

- **Data preprocessing:** understanding data characteristics and addressing data quality issues.
- **Pattern discovery:** applying clustering techniques to segment operational patterns and classify fuel efficiency profiles.
- **Process characterization:** developing systematic methods to describe the statistical and operational properties of heterogeneous bus operational and driving data.
- **Causal analysis:** employing causal inference and reasoning to identify and validate factors that influence energy-related bus operations.
- **Decision support:** designing an LLM-based recommendation module to translate analytical outputs into actionable, domain-specific insights.

8.3 Data Foundation and Framework Implementation

This section presents the data foundation and the case-specific implementation of the AI-driven decision support framework for the public transportation system. It begins with an overview of operational data collected from the bus fleet, which serves as the empirical basis for the analysis. The dataset integrates heterogeneous information from multiple sources, including vehicle sensors, CAN bus systems, GPS tracking, and journey records, covering key parameters related to driving behavior, vehicle dynamics, and route conditions.

Building on this data foundation, the section describes how the conceptual framework introduced in Fig. 5.1 (Sect. 5.1) is operationalized for the transportation domain. The algorithms and sub-frameworks developed in Chap. 6 are systematically integrated to create a unified analytical pipeline. The objective is to demonstrate how diverse and complex bus-operation data can be transformed into interpretable, decision-ready insights that support fuel-efficiency optimization and eco-driving strategies across the fleet.

8.3.1 Data Sources and Variables

The dataset comprises one week of driving records collected between *"07.08.2023"* and *"13.08.2023" (dd.mm.yyyy)*. Data is obtained from multiple buses, with each day's records stored in separate sub-folders. Each independent dataset corresponds to the operational data of a single bus over a single day. Table 8.4 shows the basic information of the datasets.

Table 8.4 Basic information on the transportation datasets

Date folder	Days of the week	Number of buses
7	Monday	112
8	Tuesday	114
9	Wednesday	114
10	Thursday	112
11	Friday	110
12	Saturday	53
13	Sunday	52

The data are sampled at a one-second interval. Table 8.5 presents the variables selected for the case study, grouped into seven categories: acceleration data, GPS data, speed data, CAN bus data, driver information, bus status information, and journey data. Each dataset, corresponding to the operation of a single bus on a given day, contains all variables presented in the table, along with their units and descriptions.

Table 8.5 Variables and description of transportation datasets

No.	Variable	Unit	Description
Acceleration data			
1	Acceleration	m/s^2	Acceleration
2	LateralAcceleration	m/s^2	Lateral acceleration
GPS data			
3	Speed	km/h	Bus speed
4	Altitude	m	Altitude
Speed data			
5	SpeedLimit	km/h	Speed limit
CAN bus data			
6	AccPedalPosition	N/A	Acceleration pedal position
7	AmbientTemp	°C	Ambient temperature
8	CurrentGear	N/A	Current gear
9	EngineLoad	%	Engine load
10	EngineSpeed	rpm	Engine speed
11	EngineTorque	Nm	Engine torque
Driver			
12	DriverId	N/A	Driver's ID
Bus Status Information			
13	Right	Binary	Turing right status (on/off)
14	Door	Binary	Door status (open/close)
15	Stop	Binary	Stop button (on/off)
16	Reverse	Binary	Reverse status (active/inactive)

(continued)

Table 8.5 (continued)

No.	Variable	Unit	Description
Journey data			
17	RouteName	N/A	Route name
18	AtStop	Binary	At stop (right/false)
19	Delay	s	Time of delay
20	NextStopName	N/A	Next stop name
21	Destination	N/A	Destination name
22	State	N/A	State of journey

8.3.2 Framework Overview

Similar to Fig. 7.3 in Case Study 1, Fig. 8.2 illustrates the AI-driven decision support framework adapted for improving fuel efficiency in the public transportation sector. Building on the conceptual foundation outlined in Fig. 5.1 (Sect. 5. 1), the framework comprises five interconnected modules that progress from data acquisition and preprocessing to pattern discovery, causal inference, and decision support.

Module 1 focuses on data collection and acquisition. Transportation data are distributed across multiple buses and encompass heterogeneous sources, including meter readings, GPS data, CAN bus records, driver identifiers, and journey information. Consolidating these diverse streams establishes a continuous acquisition pipeline that aligns real-time measurements (e.g., speed, acceleration, engine load, ambient conditions) with contextual records. This integration ensures data breadth, accuracy, and integrity, providing a robust foundation for subsequent analysis.

Once collected, the data should be transformed into a form suitable for analysis. Transportation datasets are inherently noisy and prone to gaps, outliers, and inconsistencies; fuel consumption measurements, in particular, are often imprecise in real-world conditions. This module evaluates data quality, detects anomalies, and applies systematic cleaning and transformation steps. Synchronization, contextual annotation, and feature engineering ensure that the most relevant variables are consistently represented, reconstructing fragmented records into a high-quality dataset suitable for analysis.

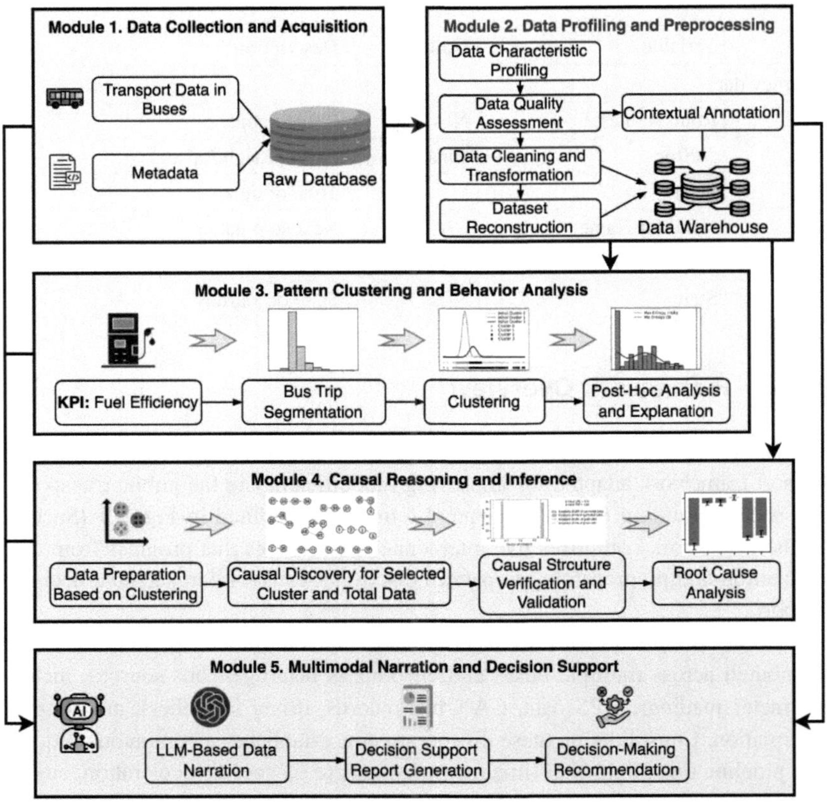

Fig. 8.2 Decision support framework for improving fuel efficiency in the public transportation system. It is a realization based on the conceptual framework in Fig. 5.1

With the data prepared, the framework proceeds to pattern clustering and behavior analysis. Bus trips exhibit substantial variability in fuel efficiency due to differences in routes, drivers, and traffic conditions. In this module, bus trips are segmented, fuel efficiency is calculated for each segment, and clusters are formed based on similarity. Comparative analysis across clusters enables the identification of efficient practices and inefficient operating modes. Post-hoc analyses further examine the distribution of route types, drivers, and operational conditions across clusters, providing insight into how different strategies translate into measurable outcomes.

While clustering reveals fuel-efficiency patterns, it does not explain their underlying causes. Module 4 applies causal inference to uncover cause-effect relationships within clusters and across operational contexts. Root cause analysis, supported by intervention-based reasoning, isolates the key drivers of fuel consumption, including acceleration behavior, gear usage, idling, and stop frequency. By moving beyond correlation, the framework identifies actionable levers that decision-makers can adjust with confidence to improve efficiency.

The final stage concerns translating analytical findings into decision support. Analytical outputs such as clusters and causal structures are often inaccessible to practitioners without advanced data science expertise. This module leverages multimodal LLMs to translate results into interpretable narratives and visualizations. The reports contextualize findings, highlight priorities, and present evidence-based recommendations for drivers, fleet managers, and planners, ensuring that analytical insights are transformed into actionable strategies for fuel efficiency.

Collectively, the five modules form an integrated pipeline tailored to the challenges of the transportation sector. The framework enables systematic progression from fragmented bus-trip data to validated causal knowledge and, ultimately, to decision support outputs that are transparent, interpretable, and actionable.

Table 8.6 demonstrates the selection of algorithms and sub-frameworks from Chap. 6 used to implement the decision support framework in this case study.

Table 8.6 The algorithms or sub-frameworks to implement the framework in the transportation case study

Module	Algorithm or sub-framework
1	• The STREAM pipeline (Sect. 6.2)
2	• Data characteristic understanding framework (Sect. 6.3)
3	• GMM clustering algorithm (Sect. 6.4.1)
4	• Bagging DAGMA-DCE algorithm for causal discovery (Sect. 6.5.2) • Method for evaluating causal graphs without ground truth (Sect. 6.5.6) • Method for root cause analysis (Sect. 6.5.7)
5	• LLM-based data narration and insight generation framework (Sect. 6.6)

Most experimental stages of this case study draw directly on the algorithms and sub-frameworks validated in Chap. 6, while only a small subset required domain-specific adaptation. In the transportation context, several specialized algorithms have been developed, including data preparation and reconstruction (Sect. 8.3.3), and bus trip segmentation (Sect. 8.3.4).

8.3.3 Sensor Data Preparation and Feature Engineering

The pipeline illustrated in Fig. 8.3 applies the generic data characteristic understanding framework introduced in Sect. 6.3, extended with domain-specific adaptations tailored to the transportation context to complete the data preparation process.

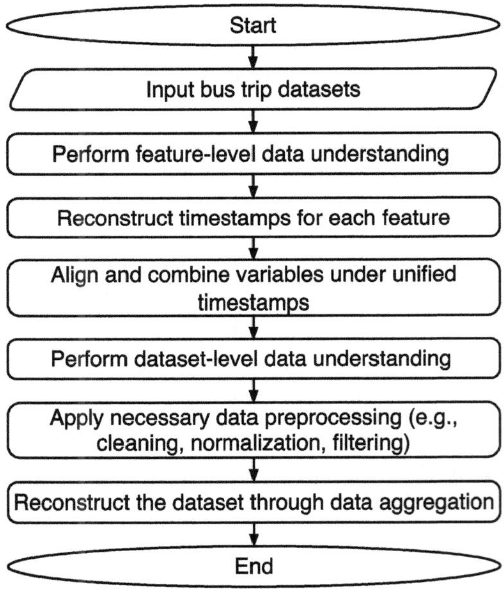

Fig. 8.3 The procedure of transportation data preparation

The preparation process begins with feature-level data understanding, where each variable in each dataset is examined individually. This includes reconstructing and aligning timestamps, detecting anomalies, and validating the statistical properties of the signals. Particular attention is given to timestamp reconstruction. Although the nominal resolution of the dataset is one second, sensors operate independently, and communication delays between physical sensors and the data storage system can introduce minor temporal misalignments. For instance, one sensor may record a value at "17:10:12.994", while another records the same event at "17:10:13.065". To ensure consistency, timestamps are rounded to the nearest second "17:10:13", thereby synchronizing signals across all variables.

Once timestamps are aligned, variables are consolidated under unified time indices, enabling consistent cross-variable comparisons and joint analyses.

Dataset-level understanding is then performed to evaluate statistical distributions, correlations, and overall data integrity. Preprocessing steps, including cleaning, normalization, and filtering, are subsequently applied. Finally, aggregation procedures are conducted to generate holistic representations such as averages, sums, and trends. This step is particularly important given the presence of multiple datasets across different buses and routes, as it produces a single integrated dataset suitable for analysis.

The resulting dataset is cleaned, well-structured, and analytically ready, preserving essential operational information while ensuring quality and consistency. It forms the foundation for the clustering, causal analysis, and decision-support tasks presented in subsequent sections.

8.3.4 Bus Trip Identification and Segmentation

Bus trip segmentation is a critical step in data analysis and is inherently domain-specific, as this case study focuses on bus trip-level analysis. To meet this requirement, a dedicated segmentation algorithm (Algorithm 8.1) is proposed, as presented in Listing 8.1.

Listing 8.1 Pseudocode of bus trip segmentation

Algorithm 8.1: Bus Trip Segmentation

Input:
Destination sequence: D = $\{d_1, \ldots, m_k$.
State sequence: S = $\{s_1, \ldots, s_k\}$.
Timestamps: T = $\{t_1, \ldots, t_k\}$.

Output:
Set of bus trips: B= $\{b_1, \ldots, b_k\}$,
where each cycle $b_k = [T_{start}[k], T_{end}[k]]$.

Procedure:

```
Initialize k ← 0, B ← ∅, 𝒥 ← {1}
for i = 1 to n − 1 do
    if d_i ≠ d_{i+1} then
        𝒥 ← 𝒥 ∪ {i + 1}                    ▷ Set of trip boundaries
    end if
end for
for each consecutive pair (i, j) in 𝒥 do
    while s_i = "wait" do
        i ← i + 1
    end while
    T_start[k] ← i
    T_end[k] ← j − 1
    b_k ← [T_start[k], T_end[k]
    B ← B ∪ {b_k}
end for
Return B
```

Algorithm 8.1 in Listing 8.1 formalizes the segmentation of bus trips based on destination changes and operational states. The input consists of three synchronized sequences: the destination data, the state data, and the corresponding timestamps. The algorithm outputs a set of bus trips B, where each trip is defined by a start and end timestamp T_{start} and T_{end}.

The procedure begins by scanning the destination sequence to identify indices where the destination changes. These indices serve as candidate trip boundaries. For each consecutive boundary pair, to refine the trip start, the state sequence is evaluated to exclude periods where the bus is in the "wait" state. The start time is updated to the first timestamp after this idle phase, ensuring that each trip reflects actual movement rather than idle periods at stops or depots. The finalized interval $[T_{start}, T_{end}]$ is stored as one bus trip and appended to the trip set B.

This algorithm guarantees that all trips are systematically segmented according to destination transitions, while state information provides an additional layer of refinement to ensure operational accuracy. The resulting set B provides a coherent representation of trips for subsequent analysis.

8.4 Results and Analysis

This section presents the results and analysis of implementing the AI-driven decision support framework for improving fuel efficiency in public transportation systems. The results are organized to reflect the framework's modular structure, encompassing data preparation (Sect. 8.4.1), feature reconstruction (Sect 8.4.2), clustering (Sect 8.4.3), causal inference (Sect 8.4.4), and multimodal decision support (Sect 8.4.5). Together, these components demonstrate how the proposed framework processes heterogeneous bus-operation data, uncovers operational patterns, identifies causal drivers of fuel consumption, and translates analytical findings into actionable recommendations for drivers and fleet managers.

8.4.1 Exploratory Data Preparation Results

Note: Parts of this section are based on the author's first-author journal article: *"A systematic data characteristic understanding framework towards physical-sensor big data challenges"* [115].

This section presents the results of data characterization and preparation in the transportation case study. The collected data comprise over 100 bus-specific datasets, each containing multiple features. While every dataset and feature was assessed at this stage, it is not feasible to present all results within this thesis. Instead, a single representative dataset with 10 features is selected and reported as an illustrative example. The dataset in this case study involves one day of operational data. The recording period is from 6:36:15 on August 7, 2023, to 21:12:12 on August 7, 2023, and the default time interval is 1 second. The ten features of the dataset are encoded as "R1"-"R10", as shown in Table 8.7.

Table 8.7 Feature name encoding in the selected transportation dataset

Original name	Encoded name
TimeToLastMoment	R1
Speed	R2
CurrentAcceleration	R3
ProcessedAcceleration	R4
ConsumptionLastSecond	R5
ComsumptionTotal	R6
FuelRate	R7
InstantFuelEco	R8
TotalFuelUsed	R9
TotalregenerativeEnergy	R10

First of all, the systematic data characteristic understanding is conducted to analyze the data quality based on the 6 V's model and data characteristic indicators and evaluation metrics defined in Sect. 6.3.2. Table 8.8 displays the evaluation scores of the 6 Vs data characteristics quantified by the metrics from Sect. 6.3.2. The findings reveal a large data volume, a wide variety of data, and high data velocity. The low score in data veracity suggests commendable accuracy and reliability of the dataset. However, the score for data value indicates a medium level of comprehensive representation, while the score for data variability indicates medium data variability and medium informativeness.

Table 8.8 Evaluation scores of the data characteristic understanding of the transportation dataset

6 Vs	Volume	Variety	Velocity	Veracity	Value	Variability
Evaluation metrics	Vol	Varie	Vel	Ver	Val	Varia
Scores	435,230	$+\infty$	1s	3.818e-3	0.36	0.4229

Table 8.9 shows the results of the data characteristic understanding of the transportation dataset, which is generalized based on the data characteristic indicators under the 6 Vs illustrated in Fig. 6.3.

The data volume includes indicators NF and NI, which represent the number of features and instances in the dataset, respectively. The results in the data variety indicate that all records in this dataset are structured. Data velocity shows an update rate of one second due to the default settings of the IoT system monitoring the vehicle's operations.

Data veracity comprises metrics on data formats, time intervals, duplicate times, abnormal spikes, and missing values. The results show that all data formats in this dataset are correct, and 99.99% of time intervals in all features follow the default settings. There is no duplicate timestamp in the dataset.

The abnormal spikes observed in "R1" are attributed to variations in recording gaps resulting from changes in vehicle operating modes. The irregular acceleration and braking patterns might result in the abnormal spikes detected in "R3" and "R4". Due to limited domain knowledge at this stage and because the identified abnormal spikes do not compromise subsequent analysis of data characteristics and quality, these spikes are retained to preserve data integrity and avoid premature exclusion.

The rate of missing values is evaluated in two datasets. The PMV (old) metric calculates the proportion of missing values in the raw dataset, whereas the PMV (new) metric measures the proportion of missing values in the adjusted dataset, where timestamps are realigned according to the pipeline introduced in Fig. 6.3. The adjusted dataset shows a higher proportion of missing values because some timestamps are missing in the raw data. This arises primarily from sensors being deactivated under specific driving conditions. In this case study, missing spans are categorized as follows: short-term ($\leq$1 minute), medium-term (1 minute-30 minutes), and long-term (>6 hours). Fig. 8.4 demonstrates the completeness of the adjusted furnace dataset.

Table 8.9 Indicators of data characteristic understanding of the transportation dataset

Volume	**NF**	10	**NI**	43,523							
Variety	**PSD/PUD/PSSD**	**R1**	**R2**	**R3**	**R4**	**R5**	**R6**	**R7**	**R8**	**R9**	**R10**
		100%/0/0	100%/0/0	100%/0/0	100%/0/0	100%/0/0	100%/0/0	100%/0/0	100%/0/0	100%/0/0	100%/0/0
Velocity	**SDP**	1s									
Veracity	**Features**	**R1**	**R2**	**R3**	**R4**	**R5**	**R6**	**R7**	**R8**	**R9**	**R10**
	CDF	Yes	Yes	Yes	Yes	Yes	Yes	Yes	Yes	Yes	Yes
	PCDF	100%									
	NAS	62	0	347	245	0	0	0	0	0	0
	PTI	99.99%	99.99%	99.99%	99.99%	99.99%	99.99%	99.99%	99.99%	99.99%	99.99%
	DTS/DTD	0/0	0/0	0/0	0/0	0/0	0/0	0/0	0/0	0/0	0/0
	PMV old	0%	0%	13.60%	0.039%	0.005%	0.005%	0.005%	0.005%	0.005%	0.005%
	PMV new	17.15%	17.15%	28.42%	17.18%	17.15%	17.15%	17.15%	17.15%	17.15%	17.15%
	SMS/MMS/LMS	0/0/1	0/0/1	388/0/2	1/0/1	1/0/1	1/0/1	1/0/1	1/0/1	1/0/1	1/0/1
Value	**Statistical metrics**	See Table 8.9									
Variability	**std**	See Table 8.9		**cross correlation**		See Figure 8.4					
	outlier rate	**F1**	**F2**	**F3**	**F4**	**F5**	**F6**	**F7**	**F8**	**F9**	**F10**
		2.521%	0%	54.67%	52.73%	0.466%	0%	0%	0%	0%	0%

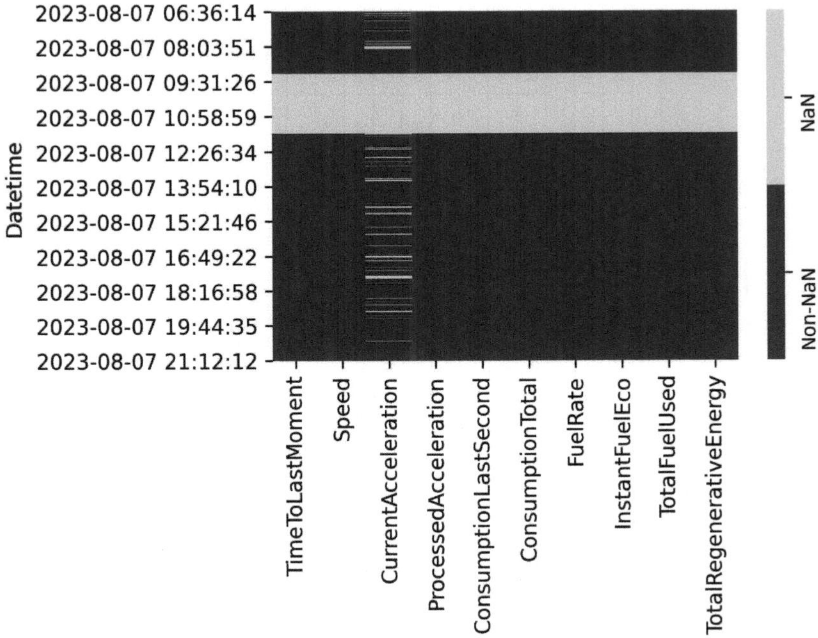

Fig. 8.4 Data completeness of the adjusted transportation dataset, where blue denotes available data and yellow indicates missing values

As shown in Fig. 8.4, no data are recorded between approximately 9:30 and 11:30, corresponding to a period when the bus is not in operation. Table 8.9 and Fig. 8.4 indicate that only the "CurrentAcceleration" feature exhibits substantial missing values, while the other features exhibit short-term gaps at the beginning of the dataset due to asynchronous sensor initialization. To address this, the initial seconds of each record are removed. Furthermore, the feature "R3" is discarded via redundant-feature elimination, as "R4" captures the same acceleration signal without missing values. The correlation matrix in Fig. 8.5 shows a perfect correlation (1.0) between "R3" and "R4", validating the feature substitution and ensuring no information loss during preprocessing.

Next, the metrics in the data value dimension are recorded in Table 8.10. The data validity dimension involves the standard deviation in Table 8.10, cross-correlation in Fig. 8.5, and outlier rate. The results show that the features "R1",

"R3", "R4", and "R5" contain outliers, whereas the others do not. In the data preprocessing phase, it is imperative to replace these outlier values with appropriate and reasonable substitutes.

Table 8.10 presents the statistical characteristics of each feature in the furnace dataset, representing the results of the data value dimension analysis. These metrics provide insights into the distributional properties of individual features. The time series exhibits no seasonality and is stationary. Features "R7", "R8", and "R10" contain only zero values, indicating no informational content and thus limited analytical utility. The feature "R5" ("ConsumptionLastSecond") alternates between values of 0 and 0.5, reflecting that fuel consumption is recorded in discrete increments of 0.5 liters.

Table 8.10 Statistical values of each feature in the transportation dataset

	R1	R2	R3	R4	R5	R6	R7	R8	R9	R10
cardinality	52	7579	29290	30036	2	201	1	1	201	1
min	0	0	−3.0	−8.44	0	374940.5	0	0	749881.0	0
max	1066	87.83	4.62	19.49	0.5	375040.5	0	0	750081.0	0
mean	1000.6	22.5	−0.02	−0.07	0	374998.5	0	0	749997.0	0
median	1001.0	12.77	0	0	0	374996.5	0	0	749993.0	0
std	6.99	25.04	0.43	0.5	0.03	31.23	0	0	62.46	0
skewness	−134.67	0.76	−0.55	0.66	14.5	−0.09	N/A	N/A	−0.09	N/A
excess kurtosis	19275.8	−3.69	3.14	59.16	206.4	−4.3	N/A	N/A	−4.3	N/A
1st qrt	1000	0.03	−0.17	−0.24	0	374965.5	0	0	749931.0	0
3rd qrt	1001	46.17	0.16	0.14	0	375034.0	0	0	750068.0	0
seasonality	No	No	No	No	No	No	No	No	No	No
stationary	Yes	Yes	Yes	Yes	Yes	Yes	Yes	Yes	Yes	Yes

Figure 8.5 illustrates the cross−correlation among the dataset's features. As no prior domain knowledge is available regarding appropriate time lags, a lag of 15 is selected, corresponding to a delay of 15 seconds. It indicates a strong correlation between features "R3" and "R4", as well as between features "R6" and "R9". "R3" and "R4" represent two different measurements of acceleration, while "R6" and "R9" are two different detection methods of fuel consumption. By contrast, "R7", "R8", and "R10" exhibit no correlation with other features, consistent with their constant zero values.

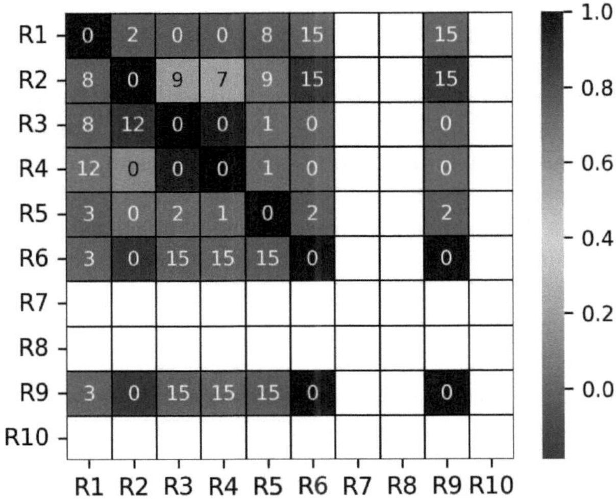

Fig. 8.5 Cross-correlation of different features in the transportation dataset. Cell colors correspond to the correlation values shown in the color bar, while the values within the cells indicate the time lag at which the maximum correlation occurs

Figure 8.6 reflects the behavior of the feature "ConsumptionLastSecond", where fuel usage is logged in increments of 0.5 liters. Consequently, the fuel consumption data are discrete rather than continuous, making them unsuitable for direct time-series analysis compared with continuous variables such as speed or acceleration.

Fig. 8.6 The example of the recorded total fuel used in liters

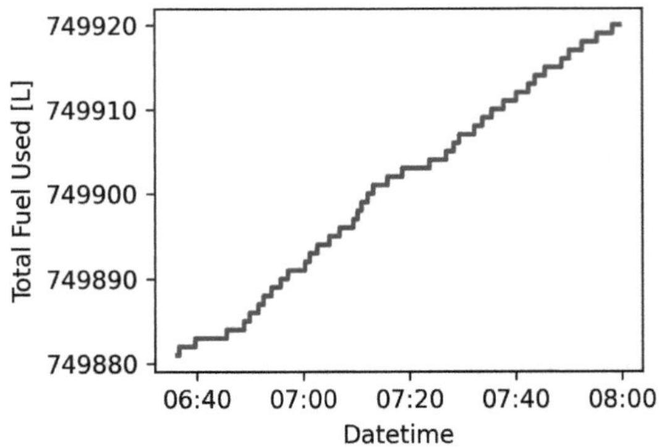

This section has examined the characteristics of the collected furnace operation data. Data quality has been assessed, and the necessary preprocessing steps, including missing value treatment and feature selection, have been performed. The analysis revealed that fuel consumption data are recorded in discrete increments, making them unsuitable for direct time-series analysis. Consequently, characteristic features should be extracted from the datasets to enable a meaningful analysis and assessment of fuel efficiency.

From an operational standpoint, the exploratory data analysis highlights the complexity and richness of modern telematics data in public transportation. The identification of missing values, redundant features, and discrete fuel-consumption recordings demonstrates the importance of systematic preprocessing to ensure data reliability. For fleet operators, this process ensures that subsequent analytics and decision-support outputs are grounded in clean, synchronized, and trustworthy datasets. It also establishes confidence that technical recommendations on fuel efficiency will reflect genuine operational conditions rather than artifacts of poor data quality or sensor inconsistency.

8.4.2 Feature Reconstruction and Dataset Preparation

As outlined in Sect. 8.4.1, feature engineering is conducted to extract characteristic variables from the datasets, enabling a meaningful analysis of fuel efficiency. Informed by domain knowledge and prior literature [319, 326, 327], 50 domain-relevant features are derived, as summarized in Table 8.11.

To reconstruct the dataset based on the extracted features, all records are first segmented into individual bus trips using Algorithm 8.1 (Listing 8.1), resulting in 4,198 identified trips. Rule-based outlier detection is then applied to ensure data validity: trips with "fuel_efficiency" equal to 0 or exceeding 160 are classified as outliers and removed. Following this procedure, 4,006 valid trips are retained for subsequent analysis.

For each bus trip, feature extraction is performed to generate trip-level representations. Specifically, the 50 features listed in Table 8.11 are computed from the recorded sensor time-series data described in Sect. 8.3.1, based on the variable definitions in Table 8.5. The resulting reconstructed dataset consists of 4,006 trip instances, each characterized by 50 features, providing the foundation for subsequent clustering and causality analyses.

Table 8.11 Summarization of extracted characteristic variables in the transportation case study

No.	Feature	Unit	Definition
1	speed_max	km/h	Maximum speed
2	speed_ave	km/h	Average speed
3	speed_std	km/h	Standard deviation of speed
4	speed_lim_min	km/h	Minimum speed limit
5	speed_lim_max	km/h	Maximum speed limit
6	speed_lim_ave	km/h	Average speed limit
7	speed_lim_std	km/h	Standard deviation of speed limit
8	acc_pedal_max	%	Maximum acceleration pedal position
9	acc_pedal_ave	%	Minimum acceleration pedal position
10	acc_pedal_std	%	Standard deviation of pedal position
11	acc_min	m/s^2	Minimum acceleration
12	acc_max	m/s^2	Maximum acceleration
13	acc_ave	m/s^2	Average acceleration
14	acc_std	m/s^2	Standard deviation of acceleration
15	lat_acc_min	m/s^2	Minimum lateral acceleration
16	lat_acc_max	m/s^2	Maximum lateral acceleration
17	lat_acc_ave	m/s^2	Average lateral acceleration
18	lat_acc_std	m/s^2	Standard deviation of lateral acceleration
19	gear_max	N/A	Maximum selected gear
20	gear_ave	N/A	Average selected gear
21	gear_std	N/A	Standard deviation of selected gear
22	engine_load_ave	%	Average engine load
23	engine_load_std	%	Standard deviation of engine load
24	engine_speed_max	rpm	Maximum engine speed
25	engine_speed_ave	rpm	Average engine speed
26	engine_speed_std	rpm	Standard deviation of engine speed
27	engine_torque_max	N·m	Maximum engine torque
28	engine_torque_ave	N·m	Average engine torque
29	engine_torque_std	N·m	Standard deviation of torque
30	ambienttemp_min	°C	Minimum ambient temperature

(continued)

Table 8.11 (continued)

No.	Feature	Unit	Definition
31	ambienttemp_max	°C	Maximum ambient temperature
32	ambienttemp_ave	°C	Average ambient temperature
33	ambienttemp_std	°C	Standard deviation of ambient temperature
34	altitude_min	m	Minimum altitude
35	altitude_max	m	Maximum altitude
36	altitude_ave	m	Average altitude
37	altitude_std	m	Standard deviation of altitude
38	driverid	N/A	Driver id
39	right%	%	Percentage of turning right
40	door_open%	%	Percentage of opening door
41	stop%	%	Percentage of fully stopping
42	reverse%	%	Percentage of reverse
43	routename	N/A	Route name
44	at_stop%	%	Percentage of parking at stops
45	delay_min	min	Minimum delay minutes
46	delay_max	min	Maximum delay minutes
47	delay_ave	min	Average delay minutes
48	delay_std	min	Standard deviation of delay minutes
49	num_stop	N/A	Number of stops
50	fuel_efficiency	L/100 km	Fuel efficiency

From an operational perspective, the reconstructed dataset converts complex, high-frequency telematics signals into interpretable indicators that reflect driver behavior, vehicle performance, and route characteristics. This transformation enables transport managers to evaluate performance systematically across trips and drivers, identify variability in eco-driving practices, and benchmark operational efficiency at the fleet level. By bridging raw sensor data and managerial insight, the dataset establishes a reliable foundation for informed decision-making and continuous improvement in fuel-efficient transport operations.

8.4.3 Clustering and Operational Pattern Analysis

Note: Parts of this section are based on the author's first-author conference paper: *"Fuel Efficiency Analysis of the Public Transportation System Based on the Gaussian Mixture Model Clustering"* [276].

This section demonstrates the results of clustering and pattern analysis for the selected energy consumption KPI. Fuel efficiency, expressed in liters per 100 kilometers (L/100 km) according to the EU standard [328], is chosen because it normalizes fuel use relative to distance traveled, enabling consistent comparisons across trips of different lengths. Its standardized definition and broad acceptance in both research and practice make it a robust and interpretable indicator of operational energy performance.

Figure 8.7 visualizes the distribution of fuel efficiency using a histogram.

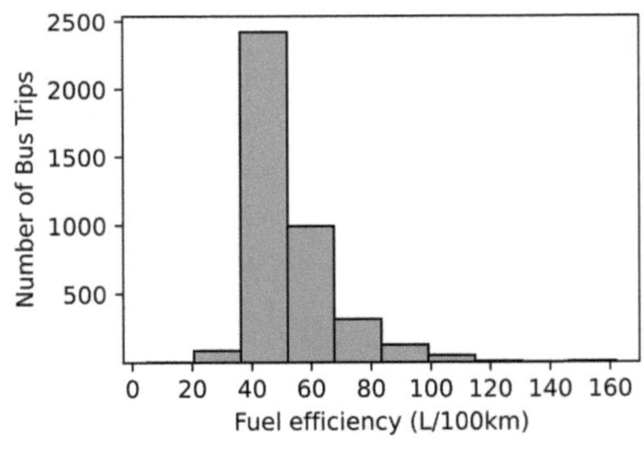

Fig. 8.7 The distribution of fuel efficiency of 4,006 bus trips. The horizontal axis represents fuel efficiency (L/100 km), and the vertical axis indicates the frequency of trips within each fuel efficiency interval. Each fuel efficiency group is represented by a light blue bar

Next, GMM clustering is applied to analyze the fuel efficiency of the 4,006 bus trips. The implementation details of the GMM algorithm are provided in Sect. 6.4.1.1, while the procedure for determining the optimal number of clusters is described in Sect. 6.4.1.2.

The optimal number of clusters is selected from the range [2, 9] and Table 8.12 demonstrates the ranking of clustering performance under different cluster numbers. The average ranking indicates that using three clusters yields the best performance across both cohesion and separation properties.

Table 8.12 The ranking of GMM clustering performance under different numbers of clusters in the transportation case study

No. Clusters	2	3	4	5	6	7	8	9
SIL	**1**	2	7	5	8	3	4	6
CHI	2	**1**	3	4	6	5	8	7
DBI	2	**1**	4	3	8	6	5	7
Average	1.7	**1.3**	4.7	4.0	7.3	4.7	5.7	6.7

In the next step, a GMM model with three clusters is employed to cluster the 4,006 fuel-efficiency samples. Figure 8.8 illustrates the clustering results in both the Gaussian distribution curve of each cluster and the scatter points.

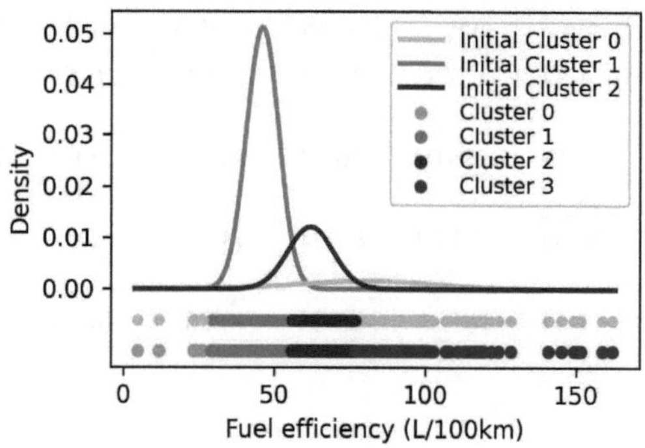

Fig. 8.8 GMM clustering results of fuel efficiency. The top scatter points and Gaussian curves represent the initial clusters (Initial Cluster 0–2), with each point assigned to the cluster with the highest posterior density. Points and curves of the same color correspond to the same cluster. The bottom scatter points show the optimized clustering solution, comprising four clusters (Cluster 0–3), where one initial cluster is subdivided into Cluster 0 and Cluster 3

As shown in Fig. 8.8, Initial Cluster 0 (the yellow one) represents bias, including extremely low and high fuel consumption. Initial Cluster 1 (the green one) and Initial Cluster 2 (the purple one) represent normal and high fuel efficiency, respectively. In the initial clustering, Initial Cluster 0 exhibits a separable internal structure, suggesting a potential for further division into two subgroups. The data points in this cluster are completely partitioned into two parts by other clusters. Afterward, the initial Cluster 0 is divided into the new Cluster 0 and Cluster 3, as shown in the bottom scatter points. The scatter points with the same color are assigned to the same cluster, as shown in the legend. The new Cluster 0 (the orange one) represents extreme fuel efficiency, and the new Cluster 3 (the brown one) represents extremely low fuel efficiency.

Table 8.13 shows the statistical values of each new cluster. The minimum and maximum values suggest that all data points are separated and do not overlap within the range. Most data points are assigned to Cluster 1 and Cluster 2, indicating that the fuel efficiency of most trips falls within the range [29.16, 77.01] L/100 km. However, the standard deviation of data points in Cluster 3 is significantly greater than that in other clusters, indicating the presence of outliers in Cluster 3.

Table 8.13 Statistical values of each cluster of fuel efficiency in the transportation case study

Clusters	num	min	max	mean	median	std	Explanation
Cluster 0	11	4.84	26.35	21.73	24.04	6.55	Extreme fuel efficiency
Cluster 1	2857	29.16	56.02	46.03	46.25	5.02	Normal fuel efficiency
Cluster 2	908	56.04	77.01	63.94	63.31	5.61	Low fuel efficiency
Cluster 3	230	77.44	161.9	95.05	90.86	14.79	Extremely low fuel efficiency

Figure 8.9 demonstrates the distribution of each cluster, including its outliers, using boxplots. Samples in Cluster 1 and Cluster 2 are concentrated in a specific range without any outliers. However, Cluster 0 contains two outliers, and Cluster 3 exhibits several outliers. This observation indicates that extreme fuel consumption is atypical in bus operations.

Next, a brief analysis is conducted to examine whether individual driving behavior and route conditions significantly influence fuel efficiency. The distributions of drivers, routes, and road types across the four clusters are analyzed, and entropy is calculated to quantify their effects. Lower entropy values indicate that a variable is unevenly distributed across clusters and thus more strongly associated with fuel efficiency, whereas higher entropy values reflect a uniform distribution and a weaker association with fuel efficiency.

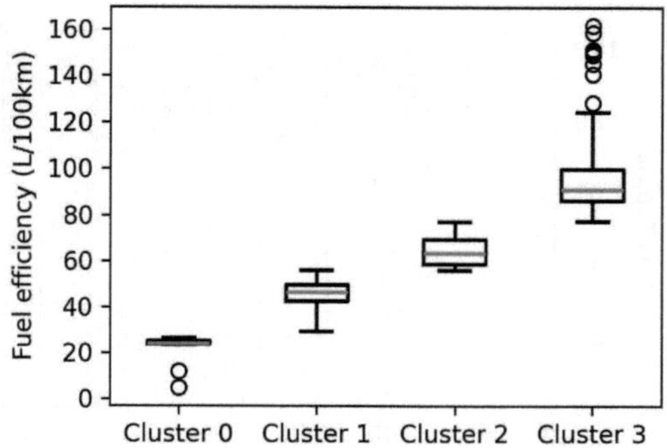

Fig. 8.9 Boxplots of each cluster of fuel efficiency. Each boxplot from left to right refers to the distribution of Cluster 0–3, respectively, and the black hollow circles denote the outliers

First, the fuel efficiency of 202 drivers across 4,006 recorded trips is examined using the "DriverId" feature. Each driver is uniquely identified in the management system and is encoded as an integer between 0 and 201 in this study.

To evaluate variations in fuel efficiency, the proportion of each driver's trips in the four clusters is compared with the overall average distribution. This allows identification of drivers whose performance deviates from the expected average. Figure 8.10 presents a bar chart showing the proportion of each driver's trips across the four clusters. Each bar is divided into segments corresponding to the percentage of trips in a given cluster. The dashed lines indicate the average trip proportions for each cluster across all drivers, enabling direct comparison between individual and overall patterns.

To further quantify the distributional characteristics, entropy is calculated for each driver based on their trip proportions across the four clusters shown in Fig. 8.10. Specifically, if a driver's trips are distributed with proportions a, b, c, d (where $a + b + c + d = 1$), the entropy H is computed as:

$$H = -(a\ln a + b\ln b + c\ln c + d\ln d) \tag{8.1}$$

This measure captures the degree of concentration or dispersion in a driver's cluster distribution. A low entropy value (close to zero) indicates that most trips are concentrated in a single cluster, while a higher entropy value reflects a more balanced distribution across clusters. For reference, the entropy of the overall distribution of all bus trips across the four clusters is 0.758, which serves as a benchmark for evaluating individual drivers' distributions

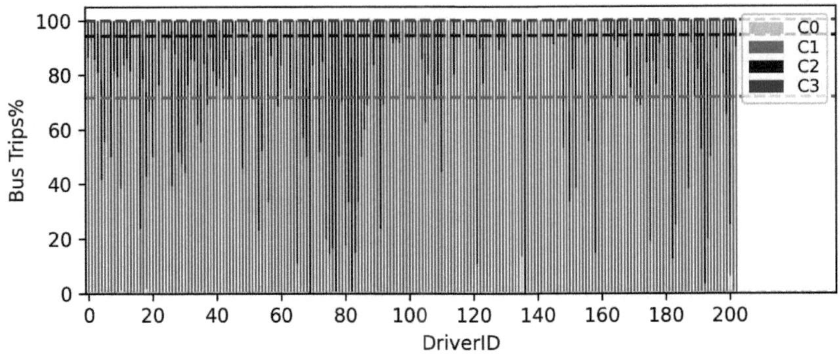

Fig. 8.10 Proportion of drivers' participation in bus trips across four clusters. The x-axis represents driver IDs, and the y-axis indicates the percentage of each driver's trips assigned to each cluster relative to their total trips. Bars are segmented by percentage of trips within clusters (C0-C3), as indicated in the legend. Dashed horizontal lines in cluster-specific colors mark the upper boundary of the average percentage of trips within each cluster

Figure 8.11 shows the distribution of drivers' entropy values. Approximately 30% of drivers exhibit entropy values close to zero, suggesting that their trips are almost entirely concentrated in one cluster. A notable proportion of entropy values falls between 0.4 and 0.6, indicating a moderate level of dispersion, though still below the overall trip distribution entropy (0.758). This contrast implies that, compared to the global distribution of all bus trips across the four clusters, most individual drivers demonstrate a more concentrated pattern, with their trips skewed toward specific clusters rather than evenly distributed.

Together, Fig. 8.10 and Fig. 8.11 highlight that individual driving behavior has a substantial influence on fuel efficiency. Many drivers consistently operate in a manner aligned with specific fuel-efficiency clusters. In particular, the dominance of Cluster 1 or Cluster 2 in many drivers' distributions underscores the strong role of individual driving practices. Overall, the analysis demonstrates significant heterogeneity across drivers, with most concentrating on their trips in a single cluster, thereby confirming the impact of driving behavior on fuel efficiency outcomes.

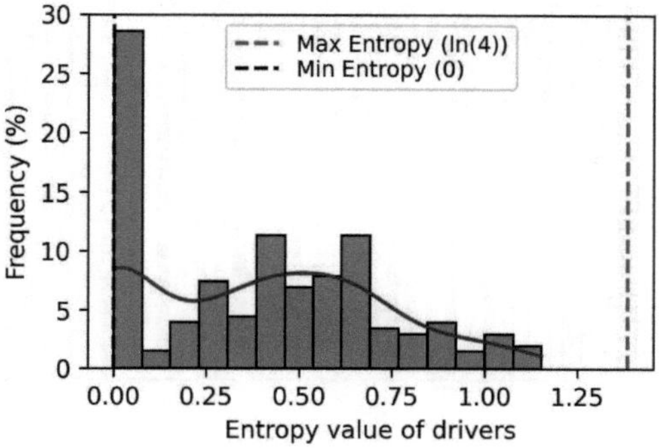

Fig. 8.11 Distribution of entropy values for drivers' participation in bus trips across four clusters. The x-axis represents entropy values, and the y-axis shows their relative frequency (%). The histogram illustrates the distribution, with the overlaid curve representing the kernel density estimate (KDE). The black and red dashed lines indicate the minimum and maximum potential entropy values, respectively

Second, the fuel-efficiency performance of 44 routes across the trips is examined using the "RouteID" feature. Each route is uniquely identified in the management system and is encoded as an integer between 0 and 43 in this study.

To evaluate variations in fuel efficiency, the proportion of trips on each route across the four clusters is compared with the overall average distribution, thereby identifying routes whose performance deviates from the expected baseline. Fig. 8.12 presents a bar chart of the cluster proportions for each route. Each bar is segmented by the percentage of trips in each cluster, while dashed lines indicate the average proportion of trips in each cluster across all routes, allowing direct comparison between individual and overall patterns.

To further quantify the distributional characteristics, entropy is calculated for each route using the same formulation as in Equation 8.1, based on the proportions shown in Fig. 8.12. For reference, the entropy of the overall distribution of all bus trips across the four clusters is 0.758.

Figure 8.13 displays the distribution of entropy values across routes. Approximately 25% of routes exhibit entropy values close to zero, indicating that their trips are concentrated in a single cluster. A substantial proportion of routes fall within the range 0.25–0.75, reflecting moderate dispersion but still below the global entropy benchmark of 0.758. This contrast shows that most routes exhibit more concentrated fuel-efficiency patterns compared to the overall trip distribution, with trips disproportionately allocated to specific clusters.

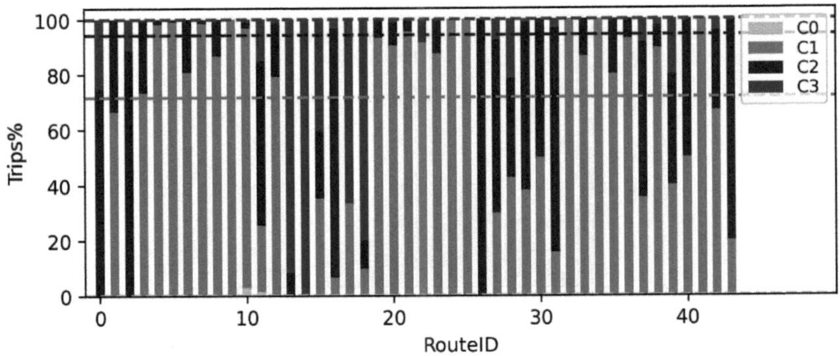

Fig. 8.12 Proportion of routes in bus trips across four clusters. The x-axis represents route IDs, and the y-axis indicates the percentage of the trips of each route assigned to each cluster relative to their total trips. Bars are segmented by percentage of trips within clusters (C0-C3), as indicated in the legend. Dashed horizontal lines in cluster-specific colors mark the upper boundary of the average percentage of trips within each cluster

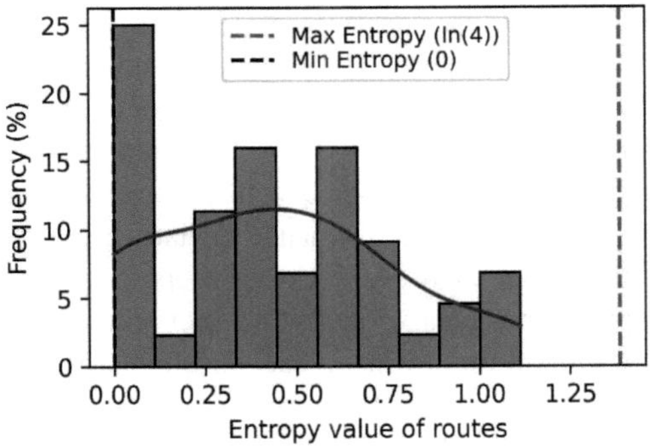

Fig. 8.13 Distribution of entropy values of routes in bus trips across four clusters. The x-axis represents entropy values, and the y-axis shows their relative frequency (%). The histogram illustrates the distribution, with the overlaid curve representing the KDE. The black and red dashed lines indicate the minimum and maximum potential entropy values, respectively

Taken together, Fig. 8.12 and Fig. 8.13 demonstrate that route conditions strongly influence fuel efficiency. Many routes consistently align with particular fuel-efficiency clusters. The observed heterogeneity across routes confirms that route-specific characteristics significantly shape fuel-efficiency outcomes, with most routes dominated by a single cluster rather than displaying evenly distributed performance.

Third, fuel efficiency is examined across different road types. Road types are classified as urban, rural, or highway based on the "SpeedLimit" feature: urban roads correspond to speed limits below 80 km/h, rural roads to limits between 80 and 100 km/h, and highways to limits of 110 km/h or above.

To evaluate variations in fuel efficiency, the proportion of road types in each trip across the four clusters is illustrated in Fig. 8.14. In Cluster 1, most trips consist of 30–60% urban roads, with some trips showing a balanced distribution among all three road types, while others concentrate on urban and rural segments. In Cluster 2, highway proportions are generally low (0–10%), with trips dominated by urban and rural roads. Cluster 3 exhibits an even stronger concentration, with almost no highway segments, and trips are predominantly urban with smaller contributions from rural roads.

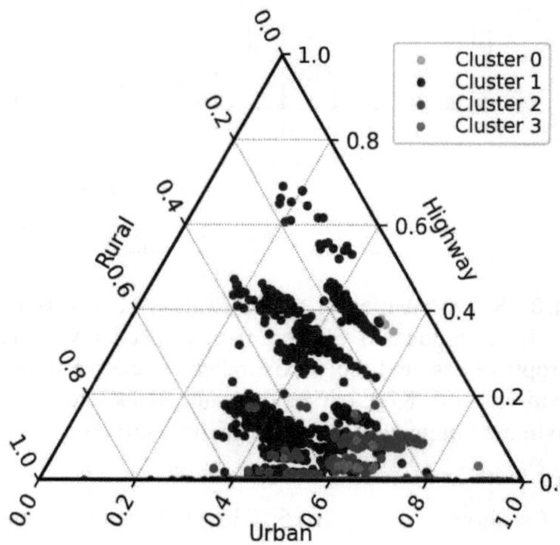

Fig. 8.14 Ternary plot of the proportions of trips across urban, rural, and highway road types. Each scatter point represents a bus trip, with colors indicating cluster assignment as shown in the legend. The three axes represent the percentages of road types (urban, rural, and highway) for each trip

To further quantify the distributional characteristics, the entropy of road types is computed for each trip using the same formulation as in Equation 8.1, adjusted for three elements corresponding to the three road types shown in Fig. 8.14. In this case, the minimum entropy value is 0, indicating that all road segments of a trip belong to a single type, while the maximum value is $\ln 3 \approx 1.099$, which corresponds to an equal distribution across the three road types.

Figure 8.15 presents the distribution of entropy values of road-type proportions within each cluster.

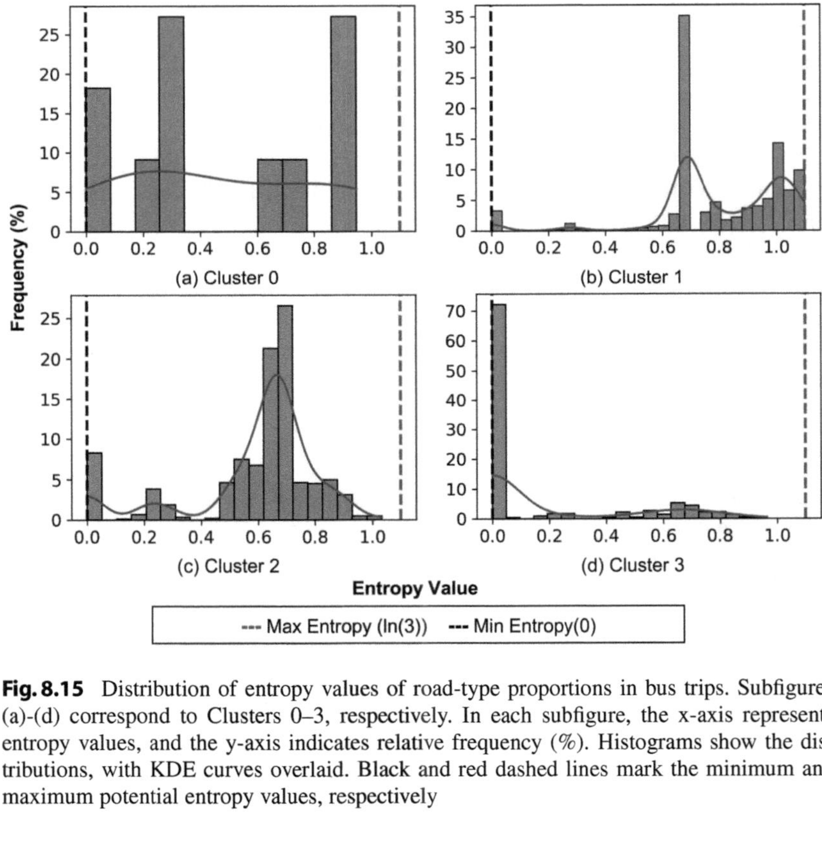

Fig. 8.15 Distribution of entropy values of road-type proportions in bus trips. Subfigures (a)-(d) correspond to Clusters 0–3, respectively. In each subfigure, the x-axis represents entropy values, and the y-axis indicates relative frequency (%). Histograms show the distributions, with KDE curves overlaid. Black and red dashed lines mark the minimum and maximum potential entropy values, respectively

As shown in Fig. 8.15, Cluster 0 contains only 11 trips, and its entropy distribution shows no clear concentration. In Cluster 1, approximately 35% of trips exhibit entropy values around 0.7, while the majority fall between 0.8 and the maximum, suggesting that many trips involve a relatively balanced mix of road types. In Cluster 2, more than half of the trips have entropy values between 0.6 and 0.7, reflecting moderate variability in road-type composition, whereas around 10% are close to 0, indicating trips dominated by a single road type. In contrast,

Cluster 3 is highly concentrated, with more than 70% of trips showing entropy values near 0, meaning these trips occur almost entirely on one type of road, most often urban.

Collectively, Fig. 8.14 and Fig. 8.15 demonstrate that road-type composition has a decisive influence on fuel-efficiency outcomes. Clusters 0 and 1, which are associated with the highest efficiency, are characterized by either balanced distributions or diverse mixes of road types, suggesting that efficiency is supported when trips span multiple road environments. By contrast, Clusters 2 and 3, which exhibit lower efficiency, are dominated by urban segments and display low entropy values, underscoring the detrimental impact of homogeneous urban driving conditions on fuel performance.

From a decision-support standpoint, the clustering outcomes provide actionable intelligence for transport operators. Efficient clusters reveal best-practice driving patterns and favorable route conditions that can be standardized and replicated, while inefficient clusters expose behavioral and operational bottlenecks requiring intervention. Managers can use these insights to design targeted driver-training programs, adjust route scheduling, and evaluate infrastructure improvements, thereby converting analytical results into strategies for enhancing fuel efficiency.

8.4.4 Causality Analysis of Bus Operations

Note: Parts of this section are based on the author's first-author journal article *"Data-Driven Causal Reasoning for Eco-Driving Behavior Analysis in Public Transportation Systems"* [165].

This section investigates the causal structure of the transportation system, with particular emphasis on the interdependencies among fuel efficiency, driving behaviors, and road conditions. The analysis considers both variable-level causal relationships within clusters and root causes across clusters. The analysis follows the causal inference pipeline introduced in Fig. 6.9 (Sect. 6.5.1). The Bagging DAGMA-DCE method (Sect. 6.5.2) is then applied to uncover causal dependencies among the 50 variables listed in Table 8.11 for each cluster. The resulting DAGs are evaluated through a permutation-based falsification test (Sect. 6.5.6) [202] and revised according to the test outcomes. Finally, targeted interventions are conducted to identify the root causes of variables related to fuel efficiency, as described in Sect. 6.5.7 [201]. Together, these steps ensure that the framework uncovers the underlying mechanisms governing fuel consumption and efficiency in transportation systems. The falsification test and root cause analysis are conducted using the python library *DoWhy-GCM* [291], an extension of the *DoWhy* [315, 316] Python library (*version 0.8.1*).

Since Clusters 0 and 3 represent extreme cases of efficiency and inefficiency, causal structures are inferred only for Clusters 1 and 2. For comparison, a causal structure is also derived from all trips combined. Table 8.14 summarizes the assessment results and corresponding validation recommendations for the three DAGs. The number of permutations is set to 100 for the falsification test.

Table 8.14 Assessment results and validation suggestions for each of the three DAGs in the transportation case study

Cluster	p-value LMC	p-value TPa	Suggestions
1	0.0	0.0	N/A
2	0.02	0.0	N/A
all	0.0	0.0	N/A

The results of Table 8.14 indicate that all three DAGs are informative and highly trustworthy. Next, the three DAGs are illustrated in Figs. 8.16–8.18.

Figure 8.16 presents the causal discovery results for bus trips in Cluster 1, representing trips with normal fuel efficiency. Most causal links appear among variables derived from the same sensor time series. For example, variables 34–37 are generated from GPS altitude records, and variables 45–48 from delay-time records. Nonetheless, several cross-variable relationships provide notable insights. The chain "speed_limit_max → speed_limit_std → speed_std → speed_max" (5 → 7 → 3 → 1) suggests that variations in posted speed limits translate into speed variability and ultimately influence maximum speed, reflecting how regulatory constraints shape actual driving performance. The path "engine_torque_std → acc_pedal_std → acc_pedal_ave" (29 → 10 → 9) indicates that fluctuations in engine torque drive accelerator pedal behavior, highlighting the interaction between power demand and driver response. Similarly, the finding that engine load (22, 23) causes engine torque (28) aligns with mechanical principles of combustion engines, while the link "speed_ave → engine_speed_ave" (2 → 25) confirms the expected dependency between vehicle speed and engine operating speed.

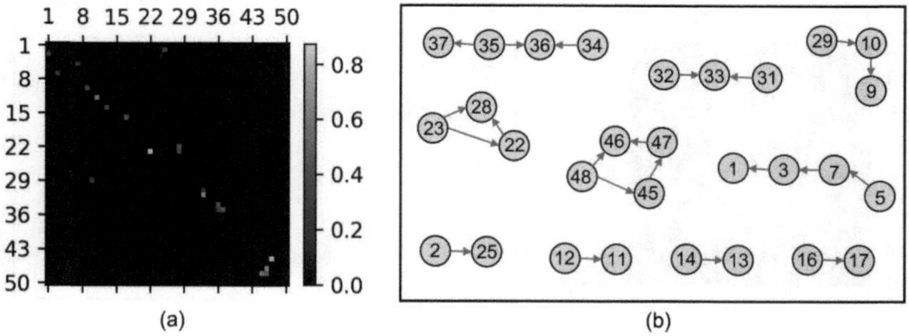

Fig. 8.16 Causal structure of bus trips in Cluster 1. Subfigure (a) shows the quantitative causal strength matrix, where each block at position (x, y) indicates the strength of the causal effect from x to y, with color intensity reflecting effect magnitude. Subfigure (b) presents the corresponding DAG, where blue nodes represent variables and directed blue arrows (x → y) denote inferred causal relationships. Axis values in (a) and node labels in (b) correspond to variable IDs listed in Table 8.11

Figure 8.17 presents the causal discovery results for bus trips in Cluster 2, representing trips with low fuel efficiency. Compared with Cluster 1 (Fig. 8.16), fewer causal links are identified. Most links remain confined to variables derived from the same sensor time series, but several cross-variable relationships are noteworthy. As in Cluster 1, the link "speed_ave → engine_speed_ave" (2 → 25) confirms the dependency between vehicle speed and engine operating speed. However, unlike Cluster 1, a new link 28 → 29 appears, which then connects to accelerator pedal behavior. This causal chain reflects the pathway "engine load → engine torque → accelerator pedal", indicating that in low-efficiency trips, fluctuations in engine load propagate through torque to driver input.

Figure 8.18 presents the causal discovery results for all bus trips in the case study. Compared with Clusters 1 and 2, the combined dataset yields a denser causal structure with more identified links. Notably, "speed_ave" (2) emerges as a central driver, causing five variables: "speed_lim_ave" (6), "gear_ave" (20), "engine_speed_ave" (25), "right%" (39), and "fuel_efficiency" (50). Additional relationships include "ambienttemp_ave → delay_std" (32 → 48) and "engine_torque_std → acc_pedal_std" (29 → 10). Interestingly, the latter direction contrasts with Clusters 1 and 2, where the relationship appears reversed (10 → 29), highlighting potential differences in how torque variability and pedal behavior interact when considering the full dataset.

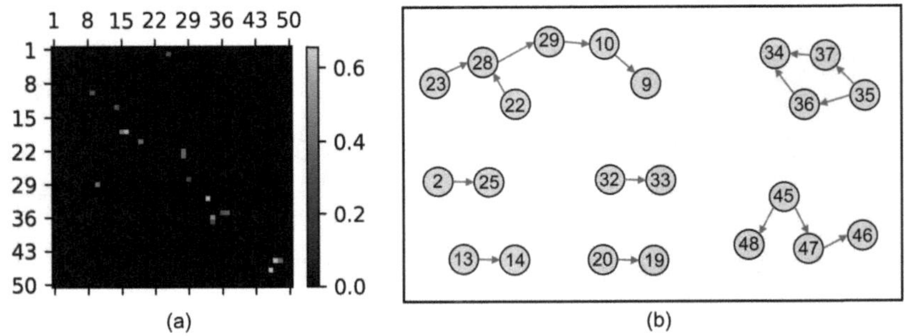

Fig. 8.17 Causal structure of bus trips in Cluster 2. Subfigure (a) shows the quantitative causal strength matrix, where each block at position (x, y) indicates the strength of the causal effect from x to y, with color intensity reflecting effect magnitude. Subfigure (b) presents the corresponding DAG, where blue nodes represent variables and directed blue arrows (x → y) denote inferred causal relationships. Axis values in (a) and node labels in (b) correspond to variable IDs listed in Table 8.11

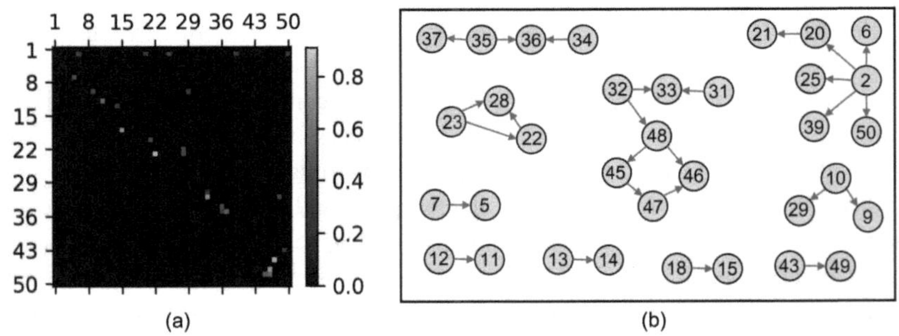

Fig. 8.18 Causal structure of total bus trips. Subfigure (a) shows the quantitative causal strength matrix, where each block at position (x, y) indicates the strength of the causal effect from x to y, with color intensity reflecting effect magnitude. Subfigure (b) presents the corresponding DAG, where blue nodes represent variables and directed blue arrows (x → y) denote inferred causal relationships. Axis values in (a) and node labels in (b) correspond to variable IDs listed in Table 8.11

After identifying the causal relationships, the root causes of key variables related to fuel efficiency are further examined [165, 201]. In each test, the main drivers are identified through interventions that perturb variable distributions using the mean values from the intervention dataset. Since only the overall causal structure in Fig. 8.18 reveals a direct link to fuel efficiency, the first analysis uses the causal mechanism of all trips as the baseline, with Clusters 1 and 2 serving as intervention datasets. Subsequently, guided by the literature [319], additional root-cause analyses are performed on variables known to influence fuel efficiency, including speed, acceleration, engine parameters, and other driver behaviors from the DAGs.

First, the causal mechanism of all trips is set as the baseline, with Clusters 1 and 2 serving as intervention datasets. Three key variables, including "fuel_efficiency" (50), "engine_torque_ave" (28) and "delay_max" (46), are selected to analyze their causal drivers. These variables are chosen because they are directly related to fuel efficiency or influence it, and because they have been identified as causal antecedents among other time-series variables within the overall causal mechanism. This makes them suitable for uncovering system-level insights.

Figure 8.19 illustrates the contribution of each variable arising from differences in its causal mechanism to the change in mean values between all trips (baseline) and Cluster 1 (intervention).

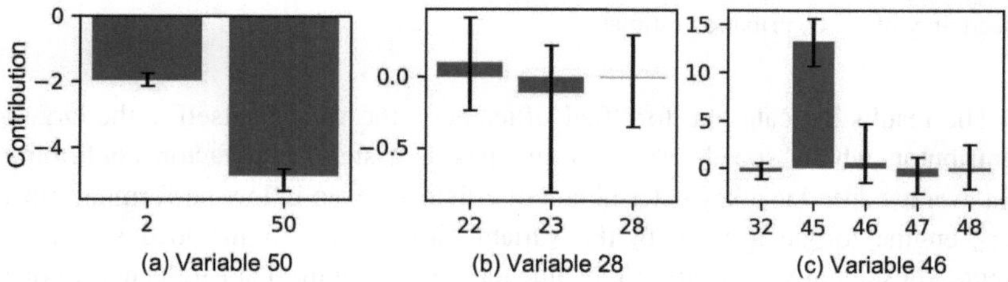

Fig. 8.19 Contribution of each variable arising from differences in its causal mechanism to the change in mean values between all trips (baseline) and Cluster 1 (intervention) in the transportation case study. Subfigures (a)-(c) correspond to different target variables in the DAG. Each bar represents the mean contribution score, while each error bar denotes the uncertainty of the contribution estimate

The results show that for "fuel_efficiency," the largest contribution comes from the variable itself, indicating a primarily self-dependent effect. This suggests that trips in the normal-efficiency range maintain their performance largely due to intrinsic efficiency characteristics. However, "speed_ave" also emerges as a meaningful contributor, highlighting that managing average speed is a practical lever for sustaining or improving fuel efficiency within this cluster. For "engine_torque_ave," no strong contributors are identified, implying that average torque in normal-efficiency trips is relatively stable and less influenced by other variables. For "delay_max," the main contributor is "delay_min," which indicates that variability in delay patterns can influence operational efficiency.

Figure 8.20 illustrates the contribution of each variable arising from differences in its causal mechanism to the change in mean values between all trips (baseline) and Cluster 2 (intervention).

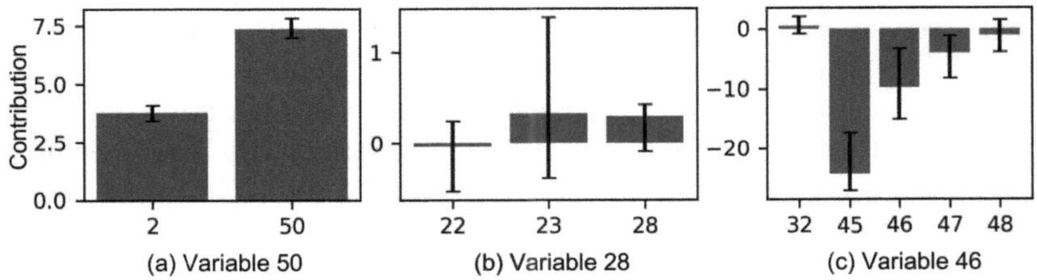

Fig. 8.20 Contribution of each variable arising from differences in its causal mechanism to the change in mean values between all trips (baseline) and Cluster 2 (intervention) in the transportation case study. Subfigures (a)-(c) correspond to different target variables in the DAG. Each bar represents the mean contribution score, while each error bar denotes the uncertainty of the contribution estimate

The results indicate that for "fuel_efficiency," the variable itself is the largest contributor, while "speed_ave" also emerges as a significant factor, confirming that average speed is a key determinant of efficiency even in low-performing trips. For "engine_torque_ave," both the variable itself and "engine_load_std" contribute substantially, indicating that fluctuations in engine load influence torque dynamics under inefficient operating conditions. For "delay_max," the largest contributor is "delay_min," followed by the variable itself and "delay_ave." This suggests that there is greater variability in delays, both at the extremes and in the averages.

Second, the causal mechanism of normal-efficiency trips in Cluster 1 is set as the baseline, with low-efficiency trips in Cluster 2 serving as the intervention dataset. Two key variables, "speed_max" (1) and "acc_pedal_ave" (9), are selected for analysis because they are closely related to fuel efficiency and have been identified as causal antecedents in the baseline mechanism. Figure 8.21 illustrates the contributions of causal drivers to changes in mean values when shifting from Cluster 1 (baseline) to Cluster 2 (intervention).

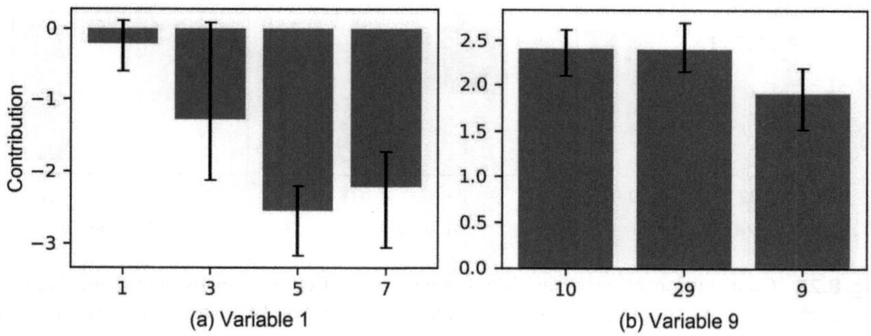

Fig. 8.21 Contribution of each variable arising from differences in its causal mechanism to the change in mean values between Cluster 1 (baseline) and Cluster 2 (intervention) in the transportation case study. Subfigures (a)-(b) correspond to different target variables in the DAG. Each bar represents the mean contribution score, while each error bar denotes the uncertainty of the contribution estimate

The results show that for "speed_max," the largest contributor is "speed_lim_max," followed by "speed_lim_std" and "speed_std." This indicates that maximum speed is strongly shaped by road speed limits and their variability. For "acc_pedal_ave," the main contributors are "acc_pedal_std" and "engine_torque_std," with the variable itself also exerting a significant influence. These findings suggest that in low-efficiency trips, inefficiency arises from greater variability in both speed control and accelerator pedal behavior, closely linked to torque fluctuations.

Third, the causal mechanism of low-efficiency trips in Cluster 2 is set as the baseline, with normal-efficiency trips in Cluster 1 serving as the intervention dataset. Three key variables, "acc_pedal_ave" (9), "engine_speed_ave" (25), and "engine_torque_std" (29), are selected for analysis, as they are closely related to fuel efficiency and have identified causal antecedents in the baseline mechanism. Figure 8.22 illustrates the contributions of causal drivers to changes in mean values when shifting from Cluster 2 (baseline) to Cluster 1 (intervention).

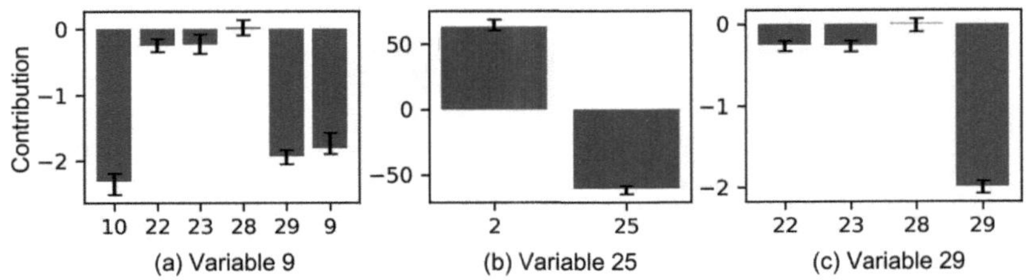

Fig. 8.22 Contribution of each variable arising from differences in its causal mechanism to the change in mean values between Cluster 2 (baseline) and Cluster 1 (intervention) in the transportation case study. Subfigures (a)-(c) correspond to different target variables in the DAG. Each bar represents the mean contribution score, while each error bar denotes the uncertainty of the contribution estimate

The results indicate that, for "acc_pedal_ave," in addition to self-dependence, the main contributors are "acc_pedal_std" and "engine_torque_std," reflecting the roles of pedal-use variability and torque fluctuations in shaping average accelerator behavior. For "engine_speed_ave," both the variable itself and "speed_ave" emerge as strong contributors, underscoring the close relationship between vehicle speed and engine speed. For "engine_torque_std," the primary contributor is the variable itself, suggesting that torque variability is largely self-driven in the transition from low- to normal-efficiency trips.

For fleet managers and policy makers, these causal findings reveal concrete levers for intervention. Stabilizing average speed through traffic-signal coordination, monitoring engine-load variability, and providing driver feedback on acceleration behavior can directly reduce fuel consumption. Unlike descriptive statistics, causal reasoning identifies the causes of inefficiencies, enabling operators to prioritize the most influential variables and design evidence-based eco-driving and scheduling strategies that deliver measurable fuel savings.

8.4.5 LLM-Based Decision Support Outputs

This section presents the multimodal LLM-based decision support mechanism. While Sects. 8.4.1–8.4.4 reported the results of Modules 2–4 in Fig. 8.2, the focus here is on Module 5, which leverages the multimodal LLM multi-agent framework developed in Sect. 6.6 to automatically interpret inputs from the preceding data analytics.

In this module, multimodal inputs, such as background context, charts, and tables, are first transformed into textual explanations through an LLM-based data narration process. Building on these narratives, the system then generates recommendations for decision-making. Similar to Sect. 7.4, in the present case study, three categories of recommendations are produced: (i) recommendations for improving data quality, (ii) fuel-efficiency recommendations derived from clustering analysis, and (iii) fuel-efficiency recommendations based on causal analysis.

The first stage, multimodal data narration, is applied to a large set of inputs, the majority of which have already been presented in Sects. 8.4.1–8.4.4. To avoid redundancy, this section concentrates on the subsequent stage, namely the LLM-generated recommendations. A representative subset of the multimodal data narration results is provided in Listing A.6 in Appendix A.2 in ESM.

Listing 8.2 presents the LLM-generated recommendations aimed at improving the quality of bus operation data. These recommendations are derived from the multimodal results in Module 2 (Sects. 8.4.1 and 8.4.2).

Listing 8.2 LLM-generated recommendations for improving the quality of bus operational data

```
Based on the data characterization and quality assessment, the following recommendations are proposed
to enhance data quality in bus transport systems:
1. Sensor Synchronization and Initialization:
  - Implement standardized sensor startup protocols to minimize asynchronous initialization and reduce
missing data at the beginning of recordings.
  - Employ real-time monitoring to detect and correct sensor desynchronization promptly.
2. Handling Missing Data:
  - Develop imputation strategies tailored to the temporal patterns of missingness, distinguishing between
operational and non-operational periods.
  - For short-term gaps, interpolation methods can be applied; for longer gaps, data should be flagged and
excluded from time-sensitive analyses.
3. Outlier Detection and Treatment:
  - Establish automated outlier detection pipelines using domain-informed thresholds and statistical
methods.
  - Replace or smooth outliers with contextually appropriate values to maintain data integrity without
discarding valuable information.
4. Enhancing Data Granularity for Fuel Consumption:
  - Upgrade fuel consumption measurement systems to capture continuous rather than discrete
increments, enabling more precise time-series analysis.
  - Alternatively, derive aggregated features that better represent fuel efficiency dynamics despite discrete
recording.
5. Feature Redundancy Management:
  - Continue leveraging correlation analyses to identify and remove redundant features, reducing data
dimensionality and computational load without losing information.
6. Data Completeness Monitoring:
  - Implement dashboards to track data completeness and quality metrics in near real-time, facilitating
proactive maintenance and data governance.
7. Integration of External Data Sources:
  - Incorporate traffic flow, weather, and road condition data to enrich datasets and improve explanatory
power for fuel consumption variability.
```

Listing 8.3 presents the LLM-generated recommendations for improving fuel efficiency in public transportation systems, derived from the clustering analysis results in Module 3 (Sect. 8.4.3). These recommendations translate the identified bus operational patterns into actionable guidance.

Listing 8.3 LLM-generated recommendations for improving fuel efficiency in public transportation systems based on clustering analysis

```
Based on the data-driven insights, the following recommendations are proposed to stakeholders for
enhancing fuel efficiency in bus transport systems:
3.1 Driver Training and Monitoring
 - Targeted Training: Develop customized training programs focusing on drivers whose trips predominantly
fall into low or extremely low fuel-efficiency clusters. Emphasize smooth acceleration, optimal gear
shifting, and anticipatory driving to reduce fuel consumption.
 - Performance Feedback: Implement real-time monitoring and feedback systems to inform drivers about
their fuel efficiency performance relative to peers, encouraging adoption of best practices.
 - Incentive Programs: Introduce incentives for drivers demonstrating consistent fuel-efficient driving
patterns to motivate behavioral change.
3.2 Route Optimization
 - Route Assessment: Conduct detailed evaluations of routes with low fuel efficiency to identify
contributing factors such as frequent stops, traffic congestion, or challenging terrain.
 - Schedule Adjustments: Modify scheduling policies to reduce delays and idling times, particularly on
routes with high delay variability.
 - Alternative Routing: Explore alternative paths or route modifications that incorporate more rural or
highway segments where feasible, to improve fuel efficiency.
3.3 Infrastructure and Traffic Management
 - Traffic Signal Coordination: Collaborate with city traffic management to optimize signal timings along
bus routes, minimizing stop-and-go conditions in urban areas.
 - Dedicated Bus Lanes: Advocate for dedicated bus lanes to reduce congestion-related delays and
improve steady driving conditions.
 - Stop Optimization: Review bus stop placement and frequency to balance accessibility with operational
efficiency, potentially consolidating stops in low-demand areas.
3.4 Vehicle and Technology Enhancements
 - Sensor Utilization: Leverage existing sensor data to develop predictive models for fuel consumption,
enabling proactive operational adjustments.
 - Fleet Modernization: Consider upgrading to more fuel-efficient or hybrid buses, especially on routes
with consistently low fuel efficiency.
 - Maintenance Programs: Ensure regular vehicle maintenance to optimize engine performance and
reduce fuel wastage.
```

Listing 8.4 presents the LLM-generated recommendations for improving fuel efficiency in public transportation systems, derived from the causality analysis results in Module 4 (Sect. 8.4.5). These recommendations emphasize the key causal drivers of fuel efficiency, such as speed control, acceleration control, and delay management.

Listing 8.4 LLM-generated recommendations for improving fuel efficiency in public transportation systems based on causality analysis

```
Based on the data-driven insights, the following recommendations are proposed to improve fuel efficiency
in bus transport systems:
1. Optimize Average Speed Management:
  Since average speed is a key determinant of fuel efficiency, implementing driver training programs
focused on maintaining consistent and moderate speeds can reduce fuel consumption. Real-time feedback
systems could assist drivers in adhering to optimal speed ranges.
2. Enhance Speed Limit Compliance and Infrastructure:
  The causal link between speed limit variability and maximum speed suggests that harmonizing speed
limits along routes and improving signage clarity can reduce speed fluctuations, contributing to smoother
driving patterns and better fuel economy.
3. Reduce Engine Load Variability:
  Fluctuations in engine load and torque negatively impact fuel efficiency, especially in low-efficiency trips.
Maintenance programs ensuring engine components operate optimally and strategies to minimize abrupt
acceleration or deceleration can stabilize engine load.
4. Manage Accelerator Pedal Behavior:
  Variability in accelerator pedal use is linked to inefficiency. Driver coaching emphasizing smooth pedal
application and avoidance of sudden throttle changes can improve fuel consumption.
5. Address Delay Variability:
  Operational delays and their variability affect fuel efficiency. Improving scheduling accuracy, traffic signal
prioritization for buses, and real-time traffic management can reduce delays and associated fuel waste.
6. Leverage Data-Driven Decision Support Tools:
  The availability of detailed sensor data enables the deployment of analytics platforms that monitor key
performance indicators and provide actionable insights to drivers and fleet managers.
```

The LLM-generated recommendations demonstrate the framework's capacity to translate complex analytical outputs into transparent, context-aware, and operationally meaningful guidance. They show how data-driven insights can be integrated into daily workflows such as sensor maintenance, production scheduling, and thermal control. Although not yet validated with operators, the results highlight the potential of explainable AI to bridge the gap between advanced analytics and practical decision-making.

In the transportation domain, the LLM-based module enhances real-time fleet management by delivering concise, evidence-based recommendations through existing dashboards. This enables users to act on insights without technical expertise, supporting dynamic decisions that optimize routes, reduce inefficiencies, and embed continuous improvement into routine operations.

8.5 Framework Evaluation and Discussion

This section evaluates the implemented AI-driven decision support framework for improving fuel efficiency in public transportation systems. The evaluation follows the criteria defined in Sect. 4.3.2, which provides a balanced basis for assessing both methodological soundness and practical relevance. The five criteria (capabilities, robustness, explainability, domain integrity, and iterative validation potential) together capture the analytical, technical, and operational dimensions of framework performance.

Table 8.15 shows the results of the defined quantitative metrics in Table 4.1 (Sect. 4.3.2) for each criterion.

Table 8.15 Integrated qualitative and quantitative evaluation results for the transportation case study

Criterion	Quantitative metrics	Results
Capabilities	1) Decision-task coverage rate 2) Customization rate	100% 100%
Robustness	1) Unexpected condition solving rate	100%
Explainability	1) Rate of recommendations with traceable rationale	100%
Domain Integrity	1) Rate of compliance with domain rules	100%
Iterative Validation Potential	1) Iterative validation rate	100%

Capabilities

The framework demonstrates comprehensive capability in addressing the full spectrum of decision-support tasks related to fuel efficiency in bus operations. It covers every analytical stage from data preparation and feature extraction to clustering, causal reasoning, and recommendation generation, ensuring end-to-end functionality. Its adaptability is a major strength: stakeholders such as fleet managers, drivers, and policymakers can easily tailor the analytical pipeline by redefining KPIs, adjusting model parameters, or refining LLM prompts to suit specific operational needs. This flexibility allows the framework to remain relevant under different policy objectives or fleet characteristics while maintaining methodological rigor.

However, one limitation is that the evaluation is conducted using historical data. Extending the framework to real-time applications could further enhance responsiveness to dynamic conditions such as traffic flow, weather variations, or route congestion.

Robustness
The framework performs reliably across varied driving and operational conditions. It effectively addresses common data challenges in transportation systems, including asynchronous sensor data, missing values, and route heterogeneity. Robustness is achieved through a structured design:

- Systematic data characterization ensures quality and coherence.
- Domain-specific segmentation isolates meaningful bus trips.
- Feature reconstruction produces consistent analytical inputs.

This design minimizes analytical instability and ensures consistent model performance even under noisy or incomplete data conditions. Nevertheless, the framework's robustness should be further validated through cross-fleet testing and multi-route scenarios to confirm its generalizability beyond the studied network.

Explainability
Explainability is one of the framework's defining strengths. Unlike conventional black-box AI systems, it integrates interpretability throughout all modules. Data characterization clarifies sensor reliability and preprocessing decisions; clustering identifies driver, route, and traffic patterns influencing fuel efficiency; causal reasoning reveals how behaviors and environmental factors interact; and the LLM-based narrative layer translates these findings into accessible, evidence-based recommendations for practitioners.

This multi-layered explainability ensures that every recommendation has a clear analytical rationale. For instance, the system explicitly explains why maintaining stable speeds reduces fuel consumption or how variability in engine load impacts efficiency. By offering transparent, traceable logic, the framework builds trust and facilitates informed decision-making among non-technical stakeholders.

Domain Integrity
The framework exhibits strong domain integrity by embedding transportation-specific terminology, operational constraints, and behavioral factors within its analytical logic. Recommendations are grounded in real-world bus operations and

align with established best practices, such as optimizing routes, moderating acceleration, reducing idling, and coordinating traffic signals. This grounding enhances the credibility and acceptance of the framework within the transportation domain.

However, as the case study focuses on a single city and bus fleet, further validation across different geographic regions, vehicle technologies (e.g., hybrid or electric buses), and regulatory contexts would be valuable to confirm broader applicability.

Iterative Validation Potential

A distinctive feature of the framework is its ability to continuously validate and learn. The integrated feedback mechanism allows results to be refined as new data are collected and operational conditions evolve. For example, fleet managers could iteratively test the framework's recommendations, measure fuel savings, and retrain the analytical models using updated driving and route data.

This dynamic feedback cycle aligns with agile AI deployment practices, ensuring that the system evolves with real-world usage. It also provides a foundation for participatory decision support, where drivers and managers co-adapt strategies over time. This iterative learning process ensures that the framework remains both technically accurate and practically relevant in a changing operational environment.

Overall, the evaluation confirms that the proposed AI-driven decision support framework demonstrates methodological rigor, operational robustness, and high interpretability, thereby enhancing fuel efficiency in public transportation systems. Quantitative results and qualitative discussion indicate complete decision-task coverage, adaptability across user roles, reliable performance under variable conditions, and full compliance with domain-specific constraints. By combining technical depth with practical accessibility, the framework establishes a credible foundation for data-driven management of fuel efficiency and eco-driving in public transportation. Its strong performance across all evaluation criteria indicates readiness for real-world deployment and scalability to larger transportation systems.

8.6 Summary and Key Contributions

This chapter has presented a case study that applies the AI-driven decision support framework to the public transportation sector, focusing on improving fuel efficiency and eco-driving in bus operations. Addressing one of the most energy-intensive and environmentally critical areas of city mobility, the study demonstrates how data-driven analytics can generate actionable insights for sustainable transportation management.

The key contributions are as follows:

- Data foundation and preprocessing: A systematic procedure has been developed for preparing and integrating heterogeneous transportation datasets collected from vehicle sensors, CAN bus systems, GPS devices, and journey records. The procedure ensures temporal synchronization, consistency, and reliability across multiple buses and routes.
- Feature extraction and pattern discovery: Through domain-informed feature engineering and GMM clustering, the framework identified distinct operational patterns that characterize variations in fuel efficiency across trips, routes, and drivers. These patterns revealed both efficient and inefficient driving behaviors, enabling the benchmarking of eco-driving practices and route-specific performance.
- Causal analysis and behavioral insights: The integration of the Bagging DAGMA-DCE algorithm with root-cause analysis enables the framework to uncover causal drivers of fuel consumption, such as acceleration behavior, speed variability, and engine load fluctuations. This causal reasoning provides transparent explanations for inefficiencies and targeted levers for improvement.
- Decision support and explainability: The multimodal LLM-based narration translates analytical outcomes into interpretable, stakeholder-oriented recommendations for drivers, fleet managers, and planners, supporting speed management, route optimization, and driver training. It bridges the gap between advanced AI analytics and everyday operational decision-making.
- Evaluation and validation: The framework is rigorously evaluated against five criteria, including capabilities, robustness, explainability, domain integrity, and iterative validation. Results confirmed its methodological soundness, adaptability, and relevance for real-world application, while also highlighting areas for future improvement.

Despite these contributions, several limitations remain. The analysis is based on one week of historical data from a single transportation network, limiting the generalizability of findings. Real-time testing under live operational conditions and across larger, more diverse fleets would further validate the framework's robustness and scalability. Additionally, while the causal models provide valuable interpretability, future work should explore hybrid human-AI validation approaches involving drivers and dispatchers to refine the causal pathways and ensure behavioral relevance. Finally, integrating external data sources such as traffic flow, weather, and road surface conditions could enhance predictive accuracy and contextual awareness.

In summary, this chapter demonstrates the feasibility and value of applying the AI-driven decision support framework to eco-driving and fuel-efficiency management in public transportation systems. By establishing a pipeline from raw bus sensor data to interpretable, actionable recommendations, the study advances both the theoretical foundation of data-driven decision support and its practical application for sustainable mobility. The next chapter extends this work by discussing cross-domain insights and synthesizing lessons from both industrial and transportation case studies, highlighting the framework's adaptability and transferability across sectors.

9 Discussion

This chapter provides an integrative and critical synthesis of the research conducted in this thesis, drawing together its conceptual, methodological, and empirical contributions. It culminates in a comprehensive discussion of the proposed AI-driven decision support framework, including its theoretical grounding, technical implementation, and demonstrated performance across multiple application domains. The conceptual design of the framework has been introduced in Chap. 5, the implementation and algorithmic development have been elaborated in Chap. 6, and the empirical validation has been undertaken through two case studies in Chaps. 7 and 8.

Building on these preceding chapters, the discussion interprets the overall research outcomes, compares the results of the two case studies, and evaluates how effectively the research objectives and questions defined in Chap. 1 have been addressed. It also assesses the framework's scientific and practical contributions, with particular emphasis on its methodological rigor, explanatory capacity, and potential for generalization across domains.

The remainder of the chapter is organized as follows: Sect. 9.1 evaluates the AI-driven decision support framework, including a cross-domain comparison of the case studies and a discussion of its generalization potential. Section 9.2 addresses the research questions; Sect. 9.3 reviews the achievement of the research objectives; and Sect. 9.4 examines the study's validity and limitations.

Z. Ma, *Artificial Intelligence-Driven Decision Support Framework for Improving Energy Efficiency in Industry and Transportation*,
https://doi.org/10.1007/978-3-658-51965-0_9

9.1 Evaluation of the AI-Driven Decision Support Framework

9.1.1 Evaluation Against Framework Criteria

This section evaluates the proposed AI-driven decision support framework using the assessment criteria outlined in Sect. 4.3.2. The evaluation framework comprises seven criteria. The first five, including capabilities, robustness, explainability, domain integrity, and potential for iterative validation, are applied in each case study to assess domain-specific performance. The remaining two criteria, including cross-sector applicability, and adaptability and scalability, are used to assess the framework's generalizability across domains. Detailed evaluations of the first five criteria are presented in Tables 7.13 and 8.15 for the foundry and transportation case studies, respectively. This section provides a summary of those findings and offers a more detailed cross-case analysis of the final two criteria.

The evaluation results indicate that the framework meets or exceeds all defined criteria, with some areas identified for future enhancement. A summary of the evaluation is presented in Table 9.1. The quantitative metrics and corresponding targets are defined in Table 4.1 (Sect. 4.3.2). "Result 1" and "Result 2" refer to the evaluation outcomes from the foundry and transportation case studies, respectively. The assessment integrates both quantitative metrics shown in Table 9.1 and qualitative evaluations are discussed for each criterion below.

Capabilities

The framework provides comprehensive decision-support capabilities across both domains, achieving full coverage of the targeted decision-making tasks. In the foundry case, it supports the complete data-to-decision pipeline, including data quality assessment, pattern discovery, causal analysis, and energy-efficiency recommendations. In the transportation case, it similarly addresses all analytical stages, from data integration and feature engineering to trip clustering, causal inference, and the generation of fuel-saving guidance. This end-to-end functionality ensures that no essential component is omitted and that stakeholders are supported throughout the decision-making process. The framework also provides a high degree of adaptability to user-specific requirements. Analysts can configure the system by selecting relevant performance indicators, such as furnace temperature or energy per tonne in the foundry, and fuel consumption per kilometer or per trip in transportation. They can also adjust model parameters to align with distinct operational objectives. This flexibility ensures the framework remains effective across a range of decision contexts.

Table 9.1 Summary of framework evaluation across case studies

Criterion	Quantitative metrics	Result 1	Result 2	Target
Capabilities	• Decision-task coverage rate • Customization rate	100% 100%	100% 100%	≥ 90% ≥ 80%
Robustness	• Unexpected condition solving rate	>90%	100%	≥ 90%
Explainability	• Rate of recommendations with traceable rationale	100%	100%	≥ 90%
Domain Integrity	• Rate of compliance with domain rules	100%	100%	≥ 90%
Iterative Validation	• Iterative validation rate	100%	100%	≥ 90%
Cross-Sector Applicability	• Number of sectors tested without major redesign	2		≥ 2
Adaptability & Scalability	• Number of data modalities supported • Maximum data volume processed	>3 N/A		≥ 3 >10xbaseline

A minor limitation is that evaluations rely on historical, offline data. Real-time deployment remains a future direction for demonstrating responsiveness to dynamic conditions. Nonetheless, the framework performs strongly in both scope and adaptability. Quantitative results confirm complete task coverage and full customization in both case studies.

Robustness

Both case studies demonstrate that the framework operates reliably and consistently under varied and challenging conditions. In the foundry case, it effectively manages noisy, asynchronous sensor data, missing values, and diverse operating modes. Over 90 percent of unexpected data and process anomalies are resolved through rigorous preprocessing, including outlier removal, timestamp alignment, process-specific segmentation of melting cycles, and targeted sub-setting for causal analysis. In the transportation case, the framework addresses irregular sensor sampling, missing data, and variability across routes and drivers by reconstructing the datasets. Data quality checks and normalization routines standardize diverse data sources, enabling stable system performance. The framework maintains model accuracy and recommendation quality despite the absence of high-quality time-series fuel consumption data.

A noted limitation is the instability of certain causal graphs in the foundry application, indicating sensitivity to specific data configurations. While this does not undermine the overall framework, it highlights an area for refinement, such as adopting ensemble causal methods or incorporating expert review. To further validate robustness, future work should test the framework in different operational contexts, such as additional foundries or transit fleets. Overall, the framework meets the robustness criterion, demonstrating stable performance across both domains with only minor limitations.

Explainability

Explainability is a key strength of the proposed decision support framework, achieved through integrated interpretability at four levels: data quality assessment, clustering explanation, causal inference, and LLM-based narration. This multi-layered approach enables users to understand, verify, and apply the system's outputs with confidence.

In the foundry case, the data characterization module identifies outliers, quantifies missing values, and provides interpretable quality metrics, ensuring transparency from the outset. Clustering results are accompanied by post-hoc analyses that describe operational patterns. Causal inference reveals performance drivers, such as delayed effects of cooling on temperature stability. The LLM-based narrative module synthesizes these results into plain-language recommendations, each directly linked to specific analytical outputs. This design yields a 100 percent traceability rate, with every recommendation grounded in documented evidence. In the transportation case, similar levels of explainability are achieved. Clustering outputs are interpreted using route, driver, and road-type profiles. Causal models highlight the influence of driving behavior and road conditions. These insights are communicated in accessible language tailored to practitioners.

This layered interpretability enhances trust and enables expert engagement with system outputs. The framework fully satisfies the explainability criterion. Future research should include real-world tests and feedback to assess how well the explanations support understanding and decision-making in practice.

Domain Integrity

The framework demonstrates strong domain integrity by embedding sector-specific knowledge, constraints, and terminology into its analysis and outputs. In both case studies, the decision-support recommendations align closely with established operational practices. In the foundry case, recommendations such as stabilizing furnace temperature, optimizing charge schedules, and maintaining cooling system efficiency reflect industry norms grounded in metallurgical principles. The framework integrates process-specific rules, including quality thresholds and equipment limitations, ensuring all outputs are operationally and physically plausible. In the public transportation case, the framework incorporates transportation terminology and operational policies, including route structures, timetables, and adherence to schedules. Recommendations, such as reducing idling at terminals or promoting smoother acceleration, align with recognized eco-driving and fleet management strategies.

This embedded domain awareness enhances the system's credibility and acceptance. Stakeholders recognize that the framework produces actionable insights grounded in familiar concepts, rather than abstract or impractical outputs. Achieving this required the inclusion of domain heuristics and context-specific data transformations, such as defining fuel economy or segmenting melting cycles. A potential limitation is the risk of overfitting to a specific environment. However, the domain rules applied remain broadly representative, and the framework's cross-domain success suggests generalizability. The domain Integrity criterion is clearly satisfied in both sectors.

Iterative Validation Potential

The framework supports iterative validation and continuous learning, even if multi-round validation is not conducted in the present case studies. Its architecture enables feedback loops, model retraining, and analytical refinement. New data can update model outputs, and user feedback on recommendations can inform successive improvements. In the foundry case, practitioners could implement recommended changes, such as adjusting charging protocols, then assess their impact and retrain models accordingly. Similarly, in transportation, fleet managers might trial eco-driving measures, monitor fuel consumption, and refine guidance based on outcomes.

This design facilitates practitioner engagement and ensures the framework evolves with changing operational contexts, such as equipment upgrades or shifting traffic conditions. While multi-round field testing is not conducted at this stage due to practical constraints, the framework's modular design supports component-level retraining and data refresh, providing a strong foundation for iterative use. Expert feedback confirms that this capability is essential for long-term sustainability. Although current evidence is limited to historical data-driven analysis, the framework satisfies the criterion for potential iterative validation based on its design and intended functionality. It is positioned not as a static tool, but as a dynamic system capable of adapting through real-world feedback and ongoing collaboration.

Cross-Sector Applicability

Following the completion of both case studies, the framework's cross-sector applicability can be meaningfully evaluated. This refers to its ability to transfer from one domain to another with minimal redesign. In the proposed decision support framework, core components such as data quality assessment, data-driven clustering, causal discovery, and LLM-based narrative generation are reused across two sectors with fundamentally different operational and data characteristics. Despite significant differences between the foundry and transportation domains, the same architectural modules are applied successfully in both contexts. Only modest adaptations are necessary. The data preparation stage is adjusted to accommodate domain-specific formats and segmentation logic, while prompts in the narrative module are slightly tailored to reflect sector-specific terminology and performance indicators. Importantly, the core analytical algorithms, reasoning logic, and system architecture remain unchanged. This demonstrates that the framework's design is sufficiently abstract, modular, and generalizable.

The evaluation criterion for cross-sector applicability is defined as successful deployment in multiple domains without major redesign, as shown in Table 9.1. Based on this definition, the framework meets the requirement. Demonstrated functionality in two distinct sectors provides strong initial evidence of generalizability. However, two domains represent only a small subset of potential applications. Future work should extend the framework to additional sectors and explore multi-domain deployments to further assess versatility. The framework effectively manages the trade-off between domain specificity and portability by encapsulating domain logic in modular components. Rather than hard-coding sector-specific rules throughout the system, these components can be substituted or reconfigured with minimal disruption. This modular design is a key enabler of adaptability across sectors.

Adaptability and Scalability

The framework demonstrates high adaptability to diverse data types and user needs, with strong scalability potential for larger datasets and operational contexts. The foundry case involves time-series sensor data, including thermal and electrical variables sampled at ten-second intervals. The transportation case integrates multimodal data, including engine telemetry, geospatial positioning, and driver event logs. The framework successfully processes and aligns these heterogeneous inputs without performance degradation, confirming its flexibility in handling domain-specific data environments. Adaptability also extends to user roles. In the industrial domain, the framework supports engineers and plant managers, while in transportation, it serves drivers, fleet supervisors, and planners. Its modular structure and customizable outputs allow it to accommodate varying decision-making levels and stakeholder needs.

Scalability is demonstrated through the efficient processing of substantial datasets. The foundry case includes about 3,000 melting cycles, each with millions of sensor readings. The transportation case comprises over 4,000 bus trips recorded at one-second resolution across multiple telemetry variables. The system's architecture supports batch processing, parallel execution, and modular deployment, enabling seamless scaling to enterprise-level operations.

According to Table 9.1, this criterion is evaluated using two quantitative metrics, including the number of supported data modalities and the maximum data volume processed. For the first metric, the framework exceeds the target by supporting more than three distinct data modalities. In the foundry case, it processes time-series sensor data from multiple physical systems, including temperature, electrical current, and cooling flow sensors. In the transportation case, it handles a broader range of modalities, including GPS data, vehicle telemetry, and categorical event logs related to driving behaviors. This confirms the framework's capability to ingest, align, and process heterogeneous data types, demonstrating its adaptability to complex, domain-specific data environments.

For the second metric, the framework successfully processes large-volume datasets. In the foundry case, it analyzes about 3,000 melting cycles with millions of sensor observations each, while in the transportation case, it processes over 4,000 trips with one-second resolution across multiple telemetry variables. Although maximum volume is inherently constrained by available hardware and computational resources, the decision support is designed for scalability. As data volumes grow, the system can be deployed on high-performance computing infrastructure or cloud-based platforms to sustain throughput and responsiveness. Therefore, the proposed framework satisfies the adaptability and scalability criterion, offering flexible configuration across domains and the infrastructure readiness for future large-scale deployments.

9.1.2 Cross-Domain Comparison of Case Studies

The proposed AI-driven decision support framework is designed for application across a range of operational domains. This thesis implements and evaluates the framework in two distinct settings: an industrial metal foundry and a public transportation system. Both case studies demonstrate the framework's capacity to deliver effective, data-driven decision support despite differing operational dynamics, data modalities, and stakeholder needs. This section presents a comparative analysis to assess the framework's generalizability, consistency, and adaptability across sectors. Table 9.2 summarizes the comparative findings of case studies.

Table 9.2 Cross-domain comparison of the two case studies

Aspect	Industrial case	Transportation case
Domain context	Metal melting process in an industrial foundry	Bus transportation system
Data type	Continuous furnace sensor data (e.g., energy, temperature, cooling water)	Heterogeneous telemetry data (e.g., speed, acceleration, fuel rate, GPS, engine load)
Segmentation method	Customized cycle segmentation for melting cycles	Trip segmentation based on route schedules
Clustering approach	Time-series clustering on the temperature feature	GMM clustering on the fuel-efficiency feature
Causal reasoning method	Integrated PCMCI + with intervention analysis	Bagging DAGMA-DCE with intervention analysis
KPIs	Melting temperature	Fuel efficiency (L/100 km)
Duration	Over one year	One week
Data challenges	Noise, redundancy, process-specific variability	Asynchronous sensors, low-resolution of fuel consumption records
Domain-specific data adaptations	Cooling-water feature reconstruction, filtering of non-melting cycles	Reconstruct characteristic datasets
Narrative output	LLM-generated recommendations for furnace operation and energy optimization	LLM-generated recommendations for eco-driving and fleet management

In both cases, the end-to-end five-module pipeline, comprising data acquisition, preprocessing, clustering, causal reasoning, and LLM-based narrative generation, is implemented without modification to the overarching architecture. Only modest domain-specific adaptations were required, confirming the modularity and abstraction of the framework's design.

In the foundry case, time-series sensor data from thermal, electrical, and cooling systems are segmented into melting cycles using a custom algorithm. Feature engineering produces interpretable indicators such as energy consumption per tonne and temperature stability. In contrast, the transportation case involves multimodal telemetry, including GPS, engine metrics, and driving events, which are segmented into individual trips and synchronized with route schedules. Despite differing data modalities and structures, the framework ingests, aligns, and analyzes both datasets effectively with minimal reconfiguration.

Clustering analysis identifies meaningful operational patterns in each domain: in the foundry, efficient versus inefficient furnace regimes; in transportation, eco-driving versus energy-intensive behaviors. Causal inference reveals key drivers of energy performance, such as the delayed impact of thermal-cooling interactions and the influence of aggressive driving on fuel consumption. These findings directly inform context-specific recommendations. The LLM-based narration module translates analytical results into stakeholder-facing outputs. For foundry engineers, the system generates guidance aligned with best metallurgical practices, such as charge scheduling and thermal control. For transit personnel, it produces targeted suggestions on driving behavior and route optimization. In both domains, the output preserves analytical traceability and domain integrity.

Overall, the cross-domain comparison demonstrates that the proposed AI-driven decision support framework remains both flexible and transferable across heterogeneous application contexts. Despite substantial differences in data structure, operational dynamics, and performance metrics, the framework maintains consistent analytical integrity through its modular architecture and standardized evaluation criteria. The results of the two case studies substantiate the framework's ability to generalize across domains while retaining the adaptability required for domain-specific optimization and decision support.

9.1.3 Generalization Potential of the Proposed Framework

The findings from the two case studies indicate that the proposed AI-driven decision support framework has significant generalization potential and underscores the importance of targeted domain adaptation. The framework is built on a modular five-stage pipeline comprising data acquisition, profiling, clustering, causal analysis, and multimodal narration. This structure has been successfully implemented in two distinct domains: industrial manufacturing and public transportation. Despite considerable variation in data types, operational goals, and environmental conditions, the overall architecture remains unchanged, with only modest adjustments required at the module level.

This generalization capability stems from the framework's modular design. Core analytical components, such as clustering and causal reasoning, can be reconfigured using algorithms tailored to the specific application context. For example, time-series clustering is used in the industrial case, while probabilistic clustering is applied in the transportation domain. Similarly, different causal inference methods are employed depending on the nature of the data. These variations do not alter the underlying function of each module, allowing the framework to be adapted without restructuring its overall logic.

However, generalizability does not imply that the system is entirely independent of domain context. Successful deployment depends on the careful integration of domain-specific knowledge. This includes defining relevant performance indicators, establishing segmentation rules for meaningful units of analysis, and crafting prompts appropriate to the narrative generation terminology. These customization points act as bridges between the generic architecture and the unique requirements of each domain.

The selected two case studies intentionally span very different settings. The framework performs reliably in both scenarios, indicating its ability to address general challenges such as heterogeneous data structures, complex causal reasoning, and translating insights into user-centered recommendations. Nonetheless, broader validation is essential. Additional domains, such as building energy management, maritime logistics, or food production, could further test the framework's limits and refine its adaptability. Even within the same sector, different organizational settings or technologies may require additional tuning. While the framework is not designed for universal, out-of-the-box applications, it provides a foundation that supports scalability and transferability with reasonable customization.

In conclusion, the generalization potential of the proposed framework is anchored in its modular structure, methodological flexibility, and successful application across contrasting domains. It offers a robust and adaptable foundation for AI-enabled decision support in energy-intensive systems, and future extensions can build on this base by incorporating domain knowledge while preserving architectural integrity.

9.2 Addressing Research Questions

The research is guided by three central research questions (RQ1-RQ3) posed in Sect. 1.3.2, and the findings presented in this thesis offer substantive answers to each, as outlined below.

RQ1: *How can artificial intelligence techniques be coherently integrated within a modular decision support framework to enable effective, data-driven enhancement of energy efficiency in industrial and transportation systems?*

This question is addressed through the design and implementation of the framework presented in Chaps. 5 and 6. The research demonstrates that AI methods, including machine learning for pattern recognition, causal inference, and multimodal LLMs, can be systematically organized into a unified five-module decision-support system.

The integration is guided by a structured methodology, namely the DataPro data processing model. Developed as a generalization and extension of the CRISP-DM framework, DataPro offers a standardized foundation for data understanding, preprocessing, and decision-oriented analytics in complex operational environments. It addresses several limitations of the original CRISP-DM model by introducing key methodological enhancements in Sect. 5.3.1.

This ensures methodological coherence and operational interoperability. Empirical validation across two case studies confirms that AI components, such as clustering and causal analysis algorithms, and LLM-based narrative generation operate effectively as a cohesive system. Information flows logically from one module to the next, from raw data ingestion through to interpretable stakeholder recommendations. This confirms the system's coherence and reinforces its capacity to bridge the gap between raw data and actionable energy-efficiency insights. In contrast to fragmented or siloed approaches found in prior literature [39, 40, 47, 72, 74], this modular integration ensures consistency, adaptability, and transparency. The successful deployment in both manufacturing and transportation domains affirms that a modular design with common interfaces enables robust and flexible integration of AI methods for energy-focused decision support.

RQ2: *What data processing and analytical approaches are required to systematically capture, structure, and interpret heterogeneous operational data to uncover underlying patterns and causal relationships influencing energy performance?*

This question is addressed through the development of a comprehensive data pipeline and analytical strategy to manage complex, high-dimensional, and heterogeneous datasets. The framework integrates domain-agnostic data processing techniques with domain-specific modeling to transform raw operational data into structured, analytically meaningful inputs. The DataPro model is introduced to guide the management of data science workflows in complex real-world domains.

The initial stages focus on systematic data characterization and quality assessment, which inform key preprocessing tasks such as outlier removal, missing value imputation, normalization, and feature engineering. These procedures ensure data integrity and analytical consistency across the pipeline. Once the data is curated, unsupervised learning methods are employed to uncover latent operational patterns. In the foundry case, time-series clustering distinguishes different furnace operating modes, while in the transportation case, multivariate clustering identifies fuel-efficiency profiles across trips. However, pattern detection alone does not explain underlying performance variations. To uncover causal mechanisms, the framework incorporates dedicated causal inference methods: PCMCI + is applied to identify time-lagged dependencies among process variables in the foundry, and ensemble DAG-based learning is used to analyze behavioral and contextual factors in the transportation case. These methods are followed by causal verification and intervention analysis, forming a complete causal reasoning pipeline to identify the root causes of performance-critical variables.

The research underscores the need for aligning technical methods with domain context. Segmenting data into cycles or trips, incorporating physical constraints, and using domain-relevant performance indicators enhance the interpretability of results. Overall, the framework demonstrates that robust preprocessing combined with pattern recognition and causal inference enables a deep understanding of energy performance dynamics, providing a comprehensive answer to RQ2.

RQ3: *How can the proposed framework ensure reliability, explainability, and cross-domain adaptability of AI-driven analyses and recommendations, thereby enhancing stakeholder trust and practical applicability in various real-world decision contexts?*

This question focuses on the practical qualities that determine whether an AI-driven decision support system can be trusted and used in real-world settings. The proposed approach addresses these concerns by incorporating reliability, explainability, and adaptability in both its design and implementation.

Reliability is achieved through systematic validation procedures, fallback mechanisms, and robust handling of real-world data irregularities. The framework systematically improves data quality, including handling missing values and sensor errors, ensuring that recommendations are based on trustworthy inputs.

Explainability is embedded throughout the framework. At each stage, the system provides clear, context-specific outputs, ranging from interpretable clustering results to causal graphs and natural-language recommendations. The multimodal LLM-based automatic narrative module translates complex analytics into stakeholder-aligned insights, allowing decision-makers to understand the rationale behind each recommendation. This traceability helps build confidence in the system and allows users to engage critically with the outputs.

Adaptability is demonstrated through the successful deployment of the framework in two fundamentally different domains without altering its core structure. By separating domain-agnostic and domain-specific components, the system can be tailored to new contexts by adjusting only a few elements, such as KPIs and segmentation logic. This modularity ensures scalability and applicability across diverse sectors while keeping customization efforts manageable.

Overall, the framework fulfills the criteria posed by RQ3. It ensures reliability through resilient data handling and systematic validation, explainability through transparent, traceable outputs, and adaptability through a modular, generalizable design. These qualities demonstrate that the system can be trusted, understood, and effectively applied in varied real-world decision-making environments.

9.3 Achieving Research Objectives

This thesis establishes five research objectives (RO1-RO5) in Sect. 1.3.3 to operationalize the overall research aim. Each objective is associated with a corresponding hypothesis (H1–H5). The following section explains how each objective has been fulfilled through the design, implementation, and validation of the proposed AI-driven decision support framework.

RO1: *Establish a rigorous methodological foundation that integrates DSR with a data-driven process model to guide the systematic design and development of the AI-driven decision support framework.*

H1: A structured methodological approach that combines DSR principles with a formalized data-processing model will provide a coherent foundation for designing, implementing, and evaluating AI-driven decision support systems, thereby ensuring both scientific rigor and practical relevance.

This objective is achieved through the development of the DataPro data processing model, as presented in Chap. 5. The DSR framework, introduced in Sect. 4.1, comprises three interrelated cycles: relevance, rigor, and design. These three cycles ensure that the artifact's development is both practically grounded and scientifically rigorous. The relevance cycle links the research to real-world challenges in energy efficiency across industrial and transportation systems. The rigor cycle anchors the work in established research on machine learning, causal inference, and decision support. The design cycle guides the iterative development and empirical evaluation of the framework through applied case studies.

To complement this methodology, the DataPro model is formulated as a formal data processing pipeline that extends the original CRISP-DM framework. It organizes the data science workflow into four logically ordered phases: define, refine, analyze, and utilize. In addition, it incorporates technical understanding and implementation planning to support analytical readiness and practical deployment. Each module within the proposed framework corresponds to specific DataPro phases, ensuring systematic development, consistent traceability, and structured evaluation, as illustrated in Fig. 5.3.

The integration of the DSR methodology and the DataPro model provides a coherent and reproducible methodological foundation for artifact creation. This alignment between conceptual rigor and applied relevance supports the successful development, deployment, and validation of the framework in two complex operational domains, thereby fully achieving RO1 and confirming its associated hypothesis.

RO2: *Design a modular and unified AI-driven decision support framework architecture that integrates key analytical components, ensuring seamless interaction across the data-to-decision pipeline from data acquisition to interpretable recommendations.*

H2: A holistic, modular framework that integrates data preprocessing, pattern discovery, causal analysis, and explainable reporting within a unified structure will enhance the coherence, efficiency, and usability of decision-making processes compared with existing fragmented approaches.

This objective is achieved through the development of a structured and integrated framework architecture, as detailed in Chap. 5. The conceptual design introduces a five-module architecture consisting of data acquisition, data preprocessing, pattern discovery, causal analysis, and decision support, as illustrated in Fig. 5.1. Each module is clearly defined in terms of its functional role, expected inputs and outputs, and interaction with adjacent modules. Standardized interfaces are established to ensure consistent and seamless data exchange across the entire pipeline.

The architecture emphasizes both coherence and modularity. As a unified system, it enables smooth progression from one analytical stage to the next. For instance, outputs from the pattern discovery module, such as clustering results, are directly transferred to the causal analysis module as structured inputs. Simultaneously, the modular design allows each analytical component to be independently developed, replaced, or extended, provided it adheres to the predefined interfaces and data formats. This flexibility is essential for maintainability and customization. The modular-unified architecture also enhances adaptability, as confirmed by its successful implementation in two distinct domains. The ability to integrate domain-specific algorithms without altering the overarching structure demonstrates the framework's robustness and generalizability.

Therefore, RO2 is achieved in this study by presenting a well-structured, modular, and unified AI-driven decision-support architecture that enables coherent system operation, supports efficient component integration, and facilitates practical deployment across application domains.

RO3: *Develop and implement novel or adapted analytical modules that are both domain-agnostic and domain-aware for data understanding, pattern discovery, causal reasoning, and insights generation that enable systematic interpretation of operational dynamics and identification of energy efficiency drivers.*

H3: Advanced data- and AI-driven analytical methods that integrate domain-agnostic generalization with domain-aware adaptation will yield deeper insights and more reliable explanations of energy performance variations, enhancing the framework's robustness and interpretability across applications.

This objective is fulfilled through the development and implementation of a suite of analytical modules, as described in Chap. 6 and applied in the case studies presented in Chaps. 7 and 8. These modules combine general-purpose data-driven and AI techniques with tailored adaptations to address the specific characteristics of each domain.

The data understanding and preprocessing module standardizes procedures for cleaning, transforming, and preparing heterogeneous sensor data. It applies general techniques such as outlier detection, missing value imputation, normalization, and feature engineering, alongside domain-specific tasks like temporal alignment in the foundry and trip segmentation in transportation. These steps ensure consistent data quality and analytical readiness.

For pattern discovery, the framework employs TS-IDEC, a time-series clustering method designed for cyclic foundry operational data. It combines deep representation learning with centroid-based clustering to identify distinct operating modes. In transportation, the GMM clustering enhanced with features such as driver and route variability reveals fuel-efficiency profiles. Although algorithmically general, both approaches are adapted through context-specific features to enhance relevance.

The causal reasoning module applies data-driven methods. PCMCI + captures time-lagged causal dependencies in the foundry, while DAGMA-DCE supports stable causal structure learning in the transportation case. Each implementation includes intervention analysis and verification to identify and validate root causes of energy inefficiencies.

The insights generation module uses a multimodal LLM-based multi-agent framework to produce stakeholder-oriented explanations. It integrates results from clustering, causality, and performance analysis into coherent reports with visual and textual elements. While domain-agnostic in design, the language model is guided by structured prompts derived from domain-specific outputs, ensuring clarity and contextual fidelity.

The case study results demonstrate that these analytical modules effectively uncover operational patterns and causal mechanisms in both industrial and transportation domains. Therefore, RO3 is achieved by delivering a set of analytical modules that combine generalizable AI techniques with domain-specific adaptation. This hybrid approach enables interpretable, trustworthy, and actionable insights into complex operational systems, supporting energy efficiency improvements in diverse application contexts.

RO4: *Embed explainability, reliability, and cross-domain adaptability into the framework to ensure transparent, trustworthy, and transferable AI-assisted decision support across diverse real-world contexts with varying data characteristics and operational constraints.*

H4: Incorporating explainability and cross-domain adaptability into the framework will enable transparent interpretation of AI-generated insights and support reliable adaptability across domains, ensuring consistent performance and trust in diverse operational environments.

This objective is achieved through deliberate architectural and methodological choices that ensure transparency, robustness, and generalizability. Explainability is incorporated into every stage of the framework. Outputs are accompanied by interpretable elements such as traceable recommendations, labeled clustering results, validated causal graphs, and human-readable reports generated by a multimodal LLM-based narrative module. The case studies confirm that stakeholders consistently understand and verify the reasoning behind each recommendation, thereby fulfilling the transparency requirement.

Reliability is addressed through robust data handling and systematic validation and verification mechanisms embedded throughout the data processing pipeline. These include mechanisms for managing missing data, detecting anomalies, validating model outputs, and applying fallback strategies when necessary. During the development of algorithms and sub-frameworks within each module in Chap. 6, comprehensive verification techniques are employed, including ablation studies to assess the contribution of individual components, sensitivity analysis to evaluate model stability under parameter variation, and comparative analysis with SotA methods to validate performance and methodological soundness. Results from both case studies demonstrate consistent behavior and high robustness, with the framework effectively managing noise and outliers in real-world datasets. These outcomes confirm that the system operates reliably and predictably, supporting user trust.

Cross-domain adaptability is achieved through a modular architecture and abstraction from domain-specific constraints. The framework operates effectively across industrial and transportation domains without requiring fundamental structural changes. Core modules remain unchanged, while configurable elements such as KPIs, clustering parameters, and narrative prompts are tailored to each domain. Generalizable AI methods and a standardized data-processing model further enhance transferability. Results from both industrial and transportation cases confirm the framework's ability to align with sector-specific practices and generate actionable insights.

Therefore, RO4 is fully achieved. The framework exhibits explainability by generating interpretable, context-aware outputs, ensuring reliability through robust data handling and systematic validation, and demonstrating adaptability through successful implementation across multiple real-world domains.

RO5: *Establish a rigorous evaluation and benchmarking strategy to assess the framework's performance, robustness, and practical utility through quantitative metrics and qualitative validation in real-world case studies.*

H5: Systematic evaluation across multiple criteria, including analytical accuracy, causal validity, interpretability, and decision-making effectiveness, will demonstrate that the proposed framework and its components outperform existing baselines, confirming their robustness, relevance, and contribution to energy-efficient operations.

This objective is achieved through the development and application of a structured evaluation strategy, as outlined in Sect. 4.3.2 and operationalized in Chaps. 7–9. The evaluation framework defines clear criteria across multiple dimensions, including analytical capabilities, robustness, explainability, domain integrity, potential for iterative validation, cross-sector applicability, and adaptability and scalability. Each criterion is linked to both quantitative metrics and qualitative assessment guidelines to ensure comprehensive measurement of system performance.

The evaluation methodology integrates quantitative metrics, such as task coverage rates and recommendation traceability, with structured expert assessments to validate both technical performance and practical relevance. Performance data are systematically collected across both case studies to ensure comprehensive evaluation. Benchmarking is conducted by evaluating key components, such as the TS-IDEC clustering algorithm and the causal inference module, against established baselines, including k-means clustering and standard DAG-based learning methods. The results consistently demonstrate that the proposed framework provides improved insight quality and greater decision-support value. Sections 7.5, 8.5, and 9.1 provide a detailed performance evaluation and discussion. The use of two distinct case studies further strengthens the evaluation. This dual application tests the framework's utility and reliability in heterogeneous contexts and confirms its cross-domain applicability. Where limitations are observed, such as occasional instability in causal graphs, they are documented transparently as areas for future improvement.

Therefore, RO5 is achieved, as the evaluation strategy confirms that the framework meets its defined performance and usability objectives, demonstrating both scientific rigor and practical utility across multiple domains.

9.4 Validity and Limitations

This section provides a critical evaluation of the study's overall credibility and scope, examining its validity and limitations. It assesses how methodological rigor, empirical evidence, and theoretical alignment support the strength, reliability, and applicability of the findings, while also acknowledging the boundaries that condition their interpretation. Although the proposed framework is developed through a structured, theoretically grounded methodology and validated across two contrasting domains, certain design, data, and methodological constraints may limit its generalizability and practical implementation.

The discussion is organized into two complementary parts: validity (Sect. 9.4.1), which examines methodological soundness and evaluation integrity, and limitations (Sect. 9.4.2), which identifies the principal boundaries, assumptions, and contextual factors shaping the framework's applicability.

9.4.1 Validity

The validity of this study is reinforced by the evaluation of the proposed AI-driven decision support framework, the structured responses to the research questions, and the fulfillment of the defined research objectives in Sects. 9.1–9.3. This section synthesizes those discussions from a validity perspective, highlighting how methodological rigor, empirical evaluation across domains, and alignment with theoretical and practical goals support the methodological, internal, construct, and external validity of this research.

Methodological validity is ensured through the integration of the three-cycle DSR method, which includes the rigor, relevance, and design cycles, with the DataPro data-processing model. Together, they guide the iterative development and evaluation of the framework. The rigor cycle establishes theoretical grounding, the relevance cycle links the artifact to real-world problems, and the design cycle ensures systematic construction and evaluation of the artifact. Each design decision is informed by relevant literature or empirical feedback, reinforcing internal consistency and analytical rigor.

Internal validity is supported by robust data handling and systematic validation throughout the framework. Data understanding and preprocessing address missing data, anomalies, and noise, while model development incorporates ablation studies, sensitivity analysis, and benchmarking against SotA methods to verify the correctness and stability of analytical components. This continuous evaluation corresponds to the iterative refinement loops within the design cycle, ensuring that analytical reliability emerges through repeated testing and empirical adjustment.

Construct validity is upheld by aligning theoretical constructs with measurable performance indicators. Key application concepts, such as energy efficiency and operational patterns, are operationalized through well-defined KPIs, such as melting temperature and fuel economy. These metrics are grounded in business objectives and domain knowledge, ensuring analytical outputs map onto real-world concepts. This translation from theory to measurable constructs exemplifies the rigor cycle's role in maintaining conceptual integrity between the theoretical foundation and empirical representation.

External validity is demonstrated by applying the framework across two distinct domains, including industrial manufacturing and public transportation, without altering the core architecture. The successful implementation and evaluation in both contexts affirm the framework's generalizability, indicating its potential for broader applicability in other energy-intensive domains. This empirical breadth reflects the relevance cycle, which connects artifact design with diverse operational environments and validates that theoretical contributions retain applicability across contexts.

These four validity dimensions correspond directly to the three-cycle DSR structure: methodological and construct validity derive from the rigor cycle, internal validity is strengthened through the iterative design cycle, and external validity emerges from the relevance cycle. This alignment confirms that the framework's development and evaluation processes are coherent within the DSR paradigm and that validity is embedded throughout its theoretical, methodological, and practical layers.

9.4.2 Limitations

The proposed AI-driven decision support framework presents a novel and structured approach to improving energy efficiency in industrial and transportation systems. Nonetheless, several limitations remain that warrant consideration. These considerations pertain to system-level design, domain applicability, and the flexibility and interpretability of individual analytical components. Recognizing these limitations is essential to guiding future research and development efforts.

At this stage, the framework has been validated in controlled, retrospective settings using historical datasets. While these studies provide valuable insights into its feasibility and analytical capabilities, real-world deployment and operational testing have not yet been conducted. The practical utility of the decision support recommendations, therefore, remains unverified. As a result, the system's behavior under actual operating conditions remains insufficiently understood. Although such validation lies beyond the present scope, partial or simulated deployments could, in future investigations, serve to examine operational performance and usability under real-world conditions.

Furthermore, the current implementation lacks a fully developed user interface for practical deployment as a DSS. The absence of an interactive graphical user interface (GUI) may pose challenges for end-users who are not familiar with the underlying algorithms. Developing lightweight visualization or dashboard functions could be a useful extension to enhance accessibility, yet such developments are outside the current research scope.

Regarding domain coverage, the framework has so far been applied in two distinct contexts, metal foundry operations and public transportation systems. These studies demonstrate cross-sector adaptability but do not provide comprehensive evidence of generalizability. Other domains, such as building energy management and chemical processing, may introduce unique constraints, operational complexities, or data challenges that have not been examined. Further exploration across additional sectors could offer insight into broader applicability; however, this remains an open direction rather than a defined continuation of the present work. Additionally, each case study in this thesis focuses on a specific data modality: time-series process data in the foundry case, and static characteristic data in the transportation case. The integration of multiple data types within a single case study has not been attempted; combining multimodal sources (e.g., sensor, text, or image data) could provide additional analytical depth but exceeds the current study's scope.

From a methodological and algorithmic perspective, certain analytical components could benefit from increased flexibility. The proposed data characteristic and quality understanding framework currently applies a fixed set of metrics across all cases. While this ensures consistency, it may include indicators irrelevant to specific contexts. Allowing users to tailor the profiling process by selecting relevant indicators could enhance usability and minimize unnecessary complexity. Developing this module as a configurable software package would further promote reuse and adaptation across applications.

The clustering and pattern discovery module effectively identifies behavioral groupings but provides limited guidance on selecting the number of clusters. In the absence of clear criteria or user-oriented heuristics, interpreting and validating clusters may be less intuitive for end-users.

Similarly, the causal reasoning and inference module, although grounded in established methods, has not yet been validated through domain-based intervention or counterfactual testing. While the inferred relationships offer a promising basis for understanding energy-related dynamics, their real-world significance remains to be empirically verified. Addressing minor instability observed in certain causal graphs may require ensemble-based or expert-reviewed approaches, thereby strengthening robustness in future methodological refinement.

Finally, the LLM-based narration and decision support module is currently built on a zero-shot reasoning procedure without domain-specific fine-tuning. As a result, the clarity or domain alignment of generated explanations may vary. Although the model performs adequately within the tested domains, subsequent fine-tuning or prompt optimization could be considered in later work to further improve contextual precision and interpretability, without altering the system's conceptual foundation.

10 Conclusion and Future Work

This thesis has developed an AI-driven decision support framework that enhances energy efficiency in energy-intensive industrial and transportation systems. The research is motivated by the high energy consumption and emissions of these sectors, as well as the untapped potential of their expanding data streams. It aims to establish a rigorous and interpretable framework that bridges the gap between data analytics and operational decision-making in energy-intensive sectors.

Using a three-cycle DSR methodology, the study iteratively develops and validates a modular framework that transforms heterogeneous sensor data into actionable recommendations. The framework integrates advanced data processing and explainable AI techniques, including data characteristic understanding, clustering, causal inference, and multimodal LLMs. It addresses the challenges of data heterogeneity, limited causal understanding, and the need for transparent and interpretable recommendations. The inductive development across two case studies, followed by cross-case evaluation, demonstrates both generality and practical applicability.

Two real-world case studies validate the framework's performance. In a metal foundry, the system uncovers operational patterns and causal drivers of energy consumption in melting processes, providing interpretable recommendations for process adjustments. In a public transportation fleet, it identifies how driving behavior and route factors influence fuel efficiency and produces actionable eco-driving guidance. These results confirm that the framework integrates AI components coherently, captures and interprets complex operational data, and provides explainable, reliable, and transferable decision support across domains.

All three research questions have been answered, and all five research objectives have been achieved through systematic design, implementation, and

Z. Ma, *Artificial Intelligence-Driven Decision Support Framework for Improving Energy Efficiency in Industry and Transportation*,
https://doi.org/10.1007/978-3-658-51965-0_10

evaluation. The DataPro model extends the CRISP-DM process, offering structured guidance for data-driven projects in energy-intensive contexts. Within the proposed framework, several novel methods are developed: the STREAM data pipeline and sensor characterization procedure for robust data acquisition; the TS-IDEC time-series clustering algorithm for discovering operational patterns; the Bagging DAGMA-DCE and Integrated PCMCI+ algorithms for robust causal discovery; a causal reasoning module for root-cause analysis; and an LLM-based multimodal narration component for generating explainable, human-centered insights.

The novelty of this PhD research resides in developing an integrated, explainable, and cross-domain architecture that unifies multiple AI techniques within a coherent design science foundation. The resulting framework delivers an end-to-end, transparent, and causally grounded decision support process from data acquisition to interpretable recommendations.

Scientific Novelty and Contributions

The framework is scientifically novel in combining advanced data processing, unsupervised pattern discovery, causal inference, and LLM-based explainability within a unified decision-support architecture. It explicitly links AI-driven analytics with the three-cycle DSR methodology, demonstrating how the rigor, relevance, and design cycles can be operationalized to achieve both theoretical depth and practical impact. Key innovations include:

- The DataPro model extends CRISP-DM with standardized steps for data understanding, quality assessment, model development, and integration of domain expertise.
- The STREAM data pipeline enables robust acquisition, and a sensor data characterization procedure ensures understanding of the quality of heterogeneous sensor data.
- The TS-IDEC algorithm advances deep clustering for time-series data, enabling the discovery of operational patterns.
- A novel causal reasoning pipeline identifies root causal drivers of energy efficiency and inefficiency.
- The LLM-based multimodal narration module generates human-centered explanations, enhancing interpretability and trust.

Practical Contributions

Practically, the framework demonstrates adaptability, scalability, and real-world applicability. Validation in both a metal foundry and a public transportation system confirms its transferability across distinct operational contexts. In each case, the system identifies inefficiencies, provides interpretable recommendations, and supports measurable improvements in energy performance. These outcomes validate the design principles established through DSR, confirming that scientific innovation can translate into operational value. The framework also yields a set of design principles for responsible and human-centered AI in industrial decision support, emphasizing transparency, stakeholder trust, and effective collaboration between human expertise and AI systems.

Limitations and Future Work

While this research meets its objectives and demonstrates the potential of AI-assisted decision support to enhance energy efficiency, certain limitations persist. As detailed in Chap. 9, these limitations are summarized here to provide context for possible directions for extending the work.

The framework currently represents a validated research prototype rather than a fully operational industrial system. Further investigation could explore real-world deployment or simulated pilot testing to examine usability under dynamic industrial and transportation conditions. Such efforts would enable systematic assessment of reliability, adaptability, and quantifiable energy savings, supported by user feedback for iterative improvement. Developing interactive visualization tools or domain-specific dashboards could further enhance interpretability and accessibility, especially for practitioners who rely on visual insights for decision-making.

Expanding validation across additional sectors, such as building management, logistics, or process industries, could provide evidence of broader transferability, while integrating heterogeneous data sources (e.g., real-time sensor, textual, or contextual data) may reveal further analytical opportunities. These remain open avenues rather than defined commitments.

From a methodological perspective, future work could improve adaptability and configurability across analytical modules. Examples include customizable data-quality metrics and semi-automated cluster selection informed by domain expertise. Minor instability observed in causal graph generation suggests that ensemble-based or expert-reviewed causal validation may improve robustness, although such refinement exceeds the present scope. Finally, domain-adaptive explainability represents a meaningful area for conceptual exploration. Fine-tuning LLMs on sector-specific corpora or integrating user feedback mechanisms could improve contextual precision and linguistic consistency, thereby fostering greater trust in AI-assisted recommendations.

In conclusion, this PhD research establishes a comprehensive foundation for AI-driven decision support in energy-intensive sectors, demonstrating both conceptual soundness and empirical viability. The developed framework serves as a blueprint for integrating data analytics, machine learning, and explainable AI to enhance energy efficiency in complex operations. Its contributions encompass theoretical advances, algorithmic innovation, and empirical validation within the emerging field of energy informatics. By bridging AI, data science, and energy informatics, this research contributes to the evolving paradigm of digital sustainability and provides a replicable foundation for responsible AI deployment in energy-intensive systems. Building on this foundation, future scholarly work may further refine the system's capabilities, broaden its applicability, and enable field-level validation, thereby contributing to energy savings, operational efficiency, and global sustainability goals.

References

1. International Energy Agency. "Global CO2 emissions by sector, 2019–2022." https://www.iea.org/data-and-statistics/charts/global-co2-emissions-by-sector-2019-2022 (accessed September 10, 2025).
2. International Energy Agency. "Global CO2 emissions from transport by sub-sector in the Net Zero Scenario, 2000–2030." https://www.iea.org/data-and-statistics/charts/global-co2-emissions-from-transport-by-sub-sector-in-the-net-zero-scenario-2000-2030-2 (accessed September 10, 2025).
3. International Energy Agency. "Industry." https://www.iea.org/energy-system/industry (accessed August 27, 2025).
4. V. Chang and C. Martin, "An industrial IoT sensor system for high-temperature measurement," *Computers and Electrical Engineering,* vol. 95, p. 107439, 2021.
5. P. C. M. Arachchige, P. Bertok, I. Khalil, D. Liu, S. Camtepe, and M. Atiquzzaman, "A trustworthy privacy preserving framework for machine learning in industrial IoT systems," *IEEE Transactions on Industrial Informatics,* vol. 16, no. 9, pp. 6092–6102, 2020.
6. Y. Tian *et al.*, "VistaGPT: Generative parallel transformers for vehicles with intelligent systems for transport automation," *IEEE Transactions on Intelligent Vehicles,* vol. 8, no. 9, pp. 4198–4207, 2023.
7. S. Scharf *et al.*, "FOUNDRY 4.0: An innovative technology for sustainable and flexible process design in foundries," *Procedia CIRP,* vol. 98, pp. 73–78, 2021.
8. D. A. Howard, B. N. Jørgensen, and Z. Ma, "Identifying best practice melting patterns in induction furnaces: a data-driven approach using time series k-means clustering and multi-criteria decision making," in *Energy Informatics Academy Conference*, 2023: Springer, pp. 271–288.
9. X. Shan, C. Wang, and D. Zhou, "Interfering spatiotemporal features and causes of bus bunching using empirical gps trajectory data," *Journal of Grid Computing,* vol. 21, no. 1, p. 15, 2023.
10. H. Kang, T. Vo, H. K. Kim, and J. B. Hong, "CANival: A multimodal approach to intrusion detection on the vehicle CAN bus," *Vehicular Communications,* vol. 50, p. 100845, 2024.

Z. Ma, *Artificial Intelligence-Driven Decision Support Framework for Improving Energy Efficiency in Industry and Transportation*,
https://doi.org/10.1007/978-3-658-51965-0

11. K.Y. Lin, "Generative artificial intelligence–driven sustainable supply chain management: a UNISONE framework for smart logistics and predictive analytics under Industry 5.0," *International Journal of Logistics Research and Applications,* pp. 1–32, 2025.
12. R. Guidotti, A. Monreale, S. Ruggieri, F. Turini, F. Giannotti, and D. Pedreschi, "A survey of methods for explaining black box models," *ACM computing surveys (CSUR),* vol. 51, no. 5, pp. 1–42, 2018.
13. A. Cabrera, A. Acosta, F. Almeida, and V. Blanco, "A heuristic technique to improve energy efficiency with dynamic load balancing," *Journal of Supercomputing,* vol. 75, no. 3, 2019.
14. Y. Luo, M. Zeng, and H. Jiang, "Learning to tradeoff between energy efficiency and delay in energy harvesting-powered D2D communication: A distributed experience-sharing algorithm," *IEEE Internet of Things Journal,* vol. 6, no. 3, pp. 5585–5594, 2019.
15. L. Zhang and L. Zhang, "Artificial intelligence for remote sensing data analysis: A review of challenges and opportunities," *IEEE Geoscience and Remote Sensing Magazine,* vol. 10, no. 2, pp. 270–294, 2022.
16. M. U. Mehmood, D. Chun, H. Han, G. Jeon, and K. Chen, "A review of the applications of artificial intelligence and big data to buildings for energy-efficiency and a comfortable indoor living environment," *Energy and buildings,* vol. 202, p. 109383, 2019.
17. D. A. Narciso and F. G. Martins, "Application of machine learning tools for energy efficiency in industry: A review," *Energy Reports,* vol. 6, pp. 1181–1199, 2020.
18. R. H. Bonczek, C. W. Holsapple, and A. B. Whinston, *Foundations of decision support systems.* Academic Press, 2014.
19. A. R. Hevner, "A three cycle view of design science research," *Scandinavian journal of information systems,* vol. 19, no. 2, pp. 87–92, 2007.
20. A. R. Hevner, S. T. March, J. Park, and S. Ram, "Design science in information systems research," *MIS quarterly,* vol. 28, no. 1, pp. 75–105, 2004.
21. A. Hevner and S. Chatterjee, *Design research in information systems: theory and practice.* Springer Science & Business Media, 2010.
22. International Energy Agency. "The value of urgent action on energy efficiency." https://www.iea.org/reports/the-value-of-urgent-action-on-energy-efficiency (accessed October 9, 2025).
23. M. G. Patterson, "What is energy efficiency?: Concepts, indicators and methodological issues," *Energy policy,* vol. 24, no. 5, pp. 377–390, 1996.
24. International Energy Agency. "World Energy Outlook 2024." https://www.iea.org/reports/world-energy-outlook-2024 (accessed October 9, 2025).
25. International Energy Agency. "Energy Efficiency 2024." https://www.iea.org/reports/energy-efficiency-2024 (accessed October 9, 2025).
26. P. Arora, "COP28: ambitions, realities, and future," *Environmental Sustainability,* vol. 7, no. 1, pp. 107–113, 2024.
27. D. A. Howard, "Generic Digital Twin Development Framework for Enhancing Energy Efficiency and Flexibility in Industrial Production Processes," University of Southern Denmark, 2023.

28. J. Haraldsson and M. T. Johansson, "Barriers to and drivers for improved energy efficiency in the Swedish aluminium industry and aluminium casting foundries," *Sustainability,* vol. 11, no. 7, p. 2043, 2019.
29. M. T. Johansson and P. Thollander, "A review of barriers to and driving forces for improved energy efficiency in Swedish industry–Recommendations for successful in-house energy management," *Renewable and Sustainable Energy Reviews,* vol. 82, pp. 618–628, 2018.
30. K. I. Batouta, S. Aouhassi, and K. Mansouri, "Energy efficiency in the manufacturing industry—A tertiary review and a conceptual knowledge-based framework," *Energy Reports,* vol. 9, pp. 4635–4653, 2023.
31. J. Dai, U. Mehmood, and A. A. Nassani, "Empowering sustainability through energy efficiency, green innovations, and the sharing economy: Insights from G7 economies," *Energy,* vol. 318, p. 134768, 2025.
32. A. Bagaini, F. Colelli, E. Croci, and T. Molteni, "Assessing the relevance of barriers to energy efficiency implementation in the building and transport sectors in eight European countries," *The Electricity Journal,* vol. 33, no. 8, p. 106820, 2020.
33. S. Langlois-Bertrand, M. Benhaddadi, M. Jegen, and P. O. Pineau, "Political-institutional barriers to energy efficiency," *Energy Strategy Reviews,* vol. 8, pp. 30–38, 2015.
34. K. J. Shah *et al.*, "Green transportation for sustainability: Review of current barriers, strategies, and innovative technologies," *Journal of Cleaner Production,* vol. 326, p. 129392, 2021.
35. Ş. İmre, D. Celebi, and F. Koca, "Understanding barriers and enablers of electric vehicles in urban freight transport: Addressing stakeholder needs in Turkey," *Sustainable Cities and Society,* vol. 68, p. 102794, 2021.
36. F. Burstein and C. W. Holsapple, *Handbook on decision support systems 1: basic themes*. Springer, 2008.
37. D. J. Power, "Decision support systems: concepts and resources for managers," *Studies in Informatics and Control,* vol. 11, no. 4, pp. 349–350, 2002.
38. D. J. Power, "Web-based and model-driven decision support systems: concepts and issues," *AMCIS 2000 Proceedings,* p. 387, 2000.
39. Y. Duan, J. S. Edwards, and Y. K. Dwivedi, "Artificial intelligence for decision making in the era of Big Data–evolution, challenges and research agenda," *International journal of information management,* vol. 48, pp. 63–71, 2019.
40. M. Elhaddad and S. Hamam, "AI-driven clinical decision support systems: an ongoing pursuit of potential," *Cureus,* vol. 16, no. 4, 2024.
41. A. E. Johnson, M. M. Ghassemi, S. Nemati, K. E. Niehaus, D. A. Clifton, and G. D. Clifford, "Machine learning and decision support in critical care," *Proceedings of the IEEE,* vol. 104, no. 2, pp. 444–466, 2016.
42. H. Taherdoost, "Deep learning and neural networks: Decision-making implications," *Symmetry,* vol. 15, no. 9, p. 1723, 2023.
43. E. Hossain *et al.*, "Natural language processing in electronic health records in relation to healthcare decision-making: a systematic review," *Computers in biology and medicine,* vol. 155, p. 106649, 2023.
44. J. Huang *et al.*, "Foundation models and intelligent decision-making: Progress, challenges, and perspectives," *The Innovation,* 2025.

45. X. Xiao, P. Chen, B. Qi, J. Liang, J. Tong, and H. Wang, "A novel scenario-driven method for enhanced dynamic emergency decision support in nuclear power plants," *Progress in Nuclear Energy,* vol. 189, p. 105908, 2025.
46. R. Sapkota *et al.*, "Multi-modal LLMs in agriculture: A comprehensive review," *IEEE Transactions on Automation Science and Engineering,* 2025.
47. R. Rosati *et al.*, "From knowledge-based to big data analytic model: a novel IoT and machine learning based decision support system for predictive maintenance in Industry 4.0," *Journal of Intelligent Manufacturing,* vol. 34, no. 1, pp. 107–121, 2023.
48. V. Gupta, V. K. Mishra, P. Singhal, and A. Kumar, "An overview of supervised machine learning algorithm," in *2022 11th International Conference on System Modeling & Advancement in Research Trends (SMART),* 2022: IEEE, pp. 87–92.
49. F. Bröker, L. L. Holt, B. D. Roads, P. Dayan, and B. C. Love, "Demystifying unsupervised learning: how it helps and hurts," *Trends in cognitive sciences,* 2024.
50. B. M. Konopka, F. Lwow, M. Owczarz, and Ł. Łaczmański, "Exploratory data analysis of a clinical study group: Development of a procedure for exploring multidimensional data," *PloS one,* vol. 13, no. 8, p. e0201950, 2018.
51. K. R. Kashwan and C. Velu, "Customer segmentation using clustering and data mining techniques," *International Journal of Computer Theory and Engineering,* vol. 5, no. 6, p. 856, 2013.
52. L. Eckart, S. Eckart, and M. Enke, "A brief comparative study of the potentialities and limitations of machine-learning algorithms and statistical techniques," in *E3S Web of Conferences,* 2021, vol. 266: EDP Sciences, p. 02001.
53. M. M. Malik, "A hierarchy of limitations in machine learning," *arXiv preprint arXiv:2002.05193,* 2020.
54. L. Alzubaidi *et al.*, "Review of deep learning: concepts, CNN architectures, challenges, applications, future directions," *Journal of Big Data,* vol. 8, no. 1, p. 53, 2021.
55. A. Sherstinsky, "Fundamentals of recurrent neural network (RNN) and long short-term memory (LSTM) network," *Physica D: Nonlinear Phenomena,* vol. 404, p. 132306, 2020.
56. X. Wang *et al.*, "Deep reinforcement learning: A survey," *IEEE Transactions on Neural Networks and Learning Systems,* vol. 35, no. 4, pp. 5064–5078, 2022.
57. S. Liu, K. C. See, K. Y. Ngiam, L. A. Celi, X. Sun, and M. Feng, "Reinforcement learning for clinical decision support in critical care: comprehensive review," *Journal of Medical Internet Research,* vol. 22, no. 7, p. e18477, 2020.
58. K. Zhang *et al.*, "Training effective deep reinforcement learning agents for real-time life-cycle production optimization," *Journal of Petroleum Science and Engineering,* vol. 208, p. 109766, 2022.
59. K. Kadamala, D. Chambers, and E. Barrett, "Enhancing HVAC control systems through transfer learning with deep reinforcement learning agents," *Smart Energy,* vol. 13, p. 100131, 2024.
60. T. Yang, L. Zhao, W. Li, and A. Y. Zomaya, "Dynamic energy dispatch strategy for integrated energy system based on improved deep reinforcement learning," *Energy,* vol. 235, p. 121377, 2021.
61. OpenAI. "Introducing GPT-4.1 in the API." https://openai.com/index/gpt-4-1/ (accessed April 14, 2025).

62. Anthropic. "Introducing computer use, a new Claude 3.5 Sonnet, and Claude 3.5 Haiku." https://www.anthropic.com/news/3-5-models-and-computer-use (accessed October 22, 2024).
63. Google DeepMind. "Gemini 2.5 Flash." https://deepmind.google/models/gemini/flash/ (accessed May 20, 2024).
64. J. Wei *et al.*, "Chain-of-thought prompting elicits reasoning in large language models," *Advances in neural information processing systems,* vol. 35, pp. 24824–24837, 2022.
65. A. Szymanski, N. Ziems, H. A. Eicher-Miller, T. J. J. Li, M. Jiang, and R. A. Metoyer, "Limitations of the llm-as-a-judge approach for evaluating llm outputs in expert knowledge tasks," in *Proceedings of the 30th International Conference on Intelligent User Interfaces*, 2025, pp. 952–966.
66. H. Fei, Y. Yao, Z. Zhang, F. Liu, A. Zhang, and T. S. Chua, "From multimodal llm to human-level ai: Modality, instruction, reasoning, efficiency and beyond," in *Proceedings of the 2024 Joint International Conference on Computational Linguistics, Language Resources and Evaluation (LREC-COLING 2024): Tutorial Summaries*, 2024, pp. 1–8.
67. L. Wang *et al.*, "A multimodal LLM-agent framework for personalized clinical decision-making in hepatocellular carcinoma," *Patterns,* 2025.
68. S. Kim, S. Hong, J. Jin, and B. Noh, "Driving Scene Context-Augmented Trajectory Prediction with Risk-Aware Decision Reasoning Using Multimodal LLM," in *EPIA Conference on Artificial Intelligence*, 2025: Springer, pp. 192–204.
69. S. Arena, E. Florian, I. Zennaro, P. F. Orrù, and F. Sgarbossa, "A novel decision support system for managing predictive maintenance strategies based on machine learning approaches," *Safety science,* vol. 146, p. 105529, 2022.
70. K. Du *et al.*, "LLM-MANUF: An integrated framework of Fine-Tuning large language models for intelligent Decision-Making in manufacturing," *Advanced Engineering Informatics,* vol. 65, p. 103263, 2025.
71. J. Senoner, T. Netland, and S. Feuerriegel, "Using explainable artificial intelligence to improve process quality: evidence from semiconductor manufacturing," *Management Science,* vol. 68, no. 8, pp. 5704–5723, 2022.
72. G. González Rodríguez, J. M. Gonzalez-Cava, and J. A. Méndez Pérez, "An intelligent decision support system for production planning based on machine learning," *Journal of Intelligent Manufacturing,* vol. 31, no. 5, pp. 1257–1273, 2020.
73. S. K. Jauhar, S. Sethi, S. S. Kamble, S. Mathew, and A. Belhadi, "Artificial intelligence and machine learning-based decision support system for forecasting electric vehicles' power requirement," *Technological Forecasting and Social Change,* vol. 204, p. 123396, 2024.
74. S. Zakeri, D. Konstantas, S. Sorooshian, and P. Chatterjee, "A novel ML-MCDM-based decision support system for evaluating autonomous vehicle integration scenarios in Geneva's public transportation," *Artificial intelligence review,* vol. 57, no. 11, p. 310, 2024.
75. Z. Xu, T. Chen, and S. Chen, "A LLM-based Multimodal Warning System for Driver Assistance," in *2024 IEEE 27th International Conference on Intelligent Transportation Systems (ITSC)*, 2024: IEEE, pp. 1527–1532.

76. B. Wu, T. Cheng, T. L. Yip, and Y. Wang, "Fuzzy logic based dynamic decision-making system for intelligent navigation strategy within inland traffic separation schemes," *Ocean Engineering,* vol. 197, p. 106909, 2020.
77. B. Murray and L. P. Perera, "A dual linear autoencoder approach for vessel trajectory prediction using historical AIS data," *Ocean engineering,* vol. 209, p. 107478, 2020.
78. N. Ghadami *et al.*, "Implementation of solar energy in smart cities using an integration of artificial neural network, photovoltaic system and classical Delphi methods," *Sustainable Cities and Society,* vol. 74, p. 103149, 2021.
79. V. Marinakis, "Big data for energy management and energy-efficient buildings," *Energies,* vol. 13, no. 7, p. 1555, 2020.
80. E. Elbeltagi and H. Wefki, "Predicting energy consumption for residential buildings using ANN through parametric modeling," *Energy Reports,* vol. 7, pp. 2534–2545, 2021.
81. F. Jiang *et al.*, "Data-Driven Decision Support for Equipment Selection and Maintenance Issues for Buildings," *Buildings,* vol. 14, no. 2, p. 436, 2024.
82. M. Kor, I. Yitmen, and S. Alizadehsalehi, "An investigation for integration of deep learning and digital twins towards Construction 4.0," *Smart and Sustainable Built Environment,* vol. 12, no. 3, pp. 461–487, 2023.
83. M. T. Linaza *et al.*, "Data-driven artificial intelligence applications for sustainable precision agriculture," *Agronomy,* vol. 11, no. 6, p. 1227, 2021.
84. M. K. Senapaty, A. Ray, and N. Padhy, "IoT-enabled soil nutrient analysis and crop recommendation model for precision agriculture," *Computers,* vol. 12, no. 3, p. 61, 2023.
85. P. Li, F. Xiong, X. Huang, and X. Wen, "Construction and optimization of vending machine decision support system based on improved C4. 5 decision tree," *Heliyon,* vol. 10, no. 3, 2024.
86. J. B. Didden, E. Lefeber, I. J. Adan, and I. W. Panhuijzen, "Genetic algorithm and decision support for assembly line balancing in the automotive industry," *International Journal of Production Research,* vol. 61, no. 10, pp. 3377–3395, 2023.
87. E. Chatzi, I. Abdallah, K. Tatsis, S. Osmani, and I. Robles, "Using interpretable machine learning for data-driven decision support for infrastructure operation & maintenance,“ in *Bridge Safety, Maintenance, Management, Life-Cycle, Resilience and Sustainability*: CRC Press, 2022, pp. 837–845.
88. I. M. Jiskani, Q. Cai, W. Zhou, X. Lu, and S. A. A. Shah, "An integrated fuzzy decision support system for analyzing challenges and pathways to promote green and climate smart mining," *Expert Systems with Applications,* vol. 188, p. 116062, 2022.
89. H. Chen and F. Pang, "A decision-support agent framework and its application in industry," in *Proceedings of the 2024 3rd International Conference on Cyber Security, Artificial Intelligence and Digital Economy*, 2024, pp. 131–137.
90. A. Abusitta, G. H. de Carvalho, O. A. Wahab, T. Halabi, B. C. Fung, and S. Al Mamoori, "Deep learning-enabled anomaly detection for IoT systems," *Internet of Things,* vol. 21, p. 100656, 2023.
91. S. Z. Farzana, D. R. Paudyal, S. Chadalavada, and M. J. Alam, "Decision support framework for water quality management in reservoirs integrating artificial intelligence and statistical approaches," *Water,* vol. 16, no. 20, p. 2944, 2024.

92. H. Hong, J. Liu, and A. X. Zhu, "Modeling landslide susceptibility using LogitBoost alternating decision trees and forest by penalizing attributes with the bagging ensemble," *Science of the total environment,* vol. 718, p. 137231, 2020.
93. A. Kalyuzhnaya *et al.*, "LLM Agents for Smart City Management: Enhancing Decision Support Through Multi-Agent AI Systems," *Smart Cities (2624–6511),* vol. 8, no. 1, 2025.
94. R. A. Khalil, N. Saeed, M. Masood, Y. M. Fard, M. S. Alouini, and T. Y. Al-Naffouri, "Deep learning in the industrial internet of things: Potentials, challenges, and emerging applications," *IEEE Internet of Things Journal,* vol. 8, no. 14, pp. 11016–11040, 2021.
95. A. Liso *et al.*, "A review of deep learning-based anomaly detection strategies in industry 4.0 focused on application fields, sensing equipment, and algorithms," *IEEE Access,* vol. 12, pp. 93911–93923, 2024.
96. N. Talpur, S. J. Abdulkadir, H. Alhussian, M. H. Hasan, N. Aziz, and A. Bamhdi, "Deep Neuro-Fuzzy System application trends, challenges, and future perspectives: A systematic survey," *Artificial intelligence review,* vol. 56, no. 2, pp. 865–913, 2023.
97. G. Kostopoulos, G. Davrazos, and S. Kotsiantis, "Explainable artificial intelligence-based decision support systems: A recent review," *Electronics,* vol. 13, no. 14, p. 2842, 2024.
98. M. Amini, A. Bagheri, and D. Delen, "Discovering injury severity risk factors in automobile crashes: a hybrid explainable AI framework for decision support," *Reliability Engineering & System Safety,* vol. 226, p. 108720, 2022.
99. R. Machlev *et al.*, "Explainable Artificial Intelligence (XAI) techniques for energy and power systems: Review, challenges and opportunities," *Energy and AI,* vol. 9, p. 100169, 2022.
100. A. Ucar, M. Karakose, and N. Kırımça, "Artificial intelligence for predictive maintenance applications: key components, trustworthiness, and future trends," *Applied Sciences,* vol. 14, no. 2, p. 898, 2024.
101. H. D. Shoorkand, M. Nourelfath, and A. Hajji, "A hybrid CNN-LSTM model for joint optimization of production and imperfect predictive maintenance planning," *Reliability Engineering & System Safety,* vol. 241, p. 109707, 2024.
102. Y. Zhao, J. Yang, W. Wang, H. Yang, and D. Niyato, "TranDRL: A transformer-driven deep reinforcement learning enabled prescriptive maintenance framework," *IEEE Internet of Things Journal,* 2024.
103. M. Farhan Naeem *et al.*, "A novel method for life estimation of power transformers using fuzzy logic systems: An intelligent predictive maintenance approach," *Frontiers in Energy Research,* vol. 10, p. 977665, 2022.
104. S. J. Upasane, H. Hagras, M. H. Anisi, S. Savill, I. Taylor, and K. Manousakis, "A Type-2 fuzzy-based explainable AI system for predictive maintenance within the water pumping industry," *IEEE Transactions on Artificial Intelligence,* vol. 5, no. 2, pp. 490–504, 2023.
105. C. Li, D. Zhu, C. Hu, X. Li, S. Nan, and H. Huang, "ECDX: Energy consumption prediction model based on distance correlation and XGBoost for edge data center," *Information Sciences,* vol. 643, p. 119218, 2023.
106. C. Liu, A. Cichon, G. Królczyk, and Z. Li, "Technology development and commercial applications of industrial fault diagnosis system: a review," *The International Journal of Advanced Manufacturing Technology,* vol. 118, no. 11, pp. 3497–3529, 2022.

107. H. Zhang, X. Guo, and P. Zhang, "Improved PSO-SVM-based fault diagnosis algorithm for wind power converter," *IEEE Transactions on Industry Applications,* vol. 60, no. 2, pp. 3492–3501, 2023.
108. M. Fernandes, J. M. Corchado, and G. Marreiros, "Machine learning techniques applied to mechanical fault diagnosis and fault prognosis in the context of real industrial manufacturing use-cases: a systematic literature review," *Applied Intelligence,* vol. 52, no. 12, pp. 14246–14280, 2022.
109. Y. Zong *et al.*, "An intelligent and automated 3D surface defect detection system for quantitative 3D estimation and feature classification of material surface defects," *Optics and Lasers in Engineering,* vol. 144, p. 106633, 2021.
110. S. M. Lundberg and S. I. Lee, "A unified approach to interpreting model predictions," *Advances in neural information processing systems,* vol. 30, 2017.
111. M. T. Ribeiro, S. Singh, and C. Guestrin, " Why should I trust you?' Explaining the predictions of any classifier," in *Proceedings of the 22nd ACM SIGKDD international conference on knowledge discovery and data mining*, 2016, pp. 1135–1144.
112. H. Taherdoost and M. Madanchian, "Multi-criteria decision making (MCDM) methods and concepts," *Encyclopedia,* vol. 3, no. 1, pp. 77–87, 2023.
113. A. Bahadori-Jahromi, S. Room, C. Paknahad, M. Altekreeti, Z. Tariq, and H. Tahayori, "The role of Artificial Intelligence and Machine Learning in advancing civil engineering: a comprehensive review," *Applied Sciences,* vol. 15, no. 19, p. 10499, 2025.
114. A. Kovari, "AI for Decision Support: Balancing Accuracy, Transparency, and Trust Across Sectors," *Information,* vol. 15, no. 11, p. 725, 2024.
115. Z. Ma, B. N. Jørgensen, and Z. G. Ma, "A systematic data characteristic understanding framework towards physical-sensor big data challenges," *Journal of Big Data,* vol. 11, no. 1, p. 84, 2024.
116. B. A. Tolnai, Z. Ma, B. N. Jørgensen, and Z. G. Ma, "An Automated Domain-Agnostic and Explainable Data Quality Assurance Framework for Energy Analytics and Beyond," *Information,* vol. 16, no. 10, p. 836, 2025.
117. P. Niloofar *et al.*, "Data-driven decision support in livestock farming for improved animal health, welfare and greenhouse gas emissions: Overview and challenges," *Computers and Electronics in Agriculture,* vol. 190, p. 106406, 2021.
118. M. Karatas, L. Eriskin, M. Deveci, D. Pamucar, and H. Garg, "Big Data for Healthcare Industry 4.0: Applications, challenges and future perspectives," *Expert Systems with Applications,* vol. 200, p. 116912, 2022.
119. A. Gandomi and M. Haider, "Beyond the hype: Big data concepts, methods, and analytics," *International journal of information management,* vol. 35, no. 2, pp. 137–144, 2015.
120. H. Y. Teh, A. W. Kempa-Liehr, and K. I. K. Wang, "Sensor data quality: A systematic review," *Journal of Big Data,* vol. 7, no. 1, p. 11, 2020.
121. I. Taleb, M. A. Serhani, C. Bouhaddioui, and R. Dssouli, "Big data quality framework: a holistic approach to continuous quality management," *Journal of Big Data,* vol. 8, no. 1, p. 76, 2021.
122. H. Zou and K. Xiang, "A novel rigorous measurement model for big data quality characteristics," in *2022 IEEE International Conference on Big Data (Big Data)*, 2022: IEEE, pp. 2699–2708.

123. M. Naeem *et al.*, "Trends and future perspective challenges in big data," in *Advances in intelligent data analysis and applications: Proceeding of the sixth euro-China conference on intelligent data analysis and applications, 15–18 October 2019, Arad, Romania,* 2021: Springer, pp. 309–325.
124. I. A. T. Hashem, I. Yaqoob, N. B. Anuar, S. Mokhtar, A. Gani, and S. U. Khan, "The rise of "big data" on cloud computing: Review and open research issues," *Information systems,* vol. 47, pp. 98–115, 2015.
125. D. Laney, "3D data management: Controlling data volume, velocity and variety," *META group research note,* vol. 6, no. 70, p. 1, 2001.
126. A. Sinaeepourfard, J. Krogstie, S. A. Petersen, and A. Gustavsen, "A zero emission neighbourhoods data management architecture for smart city scenarios: discussions toward 6Vs challenges," in *2018 International Conference on Information and Communication Technology Convergence (ICTC),* 2018: IEEE, pp. 658–663.
127. J. J. Seddon and W. L. Currie, "A model for unpacking big data analytics in high-frequency trading," *Journal of Business Research,* vol. 70, pp. 300–307, 2017.
128. A. Sinaeepourfard, J. Garcia, X. Masip-Bruin, and E. Marín-Tordera, "A comprehensive scenario agnostic Data LifeCycle model for an efficient data complexity management," in *2016 IEEE 12th International Conference on e-Science (e-Science),* 2016: IEEE, pp. 276–281.
129. D. Bhardwaj and O. Ormandjieva, "Toward a Novel Measurement Framework for Big Data (MEGA)," in *2021 IEEE 45th Annual Computers, Software, and Applications Conference (COMPSAC),* 2021: IEEE, pp. 1579–1586.
130. M. F. Uddin and N. Gupta, "Seven V's of Big Data understanding Big Data to extract value," in *Proceedings of the 2014 zone 1 conference of the American Society for Engineering Education,* 2014: IEEE, pp. 1–5.
131. Y. K. Gupta and S. Kumari, "A study of big data analytics using apache spark with Python and Scala," in *2020 3rd International Conference on Intelligent Sustainable Systems (ICISS),* 2020: IEEE, pp. 471–478.
132. W. Hattawi, S. Shaban, A. Al Shawabkah, and S. Alzu'bi, "Recent quality models in bigdata applications," in *2021 International Conference on Information Technology (ICIT),* 2021: IEEE, pp. 811–815.
133. I. Emmanuel and C. Stanier, "Defining big data," in *Proceedings of the International Conference on big data and advanced Wireless technologies,* 2016, pp. 1–6.
134. A. Sinaeepourfard, J. Garcia, X. Masip-Bruin, and E. Marín-Torder, "Towards a comprehensive data lifecycle model for big data environments," in *Proceedings of the 3rd IEEE/ACM International Conference on Big Data Computing, Applications and Technologies,* 2016, pp. 100–106.
135. M. Ghasemaghaei, "Understanding the impact of big data on firm performance: The necessity of conceptually differentiating among big data characteristics," *International Journal of Information Management,* vol. 57, p. 102055, 2021.
136. W. Yu, T. Dillon, F. Mostafa, W. Rahayu, and Y. Liu, "A global manufacturing big data ecosystem for fault detection in predictive maintenance," *IEEE Transactions on Industrial Informatics,* vol. 16, no. 1, pp. 183–192, 2019.
137. R. Terzi, S. Sagiroglu, and M. U. Demirezen, "Big data perspective for driver/driving behavior," *IEEE Intelligent Transportation Systems Magazine,* vol. 12, no. 2, pp. 20–35, 2018.

138. S. Sagiroglu and D. Sinanc, "Big data: A review," in *2013 international conference on collaboration technologies and systems (CTS)*, 2013: IEEE, pp. 42–47.
139. J. Fan, F. Han, and H. Liu, "Challenges of big data analysis," *National science review,* vol. 1, no. 2, pp. 293–314, 2014.
140. S. Qiu *et al.*, "Multi-sensor information fusion based on machine learning for real applications in human activity recognition: State-of-the-art and research challenges," *Information Fusion,* vol. 80, pp. 241–265, 2022.
141. L. Da Xu, W. He, and S. Li, "Internet of things in industries: A survey," *IEEE Transactions on industrial informatics,* vol. 10, no. 4, pp. 2233–2243, 2014.
142. Y. Lu, "Industry 4.0: A survey on technologies, applications and open research issues," *Journal of industrial information integration,* vol. 6, pp. 1–10, 2017.
143. F. Wang *et al.*, "Privacy-aware traffic flow prediction based on multi-party sensor data with zero trust in smart city," *ACM Transactions on Internet Technology,* vol. 23, no. 3, pp. 1–19, 2023.
144. Y. Kang, R. J. Hyndman, and F. Li, "GRATIS: GeneRAting TIme Series with diverse and controllable characteristics," *Statistical Analysis and Data Mining: The ASA Data Science Journal,* vol. 13, no. 4, pp. 354–376, 2020.
145. Z. Ma, B. N. Jørgensen, and Z. Ma, "Discovering Operational Patterns Using Image-Based Convolutional Clustering and Composite Evaluation: A Case Study in Foundry Melting Processes," *Information,* vol. 16, no. 9, p. 816, 2025.
146. G. J. Oyewole and G. A. Thopil, "Data clustering: application and trends," *Artificial intelligence review,* vol. 56, no. 7, pp. 6439–6475, 2023.
147. P. Arora and S. Varshney, "Analysis of k-means and k-medoids algorithm for big data," *Procedia Computer Science,* vol. 78, pp. 507–512, 2016.
148. F. Murtagh and P. Contreras, "Algorithms for hierarchical clustering: an overview," *Wiley interdisciplinary reviews: data mining and knowledge discovery,* vol. 2, no. 1, pp. 86–97, 2012.
149. M. Subramaniyan, A. Skoogh, A. S. Muhammad, J. Bokrantz, B. Johansson, and C. Roser, "A generic hierarchical clustering approach for detecting bottlenecks in manufacturing," *Journal of Manufacturing Systems,* vol. 55, pp. 143–158, 2020.
150. J. Gan and Y. Tao, "DBSCAN revisited: Mis-claim, un-fixability, and approximation," in *Proceedings of the 2015 ACM SIGMOD international conference on management of data*, 2015, pp. 519–530.
151. R. J. Campello, P. Kröger, J. Sander, and A. Zimek, "Density-based clustering," *Wiley Interdisciplinary Reviews: Data Mining and Knowledge Discovery,* vol. 10, no. 2, p. e1343, 2020.
152. C. M. Weber, D. Ray, A. A. Valverde, J. A. Clark, and K. S. Sharma, "Gaussian mixture model clustering algorithms for the analysis of high-precision mass measurements," *Nuclear Instruments and Methods in Physics Research Section A: Accelerators, Spectrometers, Detectors and Associated Equipment,* vol. 1027, p. 166299, 2022.
153. M. Svensén and C. M. Bishop, "Robust Bayesian mixture modelling," *Neurocomputing,* vol. 64, pp. 235–252, 2005.
154. J. Paparrizos, F. Yang, and H. Li, "Bridging the gap: A decade review of time-series clustering methods," *arXiv preprint arXiv:2412.20582,* 2024.

155. D. J. Berndt and J. Clifford, "Using dynamic time warping to find patterns in time series," in *Proceedings of the 3rd international conference on knowledge discovery and data mining*, 1994, pp. 359–370.
156. M. Cuturi and M. Blondel, "Soft-dtw: a differentiable loss function for time-series," in *International conference on machine learning*, 2017: PMLR, pp. 894–903.
157. Y. S. Jeong, M. K. Jeong, and O. A. Omitaomu, "Weighted dynamic time warping for time series classification," *Pattern recognition,* vol. 44, no. 9, pp. 2231–2240, 2011.
158. J. Paparrizos and L. Gravano, "k-shape: Efficient and accurate clustering of time series," in *Proceedings of the 2015 ACM SIGMOD international conference on management of data*, 2015, pp. 1855–1870.
159. C. H. Lubba, S. S. Sethi, P. Knaute, S. R. Schultz, B. D. Fulcher, and N. S. Jones, "catch22: CAnonical Time-series CHaracteristics: Selected through highly comparative time-series analysis," *Data mining and knowledge discovery,* vol. 33, no. 6, pp. 1821–1852, 2019.
160. X. Guo, L. Gao, X. Liu, and J. Yin, "Improved deep embedded clustering with local structure preservation," in *the 26th International Joint Conference on Artificial Intelligence*, 2017, vol. 17, pp. 1753–1759.
161. A. Alqahtani, X. Xie, J. Deng, and M. W. Jones, "A deep convolutional auto-encoder with embedded clustering," in *2018 25th IEEE international conference on image processing (ICIP)*, 2018: IEEE, pp. 4058–4062.
162. J. M. Santos and M. Embrechts, "On the use of the adjusted rand index as a metric for evaluating supervised classification," in *International conference on artificial neural networks*, 2009: Springer, pp. 175–184.
163. O. Arbelaitz, I. Gurrutxaga, J. Muguerza, J. M. Pérez, and I. Perona, "An extensive comparative study of cluster validity indices," *Pattern recognition,* vol. 46, no. 1, pp. 243–256, 2013.
164. Y. Ren *et al.*, "Deep clustering: A comprehensive survey," *IEEE transactions on neural networks and learning systems,* vol. 36, no. 4, pp. 5858–5878, 2024.
165. Z. Ma, B. N. Jørgensen, and Z. Ma, "Data-Driven Causal Reasoning for Eco-Driving Behavior Analysis in Public Transportation Systems," *Complex & Intelligent Systems,* 2026.
166. Z. Ma, B. N. Jørgensen, and Z. Ma, "Uncovering Causal Drivers of Energy Efficiency for Industrial Process in Foundry via Time-Series Causal Inference," in *Energy Informatics Academy Conference,* 2025: Springer, pp. 366–381.
167. D. M. Chickering, D. Heckerman, and C. Meek, "Large-sample learning of Bayesian networks is NP-hard," *Journal of Machine Learning Research,* vol. 5, no. Oct, pp. 1287–1330, 2004.
168. M. J. Vowels, N. C. Camgoz, and R. Bowden, "D'ya like dags? a survey on structure learning and causal discovery," *ACM Computing Surveys,* vol. 55, no. 4, pp. 1–36, 2022.
169. M. Kalisch and P. Bühlman, "Estimating high-dimensional directed acyclic graphs with the PC-algorithm," *Journal of Machine Learning Research,* vol. 8, no. 3, 2007.
170. N. Harris and M. Drton, "PC algorithm for nonparanormal graphical models," *The Journal of Machine Learning Research,* vol. 14, no. 1, pp. 3365–3383, 2013.
171. E. V. Strobl, K. Zhang, and S. Visweswaran, "Approximate kernel-based conditional independence tests for fast non-parametric causal discovery," *Journal of Causal Inference,* vol. 7, no. 1, p. 20180017, 2019.

172. R. Sen, A. T. Suresh, K. Shanmugam, A. G. Dimakis, and S. Shakkottai, "Model-powered conditional independence test," *Advances in neural information processing systems,* vol. 30, 2017.
173. C. Shi, T. Xu, W. Bergsma, and L. Li, "Double generative adversarial networks for conditional independence testing," *Journal of Machine Learning Research,* vol. 22, no. 285, pp. 1–32, 2021.
174. X. Zheng, B. Aragam, P. K. Ravikumar, and E. P. Xing, "Dags with no tears: Continuous optimization for structure learning," *Advances in neural information processing systems,* vol. 31, 2018.
175. X. Zheng, C. Dan, B. Aragam, P. Ravikumar, and E. Xing, "Learning sparse nonparametric dags," in *International conference on artificial intelligence and statistics,* 2020: Pmlr, pp. 3414–3425.
176. Y. Yu, J. Chen, T. Gao, and M. Yu, "DAG-GNN: DAG structure learning with graph neural networks," in *International conference on machine learning,* 2019: PMLR, pp. 7154–7163.
177. K. Bello, B. Aragam, and P. Ravikumar, "Dagma: Learning dags via m-matrices and a log-determinant acyclicity characterization," *Advances in Neural Information Processing Systems,* vol. 35, pp. 8226–8239, 2022.
178. D. Waxman, K. Butler, and P. M. Djurić, "Dagma-DCE: Interpretable, non-parametric differentiable causal discovery," *IEEE Open Journal of Signal Processing,* vol. 5, pp. 393–401, 2024.
179. K. Butler, G. Feng, and P. M. Djurić, "A differential measure of the strength of causation," *IEEE Signal Processing Letters,* vol. 29, pp. 2208–2212, 2022.
180. J. Runge, A. Gerhardus, G. Varando, V. Eyring, and G. Camps-Valls, "Causal inference for time series," *Nature Reviews Earth & Environment,* vol. 4, no. 7, pp. 487–505, 2023.
181. Z. Ma, M. Kemmerling, D. Buschmann, C. Enslin, D. Lütticke, and R. H. Schmitt, "A data-driven two-phase multi-split causal ensemble model for time series," *Symmetry,* vol. 15, no. 5, p. 982, 2023.
182. A. Brovelli, "Statistical Analysis of Single-Trial Granger Causality Spectra," *Computational and Mathematical Methods in Medicine,* vol. 2012, no. 1, p. 697610, 2012.
183. A. Shojaie and E. B. Fox, "Granger causality: A review and recent advances," *Annual Review of Statistics and Its Application,* vol. 9, no. 1, pp. 289–319, 2022.
184. L. Schiatti, G. Nollo, G. Rossato, and L. Faes, "Extended Granger causality: a new tool to identify the structure of physiological networks," *Physiological measurement,* vol. 36, no. 4, p. 827, 2015.
185. Y. Li, M. Lei, W. Cui, Y. Guo, and H. L. Wei, "A parametric time-frequency conditional Granger causality method using ultra-regularized orthogonal least squares and multiwavelets for dynamic connectivity analysis in EEGs," *IEEE Transactions on Biomedical Engineering,* vol. 66, no. 12, pp. 3509–3525, 2019.
186. E. Siggiridou and D. Kugiumtzis, "Granger causality in multivariate time series using a time-ordered restricted vector autoregressive model," *IEEE Transactions on Signal Processing,* vol. 64, no. 7, pp. 1759–1773, 2015.
187. L. A. Baccalá and K. Sameshima, "Partial directed coherence: a new concept in neural structure determination," *Biological cybernetics,* vol. 84, no. 6, pp. 463–474, 2001.

188. A. Tank, I. Covert, N. Foti, A. Shojaie, and E. B. Fox, “Neural granger causality,” *IEEE Transactions on Pattern Analysis and Machine Intelligence,* vol. 44, no. 8, pp. 4267–4279, 2021.
189. W. Zhang, T. Panum, S. Jha, P. Chalasani, and D. Page, “Cause: Learning granger causality from event sequences using attribution methods,” in *International Conference on Machine Learning*, 2020: PMLR, pp. 11235–11245.
190. W. Peng, “DLI: A Deep Learning-Based Granger Causality Inference,” *Complexity,* vol. 2020, no. 1, p. 5960171, 2020.
191. K. Hlaváčková-Schindler, M. Paluš, M. Vejmelka, and J. Bhattacharya, “Causality detection based on information-theoretic approaches in time series analysis,” *Physics Reports,* vol. 441, no. 1, pp. 1–46, 2007.
192. L. Barnett, A. B. Barrett, and A. K. Seth, “Granger causality and transfer entropy are equivalent for Gaussian variables,” *Physical review letters,* vol. 103, no. 23, p. 238701, 2009.
193. J. Runge, J. Heitzig, V. Petoukhov, and J. Kurths, “Escaping the curse of dimensionality in estimating multivariate transfer entropy,” *Physical review letters,* vol. 108, no. 25, p. 258701, 2012.
194. K. M. Ikegwu, J. Trauger, J. McMullin, and R. J. Brunner, “PyIF: A fast and light weight implementation to estimate bivariate transfer entropy for big data,” in *2020 SoutheastCon*, 2020: IEEE, pp. 1–6.
195. J. Ma, “Estimating transfer entropy via copula entropy,” *arXiv preprint arXiv:1910.04375,* 2019.
196. G. Sugihara *et al.*, “Detecting causality in complex ecosystems,” *science,* vol. 338, no. 6106, pp. 496–500, 2012.
197. J. Runge, P. Nowack, M. Kretschmer, S. Flaxman, and D. Sejdinovic, “Detecting and quantifying causal associations in large nonlinear time series datasets,” *Science advances,* vol. 5, no. 11, p. eaau4996, 2019.
198. J. Runge, “Discovering contemporaneous and lagged causal relations in autocorrelated nonlinear time series datasets,” in *Conference on uncertainty in artificial intelligence,* 2020: Pmlr, pp. 1388–1397.
199. J. Pearl, *Causality: Models, Reasoning and Inference*, 2nd ed. Cambridge university press, 2009.
200. J. Pearl, “Causal inference in statistics: An overview,” 2009.
201. K. Budhathoki, D. Janzing, P. Bloebaum, and H. Ng, “Why did the distribution change?,” in *International Conference on Artificial Intelligence and Statistics*, 2021: PMLR, pp. 1666–1674.
202. E. Eulig, A. A. Mastakouri, P. Blöbaum, M. Hardt, and D. Janzing, “Toward falsifying causal graphs using a permutation-based test,” in *Proceedings of the AAAI Conference on Artificial Intelligence*, 2025, vol. 39, no. 25, pp. 26778–26786.
203. Z. Ma *et al.*, “Multi-Agent Multimodal Large Language Model Framework for Automated Interpretation of Fuel Efficiency Analytics in Public Transportation,” *Applied Sciences,* vol. 15, no. 21, p. 11619, 2025.
204. G. Sahu *et al.*, “Insightbench: Evaluating business analytics agents through multi-step insight generation,” *arXiv preprint arXiv:2407.06423,* 2024.

205. C. Zhang, C. Li, and S. Gao, "MDSF: Context-Aware Multi-Dimensional Data Storytelling Framework based on Large language Model," *arXiv preprint arXiv:2501.01014,* 2025.
206. J. Luo *et al.*, "Application of LLM Techniques for Data Insights in DHP," in *2024 IEEE 4th International Conference on Digital Twins and Parallel Intelligence (DTPI)*, 2024: IEEE, pp. 656–661.
207. L. Wang, S. Zhang, Y. Wang, E. P. Lim, and Y. Wang, "Llm4vis: Explainable visualization recommendation using chatgpt," *arXiv preprint arXiv:2310.07652,* 2023.
208. B. J. Tang, A. Boggust, and A. Satyanarayan, "Vistext: A benchmark for semantically rich chart captioning," *arXiv preprint arXiv:2307.05356,* 2023.
209. R. Rahman, R. Hasan, A. A. Farhad, M. T. R. Laskar, M. H. Ashmafee, and A. R. M. Kamal, "Chartsumm: A comprehensive benchmark for automatic chart summarization of long and short summaries," *arXiv preprint arXiv:2304.13620,* 2023.
210. M. S. Islam, M. T. R. Laskar, M. R. Parvez, E. Hoque, and S. Joty, "DataNarrative: Automated data-driven storytelling with visualizations and texts," in *Proceedings of the 2024 Conference on Empirical Methods in Natural Language Processing*, 2024, pp. 19253–19286.
211. D. Chen *et al.*, "Mllm-as-a-judge: Assessing multimodal llm-as-a-judge with vision-language benchmark," in *Forty-first International Conference on Machine Learning*, 2024.
212. C. Y. Li *et al.*, "Towards a holistic framework for multimodal LLM in 3D brain CT radiology report generation," *Nature Communications,* vol. 16, no. 1, p. 2258, 2025.
213. D. Zhang *et al.*, "Mm-llms: Recent advances in multimodal large language models," *arXiv preprint arXiv:2401.13601,* 2024.
214. R. Zhang *et al.*, "Let storytelling tell vivid stories: A multi-modal-agent-based unified storytelling framework," *Neurocomputing,* vol. 622, p. 129316, 2025.
215. Anthropic. "Introducing Claude 4." https://www.anthropic.com/news/claude-4 (accessed May 22, 2025).
216. Google DeepMind. "Gemini 2.5 Pro." https://deepmind.google/models/gemini/pro/ (accessed May 7, 2025).
217. OpenAI. "Introducing OpenAI o3 and o4-mini." https://openai.com/index/introducing-o3-and-o4-mini/ (accessed April 16, 2025).
218. P. Sahoo, A. K. Singh, S. Saha, V. Jain, S. Mondal, and A. Chadha, "A systematic survey of prompt engineering in large language models: Techniques and applications," *arXiv preprint arXiv:2402.07927,* 2024.
219. A. Radford, J. Wu, R. Child, D. Luan, D. Amodei, and I. Sutskever, "Language models are unsupervised multitask learners," *OpenAI blog,* vol. 1, no. 8, p. 9, 2019.
220. T. Brown *et al.*, "Language models are few-shot learners," *Advances in neural information processing systems,* vol. 33, pp. 1877–1901, 2020.
221. Z. Wang *et al.*, "Chain-of-table: Evolving tables in the reasoning chain for table understanding," *arXiv preprint arXiv:2401.04398,* 2024.
222. Y. K. Chia, G. Chen, L. A. Tuan, S. Poria, and L. Bing, "Contrastive chain-of-thought prompting," *arXiv preprint arXiv:2311.09277,* 2023.
223. B. Li, S. Lee-Urban, G. Johnston, and M. Riedl, "Story generation with crowdsourced plot graphs," in *Proceedings of the AAAI Conference on Artificial Intelligence*, 2013, vol. 27, no. 1, pp. 598–604.

224. A. Hu *et al.*, "mplug-paperowl: Scientific diagram analysis with the multimodal large language model," in *Proceedings of the 32nd ACM International Conference on Multimedia*, 2024, pp. 6929–6938.
225. J. Kim *et al.*, "Multi-LLM Collaborative Caption Generation in Scientific Documents," in *International Workshop on AI for Transportation*, 2025: Springer, pp. 142–160.
226. S. Guo, C. Deng, Y. Wen, H. Chen, Y. Chang, and J. Wang, "Ds-agent: Automated data science by empowering large language models with case-based reasoning," *arXiv preprint arXiv:2402.17453*, 2024.
227. L. Shen, H. Li, Y. Wang, and H. Qu, "From data to story: Towards automatic animated data video creation with llm-based multi-agent systems," in *2024 IEEE VIS Workshop on Data Storytelling in an Era of Generative AI (GEN4DS)*, 2024: IEEE, pp. 20–27.
228. S. Gregor and A. R. Hevner, "Positioning and presenting design science research for maximum impact," *MIS quarterly*, vol. 13, no. 2, pp. 337–355, 2013.
229. L. McCormack and M. Bendechache, "A comprehensive survey and classification of evaluation criteria for trustworthy artificial intelligence," *AI and Ethics*, pp. 1–22, 2024.
230. J. Stacy *et al.*, "Qualitative Evaluation of an Artificial Intelligence–Based Clinical Decision Support System to Guide Rhythm Management of Atrial Fibrillation: Survey Study," *JMIR Formative Research*, vol. 6, no. 8, p. e36443, 2022.
231. E. Blasch, J. Sung, and T. Nguyen, "Multisource AI scorecard table for system evaluation," *arXiv preprint arXiv:2102.03985*, 2021.
232. P. Salehi *et al.*, "Towards trustworthy AI-enabled decision support systems: Validation of the multisource AI scorecard table (MAST)," *Journal of Artificial Intelligence Research*, vol. 80, pp. 1311–1341, 2024.
233. D. J. Power, "Understanding data-driven decision support systems," *Information Systems Management*, vol. 25, no. 2, pp. 149–154, 2008.
234. Z. Ma, B. N. Jørgensen, and Z. G. Ma, "DataPro–A Standardized Data Understanding and Processing Procedure: A Case Study of an Eco-Driving Project," in *Energy Informatics Academy Conference*, 2024: Springer, pp. 136–154.
235. R. Wirth and J. Hipp, "CRISP-DM: Towards a standard process model for data mining," in *Proceedings of the 4th international conference on the practical applications of knowledge discovery and data mining*, 2000, vol. 1: Manchester, pp. 29–39.
236. F. Martínez-Plumed *et al.*, "CRISP-DM twenty years later: From data mining processes to data science trajectories," *IEEE transactions on knowledge and data engineering*, vol. 33, no. 8, pp. 3048–3061, 2019.
237. A. Osterwalder and Y. Pigneur, *Business model generation: a handbook for visionaries, game changers, and challengers*. John Wiley & Sons, 2010.
238. Z. Ma, B. N. Jørgensen, M. Levesque, M. Amazouz, and Z. Ma, "Business models for digitalization enabled energy efficiency and flexibility in industry: a survey with nine case studies," in *Energy Informatics Academy Conference*, 2023: Springer, pp. 253–270.
239. J. Pearl, "Causal Inference," in *Proceedings of Workshop on Causality: Objectives and Assessment at NIPS 2008*, 2010, pp. 39–58.
240. D. B. Rubin, "Causal inference using potential outcomes: Design, modeling, decisions," *Journal of the American statistical Association*, vol. 100, no. 469, pp. 322–331, 2005.

241. A. R. Munappy, J. Bosch, and H. H. Olsson, "Data pipeline management in practice: Challenges and opportunities," in *International Conference on Product-Focused Software Process Improvement*, 2020: Springer, pp. 168–184.
242. B. Acar, M. Berger, M. G. Augusto, T. Küster, F. Sivrikaya, and S. Albayrak, "An Agent-Based Data Acquisition Pipeline for Image Data," *IEEE Access*, 2024.
243. E. Lyard and R. Walter, "End-to-end data acquisition pipeline for the Cherenkov Telescope Array," *arXiv preprint arXiv:1709.04203*, 2017.
244. Y. Demchenko, P. Grosso, C. De Laat, and P. Membrey, "Addressing big data issues in scientific data infrastructure," in *2013 International conference on collaboration technologies and systems (CTS)*, 2013: IEEE, pp. 48–55.
245. P. Dhal and C. Azad, "A comprehensive survey on feature selection in the various fields of machine learning," *Applied intelligence*, vol. 52, no. 4, pp. 4543–4581, 2022.
246. W. Jia, M. Sun, J. Lian, and S. Hou, "Feature dimensionality reduction: a review," *Complex & Intelligent Systems*, vol. 8, no. 3, pp. 2663–2693, 2022.
247. R. H. Hariri, E. M. Fredericks, and K. M. Bowers, "Uncertainty in big data analytics: survey, opportunities, and challenges," *Journal of Big Data*, vol. 6, no. 1, pp. 1–16, 2019.
248. N. Gutacker and A. Street, "Use of large-scale HRQoL datasets to generate individualised predictions and inform patients about the likely benefit of surgery," *Quality of life research*, vol. 26, no. 9, pp. 2497–2505, 2017.
249. C. Li, Y. Chen, and Y. Shang, "A review of industrial big data for decision making in intelligent manufacturing," *Engineering science and technology, an international journal*, vol. 29, p. 101021, 2022.
250. D. Zhang, C. Yin, J. Zeng, X. Yuan, and P. Zhang, "Combining structured and unstructured data for predictive models: a deep learning approach," *BMC medical informatics and decision making*, vol. 20, no. 1, p. 280, 2020.
251. S. Kamm, N. Jazdi, and M. Weyrich, "Knowledge discovery in heterogeneous and unstructured data of industry 4.0 systems: challenges and approaches," *Procedia CIRP*, vol. 104, pp. 975–980, 2021.
252. M. Mohammadpoor and F. Torabi, "Big Data analytics in oil and gas industry: An emerging trend," *Petroleum*, vol. 6, no. 4, pp. 321–328, 2020.
253. N. J. Isaac *et al.*, "Data integration for large-scale models of species distributions," *Trends in ecology & evolution*, vol. 35, no. 1, pp. 56–67, 2020.
254. K. Batko and A. Ślęzak, "The use of Big Data Analytics in healthcare," *Journal of big Data*, vol. 9, no. 1, p. 3, 2022.
255. L. Zhu and D. J. Hill, "Cost-effective bad synchrophasor data detection based on unsupervised time-series data analytic," *IEEE Internet of Things Journal*, vol. 8, no. 3, pp. 2027–2039, 2020.
256. Y. Bai, J. Wang, X. Zhang, X. Miao, and Y. Lin, "CrossFuN: Multiview joint cross-fusion network for time-series anomaly detection," *IEEE Transactions on Instrumentation and Measurement*, vol. 72, pp. 1–9, 2023.
257. R. Sahal, J. G. Breslin, and M. I. Ali, "Big data and stream processing platforms for Industry 4.0 requirements mapping for a predictive maintenance use case," *Journal of manufacturing systems*, vol. 54, pp. 138–151, 2020.
258. S. I. Khan and A. S. M. L. Hoque, "SICE: an improved missing data imputation technique," *Journal of Big Data*, vol. 7, no. 1, p. 37, 2020.

259. W. Dong *et al.*, "Generative adversarial networks for imputing missing data for big data clinical research," *BMC medical research methodology,* vol. 21, no. 1, p. 78, 2021.
260. R. J. Little and D. B. Rubin, *Statistical analysis with missing data.* John Wiley & Sons, 2019.
261. L. Liu and Y. Liu, "Load image inpainting: An improved U-Net based load missing data recovery method," *Applied Energy,* vol. 327, p. 119988, 2022.
262. A. V. Levitin and T. C. Redman, "A model of the data (life) cycles with application to quality," *Information and Software Technology,* vol. 35, no. 4, pp. 217–223, 1993.
263. S. I. H. Shah, V. Peristeras, and I. Magnisalis, "DaLiF: a data lifecycle framework for data-driven governments," *Journal of Big Data,* vol. 8, no. 1, p. 89, 2021.
264. X. Wang, K. Smith, and R. Hyndman, "Characteristic-based clustering for time series data," *Data Mining and Knowledge Discovery,* vol. 13, no. 3, pp. 335–364, 2006.
265. J. D. Kelleher, B. Mac Namee, and A. D'arcy, *Fundamentals of machine learning for predictive data analytics: algorithms, worked examples, and case studies.* MIT press, 2020.
266. A. Blázquez-García, A. Conde, U. Mori, and J. A. Lozano, "A review on outlier/anomaly detection in time series data," *ACM computing surveys (CSUR),* vol. 54, no. 3, pp. 1–33, 2021.
267. S. Schmidl, P. Wenig, and T. Papenbrock, "Anomaly detection in time series: a comprehensive evaluation," *Proceedings of the VLDB Endowment,* vol. 15, no. 9, pp. 1779–1797, 2022.
268. E. Beard *et al.*, "Understanding and using time series analyses in addiction research," *Addiction,* vol. 114, no. 10, pp. 1866–1884, 2019.
269. S. Singh, B. Mahanty, and M. K. Tiwari, "Framework and modelling of inclusive manufacturing system," *International Journal of Computer Integrated Manufacturing,* vol. 32, no. 2, pp. 105–123, 2019.
270. H. Li and X. Lu, "Challenges and trends of big data analytics," in *2014 Ninth International Conference on P2P, Parallel, Grid, Cloud and Internet Computing,* 2014: IEEE, pp. 566–567.
271. K. S. Kiangala and Z. Wang, "Initiating predictive maintenance for a conveyor motor in a bottling plant using industry 4.0 concepts," *The International Journal of Advanced Manufacturing Technology,* vol. 97, no. 9, pp. 3251–3271, 2018.
272. Z. Li, Y. Wang, and K.-S. Wang, "Intelligent predictive maintenance for fault diagnosis and prognosis in machine centers: Industry 4.0 scenario," *Advances in Manufacturing,* vol. 5, no. 4, pp. 377–387, 2017.
273. Q. Song and M. Shepperd, "Missing data imputation techniques," *International journal of business intelligence and data mining,* vol. 2, no. 3, pp. 261–291, 2007.
274. Y. Zhang, B. Zhou, X. Cai, W. Guo, X. Ding, and X. Yuan, "Missing value imputation in multivariate time series with end-to-end generative adversarial networks," *Information Sciences,* vol. 551, pp. 67–82, 2021.
275. Z. Ma, B. N. Jørgensen, and Z. G. Ma, "A novel hybrid feature importance and feature interaction detection framework for predictive optimization in industry 4.0 applications," in *IECON 2023–49th Annual Conference of the IEEE Industrial Electronics Society,* 2023: IEEE, pp. 1–6.

276. Z. Ma, B. N. Jørgensen, and Z. Ma, "Fuel Efficiency Analysis of the Public Transportation System Based on the Gaussian Mixture Model Clustering," in *EPIA Conference on Artificial Intelligence*, 2024: Springer, pp. 209–219.
277. E. Patel and D. S. Kushwaha, "Clustering cloud workloads: K-means vs gaussian mixture model," *Procedia computer science,* vol. 171, pp. 158–167, 2020.
278. C. Savkli and C. Schwartz, "Random Subspace Mixture Models for Interpretable Anomaly Detection," *arXiv preprint arXiv:2108.06283,* 2021.
279. G. Tardioli, R. Kerrigan, M. Oates, J. O'Donnell, and D. P. Finn, "Identification of representative buildings and building groups in urban datasets using a novel preprocessing, classification, clustering and predictive modelling approach," *Building and Environment,* vol. 140, pp. 90–106, 2018.
280. A. Starczewski and A. Krzyżak, "Performance evaluation of the silhouette index," in *International conference on artificial intelligence and soft computing*, 2015: Springer, pp. 49–58.
281. X. Wang and Y. Xu, "An improved index for clustering validation based on Silhouette index and Calinski-Harabasz index," in *IOP Conference Series: Materials Science and Engineering*, 2019, vol. 569, no. 5: IOP Publishing, p. 052024.
282. S. Petrovic, "A comparison between the silhouette index and the davies-bouldin index in labelling ids clusters," in *Proceedings of the 11th Nordic workshop of secure IT systems*, 2006, vol. 2006: Citeseer, pp. 53–64.
283. J. Xie, R. Girshick, and A. Farhadi, "Unsupervised deep embedding for clustering analysis," in *International conference on machine learning*, 2016: PMLR, pp. 478–487.
284. D. Guijo-Rubio, A. M. Durán-Rosal, P. A. Gutiérrez, A. Troncoso, and C. Hervás-Martínez, "Time-series clustering based on the characterization of segment typologies," *IEEE transactions on cybernetics,* vol. 51, no. 11, pp. 5409–5422, 2020.
285. H. Nizam, S. Zafar, Z. Lv, F. Wang, and X. Hu, "Real-time deep anomaly detection framework for multivariate time-series data in industrial IoT," *IEEE Sensors Journal,* vol. 22, no. 23, pp. 22836–22849, 2022.
286. D. P. Kingma and J. Ba, "Adam: A method for stochastic optimization," *arXiv preprint arXiv:1412.6980,* 2014.
287. R. Tavenard *et al.*, "Tslearn, a machine learning toolkit for time series data," *Journal of machine learning research,* vol. 21, no. 118, pp. 1–6, 2020.
288. A. Paszke *et al.*, "Pytorch: An imperative style, high-performance deep learning library," *Advances in neural information processing systems,* vol. 32, 2019.
289. N. S. Madiraju, S. M. Sadat, D. Fisher, and H. Karimabadi, "Deep Temporal Clustering: Fully Unsupervised Learning of Time-Domain Features," *arXiv preprint arXiv:1802.01059,* 2018.
290. J. Cai, J. Fan, W. Guo, S. Wang, Y. Zhang, and Z. Zhang, "Efficient deep embedded subspace clustering," in *Proceedings of the IEEE/CVF conference on computer vision and pattern recognition*, 2022, pp. 1–10.
291. P. Blöbaum, P. Götz, K. Budhathoki, A. A. Mastakouri, and D. Janzing, "DoWhy-GCM: An extension of DoWhy for causal inference in graphical causal models," *Journal of Machine Learning Research,* vol. 25, no. 147, pp. 1–7, 2024.
292. J. Peters, D. Janzing, and B. Schölkopf, *Elements of causal inference: foundations and learning algorithms*. The MIT press, 2017.
293. J. Runge. https://github.com/jakobrunge/tigramite (accessed August 5, 2025).

294. X. Liang, K. Hao, L. Chen, X. Cai, and L. Hao, "Causal inference of multivariate time series in complex industrial systems," *Advanced Engineering Informatics,* vol. 59, p. 102320, 2024.
295. P. Guo, Y. Huang, and J. Wang, "Scalable and flexible two-phase ensemble algorithms for causality discovery," *Big Data Research,* vol. 26, p. 100252, 2021.
296. J. Pearl, *Probabilistic reasoning in intelligent systems: networks of plausible inference.* Elsevier, 2014.
297. R. D. SHAH and J. PETERS, "The hardness of conditional independence testing and the generalised covariance measure," *The Annals of Statistics,* vol. 48, no. 3, pp. 1514–1538, 2020.
298. E. Winter, "The shapley value," *Handbook of game theory with economic applications,* vol. 3, pp. 2025–2054, 2002.
299. T. M. Cover, *Elements of information theory.* John Wiley & Sons, 1999.
300. K. Zhang, J. Peters, D. Janzing, and B. Schölkopf, "Kernel-based conditional independence test and application in causal discovery," in *Proceedings of the Twenty-Seventh Conference on Uncertainty in Artificial Intelligence*, 2011, pp. 804–813.
301. M. Michalowski *et al.*, "Manually-curated versus LLM-generated explanations for complex patient cases: an exploratory study with physicians," in *International Conference on Artificial Intelligence in Medicine*, 2024: Springer, pp. 313–323.
302. Meta AI. "The Llama 4 herd: The beginning of a new era of natively multimodal AI innovation." https://ai.meta.com/blog/llama-4-multimodal-intelligence/ (accessed April 5, 2025).
303. F. Marulli, L. Campanile, M. S. de Biase, S. Marrone, L. Verde, and M. Bifulco, "Understanding readability of large language models output: an empirical analysis," *Procedia Computer Science,* vol. 246, pp. 5273–5282, 2024.
304. E. A. Smith and R. Senter, "Automated readability index," *Aerospace Medical Research Laboratories, Aerospace Medical Division, Air Force Systems Command,* vol. 66, no. 220, pp. 1–14, 1967.
305. International Energy Agency. "Direct CO2 emissions from industry in the Net Zero Scenario, 2000–2030." https://www.iea.org/data-and-statistics/charts/direct-co2-emissions-from-industry-in-the-net-zero-scenario-2000-2030-2 (accessed August 27, 2025).
306. International Energy Agency. "Steel." https://www.iea.org/energy-system/industry/steel (accessed August 27, 2025).
307. B. M'barek, A. Hasanbeigi, and M. Gray. "Global steel production costs. a country and plant-level cost analysis." https://www.globalefficiencyintel.com/global-steel-production-costs-report (accessed August 27, 2025).
308. "Total production of crude steel." https://worldsteel.org/data/annual-production-steel-data/?ind=P1_crude_steel_total_pub/CHN/IND (accessed August 27, 2025).
309. K. Benavides *et al.*, "Mitigating emissions in the global steel industry: Representing CCS and hydrogen technologies in integrated assessment modeling," *International Journal of Greenhouse Gas Control,* vol. 131, p. 103963, 2024.
310. Z. Fan and S. J. Friedmann, "Low-carbon production of iron and steel: Technology options, economic assessment, and policy," *Joule,* vol. 5, no. 4, pp. 829–862, 2021.
311. J. Campbell, *Complete casting handbook: metal casting processes, metallurgy, techniques and design.* Butterworth-Heinemann, 2015.

312. D. A. Howard, M. Værbak, Z. Ma, B. N. Jørgensen, and Z. Ma, "Data-Driven Digital Twin for Foundry Production Process: Facilitating Best Practice Operations Investigation and Impact Analysis," in *Energy Informatics Academy Conference*, 2024: Springer, pp. 259–273.
313. A. Andoni, P. Indyk, and R. Krauthgamer, "Earth mover distance over high-dimensional spaces," in *SODA*, 2008, vol. 8, pp. 343–352.
314. X. Jia, M. Zhao, Y. Di, Q. Yang, and J. Lee, "Assessment of data suitability for machine prognosis using maximum mean discrepancy," *IEEE transactions on industrial electronics,* vol. 65, no. 7, pp. 5872–5881, 2017.
315. A. Sharma and E. Kiciman, "DoWhy: An end-to-end library for causal inference," *arXiv preprint arXiv:2011.04216,* 2020.
316. A. Sharma, V. Syrgkanis, C. Zhang, and E. Kiciman, "Dowhy: Addressing challenges in expressing and validating causal assumptions," *arXiv preprint arXiv:2108.13518,* 2021.
317. J. Kramer, L. Riza, and T. Petzoldt, "Carbon savings, fun, and money: The effectiveness of multiple motives for eco-driving and green charging with electric vehicles in Germany," *Energy Research & Social Science,* vol. 99, p. 103054, 2023.
318. Z. Lv and W. Shang, "Impacts of intelligent transportation systems on energy conservation and emission reduction of transport systems: A comprehensive review," *Green Technologies and Sustainability,* vol. 1, no. 1, p. 100002, 2023.
319. Z. Ma, B. N. Jørgensen, and Z. Ma, "A scoping review of energy-efficient driving behaviors and applied state-of-the-art AI methods," *Energies,* vol. 17, no. 2, p. 500, 2024.
320. Z. Ma, B. N. Jørgensen, and Z. G. Ma, "Eco-driving intelligent systems and algorithms: a patent review," in *2023 8th International Conference on Power and Renewable Energy (ICPRE)*, 2023: IEEE, pp. 285–290.
321. D. Hörcher and A. Tirachini, "A review of public transport economics," *Economics of transportation,* vol. 25, p. 100196, 2021.
322. C. Bu *et al.*, "Achieving net-zero emissions in China's passenger transport sector through regionally tailored mitigation strategies," *Applied Energy,* vol. 284, p. 116265, 2021.
323. P. Li, P. Zhao, and C. Brand, "Future energy use and CO2 emissions of urban passenger transport in China: A travel behavior and urban form based approach," *Applied Energy,* vol. 211, pp. 820–842, 2018.
324. C. Reined, M. Smith, and P. Pearson, "Smart and Sustainable Mobility Strategy: A Pillar of the European Green Deal," *Smart Innovation,* vol. 1, 2024.
325. Reddit user MapPorn. https://www.reddit.com/r/MapPorn/comments/4aufqb/city_buses_and_rail_aalborg_denmark_2015_2480x2480/ (accessed September 25, 2025).
326. A. Liu, P. Fan, X. He, H. Lu, L. Yu, and G. Song, "CatBoost-based fuel consumption modeling and explainable analysis for heavy-duty diesel trucks: Impact of engine, driving behavior, and vehicle weight," *Energy,* p. 137485, 2025.
327. Z. Zhang, B. Ye, S. Wang, and Y. Ma, "Analysis and estimation of energy consumption of electric buses using real-world data," *Transportation Research Part D: Transport and Environment,* vol. 126, p. 104017, 2024.
328. "Information regarding fuel consumption for new cars." https://web.archive.org/web/20190908124154/http://www.bilsweden.se/miljo-sakerhet/miljo/information-gallande-bransleforbrukning-for-nya-bilar (accessed September 29, 2025).

MIX
Papier aus verantwortungsvollen Quellen
Paper from responsible sources
FSC® C105338
FSC
www.fsc.org

If you have any concerns about our products,
you can contact us on
ProductSafety@springernature.com

In case Publisher is established outside the EU,
the EU authorized representative is:
Springer Nature Customer Service Center GmbH
Europaplatz 3, 69115 Heidelberg, Germany

Printed by Libri Plureos GmbH
in Hamburg, Germany